Odense University Studies in History
Jørgen Hæstrup: Secret Alliance. V

MW00721087

Jørgen Hæstrup

Secret Alliance

A Study of the Danish
Resistance Movement 1940–45

Vol. 1

Translated by
Alison Borch-Johansen

Odense University Press · 1976

Printed by Andelsbogtrykkeriet i Odense

ISBN 87-7492-168-1

Contents

Foreword

The books about the Danish Resistance Movement, now to be published in English, were written in the years from 1951 to 1959. Prior to the writing and parallel with the writing I worked to collect material, which could throw light upon the hidden history of the Resistance Movement, more or less shrouded in darkness immediately after the war. The search aimed at finding contemporary documents, which might have survived illegality, and supplementing such evidence with accounts from leading members of the Resistance. Contrary to all expectations the search proved to be fruitful. More Resistance people than I had expected proved to have founded and kept archives, some necessarily fragmentary, others more complete. In most cases the material was coded Altogether I was lucky enough to find c. 70 private archives, and in addition I was able to get c. 200 accounts, some short, others more extensive. As far as there were holes in the archives, which was more than natural, the accounts were able in a high degree to cover these holes. Altogether a rather solid basis was procured for a scholarly study of the Resistance Movement. Apart from an extensive literature my books are based upon the collection mentioned, which in due time was handed over to the National Archives in Copenhagen (Rigsarkivet), arranged, explained and decoded.

A description of this search and its results is omitted in this English translation of the books. Interested students can find such a description in the Danish editions or in my book: "Dørene åbnes", published in 1973. The scope and the character of the collection will materialize in the notes in the three volumes, now published in English. The collection is available in Rigsarkivet in Copenhagen.

The text of the three volumes is almost identical with the original Danish text. Minor alterations and additions have been made, especially in the first volume, as new material was discovered between the publication of that volume (in 1954) and this English version. Small modifications will also appear in the second and the third volume as a result of new research by myself and others. But basically I have adhered to the original text.

For many years I have been able to register from abroad a surprising interest in Danish affairs during the war. Several books, many articles and radio and TV programmes etc. have seen the light of day. But in spite of long conversations with foreigners, an extensive correspondence and corrections of manuscripts it has been unavoidable that quite a few misunderstandings have appeared here and there. I have often been met with justified complaint from abroad that no exposition of Danish history during the Occupation existed in an international language.

I am therefore most grateful to the many, who have made this publication in English possible. My sincere thanks go to "Tuborgfonden", to "Fonden til Fædrelandets Vel", to "Frihedsfonden", to "Ebbe Munck-fonden" and to Odense University and Odense University Press, who have all combined to make this publication a reality. I also thank Mrs. Alison Borch-Johansen for an excellent translation.

The volumes will appear separately, the first volume in June 1976, the second in autumn 1976, and the third in spring 1977.

Sct. Klemens, January 1976.

Jørgen Hæstrup

The political Background

Denmark was occupied on 9 April 1940. While German troops marched across the Danish frontier – without warning – and made landings in various coastal towns, as well as in Copenhagen, and while waves of German bombers filled the skies and bombed out the most important military airfield, the German Ambassador handed an ultimatum to the Government, demanding Danish recognition of the Occupation and immediate cessation of military resistance. The Note emphasized that the Occupation was carried out as a protective measure against alleged plans of attack from the Western Allies, and also contained an undertaking that the Germans would guarantee Danish sovereignty and territorial integrity, as well as Danish neutrality, on condition that all resistance be discontinued forthwith.

The Government had to make its decision in about two hours, during which the occupation was in full progress, and it had to act under the threat of bombardment of Danish towns.

In the judgement of the Government, Denmark had no military possibility of defending the country, or even delaying the occupation. The defence forces were few and insufficiently equipped, and geographically there was easy access for the German troops. In addition to this, the Government had been informed in advance that in the event of German attack, Denmark could not count upon support from without. In these circumstances, the King decided, after consultation with a few members of the Government, hastily assembled, and the Commanders-in-Chief, to yield to the German demand and call off the scattered fighting in which Danish covering forces were engaged. Under protest, the demands in the German Note were accepted. The Occupation was a fact, and in the years which followed, running negotiations between the Government and the German Occupying Power became the political order of the day.

The Government was a coalition of the Social Democrats and Radicals, with a solid parliamentary basis, under the leadership of the Social Democrat Prime Minister, Thorvald Stauning, and with the Radical Peter Munch as Foreign Minister. This Government had been in power from 1929, with a solid, continuous parliamentary majority. On 9 April it was immediately supplemented with "Control Ministers", as they were called, from the two largest parties in Opposition, the Left (the farmers' party) and the Conservatives. Thus the main parties were all represented in the Government, and shared the responsibility for the policy which was now instituted, the chief object of which became the creation of a screen between the population and the occupying power. The task was mainly to ensure the country's economy, to protect Danish citizens against juridical or other violations by the occupying power, and especially to prevent the small Danish Nazi Party from being swept into power behind the German bayonets. The policy was now instituted which, depending upon the attitude of the adjudicator, was described as the policy of negotiation, the policy of concession, or the policy of collaboration. It was to last until 29 August 1943, and became the political condition under which the Resistance Movement sprang up.

In terms of International Law, it was a question of a so-called "occupatio pacifica", for which there hardly existed a precedent. Formally, Denmark was an independent and neutral state, in normal contact with Germany via the Foreign Ministries of the two countries, through which all decisive negotiations were channelled. In reality, Danish independence and territorial integrity were fictions, and the claim of neutrality could be contested at any moment. This never occurred, however. The Allies bore with the Danish-German arrangement, in recognition of the fact that Denmark had acted under duress, and Denmark therefore came to live through the Second World War without a state of war existing with any of the belligerents. Denmark became an exception, and the special position of the Danish Resistance Movement was undefined and undefinable.

As an immediate consequence of the Occupation, negotiations began between Danish and German authorities. These at once took on the character of German wishes and demands, and it became the duty of the Government to try to get these modified or deflected, so that Danish interests were respected as far as possible and the fiction of the country's independence and neutrality maintained. The negotiations could only be onesided, however, stamped by German initiative and pressure, and the political problem for the Government became a question of the pace and extent of concessions. In this situation it was of decisive importance that a united Danish front should be created, and this led in July 1940 to a reconstruction of the Government. Under Stauning's leadership, the four largest parties in the country formed a Coalition Government, which thus had the overwhelming majority in Parliament behind it. One or two non-political members were also appointed to the Government. The Foreign Minister Munch was replaced by Erik Scavenius, who had been Foreign Minister during the First World War, and was presumed to be well qualified to create a favourable climate for Danish-German negotiations. The change involved an alteration in accentuation, but not a break, in the country's foreign policy. Munch had chosen to remain passive, and met the German demands with negotiation, as these demands were made. Scavenius, on the other hand, believed that in Danish interests the situation demanded enough Danish initiative for the German wishes to be forestalled, before they became imperative demands. Scavenius was a pragmatical politician and assessed the Danish possibilities for negotiation as small, but estimated that these would improve in the degree that Danish good-will was evident in advance. This did not of itself entail any change of objective for Danish policy, but the Scavenius appointment and the Government declaration of foreign policy which he demanded and had approved, which definitely stated, both in form and content, the Danish willingness to negotiate, even to an excessive degree, heralded a new style in the Danish-German negotiations. This, added to Scavenius' often arrogant behaviour towards his ministerial colleagues, and his marked contempt for public opinion and any attitude tinged with feeling, soon created distrust of him, and contributed in the years that followed to causing a series of crises. These were partly crises between him and his colleagues, and partly a growing crisis of confidence between him and ever-increasing groups of the population. In spite of this, Scavenius continued as the leading Danish negotiator, first as Foreign Minister and from November 1942 as Prime Minister, and he came to personify and to bear the main burden of the policy which, up to the 29th August 1943, was the consequence of the Danish capitulation of the 9th April. Scavenius became chained to his office so to speak, as any alteration would mean, from a Danish standpoint, a change for the worse.

Negotiations, then, became mostly one-sided, marked by constantly escalating German demands. In view of the relative strengths of the two parties, they could but lead to concessions. The standing problem was how far these should go, taking into consideration national self-respect, political and human standpoints, public and world opinion. The situation involved a certain inertia. Having once accepted the odium of capitulation, it could be difficult to provoke a rupture on lesser questions, and the result, therefore, was usually modified concessions. The problem became a question of how far one should and could concede. It was clear for all responsible politicians that there must be a limit. Surrender of the Jews, the death penalty, Danish participation in the war on the side of the Germans, and Nazi influence in the Government, for example, lay beyond this limit. It should be emphasized, that the policy which had been chosen and the maintenance of all administration in Danish hands did bring advantages, in spite of all concessions, for example in the form of better economic conditions, protection of the country's cultural life against Nazi influence, and to a great extent the maintenance of the juridical rights of citizens. This last advantage benefitted the Danish Jews, but on the other hand, could not be extended to a large group of Danish Communists, who were interned in June 1941, in a Danish internment camp up to 1943, and from October 1943 in German concentration camps. The advantages of the policy of negotiation were not confined to those mentioned. As long as a Danish Government

11

was maintained, it was possible to reduce and in several cases to refuse German demands, and in the political camp, right up to August 1943 and regardless of differences of opinion on specific questions of negotiation, there was unanimity that this policy should be adhered to as long as possible.

The German demands came in all departments, economic, military, political, juridical and cultural. Periods of crisis with many serious demands alternated with quieter periods. There was a long series of demands regarding the replacement of personalities in leading positions, ministers, politicians, editors, etc. For example, in the autumn 1940, the Germans had already demanded the replacement of the Conservative Minister of Trade, Christmas Møller, after a number of anti-German speeches, as well as his removal from all public activity. Other ministers also had to be replaced, and the influential Social Democratic politicians, Hedtoft Hansen and H. C. Hansen, had to resign their seats in Parliament and withdraw officially from political life. But the worst demands were for the surrender of Danish military equipment, for drastic measures against the Danish Communists, for Danish endorsement, although with qualifications, of the Anti-Comintern Pact, and the attempt at interference in Danish jurisdiction. To the extent that the Government had to yield on these and other questions, its authority declined, and this process was accelerated by developments on the battle fronts, and from 1942 by the agitation of the Resistance Movement against the policy of concession. By August 1943 the policy of negotiation had exhausted its possibilities, and after a violent wave of sabotage and strikes, the Government had to give up, and refuse a German ultimatum, which contained amongst other clauses, the demand for the death penalty for saboteurs. The Government tendered its resignation and a German assumption of power, with the introduction of martial law, was the inevitable consequence – the consequence hoped for by the Resistance Movement. The Danish Army was disarmed after some scattered fighting, whereas the Navy succeeded in scuttling the Fleet. Officers and men from both Services were interned.

In the period up to then, the Government had repeatedly changed their gallery of personalities, partly as the result of German demands, partly owing to Danish internal conditions. In May 1942, the Prime Minister Stauning died, and the Social Democrat Vilhelm Buhl took his place. This did not lead to any important change in government policy. In the autumn 1942, however, there came the so-called "telegram crisis", caused in reality by the German dissatisfaction with the state of affairs in Denmark, but formally on account of a short telegram from the King in reply to a birthday greeting from the German Fuehrer. The German Ambassador in Denmark was recalled and the Danish Ambassador in Berlin sent home, and for about one and a half months it was uncertain whether a German take-over was imminent in Denmark. The crisis ended, after lengthy negotiations,

partly in Berlin, partly in Copenhagen, with a German demand that Scavenius take over the office of Prime Minister, and that the Government be
reconstructed with fewer political members and more Members drawn from
outside the political parties. A demand for the inclusion of Nazis in the
Government was refused by Scavenius, and a German demand for the Government to have considerably increased powers was negotiated out of the
picture. The King and the Coalition Parties accepted the new Government,
which in reality continued the previous policy. The Scavenius Government
came to power on the demand of the Germans, but it retained parliamentary cover, with about 95 % elected Members behind it. The Government was therefore placed in the peculiar half-way position, of being
created contrary to normal parliamentary practice, but without, on that account, lacking parliamentary backing.

During these political developments, the nation's attitude gradually
changed. The decisions of the 9th April were by and large understood and
accepted as inevitable, and as the lesser of two evils, but during the long
processes of negotiation, with increasing concessions, a more critical attitude
grew up, fed not so much by the capitulation itself as by the conduct of
the Government in the concrete instances where concessions were yielded.
The original paralysis was replaced by a strongly national popular unrest,
which from demonstrations and protests gradually passed to approaching
open resistance, the illegal Press, sabotage, strikes, etc. Up to August 1943,
when the unrest broke through in earnest and made it impossible to continue the policy of negotiation, it was the Resistance Movement's main objective to achieve an open breach with the occupying power, and prevent
official Denmark from negotiating further.

This was achieved, when the Government on 28 August 1943 refused the
German ultimatum and resigned. From then on, an official Danish policy
no longer existed. The chief administrators carried on their duties, each of
them responsible to his own Ministry and his own conscience, but this only
hid the object of maintaining the administration in Danish hands, and
only in cases where administration could be carried out according to Danish
Law. In all other instances, the German authorities had to act by the law
of might. Negotiations continued until May 1945, often with results which
were valuable from a Danish point of view, but this continuation of the
Administration was devoid of political consequences. Danish politics went
into hibernation, and it was the Resistance Movement which came to design
the political course of the country, both at home and abroad, for the period 1943–45.

1. The 9th of April – Seen from Without

When news of the events of the 9th of April reached the free world, only the scantiest attention was paid to Denmark. Norway stole the picture[1] from the start. There was nothing strange in this. As we now know,[2] and as the experts knew even then, the German offensive was directed principally at Norway, and at the important strategic advantages which an occupation of Norway could provide. Denmark was only the corridor for this attack. In itself, an occupation of Denmark was of small and doubtful advantage to the Germans. Equally, it was to Norway that the Allies turned their gaze. Today it is well known that political and military circles in France and England were extremely interested in North Scandinavia, and that extensive plans for the region were discussed and completed by the French and British Governments and military staffs, during the winter months 1939–40.[3] Denmark and the possible political and military consequences for her of an intervention in Scandinavia seem at no period to have engaged the Allies' attention. All expositions of the subject are concentrated upon Norway. Winston Churchill's description of the period, in "The Second World War", covers the occupation of Denmark and the events of the 9th of April in two lines.[4]

How little interest was aroused by possible developments in Denmark, in the event of collision between the warring powers spreading over Scandinavia, is shown, not only by the pregnant silence at the time but, plainly, by some remarks of Churchill's, made at a confidential meeting with Scandinavian war correspondents on 2 February 1940:[5] "I cannot reproach Denmark for anything. The others (Norway and Sweden) have at least a pit, over which they can feed the tiger, but Denmark is so frightfully near Germany that it would be impossible to bring help. I, at all events, would not take the responsibility of guaranteeing Denmark." In only two respects – but these two were important – did Denmark offer interesting possibilities: Danish ships and Danish positions in the North Atlantic.

There is therefore nothing strange in the fact that Denmark found herself on the periphery of public interest in the free world, in the period following 9 April. A decisive role was played in the formation of public opinion by the fact that Norway was fighting, and it was there the drama was being played out. Denmark's attitude, if it was noticed at all by the man in the street, was generally misunderstood. This applies to Denmark's

15

special geographical position, and Denmark's political and military isolation, which left her no choice, when the German invasion took place. The general public, outside Denmark, had no idea of the background for the situation, and could have no balanced comprehension of the position into which Denmark was forced. When Christmas Møller came to England two years later, it was his task "to explain and defend" not only the capitulation itself, but also its unavoidable consequences, as they had arisen in the intervening period.[6]

Quite apart from the negative aspect – the lack of news that reached the Press and Radio in the free world on Denmark and Danish conditions during the first years of occupation – there are, in the archives of those days, direct statements of the low esteem in which Denmark was held abroad, after the capitulation on 9 April. The analysis of opinion in the USA which Henrik Kauffmann, the Danish Ambassador, sent to the Danish Foreign Ministry on 4 September 1940 must carry special weight. It reads in part:[7] "Knowledge of Denmark is uninformed and superficial, and Denmark is often believed to be dependent upon Germany to a far greater degree that is the case in reality ... Even though the soil in the USA was not the best for receiving the news that the Danes had yielded without resistance, I nevertheless believe that we have succeeded, in wide and at all events the more important circles, in achieving, if not approval of the Danish Government's attitude, at least a certain understanding of it. However, it has not been possible to do this everywhere ... Not once, but many times, in the days following the occupation, I had to explain why the Danes, in contrast, for example, to their Norwegian brothers, did not fight; the cadets in uniform from the training ship "Danmark" were met with shouts of contempt when they landed; in the sports news, it was said of a boxer: "He lay down without a fight, like a Dane." ... It has been somewhat difficult to explain here, that Denmark seems to have been so utterly unprepared, when the day before, the American Press had long telegrams about the great fleet of German ships which was sailing up through the Belts. I have had to hear, several times and from very prominent groups, that the occupation can hardly have come so unexpectedly for everyone in Denmark as it did for the bulk of the population, and even though I have naturally done my utmost to combat such rumours, they unfortunately continue. Here in the USA people seem to have expected a far stronger protest against the occupation ... Many Americans have therefore received the impression that after the occupation, the Danes have not practised the passive resistance, which, in spite of everything, it would have been possible to practise, but have tried to adjust themselves to it a bit too quickly, and have therefore set themselves apart from the other occupied countries ... if people in the USA get the impression that Denmark more or less voluntarily collaborates with the "Nazi Germany" so hated here, the incipient feeling that the Danish nation is spineless will unavoidably arouse reactions both in the American Government and the American public, which will be extremely detrimental to Danish interests and Danish "good will" in the USA, and seriously threaten the possibility of keeping Greenland Danish ..." One meets similar bitter remarks, though they may not be expressed so precisely, from other Danes, who experienced the problems of the Occupation in the free world.[8] It should also be mentioned, that after 9 April there was talk of stopping the BBC five minutes broadcast to Denmark, for one reason, because Denmark had given in without a fight.[9]

A more essential point than the opinion of the general public was the attitude taken by the Allied Governments, and the trend of opinion as to Denmark's position from official quarters in USA, Russia and, especially, Great Britain. The development of opinion in Britain will be considered first. As the war progressed, it was from Britain that the Danish Resistance Movement in due course received encouragement and direct help. It should be added, however, that in the last phases of the war, important American help was also received, although this was supplied through the channels which Danish–British initiative had already created, and created at a time when encouragement and help were most needed.

Danish resistance could not be built up on the basis of an illegal movement's own resources. This was particularly the case when developments in Denmark involved the disarming of the Danish Army. If the movement was to gather sufficient strength to fight the Germans actively, by force, it must rely mainly upon possible support from abroad, as regards supplies, organisation, methods, etc.; and its influence would be conditional upon the degree to which it was capable of subordinating itself to the grand strategy, which in time would wrest the victory from the grasp of Nazi Germany. None of this could be foreseen in 1940, but from the historical point of view it is quite clear that developments in Britain – and in the free world as a whole – would be of decisive importance for the possibilities for growth in a Danish Resistance Movement. Britain and British organisation became the hinge upon which all Danish resistance would one day turn to its natural place among the volunteers in the Allied ranks.

In this thesis, one of my tasks must be to follow the work of construction carried out in England in support of a Danish resistance movement. Here it is necessary to examine both the work accomplished by the British and – more especially – the work which Danes in England, and in Sweden, accomplished themselves. All other Anglo–Danish connexions will be treated only to the extent necessary for describing these organisations.

When the Germans occupied Denmark, a number of Britons in Denmark were attached to various official British offices. As several of these people later played decisive parts in the work of bringing assistance to the Danish Resistance Movement from abroad, it is reasonable to follow this circle of

Britishers a little closer. This will lead us straight into the preparatory work done for the creation of the most important Anglo-Danish resistance organisation, the Danish Section of SOE.

On 13 April 1940, this group of Britons left Denmark in a special diplomatic train, which brought them through Germany to the Dutch frontier, from where they travelled through neutral Holland and on to London.[10] Besides Mr. Howard Smith, the British Minister, who had no connexion with Anglo-Danish resistance work after he returned home, there were, amongst others on the train, four men whom we shall meet later as prominent figures in this work: the Legation Councillor Mr. Rodney Gallop, the Press Attaché, Mr. Ronald Turnbull, Commander Frank N. Stagg and Mr. R. C. Hollingworth, who were both attached to the British Legation, Commander Stagg as leader of "Navy Control Service", which supplied sailing routes for British ships leaving Denmark, and Mr. Hollingworth, working under the Naval Attaché.[11] Other Britons who later played a rôle in the Anglo–Danish organisations and who were on the diplomatic train were Mr. Reginald Spink, Mr. R. T. Taylor and Mr. Albert Christensen, all of whom were connected with official British offices in Denmark.[12]

It can be said of all these men that, because of their considerable knowledge of Danish mentality and conditions, they did not allow themselves to be fooled as regards the real content of the 9 April capitulation. They understood the military necessity for the Government's attitude, and they were also sufficiently familiar with the Danish point of view to be aware of the Danish people's anti-German feelings. Because of that realisation, and because of their understanding of what served the interests of their country best, but certainly also because of their feelings of genuine friendship for Denmark, they all became important advocates for the Danish cause in the years that followed. In his account to the Danish State Archives, Hollingworth expresses it as follows: "... during my time in Denmark I had got to love the country, and just as I wished to serve Britain in the war against Germany, so I also wished to do what I could to help the Danes to take up the fight against Germany in one way or another. We who had experienced the capitulation at first hand, and knew the country, knew and understood that Denmark could hardly have acted otherwise than she did, but at the same time, we were all quite convinced that the Danes would fight, if they got a chance to do so."[14] The other Britons in the party shared this positive attitude towards Denmark. Commander Stagg, who later became one of Christmas Møller's closest collaborators during the latter's three years stay in London, in his article for "The Book about Christmas Møller", calls himself "a friend of Denmark".[14] Spink had fairly close connexions with leading Social Democrats, from his period in Denmark, and was therefore so familiar with Danish political feelings and viewpoints that he had no doubt of the real situation,[15] and Rodney Gallop became known later through the BBC's broadcasts as "a good friend of Denmark" – a name he gave himself with reason.[16] In a broadcast to Denmark on 9 April 1942 he explained his attitude towards Denmark, and expressed the same view and feelings as those of Hollingworth: " ... I have unforgettable memories of my friends' sorrow and shame at the capitulation on 9 April, and their anxiety in case England should feel that Denmark was dishonoured for ever ... So when I came home to this free country, I felt I owed it to my Danish friends not to lose interest in their fate. Today I can look back over two years, during which I have tried to do all I could, first to explain Denmark's peculiar position to my fellow-countrymen, and next to reassure you that you were not forgotten, and to help you help yourselves ... We in England know that you will play your part, when the time comes."[17]

These Britishers did not leave Denmark without having their impression of the true feelings there confirmed in various ways. There is evidence that at least Gallop and Hollingworth were in touch with Danes in the days from 9–13 April, who assured them of the general anti-German reaction in the country. On 11 April Per Federspiel[18] managed to have a conversation with Rodney Gallop,[19] lasting several hours, in which he not only gave an account of the feelings of the great majority of Danes as he knew them, but also brought up the question of Denmark's possibilities for making her contribution on the side of the Allies in the time to come. In his account, Per Federspiel describes the conversation as follows: "... We had a conversation of several hours about the Occupation, about Gallop's disappointment at the apathetic attitude in Copenhagen of the man in the street, and the apparent absence of indignation against the Germans. I tried on that occasion, as on many previous occasions, to explain to Gallop the special reactions of the Danish national character, and promised him – although I really had no basis for this at all – that there was a strong reaction, and that there could be no doubt where the Danes stood in relation to the Germans ... During our conversation we also touched upon the question of how we could maintain contact with each other, particularly if Sweden was also involved in the Occupation. I understood from Gallop that he, for his part, had no knowledge of any plans for maintaining such contact, and that the British Legation in Copenhagen, at least, had made no preparations in relation to a possible occupation of Denmark ... Before we parted, I could declare to Gallop, that I was naturally ready to do what I could to maintain communications and in that way take part in the struggle."[20]

Mr. Hollingworth was on Langeland on 9 April, where he was to investigate the German mine-sweeping, and he hurried to Copenhagen the same day. Passing through Odense, he visited the Consul, the merchant Thorbjørn Muus, and had a conversation with him and with his son, the merchant Hans Muus.[21] During this talk, as was only natural, he received an impression of intense anger at the German occupation, and of resolution to work against German influence.[22] Finally, as the diplomatic train passed through Fredericia, a Danish staff officer threw a newspaper in through an open window of the train to a British passenger. The paper concealed authentic information on German troops on Danish soil, and with that the first sign that the British could expect active support from the Danes, as and when possibilities for it arose.[23]

These signs were all the more important in that no decisions seem to have been taken upon Danish–British co-operation in the event of a German occupation of Denmark. The newspaper editor Ebbe Munck, who is better informed than anyone else on these questions, through his close collaboration with British authorities during the war, emphasizes this somewhat surprising fact in his exposition in "Free Denmark's White Paper",[24] and in his account in "Denmark under the Occupation".[24] In his report for the Danish State Archives he adds: "At the outbreak of the great war in September 1939, we discussed with British friends what we could do in Denmark to help in general, and especially in the event of enemy occupation of the country. No actual agreement was made. The British at that period were most interested in distributing British propaganda material among the German population via Denmark, and some help was given in this. When the situation developed on and after 9 April 1940, there were, so far as I know, no definite arrangements between Danish individuals or Danish institutions on the one hand, and British authorities on the other."[25]

Both in this quotation and in his books, Ebbe Munck makes the formal reservation for his belief that no Anglo-Danish agreement had been entered into before 9 April, that such an agreement could have existed. However, there is no evidence that such was the case. On the contrary, there is extreme likelihood of the opposite. Both the scanty information on conditions in Denmark, which can be traced in the radio broadcasts from London in the first period, and the well-known difficulties in obtaining reliable information support this view. Robert Jørgensen, who was leader of the BBC radio service to Denmark, expresses it as follows: "At that time (in 1940), we had no intelligence service from Denmark apart from newspaper cuttings and the Kalundborg Radio."[26] The editor Sten Gudme, who played a leading rôle[27] in the British propaganda service to Denmark from 1941, states in his report to the State Archives: "My very first task (that is after Sten Gudme's arrival in England at the end of 1941) was to draw up a political report on the situation in Denmark – a report both to the British Foreign Office and to the Ministry of Information. As far as I know, this report was the first collected exposition the British had of the real situation in Denmark. At all events, I remember that after I had been there a month, I had a talk with Rodney Gallop, in the course of which he told me that the only information they had received in the Foreign Office up to then on conditions in Denmark had been in a private letter I had written to Tillge-

Rasmussen, which he had sent on via Portugal."[28] Everything points to the conclusion that the British were very poorly supplied with information on conditions in Denmark.[29]

Another fact which points to the lack of Anglo-Danish agreements is the enthusiasm with which the British, as we shall soon see, seize the opportunity to co-operate with the Danish Army Intelligence Section, and also, at a later stage, the purely technical difficulties which the first parachutists trained in Britain had to overcome, partly because no sure, rapid contact had been established with England even in 1941.[30] Referring to this in his account, Hollingworth states[31] that as leader of the Danish Section of SOE, he followed what was going on in Denmark to the best of his ability, and adds that at the beginning (autumn 1940) he "was occasionally sent a little, a very little intelligence material from Denmark". From February 1941 he states, in connexion with a visit to Stockholm: "No contact existed as yet between us and Danish circles, and information from Denmark was scanty and unreliable, so that we had no real knowledge of feelings and conditions in the country."[32]

It can therefore be assumed as almost certain, that Ebbe Munck was right in his opinion that no agreements did exist between Danish and British persons or institutions before 9 April 1940.

On this assumption, and even without it, the evidence of Danish will to co-operate which the various Britishers met during their few days in Denmark after 9 April must have had some value. It certainly strengthened the impression they had formed of the real conditions in Denmark. From the statements made by some of the Britishers mentioned, it also appears that during the journey on the diplomatic train, they discussed in detail how they could counter the allegations they expected of Danish pro-German feeling, or at least the lack of determination to oppose the German demands.[33] Today it cannot be established how far these discussions went, in the train, but they seem to have continued for several hours. Nothing was written down. It seems certain, however, that Commander Stagg put forward the idea of setting up an office in London, both to inform the public on the Danes' true attitude – and this might be extremely desirable, in the sceptical atmosphere which must be expected after the capitulation – and also to bring Danes together from the free world, and get them to join the fight for their country, in some way or other.[34] All accounts agree that such discussions took place, and that their starting point was the fact of Danish anti-German feeling, and the conviction that they would be willing to translate this feeling into action, if and when the possibility arose.

Commander Stagg's plan for an office was not realised, but his own account of the fate of the plan is interesting in that it shows the impression Stagg received of the British attitude towards Denmark just after 9 April. He puts it bluntly: "On the evening of 14 April 1940 I got together 7 or

8 members of staffs of the British Legation and Consulate in my room at the Hotel Gallia, Brussels, and asked if they would be willing to serve in a Danish Liaison office, which should be inter-departmental and staffed only by those were well-acquainted with Denmark, Danish and the Danish people. They welcomed the idea and promoted full collaboration, realising that Denmark was in a unique position, being neither enemy, ally or neutral. On April 16th 1940 I saw Mr. Brendan Bracken who was then Private Secretary to Mr. Churchill. He jumped at the idea and promised to take the matter up with the Foreign Office at once – and to see that none of the names of ex-officials of the Legation and Consulate at Copenhagen should be posted abroad till the matter was settled. The British Minister Howard Smith and Naval Attaché Captain Denham also started movements for the formation of this liaison office in the Foreign Office and Admiralty. Some few days later Brendan Bracken rang me up to say that the proposal had gone half way up the FO who were determined that if there was anybody who knew of Denmark they would post him to South America – and Rodney Gallop was actually posted to the South American Section."[35]

In the course of a few weeks, the war took such a dramatic and critical turn – with the German blitz invasion into Holland, Belgium and France, the British troops' evacuation from Dunkirk, the capitulation of France, and the Battle of Britain – that the question of Denmark's position receded into the background, and the budding idea of co-operation between the Britishers referred to had to wait until a later period for its realisation. Developments in Denmark, with the first Danish concessions under the growing German pressure, and with the Government statement of 8 July, were not favourable for any thought of a possible Danish effort;[36] and also, such ideas would simply drown, in the maelstrom of problems which closed about the British authorities during that summer. As we shall see later, there was also deep uncertainty in Danish circles in England, as to the course that should be set. In England, too, they needed to recover from the shock of 9 April. In England, too, the idea of resistance needed its definite, if short, incubation period.

There were very few signs of encouragement for Danish circles in England, and in the little circle of Britons with Denmark's interests at heart, during the hectic, depressing months of the spring and early summer. However, extremely important encouragement did come, from the Danish sailors. On 9 April about two hundred Danish ships were cut off from communication with the home country, and in spite of the very poor British wages, which only amounted to half of what Danish sailors earned under the Danish flag, in spite of all the dangers and hardships, the great majority chose to get to Allied ports, and about five thousand Danish sailors finally chose to serve under Allied flags.[37] The appeal to Danish ships, which was sent out repeatedly on the BBC on 9 April[38] as introduction to the Danish broadcasts from London, in which the ships were urged to seek Allied harbours, could not have received an answer which refuted more clearly all allegations – German or Allied – of any pro-German attitude.

Another piece of encouraging news came when the British Member of Parliament Mr. Mander put the following questions to the Prime Minister, Neville Chamberlain: "Whether he will include as one of the objects of the Allies in the war that of securing the restoration of the freedom and independence of Denmark," to which the Under-Secretary of the Foreign Office, Mr. Butler gave the short answer: "Yes, sir"[39] From this slender but irrefutable "Yes", the work for Denmark's cause had to seek its meagre nourishment for some time to come.

Yet, under the silent surface, this work was in full progress, in England as elsewhere in the free world, and in Denmark. The quiet initiative which the group in the diplomatic train had taken died down quickly, it is true, and its main interest is as a symptom. The actual group was being split up. Gallop, as we have seen, was caught up in the great Foreign Office machinery, Turnbull worked at the BBC until 28 May, with the establishment of the Danish broadcasts,[40] Hollingworth was posted to Iceland[41] as Secretary to the Admiral of the Occupation Force, and Spink was sent[42] to the British Consulate in Rome, while Stagg served in London, in the Ministry of Shipping, and kept himself informed[43] of the work that was developing in Danish circles in England. While the little British group's work only represented a ripple on the surface, which could vanish without leaving a trace in the final course of events, the situation was rather different as regards the initiative which Danes took in Britain and abroad generally. Here the line can be followed towards the final results. We shall move along this line in the following chapter – to a decision.

2. Among Danes in London

It is not the intention in this thesis to follow all the activities undertaken by Danes abroad in support of the fight against Nazism. Although most of these efforts benefitted Denmark and the Danish Resistance Movement in one way or another, the task here is limited to tracing activities, of which the direct purpose was to bring help to a coming resistance movement in the mother country. Thus, a description of the Danish sailors' war effort lies outside my province, as does an account of the work for the Danish cause of The Danish Council or of the various Danish legations, although one of these legations must be mentioned. This also applies in general to the Danish radio broadcasts from London, even though this work was highly influential, and directly so, in the construction and formation of Danish resistance, but here it is not possible to draw a sharp dividing line. It should be pointed out, however, that much of what must be omitted was of great importance, indirectly, to the Danish Resistance Movement. For example, the efforts of the Danish seamen, both as regards the attention they aroused in the free world, and as regards the personal hardships and sacrifices they involved for these men,[1] constituted a war effort of the first order; and this had a very marked, positive effect upon the general view of Denmark, and with it, upon the Resistance Movement at home.

The reaction to the Occupation, of Danes abroad – and here we are particularly considering Danes in England – had many similarities with the reaction in Denmark itself. In both cases the shock factor was predominant; in both cases, the first period of occupation was marked by great uncertainty as to the future: uncertainty as to the character of the Occupation; uncertainty as to the correct interpretation of information from home; uncertainty as to the attitude of the Allied Powers towards what had happened; and in particular, uncertainty as to the proper attitude for Danes, who were living outside the enclosure of occupation. Neither the effect of shock nor the feeling of uncertainty are to be wondered at. The Occupation must awaken feelings among Danes abroad which ran parallel to those of Danes at home, and it was equally natural that the swing of emotions was intensified, in many cases, by distance. For those who watch a catastrophe, sympathetically, from outside, negative emotions are not out-weighed by the strength which participation gives, or the positive feeling of belonging to a team, which is produced by common disaster. The bitter sense of impotence is often intensified if one is forced against ones will and instinct to remain an onlooker. It should also be remembered, that most of the Danes abroad were only staying there temporarily. For them, a vast amount was at stake, and for an indefinite period: contact with family, friends, work, and all the atmosphere of home. The impact of the shock must be intense, wherever they were in the free world. One finds the same horror-stricken frame of mind again and again in accounts of 9 April:

"... We sailed from Bergen early in the morning of 9 April, to meet the British escort at a pre-arranged spot outside the three-mile limit. On our way to this meeting place we met a heavily armed trawler on its way into Bergen. We knew nothing at that time of the German occupation of Denmark, and so it came as a shock when we were called to a ship's council in the Captain's cabin, and he told us what had happened."[2] "On 8 April we anchored up in Rotterdam harbour. We could be in our homes in Denmark in a few days – and we were looking forward to it. But unfortunately – too soon! The next morning we heard that Denmark was occupied by German troops ... It made an overwhelming impression on us all, and a feeling of gloom and sorrow spread over us. Low-toned and serious, we discussed these events with all their implications – and that morning I saw grown men weep."[3] Or the terse remark: "Even though events of 9 April were not unexpected, it came as a shock to hear the details on the radio that morning."[4] Flemming Muus, later to become parachutist leader, describes his feelings when he heard what had happened, in Liberia: "... The news paralysed me completely. I do not think I moved so much as a finger for the next hour. I simply sat in a chair, without thought, paralyzed by sorrow and shame."[5] And are these feelings far from the touching and very human Eskimoan message to his comrades, deep in the Arctic waste-land of Ellesmereland, scratched on a tin of pemmican: "The Germans are stealing all the meat from the Danes. The King is the only one who has not lost heart. There is no more paraffin in the shop."[6] One need not search far for evidence of horror. One does not need much imagination to understand it.

The uncertainty, which marked the first period for so many, is also understandable. In the first place, uncertainty was soon common to everyone who watched the march of events, during the spring and summer, from the free world. All accepted beliefs collapsed headlong under the onslaught. Anyone who tried to come to reasoned conclusions as to the problems in store for Denmark had, at best, only speculative theories to go upon, and these could only be based upon countless hypothetical possibilities. For many, any reasoning in such circumstances must be rash, to say the least of it. For them there was only one course open: to wait and see. In the circumstances, they could hardly have decided otherwise.

In this situation, the Danes who reacted more with their feelings and instinctive perceptions were in a stronger position in the face of what had

25

happened, than those who tried to grope their way forward in the new situation, in vain reflections over the possibilities which the future might bring. In certain situations, when complicated analyses fail to give results, action must spring from a single-minded attitude to problems, straightforwardly, and often inspired by intense feeling. Otherwise there will often be no action but that of the adversary.

While developments among the Danes abroad present many features similar to those in Denmark, in one respect they are utterly dissimilar. For many, and probably chiefly for the more activist in character, for whom problems were simple and beyond discussion, shock and uncertainty were quickly overcome, and these unhesitatingly began to think of the possibility of taking part in the open fight. This was particularly marked in the case of the Danish sailors, who in many instances were faced with the necessity for immediate decision. While the idea of resistance in Denmark needed to pass through many phases, each of which opened new flood-gates of possibilities, resistance-minded Danes in England quickly reached the point where Danish participation in the physical fight became the central and immediate goal. Here the way was not blocked to any decisive degree, by unavoidable secondary aims, collapse of the conditions for success, or the restriction of political considerations. The difference of atmosphere, alone, meant a great deal. England was in a fight to the death, open warfare was an everyday matter, and the thought of Danish participation was obvious. This looked just as natural and realistic, from England, as it looked theoretical and unrealistic from Denmark, or at least dependent upon many non-existant pre-requisites. It soon became clear that there were many considerable groups in England, whose interest for a Danish war effort grew at the same pace as Danes showed themselves willing to join in the direct fight – both on the military and the home fronts. There was friendly respect for passive resistance, but the interest was for active resistance. When activist Danish and British circles found each other, during the summer and early autumn of 1940, they started the work of building up an organisation in support of a coming struggle in Denmark. This was taking place while the Danish home front in 1940 and 1941 was working its way to the maturity upon which open war would depend.

Among the Danes who quickly reached the stage of demanding direct Danish participation in the war as the decisive aim, Major Werner Michael Iversen and Doctor Carl Johan Bruhn were to play leading rôles. If we follow their work, it will lead us straight to the heart of the set of problems which are to be examined.

On 9 April, Michael Iversen was living in England. From 1919 to 1939 he had been manager of a plantation in Malacca, and he retired in 1939 after a twenty years' contract and returned to Europe, where he settled in England with his British-born wife. He obtained a permit of residence in wartime England in January 1940. During the winter months of 1939–40 he established contact with Danish circles, partly with civil servants in the Danish Embassy, and partly with Danes in the Danish Club in London, and thus received an impression of the state of things in Denmark as they developed during the war, looked at from without.[7]

Iversen was one of the Danes for whom the situation after 9 April was quite clear. In his account for the State Archives he explains his point of view: "... When the message came, therefore, on 9 April 1940, I realised at once that there was only one thing for me to do, to find some way or other of joining the liberation struggle ... I spoke to various people in the Club to the effect that there was only one way for Danes to hold their own: to volunteer, and fight."[8] In accordance with this way of thinking, after first offering his services at the Danish Legation, he applied on 30 April to the British War Office and offered his services to the British Army: "I am most anxious to serve the Allies, as I tried to do at the outbreak (in Malacca) of war and tried to through the Field Service Centre, and I am still more anxious to place my past training and experiences at the disposal of the government in any capacity of which the Government may consider me capable ... when this country is at war and my own invaded ... I am ready to join at any time and at a moment,s notice."[9]

Iversen's attitude was clear and straightforward. It was not weighed down by reservations, red tape, or scruples. When Blytgen-Petersen describes the work of raising the Danish movement in England, and in this connexion mentions, that "some brought fire, some brought a sword, some perhaps poured on cold water",[10] Iversen was most certainly one of those that brought a sword. He did not bring it in vain.

His application was in fact declined with thanks, and a considerable number of similar applications to the British authorities, military and civil, were also turned down, during the spring and summer. But the truly untiring energy with which he sought to find an opening for making an active contribution, and particularly his intense agitation in Danish circles for raising a Danish volunteer movement was finally – in spite of all difficulties – to draw the attention of the British to his person and activities.

Iversen's second goal – to obtain a personal place in the ranks of the active – ran parallel to his main activities, and did not interfere with them. His primary aim, upon which his efforts were concentrated, was to win over Danish circles in England to a clear Danish stand, shown particularly in Danish volunteer participation in the war, on the side of Britain. In this field his work was of outstanding importance. In the process of fermentation among the Danes, which was finally to lead to the creation of The Danish Council, he, with other Danes such as Dr. Carl Johan Bruhn, was to represent the leaven, which drove the fermentation most strongly towards activism. For such men the process was incomplete, if not trivial, if it did not end in a clear manifestation of Danish will to fight. It is therefore relevant to look more closely at the developments which the Danish colony underwent in the first months after the Occupation, and at the discussions, at times hot-tempered, between its members on ways and means for Danish activities in England. The Danish Council sprang from these discussions, and parallel with it, the Danish volunteer movement, which was to have such importance for the Resistance Movement's development at home.[11]

When the news of 9 April reached England, it was naturally to the Danish Minister, Count Eduard Reventlow that all Danish eyes turned. His attitude to the new situation was bound to have decisive influence upon developments, quite apart from the importance which would be attached in general to the position taken up by Denmark's London Minister. Count Reventlow decided for the time being to remain the envoy of the Danish King and Government, and continued to represent Danish interests in Great Britain as far as possible. The rest of the Legation staff took the same attitude. In his exposition in "Denmark during War and Occupation", the Foreign Minister of that period, Peter Munch writes of Count Reventlow that he "remained at his post",[12] an expression which in Munch's careful, sober style, in addition to a statement of fact contains a short, appreciative, diplomatic characterization of Reventlow's standpoint. It is obvious that Count Reventlow's attitude, although it was only to be expected, considering the Minister's close connexion for many years with the Danish Foreign Ministry, would be felt as valuable support for the Foreign Minister, Munch, and the Danish Government as a whole. It must contribute to strengthening the Government in its decision of 9 April, and to easing the oppressive atmosphere which soon descended upon the Foreign Minister's negotiations with the Germans on the subject of the Danish legations.[13]

It is not difficult to see the reasons for Count Reventlow's decision not to commit himself, in contrast to, for instance, Henrik Kauffmann in Washington, who decided to declare that he felt himself "a free agent as regards the German-controlled Danish Government."[14] The Minister's chief motives were loyalty towards the King and the Government, and the desire not to put obstacles in the way of the policy which they had felt it necessary to pursue in Denmark. On this subject, Count Reventlow remarks in a telegram of 11 December 1941, in which he states his reason, after Denmark's signature of the Anti-Comintern Pact, for no longer accepting orders from the Danish Foreign Ministry:[15] "The line I have followed hitherto, dictated by the desire I always have and always will cherish, not to increase the difficulties at home in Denmark, I have done everything in my power to maintain as long as at all possible, in spite of very considerable difficulties." Other considerations may also have contributed to the Minister's motives. In his survey of conditions in the Danish legations, in "Denmark under Occupation", Ole Kiilerich,[16] the editor, refers to the element of uncertainty

28

implicit in the whole situation, and its development, and particularly the great uncertainty ruling in British circles as to the consequences which the capitulation would entail for British policy towards Denmark. The Under-Secretary for Foreign Affairs, Mr. Butler, stated in Parliament in 1 May 1940, that the British Government, although it could not maintain diplomatic relations with Denmark, would, however, accept that Count Reventlow continue his work in a "Semi-official capacity.[17] A Minister such as Henrik Kauffmann stood on far firmer ground in this respect, because the American State Department did not hesitate to accept his account of the Danish Government as being under German control, and therefore accepted him without reservations as representative for the free Denmark which the Occupation had brought to an end, as long as the war lasted.[18] The Foreign Office showed no corresponding certainty in determining the policy to be followed towards Denmark in April 1940.

Denmark, as pointed out previously, lay on the periphery of the British sphere of interest, and in the first months after 9 April there were certainly other and greater considerations to decide upon than Danish affairs. It was not until June when Great Britain finally stood alone, with her back to the wall, that her interest in possible allies inside Hitler's fortress was aroused in earnest, and had favourable conditions for growth. Great Britain did not bind herself, at the start, to any definite policy. One consolation in this, from the Danish point of view, was that the fiction of Danish neutrality was not contested. Consideration for the Danish ships and Danish sailors certainly carried great weight in the British deliberations.

Among the Danes in England, Count Reventlow's attitude was largely understood and accepted. It was naturally unavoidable that there should be criticism, disappointment and, especially, misunderstanding.[19] In the long run this criticism was of minor importance, and did not affect the Minister's official position in any decisive way; but it certainly affected his position in the Danish work which was now in progress. When Reventlow declined the position of "Free Danish Minister", the natural consequence was that others had to lead the effort to unite the Danes in an active policy. In the drama which was now played out in Danish circles, of which Ogier the Dane was the theme, rather than Hamlet, the Minister took his place in the audience. When he later stood up to take part in the play, it was already in progress, the plot was developing, and the important rôles were already filled.

In the first months after the occupation, feeling in Danish circles not bound by official considerations was marked by uncertainty, great indignation, sorrow and a sense of impotence. Many were burning to take action of some sort, but it was still impossible to see what was the proper action, what means could be used, and what paths would be negotiable. Danes in England, just as in Denmark, had a strong urge to be together, and they listened with intense interest to the scanty information which leaked out from Denmark or which could be picked up from broadcasts from Kalundborg Radio. Blytgen-Petersen gives the following impression of the atmosphere of those days:[20] "So we listened to the "Allsong" (the great national song meetings which were taking place in Denmark, with crowds of singers up to 100,000) took the Coalition Government as an expression of the will for national unity and for long-term policy, and we clutched at each little national manifestation in speeches or in music, with the demonstration and acclamation on the King's birthday as the climax. And then we also needed to be with our countrymen. We too met, drank coffee in the Danish Club and sang songs." The similarity between the atmosphere at home and abroad is striking.

In this atmosphere, the urge to make a free Danish war effort increased. It must have looked doubly necessary on the background of the scepticism which was shown by the British authorities towards Danish citizens, contributing further both to nervousness and depression.[21] In the discussions which now took place in the Danish Colony as to ways and means to counter the national bitterness, Major Iversen raised his voice. The actual discussions which would soon lead to the creation of the Danish Council will not be followed in detail[22] here the activities which ended in the formation of a Danish volunteer movement, only, will be described. It is here that Iversen played his decisive rôle.

He soon took the stand that "we Danes, who were living outside Denmark and in England, in any case must act in such a way that we could help the country where we were guests."[23] He very soon reached the conclusion that a Danish volunteer movement was the goal at which to aim. But he was also revolving other plans. During the summer 1940 he worked out a plan for Danes in England to undertake to reclaim a certain tract of land, where Danish man-power, stranded in England because of the Occupation, could be employed.[24] The plan was never implemented, but it is interesting in that it shows the urge for activity which inspired its author, and illustrates how the idea of a volunteer movement, even for Iversen, who agitated for it more intensely than all others, had to make a detour before finding its final form. The "agricultural plan" seems to have had its origin in an earlier plan,[25] also from June 1940, for making it possible on a long-term basis to find work for unemployed Danes, and probably depended upon the work of assistance which was started, with support from the Danish Legation, in order to find resources for Danes in need; to this Iversen contributed £100, a sum of such a size as to draw attention to him in Danish circles.[26] In his "agricultural plan" Iversen is still working from a completely civilian basis. The idea of a military Danish contribution is not yet considered as a possibility. It is stated in the plan: "The plan is therefore to find means and ways for Danes to become of positive value in spheres where circumstances allow their activities. Due to the existing particular circumstances Danes are deprived of the means to help in defensive and military activities – but not in food-producing activities." The plan stresses in conclusion that every step must be approved by the Danish Legation "from a legal and political view." The remark is interesting in that it shows that Iversen is not yet in touch with the British circles who would soon put an end to the situation, where "Danes are deprived of the means to help in defensive and military activities"; and that he still feels himself bound to the Legation's directives, at all events more strongly than was later the case.

However, Iversen would soon turn his thoughts to the fulfilment of the task which he had come to regard as decisive: collecting young Danes to fight in the Allied Forces. Such a thought was lying just ahead, and Iversen was by no means alone in contemplating it, although he became its most ardent advocate. In justice it should be mentioned, that the Trades Union representative, Børge Møller, who knew the conditions of that period extremely well, and who became the Danish sailors' spokesman in Great Britain,[27] believes that the idea of Danish participation in direct warfare can be traced back to immediately after 9 April.[28] Its crystallization in the summer can almost certainly be connected with the influence which de Gaulle's stand must have had just at that time, upon the feelings of Danes in England. There was a clear parallel between the two countries, and on 18 June 1940, de Gaulle had held his famous speech[29] to the French people, which ends: "I, General de Gaulle, who am in London at the moment, call upon the French officers and soldiers who are on British territory, or who come there, with or without weapons, and engineers and semi-skilled workers from the arms industry who are on British territory or who come there, to get in touch with me. Whatever happens, the French flame of resistance must not be extinguished, and it will not be extinguished."

After countless private discussions, which cannot be investigated today, the time for action had come. On 26 July 1940, a private meeting was convened in the Danish Club at 62, Knightsbridge. It was called by the Board of Directors of the Club, and led by the then Chairman, Allan Michelsen. It was to be of decisive importance for coming Danish developments. Regardless of the fact that it had a purely preliminary character, and that no final decisions were taken, the Free Danish Movement in Great Britain can be traced back to this meeting.[30] What had gone before, had mainly been invisible currents of feeling and thought. Now these rose to the surface for the first time. Thanks to the copious notes which Iversen took during that and the following meetings, it is possible to reconstruct events, while underlining the fact that from the start, and increasingly as time went on, Iversen represented an uncompromising and often oppositional point of view, which would soon come into the open; and that in the question of recruiting Danish volunteers, which is decisive for this investigation, he was soon to go his own way. The actual sequence of events appears clearly, however, and it is also possible to trace the increasingly close connexions which Major Iversen obtained from August onwards with British authorities.

As regards the meeting of 26 July, there is a report in Iversen's archive, written by him, with the footnote that copies have been sent to members of the exploratory committee set up at the meeting; and there is also a report written, according to a note on it in Iversen's hand-writing, by the young Dane Olaf Poulsen,[31] who was attached throughout the war to the Danish Section of the "Patriotic School", which took care of the security investigations of all foreigners coming into Great Britain.[32] The two reports confirm each other in all essentials.[33]

In Olaf Poulsen's matter-of-fact report, there is an interesting list of those present:

List[34] of attendants at the Danish meeting at the Danish club on the 26.7.40 at 2 pm. in order of speech and then the following names of people who did not speek. Next to the number indicating the speeches, the words pro and contra are written to indicate if the people who talked w[h]ere for the idea of a Danish legion or against the idea.

> Bechgaard K talks in bad danish, prefers english, PRO (1)
> Nielsen O E CONTRA (2)
> Iversen W M PRO very much applauded (3-7-9)
> Jørgensen R PRO (4-17)
> Michelsen A CONTRA (5-15)
> Mygind CONTRA (6)
> Krøyer Kielberg CONTRA (8-10)
> Nielsen Jacob CONTRA (11)
> Lunøe Engineer PRO (12)
> Palmer PRO (13)
> Willis PRO (14)
> Holdthusen (17) wanted to examine things before declaration
> Dohm PRO (18-20) applauded
> Stonner PRO (19)
> Jensen, Danish Seamans parson, PRO (21)
> Lunn Iver PRO (22)

> Duvier   Scheel, Count
> Beck   Ingerslev Engineer
> Thilge Rasmussen   Larsen
> Møller Engineer   Poulsen O
> Bendix (Hambros Bank)   4/5 names of attendances escaped me.
> Jacobsen

It also appears from the list, that the purpose of the meeting was to examine a proposal for the creation of a Danish Legion, or, to quote Olaf Poulsen's entry in full: "a Danish Legion of free and voluntary Danes wishing to join the forces of other bodies of free men belonging to Countries invaded by the Germans who wanted to fight for the sake of Great Britain."

It is not clear who moved the proposal. Iversen's report mentions that the Chairman, Allan Michelsen, opens the meeting with the announcement that "he has provided the opportunity to hold this private meeting in answer to many requests from Members, that Danes in England take steps to show their pro-British and Danish sentiments."[35] There is no real reason to look for an actual mover of the proposal. Here, as in Denmark, we find that spontaneous reactions are characteristic for the period. The many discussions set off spontaneous actions. We are in London, just before the Battle of Britain. The demand for resolute action is in the air.

The feeling of the meeting was – naturally – entirely for Britain and Britain's fight. On the other hand, it appears also from the list quoted that there were divergencies of opinion as regards ways and means. According to Olaf Poulsen's report: "The opinions differed as to the opportunity of forming a Legion. The older members believed it would do more harm than good for the sake of Denmark and those in the Home country. The younger and middle aged members were all for the idea of a Danish Legion showing the Danish colours ... The older members preconised the formation of a Danish ambulance and the collection of funds for the eventual purchase of a fighting or bombing plane to be presented to GB." This description of the opposition between the two factions is confirmed, but in vaguer terms, by Iversen's corresponding report, but it is confirmed particularly in a memorandum where Iversen outlines the main points in the work up to 7 August,[36] referring to the meeting of 26 July as follows: "Feeling amongst a certain number of the older people, the influential, is that nothing ought to be done at all, mostly influenced by diplomatic Danish wish to remain passive ... The other section support the idea that action ought to be taken, applaude my strong speech and support by J. (Robert Jørgensen) who has had this idea already since the fall of Denmark ..." Here we find, in addition to Iversen's deductions as to motives, clear indications of the divergencies which we meet increasingly, the more closely we examine the developments which resulted from the meeting of the 26th.

The result of the meeting, following a proposal by Holdthusen,[37] was that a preliminary committee of enquiry was appointed to look into the possibilities for forming a Danish Movement. The two reports differ slightly here, as Olaf Poulsen gives the aim of the committee as the examination of possibilities for the creation of a Danish "Legion", whereas Iversen notes more cautiously that the object was to examine the possibilities for a "movement which can express the Danish pro-British and Danish sentiments in a practical way." It can scarcely be doubted, however, that Iversen also has his main idea in mind, of a Danish military movement. His coming work is aimed at the realisation of this idea. Iversen expresses himself more broadly than Poulsen, and as will be seen from the work of the committee, more correctly.

The temporary examining committee was constituted as follows: the Director, S. A. Dohm, Vice-President of the Danish Club, W. M. Iversen, R. Jørgensen, O. Holdthusen and the Director I. Lunn.[38] The committee met immediately after the close of the full meeting in the Club premises. Mr. Dohm was elected Chairman, and a new meeting was fixed for 30 July. Robert Jørgensen was assigned the task of sounding British circles on the British attitude to the whole subject.

Developments were now well under weigh. At the meeting of 30 July, Robert Jørgensen[39] reported that he had enquired into the semi-official British attitude, and had met a favourable reaction to the proposal. Iversen's minutes contain the direct statement, that Robert Jørgensen had been in touch with two British civil servants, Mr. Kenny from the Ministry of Information, and Mr. Gallop, and he reports that the idea was received with favourable attention, and that it was proposed that a possible executive committee should be Anglo-Danish, and should not at first seek official recognition.[40]

When the committee of enquiry had received this information, which at least meant that there was a friendly, if non-committal attitude on the side of the British towards the efforts in Danish circles to create a free Danish movement, it proceeded to draw up the main lines for the coming work. At meetings on 5, 12, 16 and 23 August, this work continued,[41] and as it progressed, a basic disagreement was disclosed between the committee members. This disagreement is of particular interest for the present question, since its subject is the Danish volunteer movement, which Iversen advocated, and which it is our present task to follow.

As regards the general directives for the work, agreement was quickly established. After various proposals had been discussed the committee agreed, at the meeting on 16 August, on the work to be undertaken, wording it as follows:

"The work of the committee shall at present be:
1. to formulate a proposal on the main object for which it is envisaged that a new organisation shall work.
2. to examine the possibilities available for the setting up of such an organisation, including the examination of such proposals as have been or may be put forward.
3. to report the results of these enquiries to a later meeting of interested Danes, who decide thereafter for or against the setting up of a new organisation, and, if they approve, choose their own executive board."

34

On these points it can be seen that there was no essential difference of opinion. The difficulties arise over the interpretation of what followed:

"The committee shall make its enquiries with the following 4 main points as the basis for a possible organisation:

a. that it should work for the restoration of Denmark's freedom with a view to finding out in what way free Danes can give help – directly or indirectly – to the British Empire in the present situation.

b. that it should work to promote solidarity between all Danes in Great Britain and in the British Empire, and in association with all free Danes in the world.

c. that this organisation works for the strengthening of the position of official Danish representatives in England.

d. that in all public announcement(s), ... care is always taken that the wording of such announcements cannot create difficulties here or in Denmark, and thereby harm the cause."

It was the interpretation of the conditions drawn up in paragraph a. that brought the first splinters in the committee's work. Iversen interpreted this condition as meaning that, with the sanction of the British authorities, a movement of Danish volunteers should be created, who could join directly in the fight, and thus demonstrate the Danish will to take the risk of fighting side by side with the Allies. For him, this task was absolute. In a letter to Robert Jørgensen he expresses himself on this question as follows:[42] "Knowing my views, you may therefore understand perhaps, that when I feel that in the end there is a possibility for that such a voluntary force might be suppressed and come to nought, I would rather be out of it, which I understood some time, that also you preferred to be." It was this very possibility, that a Danish military force would not be created, that Iversen in August, rightly or wrongly found himself forced to face. For him this stood for the deathblow to a Danish movement. It is clear from his papers that he comes more and more decisively to the conclusion that a Danish volunteer fighting force must be raised. The idea of civilian help in agriculture, or the idea of an ambulance as it was mooted in the committee, no longer satisfies him. From a number of memoranda and notes,[43] which he draws up at the beginning of August, it is evident that he now aims at two goals, in comparison with which all else becomes immaterial or trivial: the military participation of Danish volunteers in the fighting, and the opening of a Danish house which can unite all Danes in Great Britain, including the sailors, who did not have access to the Danish Club. In his fight for these views, the antagonism between him and several of the other members increases sharply, and he soon feels himself a minority in opposition to the rest of the committee. We meet these feelings and views in a memorandum from 7 August,[44] for example:

"... we are running the risk of moving away from the mainpoint in the idea, that is up to us to present our case to the british government such, that we are willing to run risks and that we wish to run risks to help GB and thereby prove our interest in Denmarks independence. And not just talk about it or pay for it by collection to spitfires[45] and ambulances ... Only by commencing with a small military group ... can we achieve our object of giving a credulous expression for our wish to help GB and Denmark ... Also and only for this purpose could we call on free Danes in the world and obtain GB permission to let them in here or obtain permission to ... open an office in London, where Danes could call for the purpose of serving. This is the mainpoint of the whole movement and must not be lost sight of."

His papers show how his ideas for a volunteer Danish military force begin to take concrete form. In a memorandum of 11 August[46] he thinks out the administration and organisation he envisages, in some detail, and at the end of the memorandum the structure of the armed forces is described. These should be under military command only, and the officer in command should be British. A mine-sweeping section should be set up,[47] a light tank or anti-tank unit, an air force unit, Danish ambulances, a Danish hospital and possibly other detachments, depending upon the success of recruiting in Canada, USA and elsewhere. Iversen's ideas aim at the formation of regular Danish military units, incidentally on a scale which was quite disproportionate to the optimum of possible resources; but besides this the memorandum includes the point of great interest, that here for the first time we meet the idea of stimulating and giving support to the resistance which, it must be presumed, could be aroused in the mother country itself. The passage in question anticipates what was later to become a reality, in important respects, and lays down standpoints which were later to be the basis for British support for the Resistance Movement. They are therefore quoted here:

"a) Connection with BBC if possible increase number of broadcast and the time given for broadcast in Danish to Denmark.

b) If possible and as well have own transmitter for Broadcast to Denmark in Danish, encouraging Danes, during the hours most suitable to them (Danish after meals hours), to commence resistance, sabotage shortly to make the enemies occupation task as difficult as possible. Speeches should be made to rouse their national pride, to drill into them their future fate if they weaken and give in unresisting. Opposition to the *latest* danish government should be encouraged etc. etc.

c) Connection should be made with the Danish Legation in Washington ...

d) . . . .

e) *Leaflets* containing propaganda, should be written and dropped over Denmark, if possible by the Danish Aeroplane now in England."

It was on the background of these views, that Iversen came into sharp conflict, during August, with the opinion of the majority in the preliminary committee of enquiry. In particular he refused to accept the opinion that an aggressive attitude could create difficulties for the Danish Legation, could compromise the fiction of Danish neutrality, could expose Danish economic interests to danger, or call down German reprisals upon Denmark. Nor did he acknowledge the possibility that the British might not desire a Danish military war effort, or that his plans − personally or financially − exceeded the existing possibilities. When confronted with such objections, one notices his obvious irritation: "Prudence and timidity was the actual slogan behind the procedure (in the committee) and tasted very much as if it was the desire of several to prolong the move of the Danes coming out in the open before it was fairly firmly decided who would win the war."[48]

The same point of view is developed in more detail, and the same motives are attributed to his opponents, in another memorandum from the autumn 1940:[49] ". . . A question of Danish honour in fighting is not on the program, as they[50] do not wish to disturb status quo in Denmark, which is actually in their own favour . . . Their view is this, if Germany wins they have nothing against her, they have shown sufficient superficial sympathy to Britain to be left intact . . . If England wins they believe they have helped England by Red-Cross collections, etc. and by expressing their profound sympathy for the British cause, in words . . . The official attitude of the Danish Legation in London is based somehow on the latter expressed sentiment . . ." Here his irritation boils over, and he now aims his fire directly at the Legation.

It must be stated that in the heat of the battle, Iversen imputed motives to his opponents which cannot sustain a critical examination. Opportunism is by no means always engendered by ulterior motives, but can just as well be the result of justified tactical deliberations or admirable loyalty. But his notes leave no room for doubt as to the intensity and bitterness of the conflict, because we can follow it through the eyes of one of the very men who stood farthest from the centre, and on the side which we must find most interesting, because it was this side which worked deliberately towards open warfare. For the extremists, problems are simplified. Those who weigh the pros and cons are pushed into the background, and immediate basic principles, to a great extent tinged by emotions, stand out in the foreground as bases for the ungraduated standpoints which are the privilege of fighters. We are in England, but what a striking resemblance there is to conditions in Denmark, in the presentation of problems, in the argumentation, in standpoints and in feelings. The Danish Government's decision of 9 April left its mark upon discussions between Danes − also in the free world outside.

An important shift can be traced in Iversen's standpoint between June and August. In June, the idea of a Danish military war effort is quite outside the bounds of possibility, but in August it has become the indisputable aim. There can be several reasons for this shift, but one important and extremely interesting reason can be proved: Major Iversen is now in contact with British circles, for whom a Danish military war effort is not simply a possibility but a necessity. Of this contact Iversen says, himself:[51]

"In August I was already in contact with Sir Charles Hambro through Commander F. N. Stagg, R.N., who had asked to be introduced to me at the Danish Club, where he had heard of the Dane who was agitating for action." A gleam of light is also cast over this Anglo-Danish contact from contemporary sources. A report is extant among Iversen's papers of a meeting on 10 August between, on the one side, the Olaf Poulsen previously mentioned and Major Iversen, and on the other side the Mr. Bechgaard who was the first speaker at the meeting on 26 July, and who had spoken for a Danish volunteer movement at that meeting. Mr. Bechgaard was secretary to the British Member of Parliament, Mr. Strauss. The report is formed as a series of questions and answers, the object of which, throughout, is to ventilate the British point of view. It is quoted here in extenso:[52]

"Questions asked and replied given on the 10th August 1940.
Present Mrsrs. K. Bechgaard, O. Poulsen and W. M. Iversen.
Questions: Iversen
Answers: Bechgaard

1. Is the british Govern. keen on that we Danes are doing something?
   Replies: Yes!
2. Under which form?
   Reply: To be investigated!
3. What does the british Governm. want?
   Reply: Cement danish opposition!
4. Would british Governm. give us facilities to join up in British Forces to start with, as fighting soldiers – not labour – f. insts. in light Tank units or minesweeping?
   Reply: Being investigated and is under sympathetic investigation!
5. What effect will it have if our organisation look after our own countrymen only, i. e. arrange non-fighting organisation, such as unemployment exchange for Danes, social halls, shortly remain non combatant?
   Reply: Not enough, military force is required!
6. Will it satisfy if the organisation is *private* and *voluntary?*
   Reply: Yes!
7. What is the question to be brought up in the house of commons on Wednesday 14?
   Reply: Is the Government prepared to extent support and offer recognition to a body of Danes who actively work to oppose the german occupation of Denmark!"[53]

In an addenda to the report, added at the time, Iversen states that the questions "... are more or less cooborated[54] by Commander S.(tagg) as far as Questions 1.6 are concerned, whereas 7 was not discussed."[55] Major Iversen states also that Stagg has informed him that even such a detail as a battle-dress for the Danes has been discussed, and he has mentioned the English banker, Sir Charles Hambro, to him, as a great supporter of the plan, and interested in the question of a light tank unit and the training of Danish officers. This information has come as a complete surprise to Iversen, and Bechgaard's and Stagg's answers certainly go considerably beyond the hesitant British answers which, according to Iversen's papers, had been reported to the committee of enquiry up to that time. He exclaims at the end of his report: "Why have we not been told about this before?" This fresh information has apparently contributed to making Iversen even more eager for the idea of a Danish military formation to be realised. It is on the day after this meeting that he starts work on the memorandum of 11 August already quoted, in which he maps out his concrete plans.

Major Iversen had now been in personal contact with the British group who, in utmost secrecy, were building up a large scale organisation for the stimulation and support of underground activities in Europa,[56] and who, a month or two later, were to set up the Danish Section of "SOE", as the organisation was named. Charles Hambro was at this stage of the war one of the principals behind SOE, side by side with, for example, Major-General Colin Gubbins,[57] who in the spring 1940 had led the British "Scissorsforce", with great skill, in Norway.[58] It is clear that the two men had mutual need of each other, and that contact was now established between them; and it is easy to understand that the confidential conversations which now took place are not recorded in Iversen's papers, in the detail in which he reported the meetings of the committee of enquiry. There were special rules of security for work in SOE, which will be mentioned later. On 2 September 1940, however, there is a letter from Hambro: "Dear Mr. Iversen. I was very sorry to miss you last Saturday, entirely due to a misunderstanding because, while I was waiting for you at my office, you and Stagg were lunching at The Thatched House Club. I would like to see you and wonder if ... we can arrange a meeting."[59] For the sake of cohesion it can be mentioned here, that Hambro would fly to Stockholm about two months later, where he established connexions with the editor Ebbe Munck,[60] who was spinning the first threads in the fine-mesh net, which would reach over from Sweden into Denmark. The mole galleries were working their way forward, still without visible mole hills.

Contact with the British constitutes an extremely interesting background for the shift in Iversens standpoint, and helps to explain his stand. Some remarks in his letter to Robert Jørgensen, mentioned earlier, are also understandable:[61] "When you realise that the various impressions I have received from sources which I have no reason to consider unimportant are exactly of that same opinion as you and I had a little while ago, and which I hope we both still have, namely: that it is absolutely essential that we Danes show we are willing to run the risk of fighting as a corps for our freedom, as all other signs ... are not alone wasted but quite in vain ... If the British Government finds there is a real honest will behind our efforts ... they will not alone welcome this movement, recognise its existence and also give us all the help we want ..."

The stiffening of Iversen's attitude may, however, be due to other reasons beside the meeting with the British. He comes into contact at this stage with the spokesman for the Danish sailors in Newcastle, the trades union representative Børge Møller,[62] through whom he meets a kindred activist attitude among the sailors. From a series of letters exchanged between the two men, it emanates that they share the same outlook, and also that Børge Møller is in touch with Stagg. It was soon to prove that there were realities behind the words, when Børge Møller insisted that the sailors wanted action. It was the sailors, in highest degree, who were soon to fill the ranks of Danish volunteers.

Now Iversen also meets a Colonel Gibson, who was the British Liaison Officer to the Free Finns, and through him he saw a possibility of getting help towards opening a Danish house in Smith Square.[63] And finally, on the same day, he meets the Danish doctor mentioned earlier, Carl Johan Bruhn, who would become the first Danish volunteers' chief and leading personality. On 19 August he writes to Iversen:[64] "Dear Iversen. Here is my London address, and I hope, when convenient, to hear something from you as to how affairs develop and take form. It is time that certain active steps were taken and that there should be something of a "revival" of the colony, and I am convinced that many are waiting for a chance to come forward and show their true colours."

Thus the impulses which Iversen received in various ways contributed to stiffen his attitude even more. At the end of August the controversy with the other members of the committee of enquiry had reached such an acute stage, that he decided to leave the committee so that he could have a free hand.[65] After careful consideration, which lasted through the first half of September, he decided, without regard to the continuing work of the committee, to take action independently, and to send out an appeal to Danes in Great Britain, in which he asked Danes to join in the establishment of a Danish house and in a Danish promise to fight side by side with Great Britain and her Allies. The appeal was first shown to Count Reventlow, who on reading it expressed anxiety that it might cause a split among the Danes.[66] It was then sent out – on 26 September, King Christian X's birthday – addressed to "Danish men and women in Great Britain" and signed by Major Iversen, and by him only, although the "we" form is used.[67] It contains a patriotic appeal to all Danes to unite for action and with their signatures back up the opening of a Danish house intended to be a centre for those Danes who wished to offer their services to Great Britain. In addition the appeal contained an application to the British Foreign Minister, in which it both asks permission to open such a house, and also promises Danish support in the common fight. The appeal, which was sent out in about 2,000 copies, received a number of letters in reply.[68]

Strangely enough, the circulation of this appeal coincided closely with the invitation on 30 September to the constituent meeting, which resulted from the committee of enquiry's deliberations, and which led to the creation of the Danish Council. At the beginning of October, the Council opened an office in premises put at its disposal by the engineer C. F. Lunøe, and on 10 October the creation of the Council was announced over the BBC.[69] Major Iversen states[70] that this coincidence in time was not accidental, but that his appeal worked as the irritant which brought the Danish circles to the point of action, and this view is put forward in Frisch's book, "Denmark occupied and liberated",[71] although it is not clear upon what Frisch bases his opinion. Such an idea seems probable, however, if only because Iversen's initiative and aggressiveness contributed to speed up developments.[72] The circulation of the appeal must have been like pepper and salt to the committee, and must have made it extremely urgent for it to act. It should, however, be stressed that there is no proof of this, and the coincidence may have been quite accidental.

Whatever the case may be in this question, one thing is certain: Iversen's uncompromising conduct[73] did not reduce the distance, which had already widened considerably, between him and the other pioneers in the Danish work. In principle, both sides very much wished to bring the discord to an end, for the sake of the cause, and after an exchange of correspondence between Iversen and the Director S. A. Dohm,[74] it was agreed that Iversen should join the Danish Council, and hand over the signatures he had collected to it. He had thus placed himself in the official Danish work, and he was very soon also attached to the secret work within SOE,[75] circumstances which, in time to come, would cause misunderstandings and complications, which were seriously to affect the Danish recruiting work which he undertook to lead.

3. The Start of the Danish Section of SOE

The developments described in the two preceding chapters have been considered entirely from the Danish point of view: partly because my subject is the Danish Resistance Movement, and not British war history; and partly because the historical material involved is Danish and does not permit any detailed examination of events, as seen from the British point of view. In this chapter, however, it seems desirable to touch briefly upon some British problems, and to clarify them to the extent that this is possible. The solution of the crucial Danish problems was, after all, closely connected with British policy and strategy.

Through all the disasters which rained down upon Great Britain in the months after 9 April, and in the stream of hasty, improvised measures, to which the changing situations gave rise, one thing stood fast, immovable: Britain would continue to fight, regardless of what had happened in France, regardless of what further dangers would have to be faced. The Prime Minister, Winston Churchill, became the personification of British resolution on this point for the whole world, and he gave this resolution expression in his great speeches of the spring and summer of 1940.[1] The decision to continue the struggle under whatever circumstances was, to use Churchill's own words, quoted from "The Second World War", "not based upon mere obstinacy or desperation" but also upon "practical and technical reasons".[2] In a Note which Churchill sends, on 16 June 1940 at the height of the crisis, to the Prime Ministers of Canada, New Zealand, Australia and South Africa, he gives a statement regarding these "practical and technical reasons" and concludes with the words: "I have given you this full explanation to show you that there are solid reasons behind our resolve not to allow the fate of France, whatever it may be, to deter us from going on to the end."[3]

In July the British stand is the same, if not even more determined. When Hitler on 19 July urges Britain to stop the fruitless struggle, his suggestion arouses no other consideration than as to how it can be rejected most categorically.[4] The Swedish King receives the same reaction to his Note of 3 August 1940:[5] "They (the British Government) firmly believe however that with the help of God they will not lack the means to discharge their task (to beat Germany)."

It was one thing, however, for British experts after careful examination of the facts, to come to the conclusion that Great Britain was strong enough to withstand German attack, but it was quite another thing for them to see how Great Britain was to perform the task of beating Germany and winning the war. It was certainly a far cry from defensive to offensive conclusions. Here again, Churchill's history of the second world war provides a solution. The book leaves no doubt of Churchill's unalterable belief, that USA will be drawn into the war in the end, and that all perspectives will then shift. At moments this is expressed directly, as in the Note to the Prime Ministers of the Dominions, and naturally also in the long excerpts from his correspondence with President Roosevelt. Quite apart from this basic dogma, however, it is evident that the question of offensive warfare against Germany and Italy was already taken up at an early stage for direct planning. During the German offensives in April, May and June, it was unavoidable that British conduct of the war involved improvisation of a defensive nature, but Dunkirk was hardly over, and a breathing space had occurred, before offensive warfare was under consideration. In the chapter "The Apparatus of Counter-Attack" Churchill gives an account of the rôle which these offensive ideas play in British military deliberations in the summer 1940. It appears from this account that Churchill was personally occupied with vistas of the liberation when opportunity is ripe";[6] but apart from this, it is clear that the offensive possibilities of the moment are limited to occasional raids with the Commando forces, now put under the command of Sir Roger Keyes,[7] and to blockade, propaganda and air bombardment. In a letter of 25 July to President Roosevelt he writes on this question: "... it is necessary to plan on the largest scale the forces needed for victory. In broad outline we must aim first at intensifying the blockade and propaganda. Then we must subject Germany and Italy to a ceaseless and ever-growing air bombardment. These measures may themselves produce an internal convulsion or collapse."[8]

A corresponding account of the British point of view is to be found in "Comes the Reckoning", where Bruce Lockhart, Leader from 1941 of PID (Political Intelligence Department), was in charge of British propaganda during the war. In this vivid account of the gradual progress of British propaganda during the war years, from unpreparedness and mistakes to effectiveness and certainty, one finds the following passage: "But the fact should be noted that in January, 1941, when Mr. Harry Hopkins came to England to find out how we proposed to win the war, he was informed that the three lines of our attack on Germany were (1) blockade; (2) bombing and (3) propaganda and subversion ... These lines of the politico-strategic conduct of the war were confirmed by the American Chiefs of Staff during Mr. Churchill's visit to Washington in December, 1941."[9]

"And subversion". Britain's interest in developments in the occupied countries and in the possibilities which the Occupation itself offered, is now aroused in earnest. During the course of the year 1940 her attention becomes focussed upon conditions in the occupied countries. This interest can also be traced in Churchill's works, when in a memorandum of 6 June 1940 he writes to General Ismay:[10] "What arrangements are being made for good agents in Denmark, Holland, Belgium, and along the French coast? Enterprises must be prepared, with specially-trained troops of the hunter class, who can develop a reign of terror down these coasts." Later in the same memorandum he demands that a comprehensive system of espionage and intelligence be built up along the whole west coast of Europe.[11]

It is easy to understand that the British had to direct their attention increasingly to developments in the occupied countries. As the Germans overran the West European countries, so their tasks of guarding these countries increased, and the possibilities for unrest in the occupied countries multiplied. With Czechoslovakia, Poland, Denmark, Norway, Holland, Belgium and France in the hands of the Germans, their forces were already spread out considerably, and the later captures were to tax the *Wehrmacht* even more noticeably. This strain depended upon the condition that the Germans did not succeed in winning over the conquered peoples. British propaganda attacked this last threat with growing skill. In 1940 they were still groping their way to a great extent, from experience to experience, but gradually a surer touch was evident in both organisation and methods. Bruce Lockhart refers to this improvement:[12] "Yet at the time (1940–41) no serious impetus was ever given to our propaganda efforts from on top. It was due, I think, partly to the pressure of graver events and partly to ignorance of the subject in Whitehall", or in another place: "But 1942 was to see a great change. Frustration was to be replaced by the tense excitement of action. Order was to be brought into the chaos of our propaganda."[13]

On the basis of the views described above, Great Britain began to prepare in the summer of 1940 for "subversive operations". These plans were included in the Staff talks, between British and American staff officers, which were held from the summer 1940, and which, in the months of January to March 1941, resulted in the ABC-1-plan, which operated with, for example, blockade, bombing, propaganda and subversion, as preliminary measures in an offensive strategy, which was to prepare a British return to the European continent, possibly with the Americans. The immediate result of these deliberations was the creation, in mid-July 1940, of the British organisation: Special Forces Executive (SOE), the purpose of which was to support and develop resistance movements in the occupied countries, so that their activities in the form of intelligence, sabotage, assassinations, the creation of underground armies, etc., could be co-ordinated with British strategy, both short-term, and also in their vision of the future, possibly long-term.[14] It is from August 1940 that one of the leaders behind this organisation, Sir Charles Hambro turns his attention to setting up a Danish section, also.

There were formidable difficulties to face in all the occupied countries and particularly in Denmark. As I have pointed out, Denmark lay on the periphery of the British sphere of interest; the prestige of the country was not unaffected by the capitulation; Britain had not formally broken with the fiction of Danish neutrality; there was no exile government which could carry out the required recruiting; the resources of Danes abroad were extremely limited, etc., etc.; and added to this was the circumstance that Britain's own resources were very much reduced at that moment, and stretched to their uttermost. It was an imperative necessity to concentrate on the immediate possibilities, where early results could be expected. There was no desire, either politically or militarily to take on more responsibilities than the country could bear, at least not finally. We shall later see how the shortage of British resources and the lack of confidence among British military circles in the work in Denmark would obstruct British help to the work of resistance, for a long time to come.[15] On the other hand, there was no wish categorically to cut off possibilities for future developments. It was therefore best to keep the situation floating for the time being, without final commitment. It is in these very inauspicious circumstances that the Danish Section of SOE comes into being. Future developments on the great war fronts, and on the Danish home front, were to decide its fate – extremely favourably, as we shall see.

It is not possible, from the historical material extant, to determine whether the Danish Section of SOE was set up as a purely routine expansion of an organisation, which had to take all possibilities into account, or whether it was noticeably influenced by Danish initiative and the clear expression of Danish will to act, which we have seen formulated in London, and which, in the following pages, we shall see expressed in concrete terms elsewhere.[16] On the other hand, it is a fact that feeling towards Denmark was now changing, in the first place in the British circles engaged in the creation of SOE, who therefore turned their attention to developments in the occupied countries on the Continent. Thus, even though the auspices were unfavourable for the new section, psychologically it is not difficult to understand the turn of the tide. The long series of military set-backs in the spring and summer were brutal eye-openers for British onlookers, to Hitler Germany's overwhelming military power and ruthlessness; and on the background of the total collapse in Norway, Holland, Belgium and France, or on the background of the "miracle of Dunkirk", the absence of any real military effort on 9 April, and the decision to yield to the unavoidable, must have looked more comprehensible. There are worlds between the situation where Neville Chamberlain, as British Prime Minister, could say sarcastically of German military power:[17] "Whatever may be the reason – whether it was that Hitler thought he might get away with what he had got without fighting for it, or whether it was that after all the preparations were not sufficiently complete – however, one thing is certain: he missed the bus," and where Churchill promises "blood sweat and tears".[18] This is not simply the contrast between the two men, but between the different circumstances.

The entire continent had collapsed, and Britain stood alone. The situation behind Churchill's words could not but promote tolerance towards Denmark's attitude, a realistic understanding of her powerlessness.

In this atmosphere, the Danish efforts to change public feeling towards their country began to bear fruit. We have seen how the activists in London are getting the scent of a change in British signals, and we shall now – in Stockholm – find British intentions made clearer. Stockholm is now to be given the rôle which would become vital to the Danish resistance struggle. Here, in Stockholm, the circle closes – a circle which is essential to the coming resistance organism, and which is the clue to an understanding of this organism. Broadly speaking, the resistance struggle had three hotbeds: Denmark, Stockholm and London. The three main links in the movement were welded together, particularly in Stockholm, to a complete unit which gave the Resistance Movement strength and enabled it to become part of the greater Allied organism. To weigh or measure the importance of the three links against each other is just as impossible as it is unimportant. They are all three indispensable. It should, however, be emphasized, that Stockholm became in high degree the connecting link, of which the principal function was to forward impulses in and out of occupied Denmark. The editor Ebbe Munck, on the Danish side, and the Press Attaché Ronald Turnbull, on the British side, became the dominant figures in this work.

On 9 April 1940, Ebbe Munck was in Finland as correspondent to "Berlingske Tidende", and various Norwegian and English newspapers. At the end of May he returned to Denmark. Immediately after his home-coming, he began the realisation of far-sighted plans for getting to Stockholm and establishing a secret contact with the British Legation, so that a door could be opened from Denmark out into the free world.[19] A condition for such a connexion having any importance would naturally be that correspondingly important connexions were established in Denmark, and, as we shall see, this also took place. At the same time, Ebbe Munck, who was already interested in Greenland before the war,[20] was engaged in disclosing German plans on the East coast of Greenland. In the late summer of 1940, the Germans attempted, in conjunction with the Danish Nazi Carlis Hansen, to set up a meteorological station there. The station was discovered during a tour Ebbe Munck made in August 1940 through Norway, and British and Norwegian Marines destroyed the station before it could start working. The Germans, according to information Munck obtained, were taken prisoner, while Carlis Hansen had already returned to Norway.[21]

The negotiations which Ebbe Munck conducted in Denmark with a view to the future were, however, more important than this. An arrangement was made with "Berlingske Tidende" for Ebbe Munck to take over the post of Stockholm correspondent, so that the necessary camouflage was provided, for the stay he proposed to make in the Swedish capital;[22] and parallel with this, a number of secret negotiations were carried out, which were to have far-reaching consequences for the establishment and development of the whole Danish Resistance Movement. Immediately after his return from Finland, Ebbe Munck had contacted the officers of the General Staff Intelligence Section,[23] who possessed extensive knowledge of German military conditions and military movements, by virtue of their experience, military training, and the organisation at their disposal. According to the Danish-German agreement of 9 April, they were still allowed to carry on their work. The information they could provide would be passed on to the British via Stockholm. These officers, as mentioned previously, had already shown where their sympathies lay, when the British diplomatic train passed through Fredericia, and now they showed themselves willing to supply the desired material. In October 1940, Ebbe Munck could take the first set of micro-filmed information to Stockholm.[24]

Behind the idea of giving support to the Allies' conduct of the war in this way lay not only Ebbe Munck's private sympathies and antipathies, but also a national and political way of thinking identical to that which we shall meet within the ranks of the Resistance Movement in the years to come. In his account Ebbe Munck makes the following statement:[25] "The primary intention, even then, was to show fighting Britain in this way, that there were circles in Denmark who did not agree with the decisions of 9 April, and that as a modest start, they wished to make an effort which could be useful in a wider perspective. This, not least, since our armed forces, owing to the circumstances and the element of surprise in the situation, had been prevented from taking up the fight. The second intention for the realisation of these efforts was that the intelligence work should be placed to the credit of the Danish nation, and not of the British Secret Service itself. It is important to bear this last point in mind, as it became a leading motive for the work in the years which followed, where we continually endeavoured to have something to offer, and to do this work by our own efforts and with our own means, so that we were independent of any outside orders, and therefore able to negotiate on an equal footing, as to all conditions of importance to the war, shared by Denmark and England." Here we see the thought of resistance translated into practice at an astonishingly early stage. In that summer of indecision, Ebbe Munck and the officers of the Intelligence Section were among the relatively few whose horizon was not restricted by the physical confinement imposed by the Germans, but who were capable, not only of seeing the possibilities in the new situation, but of exploiting them. The fact that they all had special qualifications for doing so does not reduce the value of their contribution.

Ebbe Munck seems already to have completed his preparations in July 1940. In a letter of 19 July to Erling Foss, he writes: "... for one thing, I had to stay (in Copenhagen) because of some negotiations with the Ministry on the subject of conditions on the east coast of Greenland, and for another, because I could not get the lines for my future work for the paper laid down clearly ... I shall probably not be home by the time you return, as I am on the point of departure, so good-bye for the present, look after yourself till we meet. I am making a flying visit to Norway before I go to Stockholm ..."[26]

In October 1940 Ebbe Munck established himself finally in Stockholm. Before then, during his visit in the summer, he had already sought contact with the British Legation, and had agreed with the Naval Attaché, Captain Henry Denham, on setting up the Danish-British Intelligence Section outlined. Later the contact included the Press Attaché, Peter Tenant, through whom the Minister, Victor Mallet, was kept informed. Ebbe Munck brought the first information with him, when he finally left Denmark in October, and in the coming period he brought further material with him on various pre-arranged trips to Denmark "on duty".[27] As the work gradually increased, it became necessary to find qualified couriers, who could travel from Denmark to Sweden legally, and who were willing to run the risks which courier work involved. The task of finding such couriers was undertaken mostly by the Intelligence Officers in Denmark. Various well known figures in the Resistance, such as Erling Foss, Borch-Johansen, Mogens Fog and Per Federspiel acted as couriers on occasion,[28] and particularly in the case of Borch-Johansen this led to a considerable number of courier trips, which gradually involved him deeply in the work. In 1940 he was the business manager of the Coastal Shipowners Association, and his work gave him the possibility of keeping himself extremely well informed as to, for example, shipping conditions in Danish waters. On his trips to Sweden, for which his work gave him many opportunities, he passed this intelligence on to the British authorities. Out of this, an independent work of intelligence grew up which, as we shall see, was later linked to that of the Intelligence Officers.[29]

The chance of making a contribution to the Allied cause was seized eagerly, as is clear, for example, from a statement by Erling Foss: "Thanks to a coming combination of a business and hunting trip to Sweden, Volle (Gyth) brought me an innocent-looking object, which was to be delivered from the military Intelligence Service to Ebbe Munck in Stockholm. He had to tell me that there was a certain risk involved in delivering the thing, as it contained micro-film, but every safety measure was taken to reduce the risk to a minimum. The offer was naturally accepted with joy. Here at last there was something that was worth getting cracking on. Not only was this the way to give military information, but it also provided a unique chance to help the Danish radio in London to influence feelings in Denmark in the right way, against the Germans ... there was plenty of work to be done, politically."[30]

The effort to get their work put across to the British was soon to bear fruit. Shortly after Ebbe Munck's arrival in Stockholm, Sir Charles Hambro arrived unexpectedly in the Swedish capital, where, in utmost secrecy, he entered into negotiations with Ebbe Munck which were to be landmarks in Danish Resistance. There is a slight divergence between the accounts extant, on the timing of these talks. In his description in "Free Denmark's White Paper"[31] Ebbe Munck puts the conversations in October; in his more detailed account for the State Archives he puts them in November;[32] and in "Denmark under the Occupation"[33] he simply speaks of the autumn. In all three accounts, however, it is implied that London has received the first reports from Stockholm, and as these were forwarded in October, one may reasonably suppose that the conversations did not take place before the end of October, and possibly at the beginning of November. This also corresponds with the fact that it is mentioned, during the talks, that Ronald Turnbull would come to Stockholm as the local representative for SOE, and this was decided in October at the earliest, as we shall soon see, when the establishment of the Danish Section of SOE was a fact.[34] At all events, it seems certain that the Stockholm agreements took place after the decision to set up this section had been taken in London.

During these talks the British projects envisaged for Denmark were outlined for the first time, in the rough contours which belonged to this planning stage. The substance of the conversations will be quoted here from Ebbe Munck's report on them:[35] "Sir Charles outlined the plan for organised sabotage in Denmark already at that stage, pointing out that the Danes would themselves have the best possibilities for hitting the central organisations in Denmark without unnecessary damage. It was also emphasized that to the extent that Danes could themselves carry out this task, it would save Britain from bombing Denmark, and so killing many innocent people. It was admitted, in the talks, that no bombing of Danish targets was envisaged in the near future, since there were far more important targets in Germany itself, and at that stage Britain only had planes at her disposal for missions of the utmost importance. On the long view, when production of planes was in full swing, Danish sabotage, apart from the above advantages, would help to free British bombers for other purposes. Sir Charles was perfectly well aware of the fact that it would take some time before the Danish mentality was adjusted to the thought of sabotage, that it must necessarily take even longer before organisations with sufficient striking power were built up, properly manned and supplied with enough of the required sabotage material. But on broad lines, it was agreed, that we should work towards this goal, and as a help for the coming Danish organisations, the British would send a specially chosen Liaison Officer, Ronald Turnbull, to Stockholm. Mr. Turnbull had acted as British Press Attaché in Copenhagen in the months immediately preceding the occupation of Denmark, and thus had certain direct qualifications for fulfilling his mission in Stockholm. He would be attached to the British Legation in Stockholm, and would be registered with the Swedish authorities as Special Councillor on Danish matters ... Sir Charles strongly urged the continuation of the service already begun, which had made it clear to the deciding British authorities that there were circles in Denmark who wished, in spite of the official policy of neutrality and collaboration, to work with Britain. It was emphasized to Sir Charles that we insisted upon doing this work voluntarily and gratis, but that we should be very glad to see Mr. Turnbull come to Stockholm."[36]

A short report by Sir Charles confirms Ebbe Munck's statement. He places the talks in October, and writes in part: "I explained ... how it was the opinion of my government that it would be most helpful to the Allied cause if those Danes ... who were prepared to fight for their country's freedom, would start to form an Underground Organisation trained to conduct sabotage against the Germans. I made it clear at that time that it would not be in the interests of Denmark or Great Britain, if uncoordinated sabotage was to break out in Denmark at the moment."

With this, the rough preliminary outlines were drawn up for the work, which now lay before the Danish Stockholm circle – work which, in the years that followed, would take on very considerable and steadily increasing dimensions, both in extent and importance. To begin with, the most important function of the group was to forward intelligence. The stream flowed from inside occupied Denmark outwards, but the time would soon come, when the British would be prepared to make their return contribution, and then the stream would also flow in the opposite direction. Then the tasks would multiply and the work increase enormously. It should be stressed, however, at once, that at no time were later developments allowed to restrict the stream of intelligence. The work was reorganised and expanded, other men stepped in, supplementary organisations volunteered for work, but through all the vicissitudes, this source of military intelligence sent out its stream unchecked for the benefit of the Allied conduct of the war; and steadily and without a break, Ebbe Munck's Stockholm office at No. 13, Sibyllagatan, looked after the forwarding of this material, as well as numerous other tasks which the growing Resistance war effort laid upon it. From the beginning, the Danish Intelligence Organisation and its link in Sweden had an independent position, and made a contribution which added greatly to the respect which, well before 1945, would be established for Danish Resistance.[37]

At first Ebbe Munck worked alone, but before long he received the support of the Stockholm correspondent to "Politiken", the editor Sven See-husen and of the Danish engineer Jørgen Dalhof, a resident in Sweden.[38] In February 1941 Ronald Turnbull arrived. His rambling voyage is mentioned here, because its peculiarities illustrate two decisive features of the conditions of the time: the extremely modest British resources, and the slight weight attributed to Danish Resistance in the preliminary stages. The route from London to Stockholm – and one must suppose that it was the shortest available for this purpose – went by ship to South Africa, from there by plane to Egypt, and Turkey, and finally by train via Moscow to Stockhom.[39] In his report Hollingworth states that the reason for this route was that at that stage there was no air service from England to Stockholm.[40] It should probably be added, not, at least, for a voyage of such relative unimportance as this, in connexion with Danish affairs. It is interesting here to note that Sir Charles Hambro had flown to Stockholm, but in a Polish plane, which on the return flight took too southerly a course and ran into German flak over the island of Silt.[41] Generally speaking, it should be underlined that for a considerable period the air service between London and Stockholm was both meagre and greatly overstrained. One of the first planes came through just after Turnbull's arrival, and when the editor Sten Gudme left Denmark in May 1941, only two or three planes had flown to Stockholm. Sten Gudme was the first Dane to be given permission to use this service. His flying permit, dated 17 May 1941, is attached as an appendix to his written account.[42]

With Ronald Turnbull's arrival in Stockholm, a direct, quick contact was opened to the British authorities. From now on, the work began to take on a more definite character. The arrival of a British Legation civil servant, previously attached to the Legation in Copenhagen, naturally did not pass unnoticed by the Germans. In his account, Sten Gudme, who at that time was editorial secretary at "Politiken" and had to do with editing the foreign policy material, states that at the end of February and beginning of March "growing nervousness was noticed among the Germans" and adds: "I believe that I can say that this nervousness was intensified after they received news that Turnbull had arrived in Stockholm, and that in this connexion they expected increased English activity in Denmark."[43] If there was any nervousness, or at least speculation, among the then so exceedingly self-important Germans, it was not altogether unfounded.

Future events would demonstrate this.

We have now traced, both in London and Stockholm, how British attention is drawn to Danish conditions during the late summer and autumn 1940, and we have seen how British intentions are disclosed to Ebbe Munck for the first time. We have looked at the developments as they took form, from a Danish point of view, and have studied the traces they left inside the narrow limits of the preserves to which the few Danish observers had access. It is time now to pay a visit to SOE headquarters, and get an impression there of the situation at the start of the Danish Section. We can follow the start, as it was shaping for Lieut-Commander Hollingworth, the man who would lead the work of the section, with apparently unquenchable optimism, and with skill and wisdom, through the first years of disappointment to final victory.

In October 1940, Hollingworth was in Iceland, where he had been serving since the British occupied the country on 10 May, as Secretary to the Admiral.[44] He was now called home with orders to report to Commander Stagg in London. He then received orders to await further instructions at his home at Leicester, and after a few days there, the path led to one of SOE's training schools for underground activities. During the training which was begun here, no information whatever was given on the ultimate object of the exercise. All the work and the atmosphere which surrounded it was shrouded in the deep mystery, which characterised it thereafter. Listening to Hollingworth's own account, one is transported to the criminal world of detective novels, and readers of later times may find it difficult to enter into the peculiar atmosphere of mystery, in which the work of this organisation was steeped, from its most trivial to its most vital part. It is easy to find other accounts than that quoted below which confirm the atmosphere and methods ruling,[45] and for the sake of clarity, one should understand the immediate psychological reasons why all connected with this work, including the leaders, should from the start have woven a covering of mystery around this organisation, because, if for no other reason, such a covering was a protection against natural forgetfulness. Strangely, but understandably enough, the security insisted upon from the British side was perhaps taken more seriously in Great Britain and by the British than by the trainees who would one day find themselves working in the field. There one could adjust oneself better to the actual dangers and was reminded, by the work itself, of the danger of too much frankness. In free Great Britain, this protection had to be carried out according to fixed principles, and it may be that the magnitude of the problem increased with the distance to the battlefield.

Hollingworth's account reads:[46] "... I was to go to London and report at a given address, bring two sets of old clothes. At the adress in question I met ... Stagg, and Turnbull also arrived, with me ... Stagg was extremely secretive, and said that all that he could tell us was that we would now be brought to a place which he called "The Thieves Kitchen". Here we would get further instructions. A little later, a chauffeur arrived, who took us on a long drive, to an unknown destination. It turned out to be an old manor house in the country. Here we were told to ring the bell, and the door was opened by an oldish servant, who asked for our names. When we gave them, he stopped us and whispered two other names, which we understood we were to use in the future instead of our own."

After a short period of training,[47] the two Britishers received orders to report to an office in London, where they now met Sir Charles Hambro. He told them that their mission was to "seek to raise a Resistance struggle in Denmark, and organise it." One of them was to travel to Stockholm, and establish communication with Denmark from there, the other was to remain in London and set up a Danish Headquarters for SOE. The distribution of the rôles we already know. No detailed instructions as to ways and means were given. The task was completely open, with every opportunity for free initative and imaginative improvisation, by no means an unbritish way of tackling problems, and thoroughly typical of the talent for improvisation which characterized British warfare in 1940. A breeze from the spirit of Dunkirk meets us, in the way the Danish Section came into being.

4. Teething Troubles

Before studying the build-up of the work in the Danish Section of SOE more closely, it will be relevant to outline the framework of this whole organisation.[1]

SOE was under the Ministry of Economic Warfare. The Minister was Hugh Dalton, from the beginning of the war until February 1942, when he was replaced by Lord Selborne,[2] during a reconstruction of the British Cabinet. The most important responsibility of this Ministry, in co-operation with the Admiralty, was the constant vigil to ensure that the stranglehold of the blockade, which Great Britain had been seeking to close about the throat of Germany since the war started,[3] was not loosened. From July 1940, when Britain turned her attention to the possibilities offered by underground warfare, and SOE was established, the new organisation was placed under this Ministry. Owing to the top secrecy of this special work, the new body was kept separate from the actual Ministry, and placed under the direct orders of the Minister as a separate department. For a short time, the organisation was formally the responsibility of the Ministry of Shipping, as an administrative arrangement which was intended to camouflage the real facts.

SOE developed quickly and almost explosively, and at its start there were many changes of leadership. For the Danish work, Sir Charles Hambro came to play an important rôle, as leader of the West European Section of SOE, but before long, Major-General Sir Colin Gubbins[4] became its chief for all operational work. As such, he was Hollingworth's immediate superior in operational matters.

The work of SOE was for all the occupied countries, as they fell into the enemy's hands, not only in Europe but also, after Japan entered the war, in Asia, the work being divided regionally. There was thus a West European Section and under this a Scandinavian Section, which originally included both Norway and Denmark. At the start of the Danish Section and for a short time thereafter, it is noticeable that the whole administrative machinery was in rapid development and had by no means found its final form. Denmark belonged to the Scandinavian Section, but this was soon altered so that Denmark became a separate, independent section, as it was recognized that the conditions, and therefore the working possibilities in Denmark and Norway were totally different from each other. For a time, however, the

Danish Section continued under the administration of the Norwegian Section, led by Colonel Wilson, before it became independent; the work of the section was then co-ordinated, as far as this was necessary, under the Chief of the West European Section, the longest in office being Brigadier Mockler Ferryman.

If the tasks, and particularly the methods of SOE are now questioned, it will be necessary first to emphasize a fundamental fact: Britain was not prepared for war, and the British war machine was largely built up during the war itself, under the pressure of its imperative requirements, and under the heavy handicaps which lack of time, lack of material, and lack of experience created. This is true in general, and it is perhaps especially true of SOE. It was years before Britain slowly squeezed her way through the countless bottle-necks which blocked the way to final victory. On the other hand, there were certain advantages in this underlying unpreparedness. It permitted an open-minded attitude to problems, and a freedom from red tape in their treatment, which had their own freshness, and which gave results in a situation which called particularly for new ideas, initiative, and inner resources.

It will not be necessary, in general, to illustrate the British unpreparedness. It shines from the pages of history, and expresses itself in countless ways, in the Army, the Air Force, the Air Raid Precautions organisation, and even in the Navy. Here I shall only add some remarks on the areas which border the SOE fields of activity. In Bruce Lockhart's account of the progress of British propaganda he pronounces a cutting judgement upon the British preparations made before the war and at the beginning of the war, for a counter-offensive against Goebbels' propaganda. His whole book, including the title,[5] pursues this theme, and it is in the spirit of the book that he takes the following quotation as his opening motto:[6] "Any country which thinks more of its ease and comfort than of its freedom will loose its freedom, and the ironical thing about it is that it will loose its ease and its comfort too." The BBC propaganda to Denmark, which we have already considered, is a good example of unprepared beginnings, the make-shift improvisations, which gave rise to considerable criticism before it acquired more certainty and skill.[7]

The experience of an associated service can also supply an example of the way in which British initiative scraped through the difficulties which surrounded it, by adding improvisation to improvisation. The German use of parachute troops in Holland and elsewhere had drawn Churchill's special attention to the fact, which incidentally speaks for itself, that Britain wholly lacked such an arm; and on 6 June 1940 he ordered a parachute force of 5000 men to be raised with the least possible delay.[8] In August he returns to the question in a memorandum to Anthony Eden, as War Minister.[9]

As the direct result of Churchill's intervention, a conference was held at the beginning of June in the Air Ministry, where it was decided to set up a parachute training school. The school was situated at the civilian air port at Ringway, near Manchester.[10] Thus the organisation was created, which was to have enormous importance for the British conduct of the war, and which would become one of SOE's most important supporting organisations, since all the parachutists who attended SOE's many schools for training[12] would receive their parachute training there. There are several detailed accounts of the work of this school, the principal one being in a book written by the leader of the school, Group Captain Maurice Newnham.[12] In this very instructive, vivid book he gives a clear account of the towering difficulties of the work, such as lack of material, lack of support and understanding from doctrinaire superiors in the various military departments.[13] But the book also gives a splendid impression of the enthusiasm and imagination which carried the school through the difficulties. On a small scale, and in one corner of the arena, this reflects the way in which Britain as a whole, after the inefficiency and unpreparedness of the preliminary phases, bungled her way through to greater and greater organising skill and technical expertise. On the training of the SOE parachutists there is the laconic remark: "Concurrently with the training of men of No. 2 Commando, which was re-named No. 11 Special Air Service Battalion, the School was also responsible for the training of secret agents and men of the Resistance movements. For obvious reasons the identity of these men was most carefully guarded and they were referred to under a collective nom-de-guerre for which I will substitute the word "Specials"."[14]

What is true of the British conduct of the war in general is also true of SOE in particular. Here it was a question of an entirely new form of warfare, and broadly speaking, no previous experience could show what could be achieved in this field. The pioneers had to find out by trial and error, what methods would prove successful. Obviously tasks as well as methods had to vary from one country to another, and from one period to another. The original presentation of problems had to be somewhat vague. Seen on the background of the lack of experience, material, and trained staff, the first operations which the new organisation and its supporting organisations ventured upon must appear as necessary experiments, and a broad margin must in all fairness be allowed for mistakes and misunderstandings. This applies to the organisation as a whole, as well as to the Danish Section. In addition, these first operations – including the first operations of the Danish Section – had often to be carried out at times where those involved were far from ready for action, but where other priorities, such as propaganda, or the need to gain experience, made the operations desirable, or indeed absolutely essential. On the one side, it was necessary to demonstrate that Britain was capable of taking the initiative, and on the other, the young organisation had to justify its existence and enforce the respect for its work, which was an absolute pre-requisite for its being able to break through the prejudices and routine thinking of many political and military leaders, which stood in the way of effective results. A superb example of how, in such conditions, these men dared, nevertheless, to go into action, is given in Newnham's book, where he describes the first parachute operation ever made from England. It was an attack carried out in February 1941 against a target in Italy.[15] Fifty men took part in the attack, led by an Italian volunteer who belonged to SOE. Newnham describes in detail the infinitely small means at their disposal at that time, and adds the following characteristic comment:[16] ". . . quite an ambitious project, nevertheless, for a completely new arm of the Services whose largest exercise up to that time had been the dropping of sixteen men from two Whitley aircraft on to Salisbury Plain a week or two previously." In his account we also meet the considerations of propaganda already touched upon, when he speaks of "the urgent necessity for a 'tour de force' to demonstrate to neutral states and the world at large that Britain was still alive and kicking and capable of aggressive action."[17] But most important of all, at that time, was the reaction in Britain. After an analysis of the operation, partially unsuccessful, he adds: "But at Ringway we continued to work and wait and wonder. What did the 'high-ups' think of the first airborne experiment? Were they impressed with the potential it offered? Would our own confidence be shared and more and more men be sent to us for training?"[18] They were.

If the corresponding teething troubles applied to SOE as a whole, they applied in a special degree to the Danish Section. For some time to come, there was great uncertainty as to the extent to which an underground struggle could be carried on at all in Denmark. There was doubt as to the attitude of the people,[19] and there was also considerable scepticism as regards the practical possibilities for an underground struggle in a country of such small square mileage, densely built up areas, and excellent communications network, which seemed to raise the most serious obstacles imaginable for such a struggle. For a long time, these quite understandable misgivings had their influence, and on the average, the scepticism in London was greater than in Denmark, even after the work was in full progress and the Resistance fight a fact. Much later, during the negotiations which took place in the spring of 1944 in Stockholm, between members of the Danish Freedom Council, created in September 1943, and representatives of SOE, London's cautious evaluation found expression. These negotiations[20] lie outside the period treated in this volume, and are only mentioned in this connexion to illustrate the difference between the British and Danish views of possibilities in Denmark. At meetings on 16, 21 and 24 April 1944, in which Erling Foss,[21] Frode Jakobsen, Ebbe Munck, Lieutenant-Col. Nordentoft and Commander Mørch represented the Danish side, and Hollingworth, Turnbull, and Ray[22] represented SOE, while the parachutist Ole Geisler was substitute for the then parachutist leader, Flemming B. Muus, the question of a Danish underground army was discussed. It was during this discussion that the difference in opinion showed itself. Frode Jakobsen, who led the negotiations as representative for the Danish Freedom Council, refers to the divergence as follows:[23] "On the British side they stuck to the opinion that it would not be possible to wage any form of guerilla warfare in Denmark. To this the Freedom Council representative (F. J.) maintained that ... one would be able to wage guerilla warfare, in the sense that under the motto: 'Hit and run' one would be able, for example, to capture and hold a station for a short time, until one had carried out the desired destruction. On the other hand, he naturally agreed that we would never be capable of taking up an open fight."

This was in 1944, after the work had made such progress as one hardly dared to dream of in 1940. At that time, the aim was very modest, and there was perhaps an exaggerated idea of the difficulties. The Danish Section became a special experiment, where the section itself had to show evidence that an underground struggle, even on an extremely modest scale, was a possibility of any kind. This background should be stressed, and also the fact that the Danish Section was the Cinderella of the organisation, until development in Demark resulted in the work gradually receiving greater and greater support. The policy of the section had to be to seek to achieve results in Denmark, first with the least possible support from Britain, or even without support, in order to be able to use these results as battering rams against the British scepticism. The advantages for the work in Denmark, which could gradually be squeezed from the British authorities, could again lead to expanding results in Denmark, with renewed pressure in England as their direct follow-up. A vicious circle had to be converted to a beneficent circle.[24]

It became Hollingworth's duty to implement this policy. It is perhaps the greatest service he rendered, that it succeeded as well as it did. From 1943 there are two letters which illustrate the problem. In May 1943, Hollingworth writes to the then chief of the organisation in Denmark, Flemming B. Muus,[25] and asks him to send consecutive reports on all the sabotage actions on which he can get information. Hollingworth adds that he wishes Muus to mark his information "Jam", "Plum Jam" and "Jam Tart", respectively, so that "Jam" is used for all sabotage actions carried out by groups with whom Muus is in direct contact, "Plum Jam" for all sabotage where Muus is only in indirect contact with the groups, and finally "Jam Tart" for all major sabotage actions where Muus has no knowledge of the identities of the saboteurs. He then writes:[26] "Remember that whatever work is undertaken by the groups with which you may have no connection it is recent run of successful operations in your sphere (Denmark) and the publicity that has been given to parachutists that has directly acted as a stimulus to other resistance groups." The intention is clear enough. Hollingworth had his own battle in London, to survive in the competition with sections of other countries; the information was to provide proof in justification of an increased share in material for the Danish Section, and – 'all's fair in love and war'.[27] Hollingworth won his war, and the section with him. In the final phases, Danish Resistance work enjoyed the highest recognition in London, and the possibilities for obtaining material gradually improved more and more.[28] The way had been long and arduous, and the goal was only reached after thankless sacrifices and pioneer work, carried out by the earliest Danish Resistance men in and outside SOE. In 1940, the final result must have looked Utopian.

A picturesque and amusing account of conditions at the start of the work is given by Hollingworth. He writes:[29] "As regards my organisation of the department at the beginning, I should like to underline the fact that I had to start absolutely from scratch. My orders from Hambro were, quite tersely, that I was to tackle the problem and get some results. How it was to be done, it was up to me to find out. I got a little office (in Baker Street) with the barest office necessities, telephone, correspondance trays, etc. – and had to find out how to set about it ... So we began studying methods in underground warfare, investigating how people elsewhere in similar circumstances had tackled things. At the same time we followed as far as we could, what was going on in Denmark ... (gradually) we began, little by little, to get hold of certain ideas about what should be done, but I would like to underline the fact that at the beginning we had the feeling that we were absolutely down to bed rock and left to our own devices.

I still remember, from the first period, the two empty trays for outgoing and incoming correspondance, and a certain feeling of loneliness." The two empty trays can stand there, as a pertinent symbol for the lean, uncertain times.

In January 1941, the staff expanded, and the portrait gallery is again supplemented with our acquaintances from the diplomatic train of 13 April 1940. Reginald Spink and Albert Christensen were attached to the work,[30] the former at the Headquarters in Baker Street, while Albert Christensen was posted as British Consul in Göteborg, with the task of establishing and maintaining contacts with Denmark, together with Turnbull. At the same time, a third acquaintance from the diplomatic train, R. L. Taylor, was appointed liaison officer between Baker Street and the Danish training schools.[31] In February 1941 Christensen left by plane for Stockholm, and Hollingworth accompanied him on the trip. Turnbull had just arrived in Stockholm, and Hollingworth decided therefore, after consultation with Charles Hambro, to go to Stockholm to confer with Turnbull on how one "in some way or other could ... get a hole pricked in the boil."[32] The conference does not seem to have had any definite result. The main problem was still to get contacts established with Denmark, as the communications already in existence with the Intelligence officers served regular military purposes, and were not to be burdened with the special SOE work. This was an understandable decision, but, as we shall see, not altogether possible to maintain. The value of the conference may therefore be seen in what the personal contact meant to the two men, with the opportunity of going through the general problems once more, and of bringing Turnbull up to date as to the progress achieved in England during his long voyage.

5. The Problem of Recruitment

When the February talks took place in Stockholm, important progress had been made in one field. Recruitment of Danish volunteers had already begun and the first group of volunteers was in uniform. A start had been made in the solution of a problem which both then and later gave rise to serious difficulties of a practical as well as a principal character. The practical difficulties originated mainly in the fact that there were only very limited possibilities for recruitment in England. There were few Danes in the country, apart from the large contingent of Danish sailors, the value of whose service was primarily in the Merchant Navy. Here, however, they were of great value for the Allied struggle, and the fact that the scale of Danish recruitment was somewhat modest must be seen on the background of the contribution in that special field, which as regards volume, type, importance and self-sacrifice were worth even very considerable military contingents.

One might ask, why no effort was made to bring suitable men over from Denmark. One reason for this was that only a very slender connexion existed with the Home Front, and another, that the transport problems at that time were almost insuperable. In addition, departure from Denmark could hardly be hidden, and this would be very unfortunate from the point of view of security. It was not until a good deal later that this possibility was seriously considered, even though men were brought over from home from time to time, to join in the work.[1] In 1943 the idea of carrying out recruitment in Denmark was put forward. By then, connexions from Denmark to Sweden and from Sweden to England had been expanded to such an extent, that the suggestion could be considered as a practical possibility. In the spring 1943, Hollingworth asked the then parachutist chief, Flemming B. Muus, whether it would be possible to recruit volunteers in Denmark.[2] Muus replied in the affirmative, and stated that he was in touch at that moment with two men who could be considered suitable, and whom he proposed to send over to Turnbull, with the message that they should be sent on to London.[3] In a later letter Muus again proposed suitable men.[4] However, the idea never had any great importance for recruitment, although it is not possible to see why it was not carried out, when the possibilities were there.[5]

In addition to the purely practical difficulties there was a problem of principle. In contrast to most of the other countries where British support for coming resistance work was being prepared, Denmark was not at war with Germany, and there was no exile Danish government or corresponding Danish authority, which could and would take the initiative or the responsibility in recruiting a Danish military unit. The proper course must therefore be to enroll Danish volunteers in the British Forces, although this also created obvious difficulties, owing, for example, to Denmark's special position as regards Germany. There was a certain parallel to the Franco-British situation, but here the British Government had on 28 June 1940 recognized de Gaulle as leader of all the Free French in Great Britain. This contributed to the solution of the French recruiting problem.[6]

For the various European sections of SOE – Denmark excepted – there were thus no difficulties of principle in raising volunteers. They could all draw to a certain extent upon the officially established forces, which were present in Great Britain in varying degrees. It was a different matter for the Danish Section. No official Danish forces existed when the section was set up. However, the problem had to be solved, and solved quickly. All future work would stand or fall on this point. The problem was further complicated by the fact that open recruitment to this work was undesirable. For reasons of security, it was preferable for all recruitment and training to be carried out as secretly as possible.

For the solution of this problem the attention of SOE was drawn to Major Iversen. In the late autumn of 1940 he agreed to help Hollingworth in the required work of recruitment:[7] "During that period (autumn 1940) I had been introduced to Commander Hollingworth by Commander Stagg ... and I agreed to join the work of recruiting suitable Danes to it (work in SOE). However, owing to the opposition which would come from the Danish side over there, because of an extremely developed fear of German spies in England, and because the names of the soldiers recruited and of their families must be protected as far as possible, owing to the dangers of the service, it was necessary for me to carry out this work extremely quietly, and cover it up by urging young Danes to volunteer for the Forces (Iversen is thinking of the regular British Army)." It was naturally a condition for Iversen being able to make his contribution to such recruitment that he should be a British officer himself, a condition which SOE undertook to fulfil. At Christmas 1940 he evidently received his application papers for a British commission through this organisation.[8] In January he is made a Captain in the British Army and can begin his work of recruitment in connexion with SOE. A few days later, on 11 January 1941, the first group of Danish volunteers were collected and began their training at a school in Market Harborough.[9]

Iversen had thus done SOE and the Danish cause an important service, in a very difficult situation, but the arrangement was neither lasting nor satisfactory; nor did it fit in with the plans for establishing an independent

Danish military unit, for which Iversen had been such an ardent spokesman. The disadvantages of the arrangement were obvious enough. There was no responsible Danish authority behind the recruitment. It had to be done in secret, and this created a feeling of insecurity, both for the recruits and in Danish circles, which naturally could not remain completely unaware that men were being recruited, and which, just as naturally, could not get any information from Iversen on the purpose or the extent of recruitment. For several reasons it was therefore desirable to reach a more permanent and less hole-and-corner agreement, and efforts were made in this direction in the spring 1941. The problem was solved with a special arrangement whereby the British regiment, "the Buffs" (the Royal East Kent Regiment), whose honorary Colonel was King Christian X, opened its doors for Danish volunteers.[10] The whole question of the Danish Council's attitude to recruitment was raised at the same time, a question which was to lead to lengthy and sad misunderstandings and disagreements between Iversen and the Danish Council, and which in 1943 would finally end in an irreparable breach between the two parties. A detailed analysis of the whole quarrel has no interest in relation to this thesis, and a description of the attempt to establish a regular Danish military unit within "the Buffs" also lies to some extent outside the frame-work of this investigation.[11] Here the rough outline of the arrangements will be sketched out, as far as this is necessary for an understanding of developments within SOE.

First of all it should be stressed that the recruitment begun by SOE in January was started without reference to the Danish Council, and was secret. Iversen, as mentioned, had temporarily joined the Danish Council, and since it was impossible to hide the fact, in the long run, that recruitment was taking place – after 1 January Iversen was in uniform, himself – questions were naturally asked by the Council. Iversen was debarred by the security rules of SOE from answering, at least fully, and even though the Council quickly accepted the standpoint that he could not give detailed information, "for military reasons", they naturally wished to have some influence upon developments. In this respect also, the solution whereby Danish volunteers joined "the Buffs" seemed to be acceptable, as recruitment for this could be carried out openly, thereafter, and in connexion with the Danish Council.

The idea for this unusual arrangement seems to have originated with Stagg, and he was particularly energetic in getting it realised,[12] so that negotiations on this matter between the Danish Council and the British military authorities could be completed in the course of the spring 1941. In a letter dated 27 March 1941 to the Danish Council, the Adjutant-General to the Forces, General H. C. B. Wemyss expresses the Regiment's willingness to accept Danish volunteers,[13] and on 5 May 1941 the War Office sends the detailed rules for recruitment. This states, in part: "The Danish Council will call for volunteers among the Danes now living in the United Kingdom. After satisfying themselves as to the general suitability and bona fides of each applicant, the Danish Council will forward names and addresses of applicants to the appropriate Army Recruiting Officers who will inform each individual when and where he shall attend for medical examination ... Those who are found medically fit will be forthwith enlisted and informed on what day they must report to a Training Unit for duty." On 26 May, the Danish Council puts forward some suggestions for alterations to this, among others: "... It is requested that Captain Iversen, who is at present on the General Service List, should be transferred to the Buffs Regiment and then seconded for special duty outside. This is considered necessary because the Danish recruits wish to feel that they will be kept as a Danish Unit, and it is therefore considered advisable that a Danish citizen, who is an officer in their own regiment, should be their liaison with the War Office ... it is suggested that applicants ... should be ordered to report to Captain Iversen, the recruiting officer of the Danish council, who will then forward suitable names to the War Office for their consideration." This proposal was accepted in principle from the British side, and on 3 June 1941 the matter was finally concluded, and detailed orders on this special recruitment were promulgated by the War Office. On 19 July Iversen was transferred to the Regiment, with the rank of Major, and the Danish Volunteer Movement thus received an official stamp.

From the point of view of SOE, this arrangement had considerable advantages. Since recruitment to the British Forces could not be concealed, it was much to be preferred, that recruitment to the regular British Army should be carried out in the light of day. Such recruitment could draw possible unpleasant German attention to itself, and serve to cover up recruitment to SOE. Through open recruitment a group of Danish volunteers was gathered together, from amongst whom it was possible, with the help of the Regiment's officers, to choose suitable candidates who could then be transferred, in utmost secrecy, to the special work of SOE. The first reason was particularly cogent for the leaders of SOE, who wished to avoid German attention being drawn to the preparations for underground activity in Denmark which were being made in Britain; and for whom it was an important advantage that coming activities could come as a surprise to the Germans, at least in the initial phases.[14] For these reasons SOE urged on the completion of the arrangement with "the Buffs", and were glad of the public attention which was thereafter directed towards the recruitment,[15] shedding crocodile tears over the sad fate which had overtaken the idea of a regular Danish unit. The new arrangement served its purpose simply as camouflage for training in SOE, whilst the size, striking power, training etc. were not particularly important to the British.

The difficulties of recruitment did not therefore end with the establishment of the arrangement with "the Buffs", and they fell upon Iversen's shoulders.

One reason was that the arrangement was not sufficiently clearly defined, to avoid misunderstandings between him and the Danish Council. It is evident, from the reply quoted above, that the Council regarded Iversen as "recruiting officer of the Danish Council", whereas he regarded himself as a British Officer, and his recruiting centre as a British office, which was connected through him to the Council.[16] The Danish Council could support recruitment according to the arrangement, as they understood it, and call upon young Danes to volunteer. Technically, however, the recruitment had to be carried out through Iversen, as a British Officer; and on the basis of his connexion with SOE, of which the Council was not informed, he had to withhold information in several cases, where the Council felt it had a right to demand it of him.[17] The conflict seemed to be unavoidable. In the spring 1943, Iversen retired from the leadership of the recruiting office, and also from the Danish work. From the autumn of 1943 he served in the British Army under 21st Army Group.[18]

If Iversen's position was difficult and unenviable in relation to the Danish Council, it became untenable in the long run vis-à-vis SOE. Here, however, the situation was reversed. In this case, it was SOE that had to withhold information from its Danish recruiting officer to which he might feel himself entitled, as responsible to the Danish volunteers. The situation can best be understood if one looks at it from the SOE point of view. This was a purely British organisation, surrounded by the impassable cordon which encircles all military activity, especially in war time. Added to this, it was a secret military organisation, where water-tight isolation was a vital necessity, from which even the slightest leakage was taken with deadly seriousness. Its sphere of operations now lay outside Britain, and this forced it to employ foreigners for work which was top secret even from British officers of high rank. The difficulties involved are obvious, particularly for the Danish Section, since this section could not establish connexions with official Danish authorities and take them into its confidence at least to some degree. The result was a compromise. SOE established the connexion with Iversen, and pushed him in between itself and Danish circles, while at the same time keeping him at arm's length, and withholding any thorough orientation on conditions within the organisation from him. As Hollingworth puts it:[19] "His intense enthusiasm for getting something active done made him a very useful man at the start, when there was a question of getting volunteers. It was his job to urge the Danes to join up ... A special difficulty arose here between us in SOE and Iversen, who was in contact with a great many Danes, in that we could not and were not allowed to give him any information as to the character of the work." Hollingworth's concluding remark must certainly be interpreted as meaning that it was not possible to give him full information on everything. Iversen was naturally informed of the main character of the work he was supporting.

From the start it was clear that SOE would not limit itself to the recruitment which started from or passed through Iversen's office. In addition to this "useful" recruitment, further recruiting quietly by-passed him. An example of this was the first group of volunteers who began their training in January 1941. Hollingworth had personally taken part in recruiting several of these men. In co-operation with Børge Møller and the local police in Newcastle, he had had a series of interviews arranged with Danish sailors who were considered suitable and willing to back up a Danish Volunteer Movement. During these talks, no precise details were given of the duties which these men would undertake. The demand for absolute secrecy had to be maintained. Hollingworth himself states concerning these conversations:[20] "The difficult part about these interviews was that I could not tell them anything about the job we wanted them for. I told them that we wanted them for a very important job for their country, and I made it clear to them all, that the job was dangerous, and they must be prepared not to be informed during training as to what their duties would be. About twenty men volunteered, of whom Mogens Hammer, Anders Lassen and Lok Linblad can be mentioned."[21] There can be little doubt that the essential point in his account, the impossibility of giving details of the real purpose ahead, refers to the painful situation he was in. Even if SOE had had a clear idea, at that early stage, of what could be done in Denmark – and this was certainly not the case – such an idea could naturally not be discussed with people of whom they knew so little. In his recruiting, Iversen had to observe the same reticence. He emphasizes this as one of the principal difficulties in the work of recruitment,[22] and it is further illustrated by the following remark of one of the volunteers mentioned by Hollingworth, Lok Linblad:[23] "During training ... we realised that the leaders seemed to have certain plans for us, which differed from the original one, which I supposed was to join 'the Buffs'.[24] When we saw what we were to learn ... we were still (after several months) not clear as to what was the purpose of the training." From the following account it appears that the purpose of the training only dawned upon this volunteer well into 1942, after several months at the special training schools.

These first recruits were drawn from the reserve represented by the Danish sailors. This could not supply any very considerable number of volunteers, since it was difficult to take Danish sailors away from their service in the Merchant Navy. A direct connexion was, however, established between SOE, with Stagg as intermediary, and Captain C. L. Heel, who was leader of the Danish "sailors' pool" with an office in Newcastle (Merchant Navy Reserve Pool, Danish Section),[25] so that the leader could, when opportunity arose, refer young Danish sailors who were interested, to SOE. There was no question of any crowded or constant stream of volunteers, but rather a poor catching, drop by drop, as the correspondance between Heel

66

and Iversen shows.[26] The following remark in a letter from Heel to Iversen[27] indicates that the stream, small as it was, periodically stopped altogether: "I will do my best to send you some more men but at the present moment the pool is very low and we are having the utmost difficulty in finding men to man the ships. When it is in its entirety I hope to be able to send you more."

We have seen how SOE, from the start of recruitment in Newcastle, addressed itself direct to possible Danish volunteers, when opportunity arose, and that they could be taken into the organisation without reference to Iversen. This practice continued, even after recruitment was established on a firmer basis.[28] An important example of this was the recruitment of Christian Michael Rottbøll, who was later to become parachutist chief, which went through SOE's Stockholm department. In 1941 Rottbøll had pretended, vis-à-vis the Danish and German authorities, that he would volunteer for service in Finland during the Finnish/Russian war. He was therefore granted an exit permit from Denmark, but volunteered at the British Legation in Stockholm for service with the British Forces. On 4 August 1941 he was flown to England, and joined the work of SOE.[29] The parachutist Arne Boelsskov also volunteered through Stockholm in March 1942, after crossing the ice from Humlebæk in Denmark to Raa in Sweden, after which he managed to get into touch with the Consul in Göteborg, Albert Christensen.[30]

The fact that recruitment took place without reference to Iversen, and that he by no means always received information on the volunteers' circumstances to which he felt he was entitled, could not but be unpleasant for him. Rightly or wrongly, he felt himself responsible towards the volunteers, and he also felt that he was the only man who could insist upon Danish standpoints, vis-à-vis SOE, should the situation demand it. As he gradually discovered that his connexions with the volunteers were cut off, and that he was prevented from having any influence or control over developments, or even that general information was witheld from him, as to what happened to the volunteers as soon as they had left his recruiting office – if they came through that office at all – he turned his accusations against SOE.[31] Knowing the sharp tone of his opposition to members of the Danish circles who did not agree with him, which had been his strength when provocation to action was needed, one can hardly be surprised that he showed his teeth now, all the more because his Danish patriotism was now challenged. A further point which contributed to this was the uncertain position he held, lacking information on developments, which led to misunderstandings between him and the volunteers, so that he felt that through no fault of his own the Danish Volunteers lost confidence in him and in the whole cause that he had worked for so ardently. Various divergencies and conflicts between Danish volunteers and British officers split the work in 1941, and uncertainty and rumours as to the purpose of the work checked it.[32]

The result was a conflict with SOE which lasted as long as Iversen held the position of recruiting officer, and which gradually developed into a stream of protests from Major Iversen,[33] protests which were quite useless, and to which SOE could and did turn a deaf ear. The opponents were not evenly matched. Total isolation, the feeling of impotence and a growing realisation of the hopeless future of his original idea – the establishment of an independent Danish unit – was therefore the sad fate which overtook this pioneer for the Danish Resistance struggle. It was doubly sad because these feelings were unfounded, considering the decisive influence which the results, though they seemed so small, finally had upon the development of Danish Resistance. This could not be foreseen, however, in London, in 1941, 1942 or 1943.[34]

6. Training

It is time to leave the offices in London, and their troubles, and look more closely at the work which, in spite of all the administrative complications, went on from week to week, out in the training schools,[1] where the Danish volunteers under SOE prepared themselves for their dangerous missions in Denmark.

The teething troubles in the work of training had been largely due to the fact that the men had to be kept so long in ignorance of the real purpose of the work. Rumours and gossip had good soil to thrive in, and the relations between the volunteers and the British officers[2] were far from always good. Major Taylor, who was in daily contact with the Danish volunteers during training, strongly emphasizes the disciplinary difficulties which marked the work.[3] It appears from his account, that the difficulties sprang chiefly from the volunteers' dislike of the restrictions which it was necessary, for reasons of security, to impose upon them,[4] and it is quite obvious that their dislike was most easily aroused when they were not thoroughly informed as to what was expected of them. This was intensified when their expectations of forthcoming action against the enemy turned out to be illusions. Discontent, lack of confidence and irritability often resulted.

In this respect, the Danish volunteers shared the fate of the British, and of the other Allied soldiers, who were subjected for years to long, humdrum military training and discipline, without the stimulus which fighting action or the possibility of forthcoming action would give. The psychological pressure of the long wait was, however, heavier for tle volunteers under SOE's various sections than for the members of the regular forces. Refugee psychosis and uncertainty of the future were factors to be reckoned with, which intensified the exiled men's impatience and irritability. The leaders of SOE were naturally not blind to the disadvantages of the repetitive training, and of their painful reticence in the face of the volunteers' desire for full details on the plans for them, and on the possibility for action; but it must be remembered that there were very few ways of satisfying their wishes. The leaders' hands were tied, so that it was either undesirable or impossible to speed up the work, for various weighty reasons: complete lack of experience; Britain's unpreparedness for action in support of the men who would be sent out into the field; the necessity for extreme thoroughness in training and preparation; the situation in Denmark, which only developed very gradually to the point where psychological and practical conditions existed for Resistance actions; the slow growth of the organisation's network, with the ramifications which later spread throughout the country, etc. etc. The progress of the war in general did not give much reason for optimism in 1941 and 1942: the constant German bombing raids; defeats in the Balkans and on Crete; retreat in the desert; the German victories in Russia in 1941/42; the defeats by Japan; and the never-ending losses which hit Britain's Merchant Fleet in the Atlantic, on the way to Malta, on the Arctic routes, or out in the Far East. It was not until the autumn of 1942 that the situation began to improve effectively and permanently. From London's point of view in 1941 and 1942, it is quite understandable that restraint was necessary. None of this could be explained clearly to the volunteers, however, and the short-term, understandable but dangerous solution was to stiffen morale with mirages, which soon vanished before the hard facts of the war.

In spite of all these troubles, and in spite of all the unavoidable bungling, the work progressed. More and more men got into hard training, at a considerable number of training schools. This training is well described by many of those who took part. Several of the accounts for the State Archives touch on the training,[5] and Flemming B. Muus gives a vivid, thorough description of it in his book "The Spark and the Flame".[6] In his account, Taylor goes through the whole programme and organisation of the training schools in detail.[7] Information from other sources is more or less haphazard and incomplete, but Taylor "was the liaison officer between the school and headquarters, and it was his task to be interpreter for the Danes and to take over their personal problems and help them in every way possible. In this connexion it was his duty to report to London on their morale."[8] Through these functions Taylor came into close contact with the training schools, and was the Britisher who had the most frequent opportunities for direct contact with the volunteers. He reports in his account:[9] "In conclusion I should like to add, that I was the British officer in the Danish section, who came most into contact with trainees ... The Danish home-school had at various times three commandants, and innumerable are the hours I have spent discussing trainees with all three."

The training of SOE's men was carried out at a considerable number of schools, most of them for the special training which was common to parachutists trained in the various national sections of SOE. The men of each section had one "home school". Normally volunteers recieved their basic training there and returned to that school after training at the various special schools; they also finished up at the "home school", when their whole training was complete, and waited there for final orders for action. In the case of the Danes, this system consisted of training at the following schools:[10]

S.T.S. 1: (Special Training Shool) Brockhall (Northamptonshire). Recruit school for general military training, normally of one month's duration.

S.T.S. 2: Balasis (Dorking, Surrey). Recruit school as S.T.S. 1, from 1 January 1944, "home school" for Danish volunteers.

S.T.S. 26: Arrisaig (West Invernesshire). Recruit school as S.T.S. 1 and 2. The school lay in a strictly military area, together with a number of other special schools.[11]

S.T.S. 45: Hatherop Castle (Gloucestershire). From 1941 to 1 January 1944 "home school" for Danish volunteers.

S.T.S. ?[12]: Beaulieu (Hampshire). A number of schools for special training in security, particularly the precautionary measures which the volunteers were to observe after arrival in enemy territory; orientation on local conditions, as far as this could be supplied in England.

S.T.S. 17: Hatfield (Hertfordshire). Instruction in industrial sabotage.

S.T.S. 51: Ringway (Lancashire). Parachute training.[13]

S.T.S. 40: (Bedford). Training in the use of Eureka and S-phones. Eureka was a direction finder, used during arms dropping, both by the men on the ground and by the plane crew. S-phones made it possible for the receivers and crew to speak to each other.[14]

S.T.S. 52: Thame (Oxfordshire). Training of radio telegraphists; periodically also training in the production and use of home made explosives; training in picking locks, and other forms of "burglar technique".

S.T.S. 61: (Huntingdonshire). Parachutists were sent to this school on completion of their training, immediately before departure for Denmark. Final instructions were given here.

This was the rough outline of the training programme in which Danish volunteers for SOE work took part. There were variations, according to the special missions entrusted to the different men, or because of other circumstances, alterations in training plans, individual cases, etc. It should be emphasized, however, that the programme represents conditions as they were when the training was fully established, i.e. from 1942. For the volunteers from the beginning of 1941, the training programme had not reached its final, definite form, and for them the constant shift from school to school, sometimes to another school with the same programme, could seem unplanned.

Training periods varied a great deal. In some cases there would be relatively short instruction, in others the training could last up to two years.[15] Selection of volunteers for service in Denmark was at first entirely in the hands of Hollingworth, as chief of the section; and it was naturally he who had the actual responsibility for decisions in this respect, during the whole period. From 1944 Major Lawrence Lassen was transferred to the Danish Section from the Norwegian, and took part in selecting the men for active service, with Hollingworth and Taylor.[16] In making these decisions Hollingworth usually followed the reports on the volunteers' suitability and general conduct, which he received during their training from the British officers of the various schools, but of course other factors also influenced his choice. Apart from the military qualifications which came to light during training, the trainees could possess special abilities and possibilities, which the training did not disclose, but which could be of decisive importance in the selection. This was particularly the case when the choice was to be made of the various leaders. Here the special "military" qualifications and skills were of minor importance, and the choice had to be based on general evaluation of a complete personality, where intelligence, general knowledge, initiative, culture, ability to negotiate, possible personal connexions in Denmark, and many other factors, which must carry greater weight than, for example, physique or sharp shooting ability. It should be remembered that it was not a question of sending saboteurs to Denmark, but contact men. It was hoped that these men would find or be able to create a home front. They must therefore be able to animate others to the formation of the home front; work as instructors and advisors; contribute to co-ordinate this front with the war effort of the free world; and obtain the weapons, explosives and other necessities for underground work. The work of co-ordination and administration of the organisation it was hoped to create was the responsibility of the leader, whose position was therefore largely administrative, and entailed a great deal of negotiation, as well as responsibility, which increased at the same pace as that of the Resistance organisations' growth. As things developed, serious political responsibility was laid upon the shoulders of the leader. The choice of such a man was naturally difficult, and could not be based upon the reports of the training schools alone, even though it was such an all-round training that these could provide important clues. It appears, also, from Hollingworth's account, that general considerations were of first importance, among the reasons for his choice of leaders.[17] The remarks which will be quoted in part were not written down until after the events, but there is no reason to suppose that they do not, in the main, sum up the considerations which motivated his choices correctly. These must have been made after long and careful assessments, and must have etched themselves permanently on his memory.

The actual selections will not be discussed nor judged. In some cases they were criticised by Danish Resistance circles, as the following description shows,[18] and this is mentioned directly in Taylor's account:[19] "The choice of Danish personnel has been severely criticised, though the critics have been unable or even unwilling to analyse the situation and make a true assessment of the facts." It is reasonable to deduce from this, that there were other difficulties in addition to those mentioned, in the selection of leaders. It should be stated at once, that the choice of candidates was small, much smaller than that upon which other SOE sections could draw. It was by no means a foregone conclusion that suitable men were willing to undertake the dangers and the burden which the special work of SOE demanded. This applies also to men who wished to take part in the fight, and has nothing to do with the courage or fighting spirit of those concerned, but can be connected with the very understandable desire for action in regular warfare. An excellent example of this is Anders Lassen, who asked for transfer from SOE to the Commandos, animated by just such a desire.[20] For others it could be connected with a general unwillingness to join in work which might seem to approach espionage, and which might appear odious, at a period when the idea of underground resistance was not well known.[21] Finally and naturally, there were those who shrank from the special risks of the work.[22] This is no cause for wonder, particularly since the British, in all propriety, did not depict the prospects as brighter than they were. Flemming B. Muus recounts a dramatic conversation with his chief, Major Spooner, where, before the start of the training, his chances for survival in the Resistance work were estimated as under 10 %.[23] Muus may possibly be dramatizing that moment, and perhaps highlights the statement for its effect, but the reality belind the situation was true enough. Hollingworth emphasizes that the danger was strongly stressed vis à-vis the volunteers.[24] In this connexion it should also be mentioned that no effort was ever made in the British Army to make parachute jumping compulsory, and it was an accepted fact that even soldiers of recognized physical courage refused to obey orders, when they found themselves face to face with the jump into the void. This only led to transfer to other forms of service.[25] Added to all this, there was the natural drop-out for all sorts of other reasons: insufficient physical qualifications; inability to learn the skills required; withdrawal of volunteers for other service; and in one case a Danish volunteer who should have been sent to Denmark was withdrawn when the supposition arose that his identity, in some way or other, had been disclosed by the German spy service.[26] All in all, it must be admitted that there is no little truth in the acute form Taylor gives the problem, when he states in his account:[27] "... in 1942 and 1943 it was either a question of using the material available to put up some kind of fight or of not putting up any fight at all." At all events, this sentence contains the quintessence of the British points of view. Their justification can hardly be denied.

When the volunteer's training was finished, and he had been chosen to be sent to Denmark, he received a routine commission as an Officer in the British Army, reckoned from the moment he left England.[28] This was done partly in recognition of the mission he was to undertake, partly to give him the protection which the appointment could provide, if he should end in German imprisonment. Economically speaking, the appointment brought a salary as officer, until he returned to England and was demobilised.

Formally the Germans did not recognize the parachutists as officers in the British Army. Cases against arrested parachutists came under the "Abwehrstelle",[29] which occupied itself with counter-espionage and combatting sabotage. In fact, however, the German authorities refrained from pronouncing the death sentence in cases where Danish parachutists were seized, and where, according to German ideas, there was a question of espionage which justified the death penalty. There can be no doubt that the Danish authorities' conduct here had decisive influence upon the German attitude.[30]

7. The first Actions

During 1941 the organisation and training of volunteers was sufficiently established to allow SOE to consider the possibility of a first operation. The importance of pressing on with this project, on evidence that underground work in Denmark was possible, has already been mentioned. There is some divergence between Hollingworth's and Spink's accounts with regard to the first more concrete plans, Hollingworth stating that the aim had been underground activity, almost from the first, and Spink referring to uncertainty, as late as the spring 1941, as to the character of the work in view, and stating that the original proposal had been for Commando raids on the Danish coasts.[1] Spink's opinion can perhaps be explained in that the Danish Section was linked to the Norwegian, and that Spink therefore had a good deal to do with the planning, under Stagg's leadership, of the Commando raid which was carried out on 4 March 1941 against Lofoten,[2] so that the idea of such raids, which in the case of Norway were practicable, may have influenced his view of possibilities in Denmark. This is borne out by Stagg's account, from which it appears that at the time of the Lofoten raid there were corresponding plans for Denmark. He writes:[3] "I felt some spectacular effort ought to be made in Denmark, since the Lofoten raid proved to be the fillip that was wanted in Norway to wake up "The Home Front" and it was hoped something similar on the coast of Jutland might have a similar effect in Denmark. A scheme was elaborated for a lightning raid with small craft dropped from destroyers in Skagerak on Hirtshals or Hanstholm in the depth of winter − not with the idea of effecting any material damage to the enemy but to make the Danes at home feel they were not forgotten by the free people."

Plans of this kind were never carried out, however, and it seems safe to assume that Hollingworth's opinion, that the object from the start had been an actual resistance struggle, is correct. Charles Hambro had already mentioned this aim during his talks with Ebbe Munck in the autumn. On the other hand, Spink's and Stagg's remarks probably indicate the fact that well into the preliminary phases of the work, the planners have turned and twisted the possibilities, and have kept their minds open for every imaginable development. During 1941, however, the concept of underground resistance took on a more definite character. Spink writes:[4] "It must have been during the summer that the idea of sending parachutists to Denmark, to try and organise an incipient Resistance Movement, particularly with a view to sabotage etc., began to take more concrete form. I am not sure about this, but I am quite sure that Bruun himself was very influential, through his talks with Hollingworth, in contributing to these plans becoming more definite." Spink's account agrees here with the viewpoints in Hollingworth's, and on the last point – Carl Johan Bruhn's influence – there is perfect agreement between the two accounts. Hollingworth, also, strongly emphasizes Bruhn's influence.[5]

One factor which made it difficult to take an uncompromising attitude to Danish problems was, as stated previously, the fact that information on conditions and feelings in Denmark was very meagre. From the spring 1941, the efforts of SOE were directed to breaching the wall which surrounded occupied Denmark. An invitation was sent in the spring 1941 to the then editorial secretary of "Politiken", Sten Gudme, a close friend of Ebbe Munck, to come to London to take part in the British work of propaganda to Denmark; and in addition to this, the idea was conceived of getting a Danish politician to come to England. One of the first tasks of SOE's Stockholm organisation was to make such contacts. Sten Gudme has himself described his departure in detail. From this it appears[6] that on 5 April 1941 he received an enquiry from Ebbe Munck through the latter's mother, who had just been visiting him in Stockholm, as to whether he would be willing to go to England, without mention of any details as to what duties would await him there. If he agreed, he was to send a letter to Ebbe Munck, composed in a special way. In full confidence that weighty reasons must lie behind Munck's invitation, Gudme decided to accept, without asking for further details. One was getting used to adjusting oneself to illegal methods and hints. As no answer arrived from Munck, Gudme decided to arrange a legal trip to Stockholm, and on 7 May he left Denmark, the editor Erik Seidenfaden seeing him off at the station. During the following week there were meetings in Stockholm, with Turnbull and Munck, and his journey to England was arranged by SOE, not without a minor complication which is illustrative of the times. By arrangement with Turnbull, members of SOE were to fetch Gudme on arrival in England. They were not on the airfield, however, but had gone in error to an airfield near by. This led to Gudme's being arrested and brought to the "Patriotic".[7] Hollingworth soon arrived there, however, and the misunderstanding with the suspect foreigner was cleared up.

After this, Gudme was attached to the work of so-called "black" propaganda to Denmark. This "black" propaganda was co-ordinated with the "white" propaganda which was sent out by the BBC. It was devoted to leaflets, to be scattered over enemy occupied territory, running alleged illegal radio stations, etc. Its two chief aims were to undermine and destroy the enemy's morale, and to raise and support Resistance in enemy occupied areas.[8]

Whilst Gudme's departure was carried out quickly, it was a long drawn-out affair to bring a Danish politician to England. Ebbe Munck writes of this in his account:[9] "One of Mr. Turnbull's first tasks was to suggest to various Danish personalities, amongst others the Members of Parliament Christmas Møller and Hedtoft Hansen, and the editor Nikolaj Blædel that they should come to London, to be at the British Government's disposal in assessing Danish conditions and events." Munck goes on to describe how, owing to an incomprehensible failure on the part of the courier, the invitation to Christmas Møller – in March 1941 – did not reach him, whilst the impression was received in Stockholm that Christmas Møller had received the invitation, but that his answer was "No". That, at least, was the message which reached Stockholm, whereas Christmas Møller, when he heard later of the earlier invitation, definitely denied having received any invitation before.[10] For the time being, the idea was dropped, and only resumed with a new invitation in August 1941.[11] On the other hand, it is apparent from Gudme's account, that an enquiry was ventilated in the spring 1941 to the editor Nikolaj Blædel. While preparing his journey to London, Gudme got in touch with Blædel on 29 April and laid the cards on the table. In the conversation which followed, Blædel told him that he had received a similar enquiry, but in view of the possibility of German reprisals against his family, he had shrunk from the idea of leaving.[12] Blædel's relations with the German authorities were already very strained, because of his series of anti-German articles and broadcasts during the 1930's so his misgivings were very understandable. The appeal to the Social Democrat member of Parliament, Hedtoft Hansen, is accounted for in more detail by Spink:[13] "In connexion with the somewhat closer contact (desired), the idea arose of bringing a Danish political figure to England, whose words carried weight among the Danish people, and who could support the ideas we cherished, as far as propaganda was concerned ... The invitations for this were originally addressed to Hedtoft, as Turnbull and I, who knew Hedtoft from earlier days, had proposed his name. I personally, through my acquaintance with him, knew that Hedtoft's words carried great weight in Danish Labour circles. My idea was therefore that the Social Democrats, as the largest Danish party, would be the most valuable to win over to an active Danish Resistance."

In June 1941, Hugh Dalton, as a fellow Labour leader, writes a letter to Hedtoft Hansen urging him to come to London, to take over the leadership of the Danish work in Britain. The latter was forwarded through Stockholm to Denmark, but Hedtoft Hansen refused the British invitation, on the grounds of weighty considerations for his party, and after consultation with the Danish Prime Minister, Stauning.[14] The illegal departure of a leading Social Democrat politician would, in the opinion of both of them, put such a burden on the official Danish policy of negotiation vis-à-vis Germany, that this would break down, and the responsible Danish political leaders did not desire a break-down of this policy as yet.

A question which was now taken up in Stockholm was the financing of the future illegal work. According to the plans which were being prepared in Stockholm, it was evident that as the work developed, it would demand considerable financial resources. In accordance with Ebbe Munck's conviction, that the work of Resistance – both intelligence and resistance work in the widest sense – should be carried out as far as possible "with our own efforts and with our own resources",[15] so that the results should be placed to the credit of Denmark at the end of the war, he now tackled this important question of finance.[16] His considerations led to a request to Per Federspiel to come to Stockholm and help in the solution of the problem.[17] Owing to various misunderstandings, some produced by the failure of two couriers, the talks on the "Grundtvig Plan", as it was called,[18] did not take place until January 1942. Per Federspiel then went to Stockholm, after receiving an outline of the plan from the editor Peter de Hemmer Gudme, who urged him to come, and took with him a considerable amount of intelligence material from the Intelligence Section. "Long discussions now followed in Stockholm with Ebbe Munck, who put me in touch with E. T. Grew who seemingly sold bicycles and other hardware from a little office in Stockholm, where he told me all the details of the Grundtvig Plan, and received my promise to take over its administration."[19]

The main result of these discussions is summed up in Munck's account, and described in more detail in that of Federspiel as follows:[20] "The Grundtvig Plan ... was to raise money in Danish crowns against the promise that the contributors would be credited a corresponding amount in Sterling in London, to be paid out without question after the war, and if desired, receipts could be deposited in Sweden. My task from now on was to be limited to finance, and my outward contacts were looked after mostly by Carl Adam (Bobby) Moltke, and after his escape to Sweden in 1943 by his cousin Adam (Toffy) Moltke ... To begin with we did not make much headway in obtaining money ... On the other hand, our needs were not great at first, and we were able to cover expenses, which as far as I remember did not exceed 15,000 crowns a month in the first period ... no definite financial plan was decided upon until after Muus arrived in Denmark, in the summer 1943. At that early stage, financial contact with the parachutists was quite haphazard, and as far as I know, there were no directives from England as to what amounts were to be paid to them, and in what way they were to be paid. Payment was left to my discretion, and I paid out the amounts which were applied for convincingly ... In 1943 it became less difficult to obtain money. This was probably due to the growing confidence in an Allied victory, and the increasing abundance of cash in the country."

In addition to this, another peculiar arrangement was made from 1942. A shipping company was founded, Nordisk Shipping & Co., which took over an estate consisting of a capital interest in a partnership of the same name. This partnership had acquired four ships, using illegal money, and these, while sailing officially with normal freights, were also available for possible future illegal work. The idea of acquiring the interest in Nordisk Shipping & Co., camouflaged as it was by normal freighting, was that in case of need, considerable sums of money could be raised quickly in loans or by the sale of the company's assets, without disclosing that such loans were for the use of the Resistance Movement. As economic requirements increased, this arrangement proved extremely useful.[21]

While the Stockholm organisation of SOE was slowly going ahead with preparations for the coming work in Denmark, the work of intelligence continued in increasing volume. Press talks between Copenhagen and Stockholm came into use, in which certain pre-arranged expressions stood for code words or phrases.[22] The number of couriers was increased, and with them, the number of established contacts. A further development was in the co-ordination of intelligence work, during the last months of the year, and this was expanded to include political and economic information, in addition to military intelligence. From December 1941, the civil engineer Erling Foss began his regular, comprehensive analyses of the situation in Denmark,[23] which were forwarded through the Stockholm organisation to England. The work was also extended, from December 1941, when the USA was drawn into the war. Through the American Minister in Stockholm Ebbe Munck was now put into touch with the Danish Minister in Washington, Henrik Kauffmann, who thereafter received reports and copies of certain parts of the intelligence material.[24]

Developments in Stockholm were thus gathering momentum, and from now on it is possible to follow this work to an increasing extent, through Ebbe Munck's quite comprehensive diary. At the end of 1941 a feeling of relief is noticeable, combined with excitement that events are at last beginning to move. For example, he writes in the diary:[25] "TB (Turnbull) comes to the weekly meeting and says that London wants him over there at once ... but as I have information that the Prince (the code name for the Intelligence Officers) can possibly be expected here in the near future, it is more important for him to stay here, or at any rate make sure that he is here, when the Prince comes. TB also offers to take me with him. I would of course like to do this, but it is not a very convenient moment: for one thing it is extremely important not to draw any attention to us just now,[26] where great plans must be laid ... The Prince has made contact with the Duke (the code name for Borch-Johansen's organisation), which I am glad of. Generally speaking there seems a possibillity now for centralizing the whole thing more, so that a few responsible people direct and pull the strings direct. The last consignment arrived by courier in the usual way. That is the fifth lot in two months, not including all the verbal intelligence – so we can't complain at the moment. Now we must get it all properly arranged, while London is really interested, and while we are in contact."

Great plans must be laid – while London is really interested. The remarks lead ones thoughts back to London again, where things are coming to the boil and will have to let off steam. We learn through Sten Gudme, who gives his impression on arrival in England, that people are burning for action, in England too, after the many toilsome preparations:[27] "When I arrived in England in 1941, it was following the instructions we received through Barman,[28] which made it clear that England wanted things activised in Denmark." This desire is very understandable, and very shortly after Gudme's arrival, in May 1941, the war was to take a turn which would quicken Britain's interest in unrest in the occupied countries. In the summer 1941 the German Army attacked Russia, and as the autumn advanced, and Russia's difficulties increased, with the German Army at the gates of Moscow, pressure was increased upon the British Government to give whatever help it could. It is apparent from Churchill's memoirs of the Second World War, that he personally was unpleasantly affected by the insufficient help, which was all that it was possible to give as things stood, at that time. Searchlights circled over the horizon, to find weak places in the enemy's armour, and also came to rest over the occupied countries, where help might be expected. In a memorandum of 18 December, Churchill's own words are:[29] "We have therefore to prepare for the liberation of the captive countries of Western and Southern Europe by the landing ... of British and American armies strong enough to enable the conquered populations to revolt. By themselves they will never be able to revolt ... but if adequate and suitably equipped forces were landed in several of the following countries, namely, Norway, Denmark, Holland, Belgium, the French Channel coasts and the French Atlantic coasts, as well as in Italy and possibly the Balkans, the German garrisons would prove insufficient to cope both with the strength of the liberating forces and the fury of the revolting peoples ... there must be a design and theme for bringing the war to a victorious end in a reasonable period. All the more is this necessary when under modern conditions no large-scale offensive operations can be launched without the preparation of elaborate technical apparatus." The situation was psychological favourable for an organisation such as SOE, which was working to create unrest behind the German lines.

The Danish Section was eager to justify its existence, and, as we shall see, there was also an intense desire among the Danish volunteers to take action, and get things going. In spite of the fact that there was still much to improve in the organisation, therefore, in spite of the fact that the contacts with Denmark were still somewhat meagre, in spite of the fact that politically and psychologically Denmark was still not ripe for the creation of an actual underground fight, and in spite of the fact that Britain's resources were still not large enough to provide reliable support, Hollingworth decided to start operations in Denmark.[30] As leader of the first parachute team which would be sent over to Denmark, he chose Carl Johan Bruhn, and his radio telegraphist, Mogens Hammer.

At the outbreak of war in 1939, Carl Johan Bruhn[31] was studying medicine in England, and would soon have finished his studies. He felt dissatisfied[32] at being debarred, because of his studies, from any immediate active war effort. This feeling was intensified during the first months of the war, and when the Finnish-Russian war broke out in the winter, he seriously considered volunteering for some capacity in the British Red Cross. After 9 April, which came as a shock to him as to most Danes abroad, these feelings became still stronger. His wife describes his feelings at that period in the following words: "... he had been deeply distressed by the occupation of Denmark, was restless and anxious to be doing something more active than studying, even although so nearly finished. He felt many another young man had had his life interrupted and his career perhaps finished, he himself had no right to sit back and study."[33]

In the summer 1940 Bruhn was called up for service with the British ARP, with which he worked through the whole German blitz of the summer and autumn, and at the same time he got into touch with Danish circles. In the autumn 1940 he was put in touch with Hollingworth by Major Iversen,[34] and he was a member of the first team of volunteers who began training in January 1941. From the start he is entered in the Army List as an officer (subaltern), and from weekly pay lists it appears that during training he acted as paymaster.[35] He soon took an undisputed lead among his comrades. His age, his wide education, and certainly not least his qualities of character made him the obvious candidate for the dangerous pioneer work which lay ahead – a heavy burden which he both would and could take upon him. All accounts are unanimous in appraisal of his abilities and his character. His immediate chief, Commander Hollingworth, gives the following description of him:[36] "... in my opinion, he was by far the most important man, SOE ever had ... He was a fine man, an idealist in all he undertook, in possession of an unblemished character and filled with a burning love for his country, for which he was willing to sacrifice everything. He was a man of brilliant talents, and he actually carried on his studies at the same time as he went through the parachute training course, so that he took his Finals as a doctor[37] a week before he was sent to Denmark. In addition to all this, he was an outstanding organiser, with a tremendous capacity for work, so that he seemed to me in every respect to be the natural leader of the work in Denmark. I should also like to emphasize his strong religious faith. He had great influence upon his comrades, and I quickly decided to train him as leader, and to let him be the first man to be sent over."

His comrades had a similar opinion of the man chosen to be SOE's first leader of the work in the field, as can be seen from one of the volunteers' reports:[38] "At that time (the summer 1941) I had also met Captain Bruhn, the man who was to be Chief of the organisation in Denmark, and it should be added, that a better man ... to lead this work did not, I believe, exist: The enormous amount of work he put into the preparations in England, his deep love of country, a strong personality, and there was a degree of respect for his efforts surrounding his personality which is only given to those who possess the proper qualities of leadership, and which he received for his skill and his work." Mogens Hammer, who was selected as radio telegraphist and assistant to Bruhn, was recruited from the Danish Merchant Navy, and, like Bruhn, had been among the eleven who started training in January 1941. He was a man who, as later events showed, possessed tremendous personal courage, a quality he was to have sore need of in his work. In accordance with the tasks he was selected to carry out, he received special training as a radio telegraphist.[39]

When the decision was taken to start operations in Denmark, Hollingworth and Bruhn held detailed discussions of the general lines of the coming tasks. Bruhn naturally had influence, through these conversations,[40] upon the ideas which from now on became the general directives from London for the whole work. It was naturally impossible at that stage to do more than sketch certain general outlines quite roughly. Detailed, precise plans had to wait until there was more established contact with the Home Front, and until the first experience was gained. It was in this particular area that Bruhn's first and most important mission lay. His task was to a great extent one of reconnaissance.

Something can be said, however, on the ideas for resistance work, as they were conceived even at that early stage. The final purpose, at that period was intensive sabotage, but the conditions for this had to be produced first, and the first aim was therefore more limited: to establish contact with resistance-minded circles in the population; to stimulate this attitude of mind generally; to establish regular radio communication with London and closer contact with the Stockholm organisation; to create and train reception and sabotage groups; to reconnoitre reception points; and in general to develop an organisation which could come into force when everything was ready, both in Denmark and in England, for real action. On one single point it seems as if the discussions went beyond these general lines. One has glimpses of a basic plan of organisation, which would later have an influence on the structure of the whole Danish Resistance Movement. Both Hollingworth and Spink mention that even then, possibly and even probably inspired by Bruhn, they discussed dividing Denmark into six regions – the exact division which became the basis, much later in 1944, upon which the illegal army was built up.[41] In Hollingworth's account he writes:[42] "... during our discussions we agreed roughly to outline such a division, so that Copenhagen became one part, Zealand and Fyn one part each, and Jutland fell naturally into three parts." Spink is a little more definite:[43] "I can also remember that Bruun was working on a division of the country into sections. This division later became, according to what Hollingworth has told me, the later division into regions. Whether this is correct I cannot remember. But at all events, I have seen Bruun's division into regions."

It seems as though this principal idea can be traced back to Bruhn, therefore. In support of this opinion it can be stated that the parachutist leader, Hans F. Hansen, who was working in Denmark in 1942, also mentions,[44] that an idea for a division into six regions was discussed at that time. Since Hans F. Hansen was taken prisoner before the end of 1942. and spent the rest of the war in German prisons and concentration camps, his memory cannot be affected by any later knowledge of the regional divisions.

Regarding the plans which were outlined before Bruhn and Hammer were sent to Denmark, it should be stressed that immediate action was not the objective. The situation was not considered ripe in Denmark, and the depressing fact had to be taken into account, that Britain's resources did not allow for extensive support for the work, and possibly would not allow for it for some time to come.[45] That it was decided, nevertheless, to send over the two men, was due to several different circumstances. One of these was the opinion[46] that in Denmark, where there was still relative law and order, and where the Germans would therefore be less alert than in other areas, workers would have freer hands during the necessary preparatory work of building up the Resistance Movement; and that the quieter conditions should therefore be exploited for such work. Another circumstance was the favourable psychological effect which it was expected would result from Danish Resistance circles feeling themselves in touch with England as early as possible, and thus receiving the stimulus, which awareness that the work in Denmark could count upon support would bring. This latter consideration was naturally correct, but it had a reverse side, that there was a risk of arousing unfounded optimism among the enthusiasts, whom it was hoped to contact in Denmark, and that these would therefore be disappointed when they saw that help from England, at least at the start, could only be on a very modest scale. For obvious reasons, in such a situation, it would be out of the question to explain the situation by referring too strongly to Britain's actual weakness. Such a situation would demand decided diplomatic talents from the leader who would be entrusted with the mission, both to urge forward and to hold back. In the event, with Bruhn's tragic death, just as the mission lay before him,[47] there is little doubt that the purely propaganda value of the operation partly evaporated.

Bruhn himself did not shrink from his difficult mission. We know that he was impatient, and burned with enthusiasm to get started. As early as 1940 there are some letters from him to Major Iversen, where he urges quick results in setting up a Danish detachment of volunteers. All his letters breathe impatience.[48] The same year he had also written to Churchill, as Prime Minister, and had developed plans for the creation of a Danish underground movement.[49] Hollingworth also speaks of his impatience when, because of bad weather, his departure for Denmark was delayed.[50]

It was not only Bruhn who was impatient. In Stockholm too, the beacon of expectation was alight. Now and then there are flashes of impatience over the lack of direct action in Ebbe Munck's diary. From January 1942 one finds such expressions as this: "Kurt defends Hedtoft. I think both he and Christmas Møller should have come long ago. Christmas was invited back in March of last year ... now he is stopped by the ice. Heavens above, there is a war on, and one must make quick decisions."[51] Behind the impatience of Ebbe Munck and the initiated Danish circles concerned, lay anxiety that the Danish policy of giving in was becoming a mortal danger to the country, more dangerous the longer it lasted, and the more it must be considered as lessening the country's chances of joining the ranks of the Allies. In 1941 this sense of danger was particularly strong. On a great many important points the year had brought serious concessions – breaking off diplomatic relations with the Soviet Union, imprisonment of Danish Communists, the formation of "Frikorps Danmark", and the signature of the Anti-Comintern Pact, to name only a few examples. The reaction abroad had at times been sharp,[52] but it had been very sharp indeed at the surrender of some Danish torpedo boats in February 1941. The episode must be mentioned here, because it probably contributed more than any other to show clearly, to the initiated, that Denmark was balancing dangerously near the edge of what Britain would accept in regard to Danish concessions,[53] and thus helped to quicken their desire for swift action.

In November 1940 this question had already been raised by Admiral Raeder, and formally the demand was made by application from the Minis:er Renthe-Fink to the Foreign Minister Scavenius.[54] The idea of such a handover aroused strong opposition from the King, the Ministry and among the Naval Command, and while the negotiations were taking place, the possible British reaction to a surrender of the torpedo boats was ventilated in all secrecy. The development of the affair will be followed here through Federspiel's and Munck's accounts, and through documents in Munck's archive. Federspiel writes:[55] "Shortly before Christmas, Blædel put me in touch with the then Cavalry Major Lunding and Major Gyth from the General Staff Intelligence Section ... It must have been just after the New Year that Blædel asked me either to apply for a visa to Sweden or get hold of a really reliable courier, who could take over a verbal message. I was to have more details through Lunding. The subject of the message was the German demand for the surrender of twelve torpedo boats ... I received my instructions through Blædel. Later they were supplemented with a few further details from Major Gyth ... The instructions were to call on the British Naval Attaché, Captain Denham ... and explain the situation to him in detail, and in particular to let him know that the naval officers were prepared to sink the torpedo boats before surrendering, but that here 'at home' there was some doubt as to how far it was opportune and in the common interest to start open sabotage so soon ... My information on the torpedo boats was telephoned immediately to London, and the next day – it was probably just after the middle of January – the reply was received by the British Legation in Stockholm ... As far as I remember, the reply was as follows: IT WILL MAKE A CONSIDERABLE DIFFERENCE TO THE ATTITUDE OF THIS COUNTRY TO DENMARK AFTER THE WAR IF THE T B'S CAN BE EFFECTIVELY SABOTAGED ... On the same occasion I met Ebbe Munck in Stockholm, and he told me about the work he was beginning, and we decided to keep in close contact with each other. I was given no details of Ebbe Munck's plans at that stage, but the idea of organising underground work in Denmark, to help the Allies in their conduct of the war was naturally one which appealed to me, and I promised the support I could contribute to it ... I declared my willingness to receive Ebbe Munck's courier post ... to the General Staff Intelligence Section ... After my return I delivered the telegram ... to Commander Evers and then to Prince Axel."

This account corresponds with the following report from Ebbe Munck:[56] "It is generally known, that the Germans had presented a demand for the surrender of the torpedo boats in question, and I had been asked, via the British Naval Attaché, to inform the Danish Navy that it would be welcomed in London, if this opportunity could be used for a demonstration which would make it clear that the Danish Navy ... would oppose the German wishes. This point of view was communicated in good time beforehand, but the surrender actually took place without the proposed demonstration."

It is not clear from this quotation, whether there is a question of two independent reports, or whether the two men refer to the same British approach. Nor is it clear from the accounts extant, how far the British point of view was known in political circles, and how far it had any influence on the political deliberations on the matter. It is, however, a fact that the Government decided on 22 January to yield to the intense German pressure, and submitted in principle to the demand.[57] This released an extremely strong British reaction in the form of a sharp statement from the

First Lord of the Admiralty, Alexander, and a no less sharp statement from the British Government, which were handed to Ebbe Munck for forwarding to the proper quarters. The two Notes read as follows:[58] "In light of present information there is public contempt for lack of guts in Danish Navy, for allowing T.Bs's to be handed over to Germans. The only way to partially redeem their honour is to make quite certain that submarines are not also allowed to fall a prey to Germany"; and: "His Majesty's Government are unable to accept reasons advanced by Danish Government for their inability to sabotage or scuttle torpedo boats particularly as they must have had prior warning of German intentions. It must now be expected that Germans will demand Danish submarines. If Danish Government do not scuttle these His Majesty's Government must regard them as acting voluntarily in German interests and H.M. Government must adapt their policy accordingly both now and when peace comes to be made." It was apparently the first of the two Notes that Erling Foss reports[59] having taken to the Ministry for Naval Affairs, after the surrender of the six torpedo boats.[60]

Both in London and Stockholm, then, SOE were ready for the start. The final decision, to send Bruhn and Hammer to Denmark, seems to have been taken in the autumn 1941. Spink, as mentioned earlier, states that plans took concrete form from now on, and this agrees with Hollingworth's estimate, that the period of waiting until the decision was implemented was about three months,[61] and with the following account in Dr. Connan's report:[62] "Shortly after he (Bruhn) was qualified (this took place in September) he called me up to London. I was amazed to see him out of uniform and that he had commenced to grow a beard. This made me fully aware that his work was of a secret nature." The direct preparations were made between September and December.

The important question now arose as to what arrangements should be made in Denmark for the reception of the two men. It was obvious in advance that no comprehensive preparations were possible, since there were far too few men initiated in the work in Denmark for such a purpose. No one had any experience at that stage of the reception technique which later became so highly developed. On the other hand, it would be of the greatest value, for the two parachutists to get into touch as quickly as possible with the activist Danish circles which were in existence, and via Stockholm SOE had some contact with these. Certain preparations were made, as the Intelligence officers had asked Borch-Johansen to prepare and lead the reception, and he had declared himself willing to do so. A suitable place was reconnoitred. Knowledge of this had reached Ebbe Munck in Stockholm and we read in his diary:[63] "We have had a major arrangement going, to organise reception of the two parachute friends (Haslev), but T.B. (Turnbull) told me today that they have already been dropped, on Christmas Eve. One of them was killed in the fall. Which of them, I do not know as yet. They were both Danes, and should have worked with the V organisation.[64] One of them was small and slight, and had jumped many times (he was a doctor by profession) and was eager to do his bit. The other was big and heavy, and there was a question of dropping him in the water, as he was a good swimmer, but it was decided that they should go together, and that they should be dropped where they knew the neighbourhood and had friends." It is evident from this entry in the diary, both that "arrangements" had been made to receive the two men, and that it had been decided, nevertheless, not to put the arrangements into force. The reason for this seems to have been that Bruhn did not want any reception, but preferred to find his contacts independently.[65] He was therefore dropped at a place where he knew the terrain.[66]

Even though it was decided to drop the men "blind", however, they were supplied with details of a few contacts, if all else failed. We read in Sten Gudme's account:[67] ". . . I was called in occasionally to meetings with men in SOE. These were always shrouded in mystery. Amongst others I was called to an unknown destination in London for a meeting. I was fetched by Hollingworth in a car with curtains, and taken to an unknown house, to a room where I met Carl Johan Bruhn and Mogens Hammer. I was introduced to them by Hollingworth, and he asked me to give these two, who were going to Denmark as parachutists, certain contacts and code words. I advised them, when they arrived in Denmark, to call on the editor, Seidenfaden, and gave them certain code words for him. These code words referred to personal things, of which only Seidenfaden and I had knowledge, so that he would understand at once that they really came from England and had been in touch with me . . . At the meeting it was also arranged how the message that they had landed in Denmark should be sent to England, by putting an announcement in 'Politiken' about a lady's handbag which was lost in a certain area, so that they could give the barest information in this way. Beyond this, nothing was discussed at the meeting as to the parachutists' mission in Denmark, and I only had a vague impression of them."[68]

Hollingworth accompanied the two men personally to the airfield and said Good-bye on the evening of 27 December 1941.[69] A few hours later, the plane reached its destination, near Haslev, in a wooded area in the centre of Zealand. The two men jumped, with the fatal result that Bruhn's parachute failed to open. He was killed on the spot. Hammer's wireless transmitter, which Bruhn was carrying was also smashed to pieces. It seems probable that the static line, which Bruhn according to the rules had himself fastened to a hook in the ceiling of the plane, had in some way become unhooked, so that the release mechanism never functioned. At least, investigations ended in this conclusion as the most probable cause. Taylor states: ". . . the case has never been satisfactorily cleared up, but it is assumed that the static line of his parachute jumped off the hook in the aircraft to which it was attached."[70] Accidents of this and similar kinds, at this period, where training and instruction of parachute troops were still in the making, and the tests of material were not yet complete and final, were not altogether exceptional in the British Army. It was just at the beginning of 1942 that there were two accidents at the school at Ringway, which aroused anxiety and doubt as to methods and material, which motivated a thorough investigation. In Newnham's book, already quoted, he writes:[71] "Higher authority was beginning to show some concern and Courts of Inquiry were ordered to investigate the two fatal accidents. (This refers to two fatal accidents which occurred during training.) All kind of rumours were beginning to circulate – the parachutes were faulty, the WAAF packers were careless; the maintenance was bad. Even the instructors were getting a bit fidgety. Everything was checked and rechecked." In this atmosphere, the investigation was made into Bruhn's death – doubly dangerous because it occurred during an operation. It ended in the given explanation, as the only possible conclusion.

Bruhn's death was a catastrophe. Not only did SOE lose the man they had chosen as the pioneer of the work, and in whose ability and character they had put such hopes, but in addition, Hammer found himself in a hopeless situation, so that the work in Denmark had a false start, with all the difficulties this dragged with it. SOE knew nothing of all this, however, until a day or two after the New Year. The plane crew had reported that they had seen Hammer's parachute open, and that they thought they had seen Bruhn's.[72] It was not until after the New Year that the fatal news came from Stockholm, that the code message had appeared in the Copenhagen newspaper "Politiken" of 1 January:[73] "Where is my bag? A green lady's handbag, lock missing, lost Vesterbrogade-Gyldenløvsgade. Reward. Apply K.520 to Politiken." In Spink's words:[74] "The telegram arrived one day when Hollingworth was not in the office. I honestly thought the whole thing was a misunderstanding. I remember quite clearly how General Gubbins called me in to give an explanation of the telegram. I said that I could not believe it was true, but unfortunately it turned out that it was true."

In London SOE now had to revise the plans, which in the circumstances meant that they had to turn to improvisation. The picture was not bright. There was no substitute for Bruhn who could take his place immediately, there was no contact with Hammer, and finally, with Bruhn's tragic death the advantage of starting the work in Denmark without the knowledge of the German counter-espionage was lost.

While these gloomy prospects were being considered in London, Hammer courageously started his own improvisations on the Home Front. The free world had opened its campaign in Denmark – and the Germans knew it.

8. Two Fronts Meet

Let us complete the picture of the tragic events at Haslev, and follow the survivor, Mogens Hammer, as far as this is possible. His path is our path for a little while longer. Let us follow his fumbling attempt, with the qualifications which he possessed, to find his way to the young shoots of resistance, which were spreading into a thick undergrowth under the shadow which the German regime had cast over Denmark. His toilsome path will lead us in to the tangled scrub he made for.

Mogens Hammer died in 1945 in Hamborg in an accident, and did not leave any direct account of what happened on that ill-fated night, after he had landed safely. Nevertheless, we have a fairly clear picture of the night's events, as Mogens Hammer's brother, Svend Erik Hammer gives a description of the tragedy in his record, which is based upon his brother's story, told him very soon after it. Mogens Hammer must also have told Hollingworth what happened, when he returned to England a few months later. In Hollingworth's record there are glimpses which can only come from Hammer's own account and which are in line with the main points in Svend E. Hammer's report. As regards the establishment of Hammer's first contacts in Denmark, Svend E. Hammer's record agrees in the main with those of the editor Erik Seidenfaden and the engineer Herman Dedichen, who were the first Danes of the Underground he contacted. These various records supply a fairly detailed decription of events. Svend E. Hammer writes:[1] "Bruun jumped first, then the wireless set was dropped, and finally my brother. When he landed, he hid his parachute in a ditch and immediately began to look for Bruun, with whom he had arranged a particular whistle signal. However, he heard no sound, and it was only by chance that he found Bruun lying dead. He had to search Bruun at once, for one reason, to take the money he had on him. This search could not but be intensely shocking for him, particularly as he had a great admiration and liking for Bruun. Bruun was smashed to pieces, and to get the money, some of which Bruun had hidden in his boots, my brother had to cut them open. Then he began the search for the radio set, but after three hours he had to give up, and then began to walk in the direction of Køge, following the railway lines. After walking for about a kilometre, he went up on to the line, turned, and walked towards Haslev. There he took the early morning train to Taastrup." It may be added, that Herman Dedichen describes in his account how, a few days later, he helped to wash the marks of blood from the money.[2]

Hammer, who had been sent to Denmark to stimulate and support whatever there might be of Resistance circles, was now himself in serious difficulties. He was alone, and we must suppose, without any intimate knowledge of the plans for the developments to come, without a wireless set and thus cut off from receiving instructions, in a situation which had not been foreseen. Added to this, as his behaviour that night seems to show, he must have realised that both German soldiers and Danish police must now be aware of his existence. That night the Haslev district was covered with snow, and his vain search for Bruhn and the radio set had criss-crossed the terrain around the dropping point with countless footprints, which with the other evidence told their own tale all too clearly as to what had happened. The "Abwehrstelle" did not ignore the writing on the wall. On 26 January 1942 they demanded the assistance of the Danish police in searching for and arresting parachute agents in a note to the Public Prosecutor, at that time Poul Kjalke. In this note[3] reference is made to the episode at Haslev: "The first case of this kind on Danish soil is the jump by two apparently English agents near Køge, on the night between 27 and 28 December 1941, of whom one was killed jumping and the other escaped. In the coming period the possibility of repetition of this event must be expected, possibly in increasing numbers."

That Hammer did not give up altogether in these circumstances says a good deal for his physical courage and psychological robustness. Faced with a desperate situation he chose to get in touch with various members of his family.[4] This was absolutely contrary to the orders he had received, and he was later rebuked by the British for it.[5] From the point of view of security his decision was probably wrong. It is a different matter that it was very understandable, and perhaps in the circumstances unavoidable. Hammer's reactions during his first days in Denmark must be seen on the background of the shock he had received. Furthermore it was quite impossible for Hammer to get a roof over his head, at least not without great risk, in any other way. He made up a story for his family, to the effect that he had been shipwrecked in a British ship bound for Archangel, but had been rescued and had reached Norway, from where he had come to Denmark via Sweden.[6] This was his story for some time to come, to people with whom he came into superficial contact, while he naturally had to give the true explanation to those with whom he entered into co-operation. Hollingworth cites this story and mentions, as does Sv. E. Hammer, that Mogens Hammer telegraphed to London to get the name of a British ship, which had actually been shipwrecked at the time. It appears from this that the story must have been in use for quite a long time, as it was some while before Hammer succeeded in making contact with London – as we shall see. His explanation can well have been used from the start.[7]

After getting himself temporarily established, Hammer started to look for members of the Danish Home Front. In this search, the conversation he had had with Sten Gudme was a great help to him. It will be remembered that Gudme had mentioned Seidenfaden's name, and it was to him that Hammer now turned. In Seidenfaden's account he writes:[8] "One fine day, a stranger rang at my door. He introduced himself as Mr. Hansen, and asked to speak with me. I was alone at home and asked him in, and he at once put his cards on the table, told me that he was a British agent, that he had just landed near Haslev, and referred, as mentioned before, to Gudme. We had a long talk, and he seemed to take it for granted that I had contacts which I did not have. He asked me, for example, whether I knew "the Princes" (the Intelligence officers) etc., all of them things of which I knew nothing."

At this first meeting between the Home Front and the Front abroad, both parties were evidently equally hesitant towards each other, and as regards the tasks which co-operation might entail. One has a similar impression of the respective positions from Dedichen's description of his meeting with Hammer, which took place the same day, after Seidenfaden had introduced Hammer to him, as Dedichen had possibilities at the time for giving Hammer practical help:[9] "We admired his courage but were surprised that they had not been able to find a more suitable man in England, for the mission which he gave us the impression was entrusted to him ... Hammer was very secretive, and to my quite natural question as to how I could help him, he made no answer at all, to begin with, or was very reserved. After a little while, however, I understood that his actual mission was to contact the branches of the Danish Resistance Movement, where they existed."

There was a natural psychological explanation for the men's mutual reserve. Hammer, in his isolated position, was certainly looking for and hoping to find Danish leaders, to whom he could attach himself, whereas Seidenfaden and Dedichen naturally expected that a delegate from England would come with British plans and projects for the future. We know that Hammer was not in a position to supply these. He lacked both general and specialized knowledge; he had no intimate knowledge of the British plans, and he was without the pre-requisites for being able to adjust himself to the new and extremely demanding situation, when it suddenly presented its exacting claims upon him. This was no fault of his, nor, really, of SOE's. In London there was consternation over what had happened, and SOE was fully aware of the untenable situation;[10] but one can well understand the scepticism with which the Danish circles would regard SOE's work, after such a start. At this first meeting between the members of the Home Front and SOE, much would have looked different, had Bruhn lived.

The first contact was made, however, and the way led now to important centres of the resistance circles of the period. After a few days, Hammer was in contact with Christmas Møller and Nic. Blædel, from whom several possible paths radiated further. Christmas Møller held a number of strings in his hands, which ran in many directions to Resistance-minded groups, and the same applied to Blædel.[11]

It would be very desirable, at this point, if it were possible to give an exact analysis of the mood and the standpoints of the Danish people, when the first direct connexion was established between the Home Front and the Front abroad; if, in one way or another, it were possible to measure in what degree the idea of resistance had gained a foothold in the collective consciousness. It would be desirable, if one could determine, not only how extensive, at that stage, were the groups in the population, who were changing or who had changed their attitude to the Danish policy towards the Germans, but also how far the process of adjustment had advanced, what plans and ideas were being considered, around the country. Unfortunately such an analysis cannot be made with any certainty, either as to quantity or quality. Nevertheless, it is possible to highlight a number of facts which do give an approximate picture of the situation.

First it will be relevant here to point to the fact that the Communist Party as an organisation found itself, after 22 June 1941, at open and declared war with the Germans. The party was not large at that period. At the election of 1939 it raised about 40,000 votes,[12] and the development of public opinion from 1939–41, after the German-Russian Pact of 1939 and the Finnish War in the winter 1939–40, was presumably to the detriment of the Communist Party. However, in the Resistance Movement's earliest days, the Communist Party had particular importance because of its special character. While the "bourgeois" activists had to find each other, in small scattered groups, which were only able slowly, step by step, to work themselves into large organised cadres, the Communist Party represented a developed organisation, with the additional advantage that it was prepared for illegality and not without experience of it. The arrests of 22 June do not seem to have made any difference to the organisation of the party, however tragic their consequences were for a number of the party members.[13]

Several facts point to the Communist Party having prepared illegality and resistance against the Germans before 22 June. First, the editor of the Communist newspaper "The Workers' Paper", Børge Houmann, mentions in his account[14] that preparations were already made in 1940 to convert the party's work to illegality; that a special committee was set up, of which Houmann was a member, for this purpose; that as far back as June 1940 the party leaders had been given illegal addresses and points of rendez-vous; and that preparations were made for illegal newspaper activities. The last point no doubt explains how it was possible, in an astonishingly short time, for the Communist Party to publish illegal papers, leaflets, etc.

92

Its organisation undoubtedly gave the Communist Party an effectiveness which meant a great deal in the illegal work, but in addition, the situation in which the party found itself, of open resistance against the Germans, brought growing numbers to the party ranks – incontrovertably during the Occupation, although only demonstrably after the Occupation, when, in the elections of 1945, the Communist Party registered a quarter of a million votes.[15] Again under the impression of Russia's bitter fight against Germany, and of the persecution of the Communists which the Germans demanded, the party could count on growing sympathy among great numbers of Danes far outside the Communist sphere. How far this altered attitude had occurred as early as the New Year of 1942, it is naturally impossible to say, but the demonstrations in November 1941 against joining the Anti-Comintern Pact, public anger at the creation of the "Frikorps Danmark", and perhaps particularly the changed attitude towards Finland show at least that it was on the way. This opinion can also be found in remarks from the period. In an attempt to analyse public feeling by Erling Foss from just that time, we read:[16] "Fear of Russia. – This has been touched upon earlier, but is taken up here again, because in the later development of public feeling it is still a haunting argument, which turns up everywhere in the monied classes, and which only a minority have shaken off. It is desirable now to point out that development has been made in a bourgeois direction, with increasing natural inequality. A repeated explanation that the Soviet has 'finished' its revolution, as the reasons for it have been removed, would have a beneficial effect." According to this contemporary analysis, at least a minority had shaken off the fear of Russia, and Foss's desire is clearly to go further along the same path.

If one now asks, what forms of resistance the Communists were considering, it appears that from the beginnng of 1942 an actual change in the party's attitude took place. In 1941 the party was on the defensive, and the main task was of necessity to organise and establish itself "underground", and to publish illegal writings. Among the latter, "Land and People" appeared surprisingly quickly with its first number on 29 June 1941.[17] In the course of the summer and early autumn 1941, two other Communist publications were issued: "Political Monthly Letters",[18] and the leaflet "Danish Tones", which contained "the speech which one of the Communist Members of Parliament would have held in Parliament during the treatment of the 'Communist Law', if the Government had not, with its unconstitutional procedure, prevented this."[19] In addition to these publications, illegal books were printed, such as, in December, Steinbeck's "The Moon is down".[20]

The fact that Communist Resistance workers had limited themselves in 1941 to illegal organisation and illegal newspaper work was due to purely tactical considerations. There is no doubt whatever that they intended to start sabotage when the situation was ripe, and from the beginning of 1942 the Communists turned to organised sabotage.[21] The decision to do this was taken at the beginning of 1942. Houmann states[22] that in "one of the first months of 1942 we had called some comrades in from the provinces, and some Trades Union people from Copenhagen to quite a big meeting, to discuss the tactics to be followed in the future. There was general support in the Party for taking other means into use than illegal papers." This corresponds with the fact that in February at the urging of the party's illegal leaders, a sabotage group, KO-PA (Communist-Partisans) was formed, chiefly drawn from earlier volunteers from the Spanish Civil War.[23] This started the development which would lead to the establishment of one of the great sabotage organisations, BO-PA (Citizen-Partisan), and so it was that the Communists were the first in the country to take the offensive, a resolution which was later to influence the attitude of Resistance circles in general. The decision was taken, however, at a time when public opinion in the country was, in the main, strongly opposed to sabotage.[24]

As yet there was no possibility of action with a wider aim or on a larger scale.[25] For that, organisation was needed, as well as training and, especially, materiel. This last in particular was a very limiting factor throughout 1942. In "Free Denmark's White Paper", Børge Thing[26] gives a description of the lack of materiel which had to be coped with in the beginning. He writes:[27] "Organised sabotage began first in the early spring ... The first weapons consisted of a couple of old-fashioned revolvers ... As far as other 'materiel' was concerned, we had only what we could lay our hands on, when the opportunity arose: petrol, paraffin, benzol, phosphor, etc. We could not even get hold of ordinary black powder in the first period ... Out of their poor resources they bought the chemicals or stole, by plain theft, what they needed to use for producing home-made igniting devices or other destructive appliances ... It was not until December 1942 that there was a real coup in explosives, but it cost four men their liberty. A patrol was sent down to Faxe limestone quarry to fetch explosives ... Still, the action did yield something, as 10–15 kilos of Aerolite were brought home."[28]

A few essential features of the Communist Resistance organisation should be mentioned here. At New Year 1942 it stands almost alone. The process of co-ordination, which was gradually carried through with the national Resistance organisations was still in embryo. It was that winter, however, that the negotiations were conducted which led to the creation of "Free Denmark",[29] and so to growing co-operation between the two camps. Here as in other instances, it was soon obvious that there was no desire, on the Communist side, for any isolated Communist Resistance struggle, but on the contrary, great interest for the creation of a common front, for the establishment of which the Communists both desired and promised all support. The development here was the same as in the great war in general.[30] It is well known, and it will be apparent later in this thesis, that close co-operation was gradually established between the Communists and the non-Communist Resistance elements, and the Communist Resistance organisation was thus linked to the Danish-British(-American) co-operation of which SOE was in charge.[31] Neither then nor later was there any sign of Russian activity anywhere in Denmark similar to that of SOE. On the contrary, a striking lack of interest in and knowledge of the special Danish situation is noticeable for most of the period of the Occupation, in Russian Government circles.[32] It is outside the framework of this book to examine this question in detail, but it may be stated in general, that in 1944, when Thomas Døssing was recognized as "Fighting Denmark's" representative in Russia, it was extremely difficult for him to refute the very summary opinion on Danish conditions, which showed little knowledge of the lights and shades of the developments in Denmark during the war. In a letter of 11 December 1944 to Ebbe Munck, Døssing writes, for example:[33] "The Soviet Union's point of view is unshakeably the same as it was six months ago, its latest very sharp expression being in an article[34] in the very prominent publication, "The War and the Working Class" for 15 November ... The article states that all Danish politicians (except Christmas Møller and a few Conservatives) have been in German service during the Occupation, and at the same time, that they seized the opportunity at home to carry out a reactionary economic and social policy at the cost of the masses. There is no differentiation here, and even the Danish Council in London (including Christmas) is attacked because it seems to be willing to negotiate with the old politicians ... This is the Soviet Union's opinion, and it cannot be changed."[35]

There were, however, other Resistance plans in preparation than those being hatched out in the Communist circles. The Communist Front has received attention first, because, on account of the Communist Party's illegal status it was the most advanced in various respects, and because it constituted a compact whole. In the case of the other enterprises, historical research is in some respects more difficult. The search must cover the whole country, and both great and small initiatives must be brought to light, most of them partially independent of each other, although they are the outcome of parallel thinking and intensified feeling. The main difficulty is that a great number of these enterprises still do not manifest themselves openly, and do not reach further than their own district. What was discussed in the homes, man to man, or in small groups and circles of acquaintances, it is impossible today, as it was then, to investigate. The various situations are only disclosed to a limited extent in the historical material. Nevertheless, although developments do not allow for exact measurement, tendencies, at least, are clearly discernable.

First of all, there is no doubt that the snowball of feeling against the

Germans was rolling. The German violations and demands during 1941 had not failed to produce reactions. This need hardly be demonstrated in detail, and is reflected in the increasing mutual irritation and in a growing number of episodes throughout the country. It is also disclosed in the increasing inclination in a large part of the population to demonstrative conduct vis-à-vis the German occupying troops. Examples are to be found in all the major expositions of the general history of the Occupation. This development is certainly due to the fact that the intensely nationalistic movement, which expressed itself in meetings and associations,[36] and which had been increasing rapidly from the autumn of 1940, was now bearing fruit. It is not possible to state definitely what rôle this activity played in the progress of a Resistance-minded attitude, but it undoubtedly had considerable influence. The scepticism with which the activitists both then and later looked upon these meetings was not altogether justified; it was perhaps based on the fear that the feelings which thus had their outlet would peter out, so that the national and democratic activity of which these meetings were expressions, would not lead to what the activitists considered the logical aim for the movement: the direct fight against the Germans. Quite apart, however, from the direct influence which the movement had upon public opinion, it certainly had indirect influence, which was almost unobserved, and which should not be overlooked or underestimated. Through it, contact was established between circles of the population which up to then had had little communication with each other, and the extended contact was of enormous value, as soon as open resistance began. It should be remembered, that many of the meetings in question were arranged on the basis of mutual trust, and this contributed in itself to building up confidence between the lecturers, the members of the audience, and, especially, the organisers of the meetings all over the country. In connexion with the official or semi-official meetings, there were often coffee parties or other forms of more informal gatherings, where the tone was free, or small parties with the committee members or exclusive groups of special guests. There is an excellent description of the atmosphere which could be created in this way, in a book commemorating one of the men who bore the chief burden of this activity, Peter de Hemmer Gudme.[37] It was a time where people were taking each others measure, and noting the standpoints which were revealed, directly or indirectly. Many of the impressions recorded in consciousness in that way were valuable when the open fight came. People knew each other.

Decisive progress had been achieved in one respect of particular importance to the Resistance. The population as a whole was anti-German, both as to the progress of the war itself, and in the little world at home. Great numbers of people were accustomed to listening in regularly to the British broadcasts, and had learned the art of reading between the lines and taking hints; a continuous stream of information was passed through open and

96

closed meetings, and thus out into the whole country, and news of developments at home was spread surprisingly widely and surprisingly quickly. Even
if the information was not always correct, and this was often the case, this
did not shake people's confidence very much. They usually allowed a wide
margin for error, while information inspired by the Germans, if it was not
immediately brushed aside, was looked at through a mercilessly critical mag-
nifying glass. German propaganda soon became powerless in the face of this
general attitude, while anti-German propaganda had, contrariwise, an easy
run. Precisely when this attitude became general in the population, it is
naturally impossible to determine, but in an analysis of public feeling in
December 1941 Erling Foss believes it can be traced back to the Battle of
Britain:[38] "In addition, the news came on the British radio of the Battle
of Britain. One wanted to believe the British figures ... From that time
onward, feeling in Denmark unified on a definitely anti-German basis. One
... listened gladly to everything unfavourable about the Germans and everything favourable about the British." Whether general opinion can be dated
precisely from that point is probably questionable. Anti-German feeling certainly spread as the war progressed. The difficulties which the Germans actually met probably had their effect, and wishful thinking did the rest.
The fiasco for the German propaganda at such an early stage is remarkable,
and is a good measuring rod of the standpoints of the population. It is in
1940 and 1941 that the German propaganda, at least as regards the progress of the war, could often boast of greater accuracy than the British. The
series of German victories made the German information more reliable than
the British, whereas the British propaganda could sink to omissions, exaggerated optimism or direct untruths. This is also brought out from the British side in Bruce Lockhart's book, already quoted.[39]

With this attitude among the Danish people, an essential psychological
condition for resistance was being created. The next task must be gradually
to prepare the soil for an active Danish war effort, and a break with the
policy of co-operation. Here the illegal Press went into action from the winter 1941–42, both the illegal Communist Press and the illegal Press started
by non-Communist circles. In December 1941 the first illegal papers published
by national groups saw the light of day. These were "The Free Danes"
and "The Statue of Liberty",[40] "The Free Danes" being started by "The
Ram Club", a Resistance group which went back to 1940. Strangely enough,
Mogens Hammer's brother, Svend Erik Hammer was already in touch with
this group when his brother came to Denmark, and in his account as well
as in an appendix to it, which covers "The Free Danes", we hear of the
start of the illegal paper:[41] "I had at that time (January 1942) already
been in contact with the circle 'The Free Danes', as I had been asked, in
October–November 1941, whether I would undertake to look through an
illegal paper which was being prepared by a group, of whom I knew two

members, Carl Holm and Chresten Lidegaard, who were on the 'Politiken'. The circle called itself 'The Ram Club', and had started in the summer 1941,[42] with the object of carrying out demonstrations against the Danish Nazis. During the work, the idea of expanding their activities and starting an illegal paper occurred to the members of the circle. As they had absolutely no experience of journalism, they asked me and Sonny Nielsen[43] to look over their first draft, which we did. After a while the circle developed into 'The Free Danes', the steward, Cajus Johansen and the painter Gilbert Nielsen, who also belonged to the group, acting as editors of the paper." We shall hear more of this group, who later had a good deal to do with SOE.

Even more important than the start of "The Free Danes" and "the Statue of Liberty", however, was the founding of the largest newspaper of the Occupation, "Free Denmark". During the negotiations on the establishment of this paper, also at the New Year 1942, the imminent possibility of co-operation between the Communist Resistance groups and those of the "bourgeois" groups, became a reality for the first time.[44] The negotiations were aimed at a co-operation, which led, on 9 April 1942, to the publication of the illegal paper, "Free Denmark".[45]

Originally, the purpose of these negotiations had been to investigate the possibilities for publishing a legal paper, in which Nazism and the policy of collaboration in the "Scavenian" form would come under the strongest pressure possible, but this plan was soon abandoned. The reason was that it was felt that such a paper, directed against both the occupying power and the Scavenius policy, would not live long, and that its only result would be to compromise those who were attached to the paper, so that they could not be used in later illegal work.[46] The experience gained by others – above all by Dr. la Cour, whose proud and uncompromising agitation in "The Frontier Guard", in leaflets, and lectures, had brought him the first term of imprisonment in July 1941,[47] and who on 22 February 1942 was imprisoned for the second time – indicated that this belief was founded on fact.

The plans to publish a legal paper, coupled with the decision to abandon the idea, are very interesting in that they show that at this precise period, there is a parting of the ways. Efforts are now directed towards illegality, as the only form in which a fight against the Germans is possible. It is evident that the situation is becoming more acute, and it is also evident that the illegality which is now deliberately chosen, allows for a far more ruthless, and therefore effective, agitation for the objects pursued.

The group which was most advanced in illegality, apart from the Communists, was the "The Danish Unity Party".[48] In the period since 9 April 1940, the party had arranged hundreds of national meetings throughout the country, and had demonstrated its strongly anti-German standpoint with important publishing activity, both of the periodical "The Third Standpoint",

98

and particularly of a series of leaflets by Dr. la Cour.[49] In July 1941 the leaflet "Words to us today" brought the author and publisher – la Cour and Arne Sørensen – eighty and sixty days' imprisonment respectively. The party came into further serious conflict with the police, when it prepared the publication of the history of Denmark by the historian of the Middle Ages, Saxo, with a caustic foreword by la Cour. The publication was stopped, and the foreword was censored and altered.[50] Finally in the summer 1941, a duplicated illegal book, "Norwegian Poems" came out. With its eyes open, the party was preparing to become illegal, and we shall see how it delegated two of its leaders to take up and develop direct communication with the parachutists, when contact was made with them in the first months of 1942.

Two more examples can be cited to illustrate the parting of the ways. In the autumn 1941, the illegal organisation "The Ring" was started, on the initiative of Frode Jacobsen, who became its leader. The idea of this organisation was[51] "to hide the real object: a nation-wide creation of groups for active fighting against the Germans ... One had expected that the political leaders would have taken up the struggle, within the various parties, but when this did not occur, one had to start, oneself." It is apparent from the article quoted, that Frode Jacobsen had been trying, since the summer 1941, to win over various politicians to the idea of an apparently legal organisation, which in reality should organise groups for active resistance; and that when this did not succeed, he pursued the project without the politicians' support. In January 1942, the first leaders met, with Erik Møller as chairman, and Frode Jacobsen as "travelling secretary". There is a sharp differentiation in the article quoted, between the "apparent aim" to spread objective, reliable information, and the "real aim" of creating a nation-wide organisation, ready for more active work when this was demanded.[52]

A similar initiative can be traced in the "Danish Youth Union", the national youth organisation started in 1940 with the theological professor Hal Koch as chairman. In an interview for "Free Denmark"[53] after the war, Hal Koch states that activism within the union started in the autumn 1941 and spring 1942;[54] and this is confirmed in information given by Dr. Hilmar Ødum, who was at that time engaged in organising small groups, within the framework of the union, prepared for illegality. Ødum writes of this: "We were reckoning from the start with DU being forbidden or stopped in some other way, sooner or later, and to cope with that situation we arranged, from the start, to live on underground ... I have been informed by personal friends since the war, that several of these groups grew and joined in other illegal work, but I have not investigated the extent of these developments. Among the lists of the fallen, executed, or deported, however, I recognize many names from 'our lists'."[55] In minutes of the business meetings of the union, attached to Dr. Ødum's account, there are several references to these "Dr. Ødum's circles".[56]

7*

In addition to these enterprises, there were large and small groups, scattered throughout the country, for whom active resistance stood as an unavoidable or perhaps directly desirable consequence of the Occupation, and which in some instances had already reached the point of action or were preparing for it. In the winter 1941–42 the famous boys of the Churchill Club carried out their actions in Aalborg; and in the course of 1941 "The Ram Club" already mentioned was engaged in minor sabotage actions; in the "Conservative Youth" organisation the formation of sabotage groups had begun; in many of the cross-country clubs, which were set up all over the country in 1940–41, members were also working with the idea of sabotage and other forms of direct resistance; and scattered, unorganised actions were carried out in many places.[57] Detailed proof is difficult if not impossible, on the basis of the material extant, and does not come within the framework of this thesis. Anton Toldstrup, however, who was later Reception Chief for Jutland, in his book, "No Victory without Fighting",[58] gives a picture of an extremely realistic cross-country exercise which he remembers, with fighting against German troops as its basis, and this description applies to feelings which were not unusual at that time.

As soon as the illegal Press came into action, it became possible to follow, to some degree, the feelings and beliefs which were dominant in the ranks of the Resistance. We shall therefore look at the first numbers of "Free Denmark" to ascertain how far that transition from passive to active resistance had gone, at this stage – spring 1942 – in setting up targets and working tactics.[59] To some extent, the possibilities available at the time are illustrated in this way, as the leaders of the dawning Resistance Movement saw them. The article stating its programme – written by Christmas Møller[60] – is very informative in this respect.[61]

After a remark to the effect that behind the publication is a little group of Danes, who have previously held widely differing opinions, he mentions what is later further stressed in the article, that one of the main objectives of the paper will be "to bring our countrymen open and honest information on what is happening." He then proclaims German Nazism and its Danish off-shoots as the enemy to be combatted. On a positive note, he offers a world created by an Allied victory: "The high ideals of life, freedom, justice, integrity, probity, truth and honesty can come to reign in the world and in our country." Again: "We should never forget, that one cannot have anything gratis in this world ... We must help, ourselves ... It must not be, that Denmark is missing in the common fight against the whole world's tyrants." The objective is clear, then: the fight against Nazism and the will to lead the Danish people into this fight.

The attitude to the policy of the Government is also clear: Hands are stretched out to all who will join the fight against Nazism, also "to the political representatives of the present Government and Parliament". The gauntlet is thus thrown down before the two non-political members, the Foreign Minister Scavenius and the Transport Minister Gunnar Larsen. The same applies to Scavenius' policy, when the declaration continues: "It is a definite and consistent resistance against the German violations, the times demand of each one of us: It is the keeping of the promises of 9 April that must be established – not a yielding and sliding such as has characterized the two years which have now passed ... We want every link in Danish society to insist upon its right ... We must face the risk." The purpose of the struggle is extended now to include a show-down with the Scavenius policy of concession, and instead of this a policy "to face the risk" is declared. Behind this stand lies the conception that "Norwegian conditions", as they were called, were a consequence one was, if necessary, willing to accept.

This view had support among the population, as events proved. This is apparent in an address[62] which was handed to the Minister of the Interior at that time, Knud Kristensen, from about 425 Copenhagen hospital doctors, in which it is stated: "We have reached the point where we believe that further compliance with German demands ... will be synomous with the surrender of our national independence ... We hereby promise the Minister the support we are able to give, up to the most absolute resistance to such demands." From Odense, also, there came similar tones in an address to the Odense Member of Parliament:[63] "... we wish to state, that the Danish Government in our firm opinion can be certain that the Danish people will stand behind the Government, even in the case that decisions should be made by it of such a kind, that the consequences could be decisive changes in the conditions under which the population has lived since 9 April ... one would rather bear the burdens which might follow this, than that consideration for the Danish outlook, freedom and honour be set aside." In conclusion, the same standpoints can be found in a statement by Erling Foss:[64] "Here is the danger, that we come through and out of this war, in a well nourished Denmark, which eats well, and has taken no serious notice of the great gangster in the south, because the country has lain in the shelter of his one velvet glove." In this last remark we meet the clear opinion that "Norwegian conditions" are an inexorable necessity.

As to the means of fighting there was considerably less clarity in the article in "Free Denmark": "We wish all our countrymen to join in the broad Danish front which already exists ... We will fight the Danish traitors with all available means ... Ways and means are different for the oppressed country and for those countries that have the good fortune to be at war for their high ideals. And we shall certainly announce the ways and means." It can be seen that in this field, ideas have not been clarified. The methods to be used are still in the melting-pot.

In the following numbers of "Free Denmark" one meets a corresponding

101

presentation of problems. A break with the Germans is advocated, and a cessation of the Government's policy of concession; but instructions as to "ways and means" are still limited to the negative – not to help the Germans. More precise instructions in this direction are given to the various categories of the population: the farmers, men in industry, businessmen, workers, etc. Even the negative form is expressive:[65] "Stop or limit the delivery of ... keep back when the occasion arises ... don't sell to the Germans ... Don't accept work ... Sabotage the employment agencies ... Don't be more zealous than ... Refrain from all co-operation ... Avoid as far as possible ... Shun all association." The limited objectives can hardly be illustrated more clearly.

The word sabotage hardly appears in the article, and where it is used, as in the passage quoted, it is in the negative meaning of the word. This is characteristic, but not strange in itself. The time was not yet ripe where it was possible seriously to advocate sabotage. For this a far more effectively expanded organisation was needed, money was needed, weapons and explosives and the knowledge of their use were needed, and even more, a completely different psychological background was needed than that which existed at that time. For the great mass of the people, the line of the negotiation policy was not yet played out. It should not be forgotten that the very thought of an organised struggle through sabotage, etc., behind the German lines must seem quite foreign to a Dane of the period, and needed gradually, and to some extent through impulses from abroad, to take on more definite form in consciousness. Even the words "Resistance Movement", in the present meaning, cover a phenomenon which did not come into being until the Second World War, and this phenomenon still, in the winter 1941–42, stood for a more or less distant mirage, even for the most clear-sighted. For the mature and responsible leaders it must have been evident, that it would depend upon many still doubtful factors, which only the future could clarify, how far a resistance struggle could be created on the basis of force. Attention was directed increasingly to this possibility, but first the soil must be prepared. This was also the opinion of such a well-informed observer as Erling Foss. His first micro-film was actually sent off in January 1942 to the BBC, partly made in December 1941, and we find in it a clear analysis of public feeling and conditions in Denmark at the time, concluding in "what should be done".[66] The conclusion is concerned particularly with the form desired for BBC broadcasts to Denmark, and finally emphasizes the possibility of limiting direct Danish production of German war material through influence of the BBC and in other ways. "Denmark must not be turned into a war arsenal for Germany! This must be the motto." Foss goes no further in his remarks, and includes the following characteristic observation in his long report: "Those who wish to carry out sabotage or direct provocation today would be rejected by nearly everyone ... The long report above has had the object of demonstrating that public feeling is not ripe for sabotage – and that the effect of sabotage carried out at the moment would only split the Danish Front."

The question as to what the Home Front looked like, when the first agents from SOE met it at the beginning of 1942, when it had been the subject of long discussions, speculations and conversations between Hollingworth and Bruhn in the autumn 1941, can now be answered in the main. It rested upon a broad basis and had roots all over the country. It was supported by clear and rapidly increasing anti-German feeling in practically the whole population. Its principal political problem was opposition to policy of concession, and just at this period it started the first illegal Press offensive against that policy. Its primary purpose was information and agitation on that basis. With a growing tendency to a demonstrative attitude towards the Germans it was approaching open struggle; and in the case of a few small groups, as well as the Communist organisations, this struggle was in preparation or had already started. The main problem for these groups was the total lack of weapons and other materiel. A very few leaders had already made fragile connexion with the free world; and inside Denmark, by shadowy paths, usually through personal acquaintances, there existed an unorganised but surprisingly reliable contact from group to group. On one central point, a victory had been partially won, with the full agreement of almost all the population. Danish Nazism was in hasty retreat, compromised and exposed to ridicule.

For Mogens Hammer and for the SOE men who quickly followed him, the main task must now be to contribute to a process of co-ordination of the scattered forces, to establish a rapid and reliable contact with England, to expand the existing communications with the Stockholm organisation, to contribute help in the training of activist groups, including training in the use of weapons and explosives, and to get hold of the necessary materiel, which alone could determine their striking power in an open fight. To the extent that this succeeded, the Danish Resistance Movement, resting personally and ideally upon the Home Front, could become an effective fighting organisation, attached to the fight of the free world against German Nazism. The parachutists took up this task, and slowly and after many misfortunes, disappointments and mistakes in 1942, the work would be crowned with success in 1943 and lead to decisive results. It would have essential importance for the developments up to 29 August 1943, and would thus leave deep traces in the history of Denmark. In justice it should be emphasized in advance, that even though the work in 1942 did not lead to the results desired, even though the disappointments were overwhelming, and the misfortunes catastrophic, it was through this work that the foundation was laid which made possible the strong, rapid advance in the work which began in 1943. By then, essential experience had been gained and important preparatory work had been done, and the situation was ripe for great events. The pioneers of 1942 must be judged on this basis, and not from a cold reckoning of their actual results, which were and must be very small. It should not be forgotten for a moment, in the examination and estimation of this work, that it was something of which no one had the slightest experience, and that the general sympathy, both at home and abroad, which was later accorded the work of resistance, did not benefit these men. It was a hard fate they tempted. It is fortunate, therefore, that it can be said, that their sacrifices – for most of them, their lives – were not in vain.

9. The first Contacts with England

We have heard how Hammer, a few days after landing, had been put in touch with Christmas Møller and Nicolaj Blædel. He had thus penetrated, surprisingly quickly, to two of the centres of early Resistance – one already established, the other in the process of establishment.

It was a foregone conclusion that Christmas Møller would be a prominent figure in the activist world. His outlook, deeply anchored in an ardent national mentality, had been stamped, right from the first days of the Occupation, by the desire for a firm Danish stand in the negotiation policy vis-à-vis the Germans. He had originally accepted this policy as a political necessity, where other alternatives had no relation to practical politics. His outspoken standpoint had soon forced him out of his official positions, first as Trade Minister, later as Member of Parliament and Chairman of the Conservative Parliamentary Group.[1] For the very reason that he had fought against the tendency towards concession in Danish politics, while he was still in a leading position, his stand had aroused particular attention throughout the country and also abroad. Everyone knew where he stood, and one could imagine what would be his aim. His extensive connexions throughout Denmark, which were by no means confined to Conservative circles, were further enlarged during the national campaign of meetings,[2] which he started while he was still Trade Minister. His influence in the formation of public opinion became very important. Professor Mogens Fog the well-known left-wing neurologist entered into close co-operation with him from 1941, in connexion with the negotiations for starting the newspaper "Free Denmark". Referring to the plans for publishing this non-party political paper he remarks that "one often received reports on what was Christmas Møller's opinion",[3] and he amplifies the fact that in circles which wanted action, one included Christmas Møller as a matter of course. He writes:[4] "It was natural that one dare not carry through such a plan without having conferred with Christmas Møller, and ensured his support." In the earliest illegal world, Christmas Møller had a stature of a special class. His position was also regarded in this way by another contemporary judge, Erling Foss. In his third report to London[5] are the words: "It must be understood that in giving up X (C.M.), we are giving up the wisest and strongest man we have here at home ... We believe it is right to delegate our best man." It should be added, that even though Erling Foss was a Conservative and a personal friend of Christmas Møller, this assessment, given for the guidance of the British, was an attempt to appraise Christmas Møller from a general and not a personal point of view.

It also meant a great deal that Christmas Møller had so many connexions, and even after resigning his official appointment he exercised very considerable influence behind the scenes. Simply as an example of this, one can mention the support which he gave to la Cour, at a moment when he was preparing his own illegal departure for England.[6]

Christmas Møller's views on political developments in Denmark are apparent, for example, from the article quoted above in "Free Denmark".[7] It should also be stated here that in January 1942, when he met Hammer as the first representative of SOE, he had made up his mind to leave Denmark, and at the invitation of the British Government, to go to London.[8] Both facts show that Christmas Møller now aimed at open warfare. His dilemma at this stage was not the question of passive or active resistance, but the purely political problem of rousing everyone to join in the war, when it was declared.

Obviously, Christmas Møller welcomed the first parachutists with open arms and celebrated their arrival as a sign full of promise – although we know it to have been premature – that the British were now ready to go into action in Denmark. In his account, Erik Seidenfaden[9] mentions Christmas Møller's eagerness to get in touch with the parachutists, and Mogens Fog[10] describes how Christmas Møller enthusiastically took part in the preparatory work for the first reception of parachutists in April 1942, and in finding accommodation for them. He gave a dinner at his home, where he and his wife, with Mogens Fog, Borch-Johansen and Ole Kiilerich, the editor from the "Free Denmark" group with their wives, celebrated the successful reception of the parachutists. He was himself on the point of leaving Denmark. His relations with the SOE men were therefore short, but they lasted long enough to show with what enthusiasm he seized this sign, that Britain was moving into action in Denmark.

The circle around Blædel was of a somewhat different nature, although its outlook was, generally speaking, the same. As was natural, it consisted mainly of newspaper men, for whom the work of information took first place, and of whom the majority were on the point of joining in the work of the illegal press, which was just starting or in preparation. In the illegal press Blædel, who in these years was working on the manuscript of "Crime and Stupidity", became a leading figure, in the sense not only that he took part in the work himself, obtained journalistic material and wrote articles, but also that he laid his enormous authority over his younger colleagues in the scale on the side of illegal journalism. "He became" writes Børge Outze,[11] "one of the pioneers of the illegal Press."

Erik Seidenfaden, who was a great friend of his, gives some facts about his work,[12] which go back to the winter 1940–41: "During the winter 1940–41, a circle took definite form around Nic. Blædel. Besides Blædel, Sten Gudme,[13] Merete Bonnesen, and Herman Dedichen, the engineer, were members' most important task was to keep each other informed, whereas such as, through Blædel, Christmas Møller's. It is my impression that the member's most important task was to keep each other informed, whereas there was no question of spreading information on conditions out to larger groups, even though a good many facts leaked out by private channels."

Per Federspiel also mentions the group around Blædel:[14] "Around Blædel a circle was formed which it was perhaps premature to call illegal, in the later meaning of the word, but which at all events cultivated information from abroad very energetically, and studied literature and other material which was smuggled in from Sweden. I was not in the picture at that time (autumn 1940) as to the details of the make-up of the circle or its aim; but I benefitted a great deal from my talks with Blædel, whose judgement on the development of the war proved extremely sound."

Direct participation in the work of the illegal Press followed at a later stage, when Blædel supported "The Free Danes", soon after it was started in the winter 1941–42, writing articles for the paper, and also "right up to 29 August instructing and advising its staff."[15] His work here led him later to start an independent publication "Danish Times", as he did not feel himself altogether at home with the special, often somewhat caustic tone, which could often stamp "The Free Danes". Seidenfaden reports on this:[16] "Discussion now (spring 1942) began to turn in general more on the start of a real Resistance Movement in Denmark. Blædel and I were rather sceptical as to the level of, for example, "The Free Danes", and this led in the case of Blædel, to his starting to build up "Danish Times" himself, with Frits Drescher."

It seems that Mogens Hammer was the connexion which brought "The Free Danes" into contact with Blædel[17] early in its existence. Through his brother, Mogens Hammer quickly joined in the work of "The Free Danes", although in the eyes of the British, this lay on or outside the periphery of what he should be doing, and led to serious anxiety in SOE's headquarters, where there was strong disapproval of Hammer running such a risk, not only to himself, but to the whole organisation. At that period, work with the illegal Press was forbidden for parachutists.[18]

The immediate and urgent task for Mogens Hammer was in some way or other to establish communications with England again – both the slow and occasional communications via Stockholm, and more important, the quick and decisive direct radio communications with London. Although Hammer's transmitter was lost, his codes were intact, and the problem here was confined, for the moment, to obtaining a new transmitter. This could be difficult enough, in the circumstances, if not impossible. Through the existing accounts and contemporary documents, we can follow his work in this respect in detail, and also reconstruct most of the dates of the various phases in this work. As regards the first point, communications via Sweden, however, only very little can be said. Spink mentions that after a time a newspaper was received via Stockholm, in which Hammer had written certain information in invisible ink, which indicated that he was alive, and that certain information would possibly be sent by the same route.[19] Apart from this, there is no information that the route via Sweden was used by Hammer.[20]

On the other hand, we know a good deal about Hammer's attempt to establish direct radio contact, and to obtain a transmitter to replace the one lost. The first attempt seems to have been made through his brother, who was, as already mentioned, connected with "The Ram Club" – in all essentials identical with the group behind "The Free Danes". Through this circle Svend E. Hammer made tentative enquiries, and through the intermediary of Cajus Johansen and Gilbert Nielsen he was promised a new radio transmitter, to be constructed by two radio technicians. The transmitter was built, and transmissions started, with members of the "Free Danes" as guards. In Svend E. Hammer's account he writes:[21] "We ... began sending with it at the end of February, transmitting "blind" at 2 a.m. from a radio shop in Valby. We transmitted three or four times without receiving any answer, and during transmissions we guarded the place as strongly as possible with about thirty armed men. We got the weapons through the "Ram Club", who by various means had got several revolvers, and my brother also had two revolvers ... After three or four transmissions we gave up the attempt. We concluded that the set did not work satisfactorily."

The two radio technicians later, on 18 January 1943, received serious sentences in Copenhagen City Court for their part in this affair.[22] This first attempt here in Denmark, to produce a reliable transmitter, ended therefore in misfortune.

About three months later, however, a transmitter was procured successfully for Hammer from Sweden. As regards this transmitter, which Hammer received through Borch-Johansen, the latter's account agrees with that of Sv. E. Hammer. Borch-Johansen writes: "But on my next trip to Stockholm[23] ... I had news of a radio set which was said to be in Denmark, brought there in a suitcase by Turnbull's sister-in-law[24] ... With this set Hammer now tried to make contact with England, but it was only after the code word for the set "Possone" had been sent to the receiving station in England, that reception was acknowledged and a reply sent."[25] Both Sv. E. Hammer and Borch-Johansen describe how thereafter regular transmissions to England were arranged. Borch-Johansen reports definitely that transmissions to and from England were normally made twice a week. The opening direct contact with England took place on 17 April. In Ebbe Munck's diary there is a laconic entry for 26 April:[26] "First direct communication goes through (by Arthur) (Hammer's alias)." From the British side it is stressed that Hammer's transmissions were difficult to decipher, partly because the transmitter was not suitable.[27]

We hear a little as to the contents of these first telegrams between Denmark and England, in the accounts for the archives. Borch-Johansen states that intelligence material was sent on shipping tonnage and transports, "as we had not previously been able to send messages so quickly that these could have operational value,"[28] and he and Sv. E. Hammer both state[29] that telegrams were also sent regarding Christmas Møller's illegal departure for England, and Borch-Johansen mentions[30] that after the skipper, Schmidt, who took Christmas Møller to Sweden, had been compromised, the attempt was made to stop his return home from Sweden by telegram to Stockholm via London, an attempt which, as we shall see, did not succeed. Nor did other attempts from Borch-Johansen's side succeed, so that Schmidt returned unsuspectingly to Denmark, where he was arrested in Frederikshavn.[31]

Mogens Hammer did not work as a radio operator for long, however. In his attempt to procure a transmitter he also succeeded in establishing contact with the Danish radio engineer Duus Hansen, who before long would take over Hammer's codes and start independent transmissions to England. This, combined with the technical and general work he also took over, quickly established his position in the minds of the British, so that SOE's Headquarters in London gradually abandoned an otherwise invariable principle, only to work with men in the field of whom they had absolute knowledge through the training they had themselves given them, and attached Duus Hansen to the work on an equal footing with the parachutists sent out from England. In particular, SOE, as they put greater and greater confidence in Duus Hansen's radio technical skill, organising ability, courage and energy, gradually placed an important part of the radio work under his leadership, and depended upon him in all questions relating to this work.[32]

The contact with Duus Hansen was to be one of the most valuable that Hammer was able to pass on to those who came after him, and it is therefore reasonable to describe here, how this contact, so decisive for the coming work, was made. In some way, which does not transpire directly from the material, Hammer had come into contact with Stig Jensen, later Reception Chief for the whole of Zealand.[33] This brought him, through Olufsen, the director of the radio firm Bang & Olufsen, in touch with Duus Hansen.[34] A peculiar circumstance in this important meeting was, that whilst Hammer was cautiously feeling his way, to find a man who could and would make an efficient transmitter, Duus Hansen on his side was on the look-out for Hammer, whom he knew to have come to Denmark without, naturally, being aware of Hammer's identity.[35] For Duus Hansen the co-operation he now arranged with the members of SOE was only the natural continuation of the work he had already started, in the hope of establishing communications with England. This preparatory work must be treated here, since it brought Duus Hansen essential experience and close connexions, particularly within the Danish Police – connexions which would benefit SOE in the time to come. We must therefore leave the description of SOE for the moment and examine a strange episode, which stands quite alone in the Danish Resistance struggle, but which in important respects had decisive influence for it. The episode is the one connected with Flight-Lieutenant Thomas Sneum's name.

Thomas Sneum was one of the Danish officers for whom the capitulation of 9 April was utterly unacceptable. With various fellow-officers and others with whom he came in contact, such as Kjeld Petersen and Chr. Mich. Rottbøll, he laid plans during 1940–41 to come to England, while at the same time, on his own initiative, he carried out extensive investigations of German installations in Denmark. He succeeded in bringing the collected information to the notice of the British via Sweden, and a plan was worked out in the winter 1940–41 whereby he would get to England by a fishing vessel. Because of the hard winter, this plan had been given up.[36] In June 1941 Sneum succeeded, however, with Kjeld Petersen, in reassembling a sports plane, and flying with it to England. The aeroplane stood dismantled and packed in a barn, out in the middle of a field, and the work of assembling the machine was done for some weeks at night inside the barn. In addition the necessary petrol was also collected. On 21 June 1941, the plane got off the ground from a short grass strip as runway, and in spite of its absolute unsuitability, reached its destination the following day in England.[37]

In England Sneum was asked by SIS to return to Denmark by parachute, and to continue his investigations of German military installations. The reports, both those received earlier and those Sneum brought with him, were very highly appreciated, and it was decided that his abilities and energy could best be used by letting him carry on the intelligence work he had started. A British assessment of his results is given by Commander Stagg, who writes:[38] "The fantastic flight of Siem (Sneum) to England in May (?) 1941 with his invaluable films of German radar at work on Fanø, gave a further fillip – but Siem came under the aegis of SIS who jealously kept him away from SOE and despatched him by submarine[39] to Denmark with consequences which were regrettable not merely for Siem but for at least two other Danes. The treatment of Siem on his return to England in May (?) 1944[40] is a disgraceful chapter in English handling of one who had given us what radar specialists then called 'the most valuable piece of intelligence yet received'."[41]

Stagg gives this characterization of Sneum on the same occasion as he speaks of the growing belief in England in the possibilities for a Danish Resistance struggle, in 1941; and there is no doubt that here Sneum's and

Kjeld Petersen's daring action played an important rôle. In spite of the fact that Sneum's intention in coming to England was to join the Armed Forces, and without paying the least regard to his situation after his flight, which had deeply compromised him in Denmark,[42] Sneum agreed to return to Denmark and landed in September 1941 on Zealand, with another Dane, Christoffersen, who was intended to be his assistant as radio telegraphist.[43]

Sneum and Christoffersen were thus the first Danes to land by parachute in Denmark, but as we have heard, not attached to SOE but with special Intelligence missions. Unlike the SOE men, they succeeded in landing without any news of them reaching the German counter-espionage. In January 1942 Sneum's presence in Denmark was still unknown to the "Abwehrstelle". Nevertheless, his mission met serious difficulties, partly because the co-operation between him and Christoffersen broke down. There can be no doubt that this was through no fault of Sneum's. Reports from two men, Duus Hansen and the merchant Werner Gyberg, who worked with Sneum and Christoffersen, are unanimous on this point.[44] At all events the disagreement between the two men led to the peculiar situation, whereby they both sought contact with a Danish radio engineer and both, independently of each other, found their way through Werner Gyberg to Duus Hansen, and asked him for radio assistance.[45] One cannot help wondering how both Sneum and Christoffersen, and later Mogens Hammer, all found their way in quite a short time to precisely the man who could and would help. In Hammer's case, the reason is to be found in the valuable contacts he quickly obtained, and which quite simply led him to the heart of one of Denmark's great radio firms. In the case of the other two men, the reason lies in one of the many trivial but strange accidents, which the history of the Occupation is rich in, and which were characteristic for much of the build-up of the organisations, where it was just such accidental connexions and acquaintances which were decisive. In Werner Gyberg's account he describes[46] how a chance acquaintance with a cabinet maker brought him into contact with Christoffersen and through him with Sneum. Here it is a triviality which decides the contact, but it seems extraordinary to read in Gyberg's account:[47] "Another chance contact I had was through my washerwoman. I had the impression that she was French, but later it transpired that she was Belgian, and one day – I think it was in 1941 – she handed me some English propaganda stuff, which she had through her son. He turned out to be a sailor, on the route to Gøteborg, where he had been in touch with the British Consul in Gøteborg (Albert Christensen). The reason for my connexion with her was quite accidental. If I remember right, it was the fact that I had whistled the Marseillaise a few times, which had called her attention to my attitude." That was how contacts could be brought about in the atmosphere of the time, and this example, chosen from among hundreds, is significant proof that such contacts could become important. The

Consul, Albert Christensen, is precisely the man whom we know to have been placed by SOE as the organisation's representative in Gøteborg. Here a British propaganda leaflet, sent out by him, floats down into the lap of a Copenhagen wireless wholesaler; this man had himself been reached already through another British initiative; and this very man, three years later, would sit in Gøteborg as leader of one of the great Danish escape organisations "Danish Assistance Service", in close co-operation with the Consul, Christensen, and therefore with SOE. In addition, the sailor mentioned would become a valuable courier between Denmark and Sweden.[48] And to complete the picture, Gyberg's partner, Robert Jensen, later so famous as "Tom",[49] was drawn into the work through the episodes just described. This digression away from the central subject, which we have allowed ourselves, may seem long, but it does seem justified to the extent that it illustrates just that law of chance, which became such an inevitable factor in so much of the underground work.

The connexion between Duus Hansen and Sneum soon led to Duus Hansen's building a transmitter for him, and with this, radio transmissions to England were started, in which Duus Hansen also took part. A detailed examination of this work lies outside the framework of our subject, but its conclusion must be touched upon, because it had important consequences for later work in SOE. At the end of the winter it was decided that Christoffersen and his brother, whom he had initiated in the work, should leave Denmark, crossing the ice to Sweden. Sneum's closest assistant, Lieutenant Oxlund was to accompany them. The night of 5 March the three men made the attempt to reach the Swedish coast at Falsterbo. In the unusually bitter weather, Lieutenant Oxlund and Christoffersen's brother died, in spite of Swedish attempts to come to their help. Christoffersen was rescued, suffering badly from exposure, by the Swedish Coast Guards.

This tragedy had serious consequences for Sneum's work. It was possible to identify Oxlund's body, and his flat was ransacked. This put the police on the track of Sneum, and Werner Gyberg and one of his business acquaintances, who had had a secondary connexion with the affair, were imprisoned under suspicion of having helped Sneum. The arrest and cross-examination of Gyberg did not bring the police any nearer clearing up the affair, apart from their realising that Sneum was somehow connected with the matter.[50] Gyberg records what occurred after this:[51] "After about a fortnight ... Roland (a Danish police sergeant, Roland Olsen) came in one day – it must have been about 25 March – and said that an order had come from the Germans that serious steps must be taken in the matter, and he advised me to reconstruct a plausible explanation." Gyberg's difficulty was to construct an explanation which could hold under cross-examination, without betraying Sneum. The problem was solved by Roland Olsen on his own initiative[52] giving Gyberg a free hand to arrange a meeting in his own flat between himself, Roland Olsen, Duus Hansen and Sneum. Roland Olsen reports on the peculiar situation: "Well, 'the prisoner was led out to the Town Hall Square', to use police report language. (Gyberg) gave me his hand with the promise that he would be back within twenty minutes. He disappeared, and I sat down and – fed the pigeons."[53] Gyberg succeeded in getting hold of Sneum, and that evening the meeting took place. A plausible explanation was agreed, while Sneum, under the impression of the untenable situation, consented to leave Denmark.[54] On 26 March 1942 he left Denmark and crossed the ice. After this the possibility was open for Gyberg's release on 1 April. What we have called "the Sneum episode" was thus terminated. The whole episode, which regardless of its great independent importance only had secondary connexion with the actual Resistance struggle, is only given here in rough outline, and only because it had consequences for the work in SOE. As a result of this episode, Duus Hansen established connexion with the Danish Police, a connexion which would become even closer in time to come, and which meant a great deal in the SOE work, in which Duus Hansen was "up to the neck". Besides this, the experience of illegal radio transmission was another of the assets which Duus Hansen contributed to the work, when he made the acquaintance of Mogens Hammer in the spring 1942. Duus Hansen writes of this meeting:[55] "We had tried without success to get into touch with the parachutist (Hammer) who had landed, and it was agreed between Sneum and myself that I should do everything to get in touch, and try and get a useful co-operation going with the man, if I succeeded. In the spring 1942 I managed to get contact with Hammer[56] ... He had lost his radio set and wanted to get in touch with people who could build him a transmitter, and help him generally with technical questions ... A set was then built for Hammer's own use, but I do not know myself what results Hammer personally achieved with it." As stated above, this was only the introduction to the great things which were to come. Soon after April 1942, when the next team of parachutists landed,[57] and two new operators were attached to the work, Hammer gave up transmitting himself, and handed over this part of the work to Duus Hansen. Duus Hansen writes:[58] "On 16 (this should be 17) April 1942, Johannesen came down with Rottbøll. Johannesen brought a transmitter and he called on me through Hammer, to get any information that could be useful to him in the work. After this Hammer himself gave up operating a transmitter, and handed it over to me, with his signal plans. I had not yet been in possession of any code myself, and therefore could only send telegrams blind, as the telegrams were delivered to me in code form by Hammer. Consequently I do not know to what extent my transmissions were received, or what the contents were. When I asked Hammer or Johannesen whether they were received, I was always told that they were, and that reception was confirmed."

Thus began the co-operation between Duus Hansen and SOE. It should be emphasized here, that SOE's task was not only to wage Britain's war in Denmark, but also to stimulate the Danish Home Front and bring support to it. The basis for developments had naturally to be the work of the Home Front, and SOE could not and did not aim at starting developments which did not evolve in Denmark itself. The effectiveness of the Danish Resistance struggle had to grow with the expansion of co-operation between SOE's representatives in the field and the leaders of the Danish Home Front, and in this co-operation the leadership had, with time, to shift naturally to the leaders of the Home Front. Duus Hansen became one of the first, and one of those who, from the nature of his work, was in closest touch with the British organisation.

When Mogens Hammer from now on gave up the actual radio work, this can hardly have been due solely to the fact that he could now hand over this work to others, but was certainly connected to some extent with his growing interest in illegal newspaper work, which seems to have become his main concern. We have already heard of his connexion with "The Free Danes", for which he wrote articles himself,[59] and several accounts mention his interest in illegal newspaper work in general.[60]

London's disapproval of this contributed to strengthening the opinion, that a new leader must be sent to Denmark at all costs, and as quickly as possible. It also seemed desirable to expand the radio service of the organisation as soon as this could be done. The little Hammer had achieved in this field showed clearly upon what a flimsy foundation the decisive, direct connexion between Denmark and England rested, and with what a minute safety margin they were operating. The weakness this represented for the organisation speaks for itself. This realisation placed the headquarters in a serious dilemma. On one side SOE had certainly no desire to let things develop in Denmark without their having a man on the spot who could follow in Bruhn's footsteps, both personally and as regards instruction. On the other side, there was no one among the Danish volunteers at that moment who was considered fully qualified for this responsible post. In this situation Hollingworth decided to ask the young Christian Michael Rottbøll to undertake the heavy responsibility, in spite of his youth,[61] and in spite of his not yet having finished the long training in S.T.S.

Hollingworth makes it clear what were his considerations before taking this decision:[62] "I chose Rottbøll as the coming leader. In my opinion he was the best man available. He was a man who could inspire confidence in people of position and influence. He was in possession of intelligence and he had, like Bruhn, the culture which was absolutely necessary for the man who was to lead the work. Next, his integrity and reliable character were above suspicion, and we could count upon his security."[63] For Rottbøll, the request to go Denmark as leader in the field was just as much an honour as a burden. His acceptance is a proof of his fidelity to what he saw as his duty. There can be no doubt that he had misgivings at the enormous responsibility, which was thrust so unexpectedly upon him, and which he can hardly have felt himself mature enough to undertake, young as he was, and with his education not nearly finished. However, the situation as it looked from London could hardly leave a man of Rottbøll's character any choice. Bitter necessity chose for him. We hear a little of Rottbøll's feelings, faced with the situation into which he was forced, from both Hollingworth and Spink.

They both mention his anxiety, not as to the danger, but as to his own possibilities for living up to the demands which would be made. It is apparent from both accounts, that Rottbøll accepted in spite of his own desires, when he became convinced that his services were needed. In Spink's words:[64] "It was Rottbøll's intention to fight as a soldier, so a good deal of discussion was needed before he took this important decision. Rottbøll was a brave man, and when he was told that a man was needed and that he was considered the most suitable, he said 'Yes'."

His 'Yes' was valuable for the cause he wished to serve, fatal for himself.

10. The Rottbøl Team and their Working Conditions

Rottbøll's path to England and to the work in SOE was not that of an adventurer. He was not seeking the thrill of the fight; he was not seeking anything for himself. The motives which led him to go to England were stamped by a high degree of idealism in his attitude towards life, and democratic political principles which inevitably placed him in the active struggle against Nazism. In Ragna Siden's book, "Chr. Mich. Rottbøll", built upon letters from Rottbøll, and upon information from those who were his close friends during his short and tragic fight against Nazism, she gives a picture of his personality and of his untiring eagerness to find himself a place in the ranks of the fighters. In all his reflections, his motives for seeking this place lie, always, outside himself. In a letter to his parents of 28 September 1939 he writes, for example: "... people must realise, before they reach that conclusion, that co-operation between *all* is the only means to peace, just order, and well-being. That is idealism, but when you have read Norman Angell's book, "The Great Illusion", you will certainly not give up hope that that time must come, even if it looks rather hopeless now. None should be grey, tepid (neutral) in this wrestling match ... If England and France decide to carry the fight further ... against two dictator states, which have little respect for the individual human being ... then I shall not wait any longer, but put myself at their disposal."[1] In another letter[2] he writes: "Thank you for letting me go where I felt drawn, to place myself at their disposal in the fight against the principle: the right of the stronger to force their will upon the weaker, by force and violence, threats or war."

At the outbreak of the war Rottbøll was in Argentina, but returned home in the autumn 1939, feeling that it was his duty "to place myself at the disposal either of the Danish Defence Forces or those who, according to my conviction, fight for morally just motives."[3] After his return to Denmark he volunteered for the Danish Battalion in Finland,[4] and when he returned from Finland to occupied Denmark, he made plans, as we have heard, to come to England. In August 1941, he succeeded.[5]

Two volunteers, trained as wireless operators, were chosen together with Rottbøll for the coming operation – the steward Paul Herman Johannes Johannesen and the Chief Officer Max Mikkelsen. These were both recruited from the Danish Merchant Navy. Both of them had first served in the British Merchant Navy for a time before volunteering, and like most of the Danish sailors, had been engaged in several actions which confirmed their determination to join the fight against Nazism.[6] It was not an untried crew that was now sent to Denmark.

In contrast to the case of Bruhn and Hammer, it was decided this time to arrange for the reception of the team, and the arrangements were entrusted to Borch-Johansen. The practical arrangements as to place, time and procedure were made via Stockholm.[7] A field on the estate, Aggersvold, in North-west Zealand, was chosen as reception point. The transfer of the three men did not go smoothly this time, either. The action was fixed no fewer than six times, and then cancelled, twice after the aircraft was over Denmark, but for various reasons had to return. We can follow events from three different sources: from the plane, where Max Mikkelsen's account recalls the atmosphere during the approach;[8] from the ground, where Borch-Johansen reconnoitres the terrain alone on a pretended ski tour, skids in his car on the ice-covered roads and lands in the ditch, and at last stands ready on 17 April;[9] and from Stockholm, where the distant observer Ebbe Munck records the main lines of the action in his diary, as they reach him a few days later. First, from 26 March, the entry runs:[10] "The Duke (Borch-Johansen) ends in the ditch with his car. It is these cursed slippery roads ... And it was lovely moonlight. Don't forget to listen tomorrow, as they usually say, and better luck for it next time." Next, from 26 April:[11] "The Proprietor (Rottbøll) got through happily, and the Duke, who had difficulties with the landing – badly dropped, scattered in the trees, one was even able to get his ticket himself – still managing. Now the gear, which was lost, is needed, they will have to bring a new lot, and at a new place. We will give it a little rest, so that it can all settle down a bit." Let us here, where it is a question of the first organised reception in Denmark, follow the events through Borch-Johansen's vivid and atmosphere-laden description, if only, in this way, to measure the distance which separates the lonely, inexperienced arrangements of 1942, from the well-organised undertakings, carried out by large groups of men in 1945. This was the way – also in other respects – of the Resistance struggle.

"I made a ski tour to Jyderup and reconnoitred the whole area, where everything was covered with snow. The layer of snow was not thick enough to cover the ridges of the plough furrows, which stuck up as sharp as knives through it, so I advised against landing in these conditions, until further notice ... Once we were on the way out,[12] as the BBC had given the start signal from England the same evening. The car we were driving broke down just after Roskilde, but it turned out that the plane had turned back." On grounds of security Borch-Johansen decided now to carry out the reception alone. – "I had worked out a system by which it would be possible for me to establish the usual triangle of lights, in time, with red and clear lights. The aircraft arrived according to plan, and the first landing went smoothly where it should. I ran out at once and met Rottbøll, and we exchanged code words, after which he set to work at once, packing the parachute and the rest of his things together, after I had shown him a small pond, where the whole lot could be submerged. I then started looking for the others. I had heard the smack of the chutes, and had seen at least one container go down, although at some distance. During my search I heard the sound of footsteps, and I now found Johannesen, who had landed in a tree, and was hurt. He was a good deal shaken, and stood with his pistol cocked. However, a couple of stiff drams soon brought him round. We then began, all three, a systematic search for the third man, and for the container. We went on, in growing desperation, combing the wood and the fields right up to the nearest village, but with no result. Finally, when it was getting light, and the smoke was beginning to rise from the cottage chimneys, we drove off and came down via Haraldsted and Borup to Ole Kiilerich's house in Greve." Borch-Johansen then records, as does Mogens Fog, that the latter had helped to get hold of a car with a driving permit, and in listening to the BBC for the special message which announced the operation.[13]

What had happened to Max Mikkelsen was that he, like Johannesen, had landed in a tree. He had hung for a moment in the branches, but then had fallen and had been knocked out. Later in the morning he recovered consciousness, and was able to reach Copenhagen by train from Holbæk. He must also have been given Erik Seidenfaden's name and address, in England, as after arriving in Copenhagen he quickly made contact, through him, with his team and with Mogens Hammer.[14]

The new arrivals naturally brought the possibility of considerably strengthened communications with England, and we see radio contacts improved from now and up to the autumn, when new misfortunes hit the organisation's work, although it never reached the degree of effectiveness and continuity which later became the rule. It should, however, be stressed that Rottbøll's arrival did not apparently make any fundamental change in the picture. This was through no fault of Rottbøll's. The situation was once again to cause a check. The background for his work was essentially the same as it would have been for Bruhn, had he lived. Conditions were still maturing, and neither in Denmark nor in England was there any psychological, organisational nor material preparedness for action. It may be said of Rottbøll's mission also, that it had the character of reconnaissance, and that there was something half-hearted in his instructions, to exploit the relative law and order in Denmark to organise, establish contacts and make preparations, all without the inspiration which lay in active struggle, and without the satisfaction of

118

being able to record real, visible results. It almost seems as if the conditions for his work were harder than those Bruhn would have had. This can be explained by referring to conditions both in England and in Denmark.

It was while Rottbøll was working in Denmark, that the whole question of Britain's attitude in regard to the occupied countries was taken up for intensive discussion, and one notices a tendency to refrain from too hasty developments, and, in the British propaganda, an understanding that it would be unfortunate to animate an optimism which the events of the war did not warrant. This tendency is quite apparent in Bruce Lockhart's comments. He points[15] to a temporary back-lash for Russian propaganda, both at home and abroad, as a consequence of an over-confident assessment of the relative strengths of Germany and Russia, after the winter offensive of 1941–42. This assessment penalized itself, when the Germans started their violent offensive in the early summer 1942, against the Caucasus and Stalingrad. On this subject he writes: "At the end of May, Brooks[16] and I had a useful meeting with the British Chiefs of Staff at which the whole problem of resistance in the occupied countries had been fully discussed ... I made the point that some considerable measure of Anglo-American military success was a necessary condition to any stronger action by the oppressed peoples. General Sir Alan Brooke[17] ... gave us what we badly needed: a clear and concise directive. What the Chiefs of Staff wanted from a military point of view was: 1) the formation and support of organisations in the occuped countries which could take charge at the moment of Germany's collapse; 2) sabotage activities by these organisations in connexion with our military operations; and 3) a continuous sabotage of a "go slow" nature by all possible means of passive resistance. As to the first two directives we should co-operate with the British organisation specially charged with these functions;[18] the third was our direct concern."

This attitude on the part of the responsible British leaders was as moderate as it was wise. One notices that sabotage activity was only to play a rôle as part of the Allied military operations. The expression is, of course, open to interpretation, but in that summer and autumn, in 1942, the British-American forces were definitely on the defensive. There were difficulties in the East, difficulties in the desert, difficulties in the Atlantic. It was not until November 1942 that British and American offensives broke through, at the Battle of Alamein and the landing in French North-west Africa respectively. Brooke's statement also laid down the correct principle, that Resistance activities had military value to the extent that they could be co-ordinated with the common Allied efforts; and it stressed the important point that the European Resistance Movements must not overstrain them-selves, but must be in a position to take action in the event of a German collapse. The moderate line we meet here was not without background in fact. In May 1942 the German State Protector in Bohemia, Heydrich, was killed by two Czechslovaks who came from England, and this, to use Bruce Lockhart's words again, "brought no comfort to the Czechoslovaks and no value to the Allied cause ... its more serious effect (was) the disruption of tle Czech underground movement and of the system of secret communications between Czecloslovakia and Britain."[19] The Norwegian Prime Minister, Nygaardsvold, was expressing the same idea when, in a radio broadcast to Norway on 6 September 1942, he gave a warning against premature actions, which could only harm the cause, through the German punitive measures they inevitably brought with them.[20]

We also hear from those engaged in the work for Denmark of the restraint which made itself felt in the summer 1942. Spink writes:[21] "When people said that Norway had advanced further than Denmark and was already at work, we pointed to the fact that there was a danger that Norway would exhaust herself too soon. In Denmark the organising was to be done first, while there was time ... Developments must first reach the correct point. In the mean time we will build up the organisation." Sten Gudme gives a more direct statement:[22] "The experience in Norway, where intense activity led to violent German pressure, had such an effect that one was afraid, for a time, that the spirit behind the Resistance would collapse; and it is my opinion that this had consequences for Denmark also, so that for a time, in 1942, there was a change-over to a more restrained line. Thus in May 1942 it was regretted, in reality, that Christmas Møller came to England, as conditions at that time were essentially different from those when the invitation was sent in 1941. At that time, the British were working with the so-called "Prince plan", that is, they wished to keep developments quiet in Denmark, and confined themselves to getting military intelligence, which they could obtain through the Prince organisation (the Danish General Staff Intelligence Section) in a relatively quiet Denmark."

The "Prince policy", which Gudme refers to here, is described in more detail in Ebbe Munck's diary and in a letter of the period to the Intelligence Officers inserted in the diary. In the diary entry for 14 February 1942 we read:[23] "TB (Turnbull) has come back from his lightening trip to London. Has had contact with Attlee[24] and Duncan[24] (the Minister of Economic Warfare, the one who decides the bomb targets) and the Chief of Imperial General Staff,[25] who keep Denmark kindly in mind. There are greeting and thanks for 'service rendered', which I shall gladly pass on when the opportunity occurs. Feeling towards Denmark is good, says TB, and we shall certainly get a chance for revenge for 9 April, when the time comes. There are fairly detailed plans already."

The recognition of the Intelligence Section's work, which Turnbull's words express, must naturally have been a great encouragement and must have contributed to underlining the value of this work; and we also notice that in that spring, 1942, there is considerable anxiety among the officers in case this work, which could record such important results, should be broken up or made difficult by aggressive developments in the growing activist circles, supported by SOE. From the standpoint that the work of intelligence, from the Allied point of view, was the essential, the circles around the "Prince organisation" (the Intelligence organisation) sought via Stockholm to keep back developments – at least temporarily. This is apparent, when one of the Intelligence officers, the Cavalry Major Lunding came to Stockholm at the beginning of March for a long-awaited discussion between himself, Turnbull and Ebbe Munck. There are no actual minutes of this meeting, but Ebbe Munck's diary refers briefly to the meeting and negotiations[26] and states definitely that "Mathis" (Lunding)[27] proposes plans which revise the previous ones completely. The work has advanced much further than previously supposed, and will certainly be impressive in the right quarters. He is splendid, and I must say we are all very surprised at what has already happened ... we agree that for the time being there cannot be anything more important than to be able to continue the work in peace. Kristian (Christmas Møller) must therefore retire into the background for the present, and we agree to postpone him. We must also see that the Duke (Borch-Johansen) does not get more than absolutely necessary, and demonstrations which have no real importance must still be avoided. On the other hand it will soon be time to let a couple of factories make the acquaintance of the bombs."

There is an even clearer account of the meeting and its results in two existing letters from Turnbull to the "Liga" (= "the Princes" = the Intelligence officers). The first is quite a short letter of 10 March,[28] where he thanks them for "most interesting and inspiring conversation"; and the second is a longer letter,[29] in which Turnbull reports London's "preliminary reactions" in detail to the standpoints and plans of the officers' group, as put forward by Lunding. This letter, dated April 11th, shows clearly what the subject of the negotiations has been, and the whole attitude taken by the "Liga" towards the British initiative in Denmark. The letter is an important historical document, and requires detailed study. Turnbull first states definitely that "the plan" has been well received, and is regarded as of such importance that it has been the subject of discussion both in the British General Staff and in the War Cabinet. The plan is still under discussion, but a preliminary reaction has been received. Turnbull then examines in detail a number of points in the P plan[30] which Lunding has laid before the meeting in Stockholm in March. Before studying Turnbull's authorised remarks, it will be necessary to outline this P plan, now proposed by the officers as a positive counterpart to the plans SOE had in mind. The P plan aimed at preparing the formation of military forces throughout the country, with the help of local officers of the Reserve. In principle the plan entailed a considerable expansion of the Army's engagement in the early illegal work,

121

in that it went beyond the Intelligence work which had previously predominated. Nevertheless, it was based upon utterly different standpoints from those of the civilian Resistance circles. Whereas the Resistance aimed at a direct struggle against the Germans, mainly by means of sabotage, the P plan confined itself to measures which would only become effective in the event of a German collapse, when it was considered necessary that the Army had forces at its disposal which could take over important guard duties and, as regards the Government, guarantee law and order in the country. The military plan was built upon the assumption that the Army could be kept intact, at least to some extent. A political break with the Germans, with the consequence that the Army would be dissolved, must therefore be avoided. The task must be to maintain and exploit the existing state of cooperation with the Germans, and to use it for organising and expanding the work of intelligence. Sabotage and other forms of open warfare must be avoided for tactical reasons.

As will appear in the following pages, this characterization of the P plan is valid, with the qualification that the plan also operated with the idea of bringing the military groups into action in a final battle, if collapse in Germany or invasion by the Allied Forces made such a battle militarily possible. And what was the British reaction to these plans? Turnbull's remarks in his letter of 11 April are in substance as follows:

London approves the P plan in principle and the policy of the "Liga". However, London reserves the right to send individual parachutists to Denmark, mostly as radio operators, instructors and organisers. This would only occur, however, with the assent of the "Liga" in each case. It is understood that the actual help will be given by Borch-Johansen. It is hoped that the "Liga" will provide some help for them, also it is hoped that the "Liga" through Borch-Johansen will "assist and encourage passive resistance and 'insaississable' sabotage and the Duke (Borch-Johansen) will agree to pay special attention to sabotage of aeroplanes, ship-building, ships, road and rail-communications for which London will supply the necessary equipment." It is hoped that the "Liga" will not disapprove of such sabotage, led by Borch-Johansen, but it is agreed, on the other hand, that such sabotage will not be carried out until it can be done in co-ordination with the full development of the P plan. The work of sabotage is to support the execution of the P plan on "the Day". The hope is expressed that the "Liga" will continue the work of intelligence.

To this was added a direct promise of a political nature: "It is agreed that London will modify its radio-propaganda in order to avoid upsetting the status quo inside Your country and steps are being taken to bring American propaganda into line. In future all unnecessary incitement to sabotage will be avoided and unnecessary attacks will not be made upon the present government." This is amplified at the end of Turnbull's letter: "With regard to propaganda as I say above this is now to be co-ordinated so that nothing will be said or done to create unsuitable conditions for the effective development of the P plan. London radio have abandoned the policy of attempting to form a split in your government and agrees that nothing must be done which might cause a change in the status quo. It is realised that the present Quisling government must remain for the time being if we are to preserve the organisation which the 'Liga' has under its control."

This is supplemented with a direct military undertaking. London agrees that sabotage which is only aimed at annoying the enemy is to be given up, and that Borch-Johansen in co-operation with Rottbøll is to concentrate on "quiet and discreet" work of organising, so that their organisation will be a part of the P plan on "the Day". In connexion with this, Turnbull states, London wishes to reassure the "Liga" with regard to sabotage work. He writes that the "Liga" is perhaps unreasonably nervous about this work. It is not London's intention to use bombs "whole-sale", and London thinks that the "Liga" will admit that they will need specially trained men with special equipment to carry out precise sabotage and "commando type of warfare" in support of military operations.

In conclusion, Turnbull makes the following statement, with parts underlined: "The Joint Chiefs of Staff Committe and the War Cabinet have agreed that absolutely no work of any kind will be done in your country *without your knowledge and without being agreed between you and the Captain (Turnbull).* No other British organisation will be allowed to work in your country and your only authentic channel of communication with the British authorities will be through the Captain and through Top (Rottbøll) and his radiomen ... All intelligence work for the British shall pass through the Capitain to London or if necessary through one of Tops radiomen."

It cannot be denied that the British reply on the P plan is bursting with glaring contradictions. It is clear that two fundamentally different points of view as to British policy in Denmark are struggling to express themselves. On one side there is a clear British desire for a continuation of the intelligence work. In consideration of this there is a promise that SIS agents will no longer be sent to Denmark. And in this connexion there is an evident British interest in the P plan's para-military forces. Both in this respect and in respect of the intelligence work, there are far-reaching concessions to the "Liga's" points of view: no undermining of the political situation in Denmark, no agitation for sabotage, no activity in Denmark without the approval of the "Liga" On the other hand, it is just as clear, that SOE's activist plans are by no means shelved. London reserves all sorts of rights. The programme will be followed of sending parachutists to Denmark, and in co-operation with civilian Danish Resistance men – Borch-Johansen alone is mentioned for the time being – they will prepare and possibly carry out sabotage actions. Turnbull makes great efforts to present that part of the programme in such a way that it will be accepted by the "Liga", but it is on that particular point that the British answer explodes. SOE's plans could not be made to agree with the officers' views in the long run, but they agree perfectly with the civilian Resistance Movement, which is now – in the spring 1942 – being established in Denmark. For the Resistance, the aim was to go into action as soon as humanly possible, and to aim at the collapse of the co-operation with the Germans and the establishment of open warfare. This was also SOE's policy. It could not be the Officers'.

The first effect of Lunding's meeting in Stockholm in March and his presentation of the P plan was, therefore, that the British held back in Denmark, for the time being, without allowing themselves to stop preparations for the long-term programme they had decided upon. It was a tactical turn in the plan – not a change of principle. Next, the negotiations had the important long-term effect, that it had now been clearly stated that the Danish officers alone, and without British interference, looked after the intelligence work,[31] and that – for that reason – they were excluded from taking part in any other work. This result was naturally not immediately as clear as it is from the historical perspective. For one thing, setting up the para-military forces of the P plan contained an element of uncertainty: to what extent could such forces be brought into the actual Resistance struggle? But this much was already a definite fact in April 1942: the "Liga" could not and would not be the immediate supporting organisation for SOE work, which Turnbull had imagined at the New Year. This was prevented by the Danish political situation and the position in which the officers were now locked.

In the civilian Resistance view, the officers' standpoints were unacceptable. The aim here was open warfare and liquidation of the policy of co-operation, regardless of the fact that the Army organisations would collapse, when the political foundation fell to pieces. In spite of the fact, therefore, that their interests coincided to a considerable degree, since the inspiration of the illegal work of both groups was anti-German, there existed nevertheless an insurmountable barrier between the two conceptions. The result was unavoidable: many instances of acute friction between the representatives of the two views, an unpleasant situation, which was not resolved until the civilian Resistance groups, supported by SOE's representatives, on 29 August 1943 swept aside the double game in Denmark, and brought the policy of open warfare to life.

The tension between the Intelligence officers and the civilian Resistance men is noticeable as a murmuring accompaniment behind the descriptions in several accounts.[32] It is quite apparent that it was just at that time – the spring 1942 – when open resistance was gathering on the horizon, that the incompatibility of the two conceptions shows itself clearly, and the parting of the ways begins. From the civilian side, Resistance men regarded the officers' work with growing distrust, while the latter, conversely, followed the increasingly uncompromising Resistance developments with mounting fear of the consequences it could drag with it. In Stockholm Ebbe Munck sat as a kind of umpire in the game, with contacts to both sides, and followed the trend of affairs with some anxiety. In conclusion, it should be remembered that open, thorough discussion of viewpoints was difficult, if not impossible. The officers, particularly, found it difficult to lay their cards on the table, and this inevitably involved misunderstandings and faulty deductions.

As we have seen, Borch-Johansen was one of the Danish Resistance pioneers, who was in closest touch with the officers of the Intelligence Service, and he was therefore one of those who felt it most strongly when the brakes were applied. He writes in undisguised terms, in his account:[33] "When the Princes learned that more parachutists (the Rottbøll team) had arrived in Denmark, they demanded very categorically to know who had come and what their mission was, and via Stockholm we received confirmation that we could initiate them in the work. They immediately took up a very strong anti-sabotage attitude, and at a meeting with Gyth and Lunding they made me personally responsible for seeing to it that nothing of the kind should be carried out before they had approved it, as they maintained that sabotage at that stage would ruin their work and compromise the P plan, which in their view would not be in the Danish interest." Borch-Johansen expresses his growing scepticism towards the officers in general and their intelligence work in particular. At the same time, both he and others, in their accounts, pour scorn on the elaborate procedure, which they found unreasonable, and which the Intelligence officers at various meetings demanded should be followed.[34]

In assessing Borch-Johansen's remarks it must, of course, be borne in mind that he was not in a position to appraise the over-all situation or the intelligence service rendered by the officers. In his position he had to take the brunt of the feelings of the civilian Resistance men, and SOE must feel that the developments they and he were aiming at were being attacked. The remarks – corroborated in what will be mentioned further on the whole subject of this divergence of opinion – illustrate clearly, that the co-operation between the officers and the civilian Resistance circles was wavering, and the cleft which divided the two conceptions could not as yet be bridged.

We also notice the difference of opinion in Duus Hansen's account, in which he states[35] that from the autumn 1942 he was placed at the disposal of the officers' section, as their radio man, with independent codes and signal plans, and with orders from London, concurrently with this, to keep contact with SOE. The officers protested at this arrangement, maintaining that he must have nothing to do with SOE as long as he was attached to the officers' special intelligence work. Later again, when Flemming Muus came to Denmark in 1943 as leader of SOE in the field, he was also affected by the divergencies of standpoint. In his book, "The Spark and the

Flame", he described the officers' opinion as follows:[36] "London had already been ... in connexion with the Army Intelligence Service for a long time, I had orders to keep away from their domain, as they already had plans for groups[37] – plans which were still in embryo ... It must ... come to divergencies between the Intelligence Service and the organisation, I was leading ... Peace, peace, peace at any price was evidently the motto of the Intelligence Service. It was only with the aid of peace and quiet that the Intelligence Service could work out the plans they were engaged in .... The objective of the Intelligence Service was to set up groups, which were gradually to be armed from the arsenals of the Army, and their task was to act as police, if there should be insurrection at the moment when the Germans had, or were in the process of retreating from the country." Although Muus in his narrative style allows himself to be lured into using unsound accentuation, the presentation of the problem is clearly the same as in 1942, the attitude also.

The divergencies in viewpoint come to light most clearly in several places in Ebbe Munck's diary. He naturally could not remain unmoved by the conflict. He was the loyal spokesman for "Liga" vis-à-vis the British, but he was at the same time an advocate for a Resistance policy which was the diametrical opposite of the standpoint of the "Liga". For a long time thereafter he can follow the Intelligence officers for tactical reasons, and based upon the over-all view of the situation, which he, above all, had the possibility of forming; but with his basic conception, he could only arrive at the desire for open warfare, when the background for it was ready. This conflict can be traced in his diary. On 28 September 1942 there is a long description of his meeting with Borch-Johansen, when, following his arrest and subsequent escape,[38] which will be described later, he comes to Stockholm. In this account Ebbe Munck's basic theme is the defence of the Intelligence officers' standpoint. It appears from the diary[39] that Ebbe Munck, in a long conversation with Borch-Johansen maintained that Christmas Møller and Borch-Johansen himself had a certain co-responsibility for the police having been able to ascertain Christmas Møller's escape route and arrest Borch-Johansen, and the diary continues: "It is true that he (Borch-Johansen) declares that the "Liga" had approved the plan and then had not helped them further – they cannot do so, as important things are at stake – but there is no excuse for ... Christian not being camouflaged[40] ... Orange (Mogens Fog) has taken over the Duke's (Borch-Johansen's) job,[41] he is the man for the job, says the Duke, which I do not doubt. But what is the use of it all, if it is not led by a central authority, which gathers all the threads together, and there can be no discussion, that that central authority must be the "Liga" ... The Duke is very bitter at the Liga, because they won't help, and he does not believe, either, that they will be able to accomplish anything later."

126

Ebbe Munck's difficult position is even more pronounced in a note dated 14–21 October 1942.[42] This reports a discussion between himself, Turnbull and Erling Foss.[43] The subject of the discussion is the future policy, and it is evident that Turnbull, on behalf of the British, has strongly stressed the desirability of now altering the directives in Denmark and urging the Danes to "take their share in the battle".[44] To this Erling Foss states that such a policy is not yet feasible in Denmark, and makes some critical remarks on Christmas Møller's BBC broadcast on sabotage in September, as he declares that the psychological background for such a policy is not yet ripe. In Ebbe Munck's diary he adds: "As spokesman for the "Liga" here on the spot, I can naturally only speak for them. I am also convinced that sabotage at the present moment – with so few experts available[45] – would have very little effect. – If it is to be done, we must have the Liga with us, and the whole thing must be organised in a different way. How long the question can be drawn out is another matter."

Finally the problem is illustrated in a letter from Ebbe Munck to Christmas Møller from that same day in October 1942. After Christmas Møller's arrival in London, he has complained at the lack of information from Stockholm, and in his reply[46] Ebbe Munck makes the following remarks, which once more stress the opinion that for the time being they must watch their step:[47] "I can well understand ... that you tear your hair in desperation that you do not get more. But the organisation[48] has other work, at least as important, and I would not be up to my job if I did not understand that security takes first place. An organisation which is smashed up half-way, is of no value, and it is therefore necessary to control ones impatience ... The said organisation ... is therefore forced to turn a cold shoulder to those who cannot respect these conditions. There are many tasks, which one would naturally very much like to bring in under the organisation, and which one would like to support, but it can't be done, as one would risk in that case making the main tasks impossible ... You may have noticed this in the period just before your departure (and the Duke has noticed it in recent months). Sentimental considerations have had to give way to practical. When your departure was discovered, this involved of necessity that we had to lie low for some time."

With the explanation for what one might call "the Prince policy" which is given here, chronological order is broken and conditions are touched upon as far in the future as 1943. This was necessary, however, because the "Prince policy" in conjunction with the great restraint which was noticeable in the spring and summer 1942 in the British attitude towards Denmark, created a part of the atmosphere in which Rottbøll came to work. But that is not all that can be said of the dismal background for his work.

It must be emphasized that Rottbøll was handicapped by somewhat vague instructions. It has already been stated that he was sent to Denmark to fill the vacuum after Bruhn's death, and that when he was sent off from England, it had not been possible to give him precise instructions.[49] Hollingworth could not count on much support from SOE's main organisation, whose chief interest lay elsewhere, and which was hampered by the general lack of material resources. Hollingworth underlines also that no more was expected or demanded from Rottbøll than purely preparatory work, and stresses the impossibility at that preliminary stage of giving men in the Field sufficient support,[50] "... because time after time, under the extremely difficult conditions, it could naturally occur that people in Denmark thought that we in London did not give them the necessary support. The truth was that in Denmark it was not always possible to assess our difficulties, which particularly in the first years were enormous. The Danish Section of SOE was only a small, and for many not a very important part of the whole machinery, and we often had to fight hard to get a proper share in the distribution of weapons, explosives and aircraft. We did our utmost in every way to further Danish interests, and particularly in the first years of the war, when Denmark was regarded with extreme scepticism in wide circles, it was very difficult for us to get a hearing for our demands, and belief in our claims that there was the right spirit in Denmark."

This is the British opinion. We meet the corresponding Danish opinion from Borch-Johansen, who writes:[51] "Rottbøll soon came to live with Stig Jensen, whom I did not know, but with whom Mogens Hammer had established contact ... I met Rottbøll regularly, and soon realised that his instructions were extremely vague. He was burning to get sabotage started, but it was doubtful in reality whether his instructions went beyond preparations for coming work ... Even when I went underground,[52] and gave up the regular work, there were still no clear instructions as to the lines on which Rottbøll was supposed to work. We asked England again and again for instructions, but received very little. Rottbøll had to confine himself mostly to acclimatizing himself, while he sat and waited for matériel ... He sometimes felt he was not accomplishing anything, but was wasting his time and his chances, although without any doubt, he worked hard building up connexions which were later very important."

In this last assessment, the historical view proves unconditionally that Borch-Johansen was right. As we shall see in the following chapters, it was in just this building up of important contacts that Rottbøll's mission came to have lasting significance for the work that followed. It may be added, that when the Resistance men, with whom SOE was in touch at that time, regarded the British organisation's weakness with some disappointment, Rottbøll managed to a great extent to reduce this feeling through the impression his personality made upon those with whom he came into close contact. He gave SOE an image and created sympathy towards the organisation. Borch-Johansen brings out his courage, aristocracy of mind, and gentleness,

Dedichen underlines his culture and intelligence, and those who worked with him speak of him as a good comrade.[53]

Finally it should be mentioned that the vagueness in Rottbøll's instructions is borne out by a further circumstance. It was London's idea that Rottbøll should take up the leadership of the work in the field, but it appears from remarks in some of the accounts[54] that the question of competence in the relations between him and Mogens Hammer were not stated definitely enough to avoid Hammer finding it difficult to accept Rottbøll as leader. It was not until May that clear instructions were given, when Hollingworth realised that there was uncertainty and conflict as to authority in the field. A series of letters and telegrams put things right.[55] In reality, from now on, London pushed Borch-Johansen between SOE and the parachutists in Denmark, as leader for their work. The arrangement may have been meant as an emergency measure, to gain control of Hammer's unwanted activities, but after Rottbøll's arrival it was decided as the permanent order. On 8 May London sent a message via the "Possone" that Headquarters recognized Borch-Johansen as leader of the parachutist organisation in Denmark, with Rottbøll as technical advisor. The message was confirmed in a letter to Borch-Johansen from Turnbull on 11 May, and the decision was further confirmed in a number of letters, which Hollingworth wrote on 16 May to Borch-Johansen, Rottbøll, Hammer, Johannesen and Mikkelsen. The whole series of letters was sent via Stockholm to Borch-Johansen, who was asked to read them before passing them on. In his letter to Borch-Johansen Hollingworth first expresses his gratitude for Borch-Johansen's work, and then defines the question of command: "May I close by telling you that London headquarters has 100 % confidence in you. We regard you as the Chief of organisation Table Top and as our link with organisation Chair. Nothing will be undertaken in your country without your knowledge ..." In the letters to the four parachutists, the same arrangement is stated definitely, in the letter to Rottbøll with the words: "In the Duke (Borch-Johansen) we have a man who is a first-class organiser, who will not take unnecessary risks and who can view the whole field of operations with a broad mind. He is a man to follow, and I sincerely hope that you and all your boys will back him 100 %. It is our wish that the Duke should be regarded as the leader for Table operations. Your position is that of Chief representative of London H.Q. and technical adviser to the Duke ... I am sure you will make a splendid team together. You are responsible to London H.Q. for the good conduct of your colleagues sent out from England and you should see that no action is undertaken except under orders of the Duke."

It appears that the arrangement with Borch-Johansen as leader of the parachutist group was not decided or discussed with Rottbøll before he left England, although London had already given Borch-Johansen a sort of command over Hammer. That the question now arose and demanded both a telegram and a series of letters from London to all those involved in Denmark was due to the fact that the arrangement was not accepted without difficulty in the Field, and therefore demanded that more formal orders should be issued than may originally have been intended. At least it is evident and not incomprehensible that Hammer did not accept London's decisions on the question of leadership. He also seems to have found it difficult to accept Rottbøll as the technical leader of the work, and the problem of leadership arose, therefore, as soon as the Rottbøll team arrived in Denmark. By the end of April the problem was acute, and Borch-Johansen referred the disagreement to Stockholm-London, in a letter which has not been preserved. This resulted both in the telegram and letters from London, and in a letter from Turnbull dated 8 May. He writes: "We are very sorry about your difficulties with Arthur (Hammer) and we quite agree with you. London has already sent a message to Arthur direct by radio saying that Little Father (Hollingworth) is sending him personal letters very soon via Stockholm. These letters will of course give Arthur instructions that he shall put himself under Top (Rottbøll) and therefore under you." Later in the letter the position is stated even more definitely, and this time with impatient irritation at Hammer: "Arthur should only keep in touch with you and take his orders from you completely. I may say that we are not in the least interested in his connections with persons unknown to you and he must stop all such stupidities. He is not fit for being a leader of large plans and he has no rights to organise anything. Arthur is a radioman and not more and he must place himself and his instruments entirely at the disposal of you and Top (Rottbøll)."

There was irritation in Stockholm, but there was anger in London. From that distance what were really quite natural disagreements took on unreasonable dimensions, conditioned by London's reaction of alarm, whenever the rigorous and theoretical security rules were disobeyed. Hollingworth wrote to Borch-Johansen on 16 May: "I don't think you will have any more difficulties with Arthur (Hammer), but if you do, and this applies to anybody who is proving a danger – I can only recommend you to use the strongest measures. We cannot afford to take risks and if a man becomes a real danger, both to himself and others, he should be liquidated." Hollingworth expressed himself to Hammer the same day in friendlier, but quite unambiguous terms. He sent his greetings and wished him good luck in the work, but then underlined that Borch-Johansen was Chief, and all orders would be given through him. He then reminded him of the fundamental order, that each man should keep to his own job and not take on other activities: "I know how difficult it must have been for you, after so many months of inactivity. You felt it was your duty to get started because you knew how important the Table organisation (the parachutist organisation) was for your

130

country's freedom and the winning of the war. You may, therefore, now find it difficult to place yourself in a position where you will receive orders rather than give them, but for the sake of your own personal safety and for the lives of many others ... it is our wish in London that each one who is sent out from England should stick to the job for which he has been trained, even though it may not always be exciting." Hollingworth then repeats his statement as to Borch-Johansen's and Rottbøll's functions of command, expresses his hope that everyone will work together in mutual understanding, and points to the fact that Johannesen's and Mikkelsen's positions are exactly the same as Hammer's. Each of them must regard himself as a "telegraph office". The command was thus determined: Borch-Johansen was Leader of the Table organisation in Denmark, with Rottbøll as technical advisor, and the other parachutists as operators. Borch-Johansen was also responsible for the Table organisation's relations with the "Liga" and for arranging the necessary co-ordination in the work and standpoints.

The whole of this arrangement, as far as Borch-Johansen was concerned, was to collapse before it had time to function as intended. The reason for this was Borch-Johansen's active participation in arranging Christmas Møller's illegal journey to London, a participation which would bring to an end his pioneer work in the history of Danish Resistance. His war effort now came to lie in the Headquarters of the Danish Section of SOE and later in active service in the British Army.

11. Towards Sabotage

The prelude to Rottbøll's work in Denmark was dramatic, and would at first increase his difficulties still further. When Rottbøll arrived on 17 April, Christmas Møller was on the point of departure for England. The preparations for the journey were complete in all essentials, and Rottbøll had no part, therefore, in carrying out this mission, although he was naturally fully informed on what was impending. As it took place immediately after Rottbøll's arrival – he just managed, as mentioned, to meet Christmas Møller[1] – and as it obviously was of extreme importance to the work of SOE, it will be relevant to describe it here.

The British approach to Christmas Møller in August 1941[2] has already been described. His answer, in principle, was "Yes", although he wished first to make sure "whether this was serious, and whether a responsible wish of the Government was behind it."[3] He therefore asked Erling Foss, while on a visit to Stockholm in October 1941, to obtain guarantees for this.[4] The reply came, according to Erling Foss's account, in November, and will be quoted from his book, "From Passive to Active Resistance":[5] "it is vitally important that at least one well-known Danish patriot should come out of Denmark to help lead Free Danes ... It has always been felt that you and a leading Socialist,[6] whose name has already been put to you, were ideally suited to lead Danish forces of liberation ... It is sufficient to say that your presence in England is desired by his Majesty's Govt. and also by individual members of the war committee ... It is wiser for me not to sign my name, but you can be sure that I have the authority to make the above statements."

Borch-Johansen, to whom the practical arrangements for the journey were finally entrusted, also refers to Christmas Møller's natural desire for complete certainty as to his formal position:[7] "... I had to go to Stockholm again and negotiate with the British Minister, Sir Victor Mallet, to get complete certainty. A meeting was arranged between Munck and Turnbull in a villa outside Stockholm late one evening, where I met Sir Victor for the first time. During an hour's conversation he stated explicitly that it was the British Government, as such, who wished to invite Christmas Møller to come to England as their guest, and they were ready to allow him political freedom to look after Danish interests as he found best, and work with the Danish Council, of which they found it natural that he should assume the leadership ... I asked Sir Victor Mallet to crystallize these conclusions in a personal message to Christmas Møller, which he did, and I afterwards brought his letter to Christmas Møller." Borch-Johansen's account is confirmed both in Ebbe Munck's diary and in his account.[8] According to the diary, the meeting can be fixed as taking place on 2 December 1941. It is not clear whether there is a question of a double answer, or whether the letter Foss quotes is the answer Borch-Johansen brought home, as courier.[9] At all events, Christmas Møller made sure of his position by various channels. He also asked the Swedish Minister in Copenhagen to take soundings.

The journey was settled, and it was decided that Christmas Møller, with his wife and son, should cross to Sweden hidden in a ship bringing a cargo of chalk from Limfjord to Sweden. The skipper, Johs. Schmidt declared himself willing to run the risk connected with the arrangement. It was an extremely hard winter, however, and the ice conditions prevented the crossing until 30 April 1942. The actual voyage from the Limfjord to Göteborg, from where the British Consul Albert Christensen arranged the next part of the journey, to Stockholm, is described elsewhere in all its dramatic details, and will therefore be omitted here.[10]

Christmas Møller's departure inevitably aggravated the political situation in Denmark and accelerated developments decisively in the open struggle which had already begun. It was of importance in that it at least temporarily laid a serious strain on the Danish-German collaboration policy, and in that it influenced public feeling in Denmark to the detriment of that policy; and first and last it had epoch-making importance through the tremendous activity which Christmas Møller now began in London. This activity was of a political character, however, and Christmas Møller had no direct connexion with SOE's military operations in Denmark. We therefore leave Christmas Møller, in this thesis, at the moment where he took up his great mission for the Resistance Movement.[11]

Christmas Møller's departure had immediate direct consequences for the organisation as regards the work in progress in the Danish Resistance. The German reaction was violent and directed primarily against the Conservative Party, particularly the Church Minister, Vilhelm Fibiger, as the party was suspected of being in support of Christmas Møller's decision, or at least having fore-knowledge of it. An emphatic declaration by the Government, followed somewhat later by a declaration by the Conservative Party, combined with energetic police activity in the affair, cleared the air more or less, however, and removed the danger of its having more extreme consequences.[12]

The psychological consequences of Christmas Møller's leaving the country cannot, of course, be determined precisely, but there is no doubt that it was great. In a report to England of 18 May 1942 Foss tries to weigh up the effect on the population, and comes to the conclusion that the first impression was both very strong and definitely positive:[13] "People's faces lit up in a smile everywhere where Christmas's name was mentioned ... Among working people Christmas's popularity is even greater than before ... It has even led to cheers for Christmas from workers in the factories ... A ... reaction which approaches enthusiasm." Foss makes a certain reservation in his analysis in the question as to the possible reaction among the farmers. In a later analysis from 18–23 May[14] he confirms and emphasizes his opinion of the favourable attitude taken by the legal Press, at a meeting with the Foreign Minister Scavenius, in connexion with the affair. The editor Hendrik Stein, in particular, protested strongly against a Foreign Ministry suggestion that the Danish Press should mark its disapproval of Christmas Møller's action, one of his arguments being that the mass of the people backed up Christmas Møller to such an extent that disapproval from the Press would simply separate them from the population.[15] Ebbe Munck makes a corresponding statement in his diary, that the first analysis of public feeling after Christmas Møller's departure and first radio talks show a favourable attitude.[16]

For the work of the organisation in Denmark, Christmas Møller's departure had direct consequences. It had already been agreed, before the journey was decided, that the work should be slowed down, and this had even led to Stockholm ventilating the idea of cancelling the journey at the last moment. This slow-down was noticeable after the journey, so much so that one even finds some deprecating remarks at its having taken place at all. On 26 April the entry in Ebbe Munck's diary includes the following[17] comments: "We have asked that Christian should keep quiet ... but I am afraid that it is too late already. The plans are quite complete and he has waited so long that he can hardly be stopped." Later, when he has made the journey, Ebbe Munck writes:[18] "Now that he has come, there is of course nothing to regret, as the game has started, and we can only wait and see what the consequences will be. Who will be hit, the Police or the Army, the Radio or the communications with Sweden ... We shall see."

In the period which follows, the diary shows clearly that Stockholm's attitude is that the work must not be forced and make the "Princes" work with the P plan difficult, and that Christmas Møller's departure and the series of consequences it has brought with it have made it even more necessary to put on the brakes. Even while Christmas Møller is in Stockholm, waiting to go on to London, this theme appears:[19] "T (Turnbull) talks the matter over with Christian, it is important that he does not barge in with plans which do not harmonize with what is already agreed ... as that is already settled, and the Princes' (the Intelligence officers') work will in any case be privileged." In the entries which follow, right up to July, he refers several times to receiving special warning signals from the Prince organisation, in the form of post cards with pictures of the Marble Church:[20] "The

Marble Church turns up ... More Marble Churches. Absolute red light ... There are two Marble Churches at the same time." And in another place:[21] "Without doubt shadowed on the street and around Sibyllen (Munck's residence). Who it is I can't be sure. Have hoved to."

Ebbe Munck was now seriously caught in the German search lights. This is also evident from the fact that the German Press Attaché, Gustav Meissner[22] now made a direct attack on him, and demanded his recall to Denmark. Erling Foss writes on this in the first week of June:[23] "The Germans are keeping a sharp eye on Ebbe Munck and Bahnsen. Meissner has asked the editors to recall them. When this was refused, they took reprisals in the form of refusing permission to bring foreign news from outside Sweden through Stockholm – also for Ritzaus Bureau ... As far as Ebbe Munck is concerned, no one expects that he will do as they ask."[24] Nor did he. Munck writes himself:[25] "Kruse[26] has come home, telephones me to come, and tells of a conversation he has had with Meissner on the subject of the Stockholm correspondents, and especially the undersigned. Meissner repeats that he knows where I come and also where I do not come ... my place is in Stockholm until they sack me – and possibly after – at least as long as it has any importance that I am here."

It is thus evident that Christmas Møller's departure brought temporary difficulties, for the Stockholm organisation, but in Denmark the dramatic journey was soon to tear deep gashes in the organisation which was in building. The police investigation of the voyage led to Borch-Johansen's imprisonment. Christmas Møller had travelled to Middelfart by train with his family, had been fetched from there by a taxi driver from Vejle, who drove the family to Aggersund, where they went on board. The police traced the taxi driver fairly quickly, and through him the skipper Schmidt, and this brought Borch-Johansen's arrest.[27] The stages of the investigation are described in Erling Foss's letters to England just after the events.[28] On 18 May, nothing disastrous has happened as yet: "The Police have not found Christmas Møller's tracks, apart from the fact that he was seen in Middelfart." But in the report for 18–23 May, things look serious: "The affair has been unravelled to the point where Østergaard (the driver) drove Christmas Møller to Limfjord. It is believed that a ship, possibly Swedish, starting from a Danish harbour in the fjord on the way to Sweden, sent a dinghy in to the shore and fetched him. It is known that the family flew from Stockholm to London." In the following report for 26 May – I June he writes: "... as it naturally did not take long to find the skipper and arrest him, his wife and assistant. The skipper insisted that he only dealt direct with Christmas Møller, but his story was patently improbable. He admitted in the end ... that Borch-Johansen was the man. He was arrested by the police immediately after."[29]

The events can also be followed in Borch-Johansen's own account:[30] "We tried to stop the skipper, Schmidt, from coming back, but did not succeed ... and on Whit Monday I received the message that he had sailed out from Sweden on the way to Nykøbing Mors. I was in Kolding at the time and immediately went to Aalborg, where I got one of my local contacts, the insurance agent Nikolaysen, to go to Hals to get a fisherman to sail out and try to stop Schmidt before he came in to land, and give him a message to return and report to the British Consul, Christensen, in Göteborg ... The next day, however, we heard that he had sailed direct to Frederikshavn, where he was arrested at once, but had denied everything. On Thursday I was rung up by the editor Niels Grunnet, who wanted to have a talk, and we went for a long walk together. He spoke of his anxiety ... as he had been informed about the work of the Police through his brother, who was leading the investigation. Unfortunately it did not dawn on me that this was a warning, and the next day I was arrested in my office by the criminal detective Grunnet and detective constable Roland Olsen."

Borch-Johansen's arrest was serious for SOE. Although he was arrested in connexion with Christmas Møller's departure, and during cross-examination insisted that he had no knowledge of anything beyond that affair, he was so deeply involved in all illegal work, and was connected to so many sides – the Stockholm organisation, the Intelligence officers, the parachutists, Mogens Fog, and his own organisation, which included Conservative Party friends, and shipping and family connexions all over the country – that his arrest must inevitably raise sinister possibilities. It is therefore very understandable that he seized an opportunity to escape, although he thereby placed the Danish Police, and particularly Roland Olsen, in an extremely difficult situation. The choice was between the lesser and greater evils, and this must particularly be the case for Borch-Johansen, who did not know of Roland Olsen's service to the Resistance. The opportunity for escape occurred while Borch-Johansen and Roland Olsen and other policemen were in his office, where he had the right to be present during the police ransacking, and to give certain directives on the work of the office. Borch-Johansen who had feigned invalidity saw his chance to slip out from the lavatory by a back staircase,[31] and went underground. In the period which followed, he could only keep himself abreast of the work to a minor extent, primarily through Mogens Fog.[32]

Borch-Johansen's active rôle in the work of the organisation in Denmark, and his rôle as one of the more permanent links between Denmark and Sweden was thus played out. His work was taken over in the first instance by Mogens Fog, who happened to be in Stockholm when these events occurred. In Ebbe Munck's diary we read:[33] "Visit from Doc (Mogens Fog). Announcement on the evening radio about Borch, the skipper, who was tricked during the cross-examination, and the boatman. The weak link in the chain was the chauffeur from Middelfart ... Conferred with R. (Ronald

136

Turnbull) on possibilities. Marble Church turns up, stop Doc., and get instructions to pass on in the new situation ... Now we must see what happens. Borch evidently fooled them (Olsen) properly ... We must hope he also destroyed all his other tracks ... Doc. says a lot of interesting things and can certainly be very useful – particularly in the present situation, he can bridge the gap as liaison. (This has happened)."

The worst consequences of Borch-Johansen's arrest were thus averted and the work could continue. In this connection it ought to be mentioned that the somewhat careless way in which Roland Olsen conducted the search, although more strict than the way in which he acted towards Gyberg and la Cour,[34] must be registered as one of Roland Olsen's many contributions to the Danish resistance, though in this case not all a deliberate one,[35] as he had no possibility of estimating the seriousness of the imprisonment. That the case from his side must stand in quite a different light from that, in which it was viewed from Stockholm or London and is viewed by posterity goes without saying. In all considerations of right and wrong in the shadowy world of the occupation the challenge to the historian is always to familiarize himself with the motives behind the actions, and these were very often hidden to the actors in the drama, who time and again were unable to unmask themselves, even towards people they could actually trust.

Whilst all these events had been occupying the general attention, the parachutists had quietly started work. One of Rottbøll's first tasks was necessarily to enter into co-operation with the Prince organisation, a co-operation which at that period, where understanding of the problems of the Resistance was far from clarified, must seem a necessity. All Rottbøll's activity, as far as this is known, points to his having believed this to be one of his most important duties. Ole Kiilerich describes in his account how Rottbøll stressed this viewpoint immediately after his arrival in Denmark, when he and his comrades met Mogens Hammer at Kiilerich's summer villa on Køgevej at Greve Strand. Kiilerich writes of this:[36] "The team ... were brought to me, early in the morning after their reception, at my house on Køgevej,[37] and the following night we destroyed the parachutes and the rest of the equipment by burning them ... During the meeting on Køgevej, where the four parachutists and I were present, it was made clear that Rottbøll had come to lead the work in Denmark,[38] establish a sensible contact with the Army Intelligence Service, and further with all reliable circles who were willing, in one way or another to co-operate with London." Later in his account, after referring to the wellknown unwillingness on the part of the Intelligence organisation to accept sabotage as a weapon,[39] "it became Rottbøll's duty here to try to fulfil the expectations London had specified of effective sabotage, without this leading to a rupture between SOE's representatives and the Intelligence Section."

In accordance with this duty Rottbøll made contact with the officers on intelligence work and here met the aversion towards sabotage which was characteristic for their attitude at that time. A meeting was arranged between all the parachutists, Mogens Fog and Ole Kiilerich and two of the Intelligence officers, Captain Gyth and Captain Winkel, to get the divergencies of viewpoints thoroughly debated, and to reach the mutual understanding which was the pre-requisite for co-operation. The meeting which took place in Hammer's illegal flat in Bellmannsgade is mentioned in both Fog's and Kiilerich's accounts,[40] and it is also referred to in Borch-Johansen's and Sv. E. Hammer's accounts. Neither of these had more than second-hand knowledge of what occurred and only mention the meeting quite briefly, while the accounts of Fog and Kiilerich give a glimpse, at least, of the discussions. They both emphasize the comprehensive security measures which the officers demanded should be respected – for example, the officers turned up masked – and this particular point is also mentioned in the second-hand reports. It is quite apparent from the remarks in all the accounts, that there is a critical attitude among the parachutists and in the circles around them towards these security arrangements, which they found not only exaggerated but frankly comical. In Hammer's account he remarks uncompromisingly:[41] "I remember that the meeting had seemed rather comical to the parachutists, whom I met later in the evening, because the arrangements which the Intelligence officers had insisted upon had been somewhat bizarre."

The actual form in which the meeting took place is naturally unessential or at least unimportant, but there is little doubt that the critical attitude on one unimportant point covered a general scepticism, which was a decisive stumbling-block for co-operation in confidence, and it does not seem as if the meeting between the two sides led to any result apart from an exchange of viewpoints. The participants did not succeed in bridging their differences. In Fog's account the conversations are reported as follows:[42] "When we had been there some time, the doorbell rang, and in walked two gentlemen, presumably two of the Princes, who were in dinner jackets, but had pulled white hoods with peep-holes over their faces ... They gave the parachutists some general instruction in illegal work and also agreed on a number of signals, which the parachutists could use in connexion with daily contact with them. Furthermore, the Princes insisted that it was important that no major sabotage actions should be carried out, or other provocations which could bring strong counter-measures from the German side,[43] as this could only lead to a break-down of the spy organisation. Incidentally this remark was one I often met later in conversations with Captain Gyth, particularly in the autumn 1942, but also quite far into 1943." Fog's descriptions agrees in essentials with that of Kiilerich:[44] "Captain Gyth said at that meeting that for the time being our job was to lie low, so as not to compromise the organisation too early, but that there would certainly be use for all the men and all the energy one could save up, and more besides. He assured us that even if things were looking bad at the Fronts, Germany would be beaten. It would never be possible for Hitler's armies to reach the Urals, and thus the war would be decided."

It is not possible to determine exactly when this meeting took place. Ole Kiilerich puts it in May 1942, whilst Fog less definitely speaks of the summer holidays.[45] Hammer's account does not give any definite clue in this respect, but Borch-Johansen remembers it as taking place a few weeks after he escaped, at the end of May, and went underground. He mentions[46] that it was because he was living underground that he did not take part in the meeting himself, but only in the preliminary discussions which led to it. From this it seems reasonable to suppose that the meeting was finally held at the height of the summer.[47] This further strengthens the impression that the work of the Rottbøll team is concentrated in mid- and late summer and in the autumn, and that the team, partly because of the disturbance after Christmas Møller's departure, and bound by the British promises to the officers, had to remain passive for some time and use the interval for overcoming their great difficulties in establishing themselves.[48]

It seems clear that Rottbøll was eager to get the meeting arranged. For him it must have been of decisive importance to persuade the officers to go in for active sabotage which he considered his most essential objective. Unfortunately it is not possible to say a great deal about the preparations he made for this, for the very reason that he did not succeed in his purpose; but in several places in the scanty documentary material there are signs that Rottbøll put sabotage on the agenda, and in particular that work was done to create the practical possibilities for sabotage.

Here the fact that Rottbøll came into contact with the Danish Unity Party played a special rôle. It should be mentioned that Rottbøll also managed to establish contact with the Communist Resistance organisation, although this did not give practical results.[49] As will be seen in what follows, developments prevented Rottbøll from getting the sabotage material for which the Communist sabotage groups were so eager. The connexion with the Danish Unity Party seems to have been one of the first results Rottbøll achieved. Immediately after his arrival in Denmark Kiilerich put him in touch with the party leader, Arne Sørensen, and through him with the Danish Unity Party. Kiilerich reports on this:[50] "In addition I approached Arne Sørensen ... to ask him to find lodging through his organisation for the parachutists, and also transmission points, and this he undertook to do. As the Danish Unity Party was still a legal organisation, Arne Sørensen chose two of his nearest colleagues, Jørgen Diemer and Børge Eriksen, to get in touch with us. These two were brought into direct contact with Rottbøll, who afterwards maintained direct contact with us himself. The connexion between the parachutists and the Danish Unity Party which was thus established was to continue, and was maintained, through many channels, until the Liberation." The account is confirmed and supplemented by Jørgen Diemer:[51] ". . . Kiilerich came to Arne Sørensen . . . and after their talk Arne Sørensen came to me and told me what was in the air . . . A few days later a meeting was arranged . . . where Kiilerich came with a young man whom he introduced as Mr. Rasmussen. He turned out to be the parachutist officer Christian Rottbøll . . . At the meeting . . . Rottbøll outlined briefly how he could make use of us."

The co-operation which was begun here gave Jørgen Diemer the opportunity of following the plans Rottbøll was working on, and he states[52] that in the summer 1942 Rottbøll started setting up groups of Danish Unity Party people with a view to sabotage, and that it was Max Mikkelsen particularly who was to take charge of this work. This corresponds with a remark in Max Mikkelsen's account, that he was working at setting up groups.[53]

The basis for Rottbøll's hopes for getting sabotage started was not of the best. We have seen how London gave a general temporary directive to put on the mutes, and how there was serious resistance to this idea in Denmark. But this was not all. It was a characteristic feature of the Resistance Movement that it repeatedly cut through the official directives; for Rottbøll and for those who stood behind him and with him, both in London and in Denmark, these directives had quite limited weight. The debate on sabotage was now in full progress, both in Denmark and in England, and for many the problem was not reduced to the simple question – for or against sabotage. It was just as much a question as to whether the time for it had come. In Denmark the great majority of the population was still far from an activitist mentality, and there is very little doubt that the mass of the people still stood behind the Prime Minister Buhl, when, in a radio broadcast on 2 September 1942, he spoke strongly against sabotage.[54] But within the narrower Resistance circles also, there was still – in 1942 – a deep division of opinion on this question. We know that the Princes fought against it, and that their opinion was supported by Ebbe Munck and Turnbull, who still, vis-à-vis London, spoke for a temporary waiting policy, on tactical grounds.

On the other hand there were several signs that the current was shifting in Denmark. Although the summer 1942 had been relatively quiet, the death of the Prime Minister Stauning in May 1942 and the consequent reconstruction of the Cabinet under Buhl's leadership hardly contributed to strengthen the Government, and its policy was gradually pulverized, as the Occupation continued, under the constant German pressure and the constant concessions. It was also damaged noticeably by Christmas Møller's activities on the one side, and the Danish Nazists on the other. Just at the time when Rottbøll came to Denmark, the chief of the "Frikorps Danmark", the Latvian-born von Schalburg, gathered increasing bitterness against himself and his corps by ruthless attacks on the Danish population, Government and Parliament.[55] Collisions and episodes between the population and members of the corps or members of the DNSAP were daily events. In circulars from the Ministry of Justice of 12 February, 14 February and 19 February 1942, the Police have to be urged to take suitable measures to protect members of the Frikorps or their families.[56] In a party order of Fritz Clausen from 14 March 1942 he makes no bones about the state of affairs:[57] "In order to stop the persecution of our SS volunteers and their relatives it is requested that information be given through the Syssel leader on every malicious action . . . such as slander (giving the source of the slander), persecution of volunteers' children at school, attacks, business boycott, violence, provocations, etc . . ." The population – led on by the writings of the illegal Press – were laying aside the velvet gloves.

There is no trace of velvet on the glove which "Free Denmark" threw down in July 1942, in connexion with the announcement that the Frikorps had been surrounded at Ilmensee, and von Schalburg killed:[58] "In these days the "Frikorps Danmark" is finishing its inglorious existence. The korps was finally brought into action at Ilmensee, where it is now surrounded . . . Only a minority of the mercenaries were organised Clausen-Nazists. The rest were all sorts of ne'er-do-wells and adventurers . . . the dregs of Danish youth . . . In the end the Russians surrounded the area where the korps was posted, and surrounds it still . . . The remnants of the korps are experiencing the long drawn-out agonies of encirclement and destruction. We hope the history of the Frikorps ends herewith." It is seldom, in Denmark, that such a merciless judgement has been pronounced, without a grain of sympathy, and it is a measure of the bitterness against the korps that the Resistance Movement's propaganda could go so far without defeating its own ends.

The Government gradually found its policy facing hopeless odds. Buhl's speech on the radio on 2 September was like water on a duck's back to the resistance-minded circles; there it was received with nothing but increased distrust of the Government. These circles now began to advocate sabotage increasingly, whilst attacks on Government policy faded gradually into the background. In the July edition of "Free Denmark",[59] "passive and active resistance on all sides" is spoken of, and in "Land and People" in September:[60] "This situation demands other and stronger fighting measures than passive situations. Voting papers and speeches on the Constitution help damned little against bayonets. Danish workers – like the whole Danish population – have a duty to make their fighting weapons and fighting methods fit the situation . . . Only one path leads to freedom . . .: the path of action." The tone has become noticeably harder since the spring.[61] They are preparing for action.

In London also, we see that sabotage is now under debate and that there is a clash of opinions. We know that during the summer 1942 Christmas

141

Møller gradually came to the conclusion that sabotage was necessary. This found expression when on 6 September 1942 he held his great "sabotage speech" on the BBC. With one stroke the discussion became public. Here he placed himself definitely on the side of sabotage.[62] The effect in London of this speech shows that Christmas Møller was ahead of developments,[63] and for some months the British held back, so that Danish voices from the BBC, including Christmas Møller's, were subdued.[64] The conflict of opinions on this speech is clearly reflected in a remark of Sten Gudme's:[65] "We tried, of course, to counter this policy,[66] working with Christmas Møller. I can quote an entry in my diary of a conversation with Barman[67] on 14 September (1942). According to this, Barman told me then: 'Christmas is unpopular in the Foreign Office, because he brings too much pressure to bear ... Gallop has great influence. We shall get him out here (WPF)[68] as soon as possible. To get the Foreign Office to change its policy, we must, besides influencing Gallop, get Kauffmann to put pressure on the Foreign Office through Lord Halifax. Christmas ought therefore to go to the USA, as soon as he can."

From the records it is not possible to decide from what quarter the opposition came, to an immediate activisation in Denmark – in Gudme's diary Barman's opinion is mentioned that Count Reventlow and Krøyer-Kielberg were against too hasty developments – but from the examples quoted from Ebbe Munck's[69] and Sten Gudme's diaries, and from the restraint of the Danish Department of the BBC, it is quite apparent that opposition existed, and that it was still able to make itself felt, and to cast a temporary damper on the ardour of the SOE's leaders. For, although Turnbull, who was closest to the Danish public feeling and therefore was influenced most easily by misgivings within the Resistance circles in Denmark, was not yet prepared for activisation, there can be no doubt that the leaders of SOE in London wished to get started as quickly as possible. It has already been pointed out[70] that it is stated in both Hollingworth's and Spink's accounts that action was wanted at the earliest possible moment, partly because the whole Section's supply position would be improved as soon as concrete results could be shown in Denmark.

All in all, the background for Rottbøll's plans for sabotage at that moment was not good. On the other hand the situation had begun to move, and he could at least count on support from his immediate superiors in London. We also see that there seem to have been plans in the late summer 1942 to get started in Denmark, in spite of the general directives. In Ebbe Munck's diary from the end of August and well into September 1942 he refers to a plan for sabotage of the Danish ferry connexions. The first time – at the end of August – he writes:[71] "It is still a delicate question with ferries etc., but it is important to hold back, otherwise the present work will be completely wrecked. I think this is understood in the right quarters, even

142

though there are certain groups who want to see immediate results." More detailed references to plans for immediate sabotage appear in a note about a fortnight later:[72] "The German communication routes through Denmark are the central problem for the moment. If we get too much going, ourselves, the whole thing will get out of control – it will be like spending 10 kr. to earn 10 øre and T.B. (Turnbull) has strongly advocated this point of view.

The latest[73] could imply that they will try after all to do it from the air, and if this is the case, it is an important concession to our standpoint. One can well understand that it is difficult to get them to revise their opinion, once they are convinced that it is important for the conduct of the war, and one can well understand that they ask for a few results from Denmark ... The whole material, not least the ferries (number and use) has been laid before them, and has possibly countered certain opinions. If sabotage gets under weigh, the Germans will naturally demand the Police, the Army, etc., which means it will be a civilians' war."

The plan for sabotage of the Danish ferry communications, referred to here, is also mentioned in the accounts of two of the three parachutists who came to Denmark in August 1942, in a dropping operation for which Rottbøll arranged the reception, and which will be described later. The statements of the two parachutists, Hans F. Hansen and Knud E. Petersen confirm each other. In Hans F. Hansen's account he writes:[74] "In the weeks before our leaving Great Britain, the first sabotage action of real size was planned: operation Barholme. The object of this sabotage was to stop the German transit through Sweden, and we were therefore to sink all ferries between Copenhagen and Malmø as well as Helsingør-Helsingborg the same night, at the same time. The preparations were made ... in England ... At the same time we drew up the preliminary lines on which the operation should be carried out." Hans F. Hansen adds that the operation was never carried out because the necessary equipment was lost in the dropping reception in Denmark. Knud E. Petersen refers to the affair quite briefly:[75] "... we were called in to Spooner and Hollingworth, who proposed an operation, called "Barholme", to us, which was to stop all the Øresund ferries, in this instance, we did a good deal of work on this operation while we were waiting impatiently to get off." It is possible that Hans F. Hansen was right in thinking that the operation was postponed because the equipment for it was lost, but it seems just as reasonable, on the other hand, to suppose that Ebbe Munck is right in believing that operations of this kind stranded on the current divergencies of opinion, as to how far the time was ripe for sabotage to be included in the programme in Denmark. Perhaps both explanations can be combined, in that SOE's top leaders had hoped to start in the summer 1942, but that on the other hand, when the material was lost, they were not able to maintain the activist line against the opposition it still met, and manage a new dropping operation.

The impression is accentuated once more, that Rottbøll came to serve in a very difficult period, where policy was not yet finally clarified, and where he came to lack active support and clear directives from his superior officers. Here is the main explanation why he himself did not manage to give active support to Danish sabotage, although he ardently desired this. He and the SOE organisation were sailing on the ebbing current of that time, just before this current brought the organisation out into mid-stream again, when the tide turned in a free and rapidly swelling rush. While he was held back, as the responsible leader, by service questions, political and tactical considerations, small private groups, particularly of Communists, decided all the questions by entering resolutely upon growing sabotage, without hesitation, with home-made materials – sabotage which in 1943 cut off all further discussion on the subject.

The reception Rottbøll arranged took place near Farsø in the centre of Jutland on 1 August 1942. Here Rottbøll made use of his contact with the Danish Unity Party. Before it was decided which reception point should be used, various places were considered. For a time reception was contemplated on Juncker's estate, Overgaard, south of the Mariager Fjord in East Jutland, as Juncker had put his manor at the disposal of the Resistance,[76] but for various reasons a suitable terrain near Farsø was finally chosen. Jørgen Diemer relates:[77] ". . . one Sunday Rottbøll came to me with Arne Sørensen and Børge Eriksen. Rottbøll brought a General Staff map with him, and we discussed several possibilities, such as a place on Fyn where we had contact with some clergymen. In the end we finished up in Jutland, possibly even at that stage at Farsø, as we already knew the vetinerary surgeon Sonne, as a good Danish Unity Party man. At all events, it was arranged that Eriksen should go to Jutland and contact Stærmose on the subject. After Eriksen's return from Jutland we supplied Rottbøll with an identity card and he went over there with Eriksen."

The preliminary arrangements were thus put into the hands of two of the Danish Unity Party's trusted members, the headmaster of Støvring High School, Robert Stærmose, and the vetinerary surgeon Aksel Sonne, Farsø, and the accounts of these two men supplement and continue the story. Stærmose's account reads in part:[78] "In the summer 1942 I had a visit from . . . Børge Eriksen, who gave me information on the parachute landing near Jyderup . . . Børge Eriksen asked me to lead some organising work for the parachutist organisation in the whole of Jutland, with the task of finding suitable people for the reception of men and materiel from the air . . . We discussed various names without going into details . . . and agreed on the rough outlines for code systems. The first mission was to be in organising a reception in West Himmerland, and I would have a visit in a day or two from an editor, Rasmussen, whom I was to help find the vetinerary surgeon Sonne in Farsø, and also to provide assistants for the latter. I at once chose

the two Viborg students Christian Ulrich Hansen and Erik Nyemann[79] ...
A few days after Børge Eriksen's visit, the editor Rasmussen, alias Rottbøll,
called on me."

It was hardly an accident, that Stærmose became Rottbøll's contact. The
two men had met each other before, and knew each others' standpoints. In
January 1940, on a journey to Finland, Stærmose had met ten Danish volunteers in the train travelling through Sweden. Among these was Rottbøll, and
both in the train and later in Finland the two had spent hours in discussions
with each other. In the summer 1940, when Rottbøll returned home, this
led to his often visiting Stærmose, and discussing with him both Denmark's
and his own personal problems. During a visit to Rottbøll's home, Børglum Kloster[80] in the summer 1941, Stærmose received the news that Rottbøll had gone to Finland again:[81] "I received the information from the
cook — Rottbøll's parents were not at home at the time — and she told me
what had happened, with the words: "He has gone to Finland — at least that's
what they say." I had often discussed the possibility of getting to England
with Rottbøll. After our conversations I knew very well that in the circumstances he would not have volunteered for the Finnish Army." Now Rottbøll was back in Stærmose's living-room, and the plans from 1940–41 were
beginning to take concrete shape.

The arrangement with Sonne had already been made by Børge Eriksen,[82]
and now it was only agreed further that after the dropping, the expected
parachutists — three in all — would be brought to Støvring High School,
where the Danish Swimming Championships were in the course of preparation, so that the school would be full of people, which would give them good
cover. It was also arranged that Sonne should telephone Kiilerich[83] as soon
as the last details were agreed between Rottbøll and Sonne, and Kiilerich
would send on the "All Clear".

On 31 July these last arrangements were agreed by Sonne and Rottbøll,
after Rottbøll had spent the previous night in a tent with Chr. U. Hansen
and E. Nyemann in a neighbouring plantation.[84] The "All Clear" was telephoned and the dropping took place the same night. It is here described in
Sonne' words: "At about 2.30 we heard the plane. It flew across the reception field, but circled several times, apparently not having seen the lights
on the ground the first time. At last we saw three parachutes dropping
quickly to the ground, and we ran after the 'chutes, which had blown some
way outside the area which was marked off. After some searching I found a
single man who stood looking around for his 'chute. We went back to the
group, who stood and signalled with a red light. Here the whole group had
collected, plus the two parachutists, one of whom had twisted his leg. The
group had retrieved one parachute plus a suitcase with a radio set, etc. But
unfortunately the parachutists had left their 'chutes and now we had to find
them. I should also mention that some containers should have been dropped,

but we had not seen anything of them and later it turned out that they had been dropped near Ranum, where they had been handed over to the Police, who had given them up to the Germans."

They did not succeed in finding the last parachute[85] then, nor did Chr. U. Hansen the next day, as it had been found by a casual passer-by on the deserted heath. This led to a police emergency call-out which nearly brought Rottbøll's arrest, but, thanks to the criminal detective Haakon Lauritzen from Aalborg warning Stærmose in time, did not end in disaster. The three men travelled by different routes to Copenhagen and were lodged there – but the precious material was lost in spite of a carefully prepared and skillfully executed reception.[86]

12. SOE hit by new Misfortunes

The reception at Farsø represented the culmination of Rottbøll's work. Immediately after this task was accomplished, he must have felt that there was a break in the clouds. The number of parachutists was now seven; there was sufficient radio material, and this had been added to with the Farsø reception; more reliable communications had been established with England; contact had been made with several of the Resistance organisations which were increasing fast; valuable experience had been gained; and a rapidly spreading illegal Press, with the BBC broadcasts strengthened by Christmas Møller's voice, were constantly undermining the possibilities for prolonging the policy of collaboration, and were preparing the soil for the active struggle, which small groups had already begun. In all this there was much to justify a cautious optimism. But Rottbøll did not live to enjoy the fair wind which would blow before many months had passed. He had hardly got the three new parachutists, Hans F. Hansen, Peter Nielsen and Knud E. Petersen established and acclimatized to illegal life before a whole series of misfortunes rained down upon the SOE organisation. Once more the foundation of the work was swept away, and the organisation reduced to total impotence for some months after. It is reasonable to suppose that this delayed developments in Denmark for several months.

Misfortunes hit the radio work first. After the arrival of the Rottbøll team, the SOE organisation had three operators at its disposal, Mogens Hammer, Max Mikkelsen and Paul Johannesen, and the extremely important connexion with Duus Hansen had been established. There seem to have been two radio sets[1] available in working order, and there were now possibilities for obtaining further sets through Duus Hansen, if this proved necessary. Each of the telegraphists trained in England was supplied with the necessary codes.

With this radio material, contact with London was now consolidated and extended. The length and frequency of transmissions cannot be determined, but it is evident that in both respects it was a difficult start, and the problem of frequent and reliable contacts with London was not finally solved until 1943. Hollingworth[2] describes the phases of development of the radio service, as seen from London, and Taylor writes:[3] "Two further W/T operators, Mikkelsen and Johannesen, were dropped in April 1942. A certain communication was established with London, though it could hardly be termed regular." In this connexion it should be pointed out that the demand for comparative passivity, laid down at about the time of Rottbøll's arrival, as well as the scant means for direct operations, were bound in themselves to limit the scope of the radio service.

This first radio service can also be followed through occasional reports from the German side, on the results of the German Counter-espionage organisation, "Abwehrstelle's" direction finders. In the report of the Ministry of Justice of 31 August 1948, on the activities of the Public Prosecutor from August 1942 to 29 August 1943 to the Parliamentary Commission, regular German direction finding of illegal radio transmissions[4] are mentioned. It is apparent from these that the German direction finders from June 1942 onwards are able to pick up illegal transmissions, and also report a certain regularity in them. The Germans believe that they can localise the transmissions as coming from certain districts of Copenhagen, and ask several times for assistance from the Danish police for the ransacking they are planning there.

With this information it should be possible to make a fairly reliable examination of the whole illegal radio service up to September 1942, when, as we shall see, it broke down for a time. Before Rottbøll arrived, Hammer had begun the transmissions with the "Possone" set. Kiilerich states[5] that Hammer's first transmission went off in time for the Rottbøll team to bring the answer with them, that the transmissions were received and understood, and this agrees with the first reports on this first transmission by Borch-Johansen and Svend E. Hammer, as well as in Ebbe Munck's diary. The exact date of the establishment of this first contact can be fixed as 17 April at the latest – the final success after many attempts with an unsuitable set.

With the arrival of the Rottbøll team, the situation alters appreciably. There are now two sets and three telegraphists. Of these, one – Hammer – soon stops operating, while the other two start transmissions, each with his own set. In addition, Duus Hansen operates "blind", without his own code and with no possibility for checking reception, which, however, Hammer and Johannesen tell him is confirmed. Max Mikkelsen mentions[6] that he made contact the first time on 1 May. Johannesen must have started his transmissions at about the same time. The German direction findings, when compared with the information in the various accounts,[7] certainly indicate that the scope of the transmissions increased throughout the months of May, June, July and August. It is true that the British accounts report the contacts of those days as very unsatisfactory, but it must be remembered, first that the British reports on the subject are brief and in general terms, and second that events are seen in relation to the great developments of later periods.

On the other hand, very little is recorded as to the contents of the transmissions, although something can be said on the subject. Borch-Johansen and Max Mikkelsen both mention that intelligence material was sent,[8] and in the accounts it is mentioned that information on Christmas Møller's departure, and on Johannesen's and Rottbøll's deaths were transmitted.[9] On one single point the contents of a transmission can be established. The start signal for the dropping over Farsø was given on the wireless. Rottbøll telephoned from the veterinary surgeon Sonne's house to Stærmose, and gave the "all-clear". Stærmose rang to Copenhagen and passed on the message, and at 18.30 the code announcement was given on the BBC that the plane would come the same night.[10] The "all clear" could only have reached London by radio.

In the facts related, the point has been brought out that the main value of the early radio service was probably that it was in latent readiness. But its value in another respect must also be emphasized. Through the pioneer work, dearly bought experience was gained, which benefitted the radio service which took up the work, particularly through Duus Hansen. There can be no doubt that the illegal radio service, in order to function satisfactorily, needed to be based upon the sum of just such laborious experience, dangerously won. The Resistance had no such experience in 1942, and this cost Johannesen his life. This sacrifice was part of the price that had to be paid, so that it should later succeed. Duus Hansen seems to be the man who can best assess this problem. He participated in the illegal radio work from the beginning, and carried it through to the end. In his account he deals with the question of the safety measures which were needed:[11] "The Germans were by now (autumn 1942) aware of the increasing wireless activity from Denmark, and began to take countermeasures against it. The Abwehrstelle (the counter-espionage organisation) had therefore brought in several direction-finding cars from Germany, and had also sought the help of the Danish Police to locate the transmission points with the object of putting the transmitters out of action. Through our connexion within the Public Prosecutor's Department for Special Affairs, Police-Sergeant Roland Olsen, we were kept informed of the Germans' views of the radio transmissions and on the results obtained by the direction finders, with details of places, times, quality of transmissions, etc. It was now obvious that far greater care must be exercised than before, and that a proper security system must be built up for the protection of the operator. The security system worked through guards who were posted in the immediate vicinity of the transmission point, and who could get in contact with the operator and warn him in case anything happened, for example if direction finders arrived, or Danish or German police, etc. The transmission times must be reduced to the minimum, and the transmission stations should be varied as much as possible – preferably a new place for every transmission, as this change of locality naturally made the Germans' work of direction finding difficult."

These views later became the standards for expanding the security system, but in 1942 they were difficult, if not impossible, to realise. For one thing

149

the workers had not yet got the necessity of such a system into their bones,[12] and for another, it required a large personnel, on call for transmissions, and such personnel did not then exist.[13] Finally, the system demanded the availability of a considerable number of scattered transmission stations, to allow for frequent changes, and it was particularly in this respect that serious difficulties seem to have set very hampering limits for the work. A few quotations will illustrate the position. Duus Hansen comments:[14] "This variation was made difficult by the general fear among the public of giving permission to use a flat. For this reason one often had to use unsuitable places as transmission stations." Max Mikkelsen mentions the same difficulty:[15] "However, I had to find most transmission places myself. At that time people were very frightened of taking part in the work, and putting their flats at our disposal, and with few exceptions they showed an astonishing lack of interest in the work." Or Knud E. Petersen:[16] "... it was difficult to find places to send from." Many of the Resistance men had to face similar experiences in the early days of the movement. The struggle took place on a narrow front, the width of which could in this case be measured through the results of the German direction finders, which could locate the transmissions to certain districts, blocks and squares of buildings, from where the transmissions were repeated. It was just such a repetition at the same place, that made the action of 5 September possible.

There is good reason to emphasize these practical difficulties very strongly. In 1942, the Resistance Movement was by no means the broad popular movement that it became later. It was rather the fight of lonely men, whose motives were not understood, and it was restricted, in a great number of trivial respects, by lack of support and understanding among the mass of the population, on whom it could later rely. Popular Resistance literature teems with examples, and in the accounts upon which this thesis is largely based, the narrators return constantly to the everlasting, trivial, underlying theme: the struggle to get lodging, ration cards, the barest requirements of money, reliable contacts, etc. etc. Depressing realities of this kind were the background of the Resistance struggle, and they must not be forgotten in describing and assessing it.

For these reasons, and as the result of the bad luck which seems to have been the all too faithful companion of the SOE organisation in its first actions in Denmark, a new catastrophe followed for the young Resistance Movement. On 5 September 1942, the German counter-espionage organisation demanded that the houses Vinkelager 2–8 and 16–24 be ransacked on the following day by the Danish Police. Direction finders had repeatedly located illegal radio transmissions in this block.[17] They were right. Aage Krebs lived at Vinkelager 8, and he had met Rottbøll through Arne Sørensen, and had put his flat at his disposal.[18] Both on 4 and 5 September, Johannesen had worked from this flat, and on 5 September at 10.30, the

German Abwehrstelle announced that transmission had started. 120 police detectives and 25 uniformed police with 4 dogs stormed the place.

The tragic consequences of the action will not be described in detail here.[19] It will simply be stated briefly that the bitter result, both for the SOE organisation and the Police was an exchange of shots between Johannesen and Detective-Sergeant Østergaard-Nielsen, during which the policeman was killed. Faced with unavoidable arrest, Johannesen managed to swallow his cyanide pill, and died quickly, thus avoiding cross-examination and the danger that he might betray his comrades. The results of this action are doubly sad, when one studies the background of what happened. The two men were close to each other in national feeling, and both acted in accordance with what they believed to be their national and service duty. Johannesen's attitude speaks[20] through his deeds; and Østergaard-Nielsen's sympathetic attitude towards the illegal work is confirmed by Erling Foss, who states, for example, that in May 1942 Østergaard-Nielsen had expressed warm appreciation of Christmas Møller's escape.[21] The two men's views of the German Occupation can hardly have been very different, and they both fell as victims of an ambiguous policy, just as this was showing signs of collapsing.

The question arises, why a successful police raid could not have been prevented, either by SOE taking security measures or by the Police sending the necessary warning. No entirely satisfactory answer to the two questions can be given, on the basis of the historical material, even though something may be said. We know that Duus Hansen had agitated for the establishment of a security service as a matter of routine, and we also know that the creation of such a service was under consideration. The difficulties in establishing the security service have been mentioned, and are apparent, for example, in that parachutists were used for this work, which lay outside their real sphere of activity.[22] Duus Hansen states that Rottbøll was aware of the desirability of building up a security system, but that it was not until the action of 5 September that he became convinced of its absolute necessity.[23] This corresponds exactly with information in Fog's account. According to this,[24] Rottbøll visited Fog after the tragedy, and reproached himself during the conversation, that he had agreed at all to Johannesen transmitting on that particular day. It had not been possible to get cover for the transmission, partly because Rottbøll could not be present himself,[25] but in spite of this Rottbøll had agreed, when Johannesen had insisted upon transmitting. At the time for the transmission, Rottbøll had become uneasy, and had gone out to Vinkelager, only to find it cordoned off, and the raid in progress, or finished. During the conversation, Rottbøll also raised the question as to whether he should have forced his way through the cordon and tried to come to Johannesen's help.

The question remains, why no warning was given by the Police. We know from Duus Hansen's account, that one of the corner stones in the security system[26] was the expectation that, for example, Roland Olsen would send such a warning. Only one of the narrators touches on this point, however – Flemming Juncker, who only had second-hand knowledge of what happened. He mentions[27] that Duus Hansen was away for a few days around 5 September, and therefore a warning could not get through, and that Duus Hansen had informed Hammer of this in advance.[28]

After Johannesen's death, misfortunes followed in rapid succession. Hammer's position was already untenable at that stage. The Germans had been preparing an action against "The Free Danes" for some time. With the help of two informers, the Germans had succeeded in finding several members of the group responsible for the illegal newspaper, and on 4 September 1942, at a meeting in Dagmarhus (the Gestapo Headquarters) the help of the Danish Police was demanded for the preliminary arrests. The following week, a number of arrests were made of people who were connected "with the Free Danes": in all, in the period up to 17 November that year, about 30 persons.[29]

As this operation accelerated, it was clear that Mogens Hammer was in such an exposed position, that it must be considered impossible for him to remain in Denmark. His arrest could be too serious in its consequences, and there was an impression that Hammer had not been careful enough, so that there was great risk of his arrest. The accounts make it plain that the decision on Hammer's flight from the country was something which, after the action against "The Free Danes", there was no way of avoiding. One of the accounts states definitely that Hammer's flight was a necessity, brought on by his own carelessness.[30] It appears also that the Germans were aware of Hammer's connexion with "The Free Danes."[31]

At the same time, there was a wish for Borch-Johansen to leave the country. He probably wished to come to England himself,[32] and London was needing a man who knew the conditions in Denmark thoroughly, and could help Headquarters in arranging the dropping of materiel in Denmark which was aimed at.[33] It was therefore decided that both men should leave the country together, and in September they succeeded in reaching the Swedish coast near Höganäs from Gilleleje on the Zealand coast, in a two-man kayak. Mogens Fog and Kaj Otting helped with the practical arrangements for the escape.[34] Its date is not stated in the accounts, but from Ebbe Munck's diary it seems that the date of their arrival in Stockholm was 23 or 24 September.[35]

There was drama in this escape, just as there was in Christmas Møller's. A long year was to pass before an escape to Sweden became, if not actually an everyday event, at least something that happened every day. Before 1942 was over, there would be a third attempt at escape, which, as we shall see, would end in tragedy, and demonstrate how far away the days still were, when the difficulties in crossing the Øresund did not hamper the

152

work. For this very reason, one of these escape attempts ought to be described in some detail. Borch-Jolansen's and Hammer's escape is a particularly good illustration of the great distance from the experimental stage to a time when the pioneer experience brought its harvest. Fog's and Borch-Johansen's accounts of this escape correspond with each other and with the report in Ebbe Munck's diary. The latter, recorded immediately after a meeting in Stockholm with Borch-Johansen, is contemporary with the events and corroborates the accounts. Here the eyewitness report of Borch-Johansen is given in his own words:[36]

"Various plans for an illegal departure to Sweden were discussed. For example, a plan was considered whereby I should jump into the sea from the Bornholm steamer in the Falsterbo canal. I personally preferred to cross in a kayak, and as Mogens Hammer, by September, was so compromised that he had to get away, we decided to cross together in a two-man kayak. This was put at our disposal by the editor Kaj Otting, at his summer villa at Vejlby Strand. Fog fetched me the night before to his mother's flat in Ordrup. The next morning I drove in an Army car, dressed in a Danish Army greatcoat, to Grib Forest, where I was to stay until the time for the evening train to Vejlby. There I was to meet Mogens Hammer, who would come via Hillerød. However, he was not at the meeting place, and I spent a couple of uneasy hours in a raspberry plantation near the road. It was swarming with cars with their headlights on, and for a time I thought that Hammer had been taken and that they were police cars. At last I heard footsteps on the road. They did not sound like Hammer's, and I saw the silhouette of a tall man, dressed in a long black overcoat, soft hat and carrying an umbrella. It was half a minute after he had passed by, that I came out of my hiding place and found that it was Hammer, very well disguised as a kind of lay preacher. He had even managed to alter his walk.

We wandered up to the house together, and broke in, but there was a strong wind, and we agreed that it was impossible to row out that evening. Instead, we examined and overhauled the kayak, when it was quite dark. The next day we hid in the house. When darkness fell, we carried the boat down the slope, stuffed the luggage in and rowed out. We got well away from the coast, but soon had to row in again, as the kayak was out of trim, because Hammer had sat down in front. We landed for a moment at Raageleje, baled the boat out, changed places, and came out again all right. Then in the distance we saw the lights of a patrol boat, bearing down on us. We turned in again to the coast, but the patrol boat came on after us, until we were right in. It was nearly five o'clock by then, and we landed on a strip of open coast. We heard footsteps, and a man came towards us, carrying a fishing rod. We lay still in the dry seaweed, until the man came and poked us, and then we jumped up with pistols cocked, and drew his attention to the fact that it would be best for him if he did not inform anyone that he had seen us. We also asked him where we were. He said we were near Gilleleje, and that patrols often came along the coast, so we rowed out again westwards. We came in to land at a wooded part of the coast, where we broke into a house, and hid the kayak. We went to bed and slept, pretty exhausted and soaked through. The next evening the weather was fair. We started just after midnight, after eating the last of our food – butter, raisins, chocolate and snaps. We set our course for Kullen until we had the lights of Höganäs east of south, and landed at about 6, just before dawn, a couple of kilometres north of Höganäs harbour. We slipped into Höganäs without being seen, and came by bus to Helsingborg without anyone speaking to us."

It was thinning out around Rottbøll. Added to his depression over Johannesen's death was Rottbøll's feeling of uncertainty and the urgent need for a complete reorganisation of contacts. New cover points needed to be found, and all previous arrangements as to meeting-places had to be cancelled. This work occupied the fortnight which was left to Rottbøll. In the words of Duus Hansen:[37] "Johannesen's death and the police investigations which followed it meant that the whole organisation had to be reconstructed. New lodgings, new contacts, etc., had to be found, as the previous lodgings and contacts must soon be presumed known to the Germans as well as the Police. The work of reorganisation took so much of Rottbøll's time, as he saw it as his duty to look after the safety of all the other members, that he did not have time nor opportunity to make sure of his own situation and his own safety. This was a contributing factor in the success of the Police in locating his lodging."[38]

The raid on Vinkelager did not only raise the problem of reorganising the connexions of the organisation, it also raised the far more serious question of principle, as to how shooting episodes between parachutists and the Danish Police could be avoided in the future. We know that this problem lay heavily on Rottbøll's mind, and that he took the definite stand in this question that such an eventuality must be avoided at all costs. We also know what he achieved in this respect. He discussed the affair with a number of his friends and nearest colleagues, and the result of the talks was that negotiations were opened, with Duus Hansen as intermediary, between the parachutists and the Police. Duus Hansen reports on these negotiations:[39] "However, I arranged an agreement between the organisation and the police to the effect that in future the situation must be absolutely avoided, where the Danish Police and persons belonging to illegal organisations[40] were embroiled in shooting, and that both sides must show caution, as well as a certain watchfulness and tolerance, so that that kind of episode could be avoided in the future ... This agreement was made in the interval between Johannesen's and Rottbøll's deaths."

On the Police side, the agreement is mentioned by Detective-Sergeant Max Weiss amongst others, during an examination after the war for the Parliamentary Commission. His evidence reads in part:[41] "I received information that the parachutists had held a meeting where it was decided that if they realised that it was the Danish Police that arrived to make an arrest, they would never open fire on them. I had to go down to Odmar and give him that explanation, and at the same time pointed out that if he did not dare send men out to make arrests, he could just send me and my mate, and we would do everything to avoid any more encounters of that kind happening."[42]

The decision that no one must open fire on the Danish Police was the last important decision Rottbøll made. For this patriotic man, it must have been an unbearable thought, that fellow-countrymen should fire at each other. The fate which overtook him is therefore doubly tragic.[43] On the demand from the German counter-espionage organisation on 25 September 1942, a squad of Danish police was sent to Øresundsgade 19 the same day, consisting of five criminal investigation detectives and two uniformed police-men with dogs, led by the police officer A. F. Øst. As they did not find Rottbøll at home, they came again early on the morning of 26 September. Incomprehensibly, the policemen had not received instructions on the con-fidential agreement. The owner of the flat, the agent Johan Balslev, let them in, and after sending him into one of the other rooms, the police knocked on the door of Rottbøll's room, possibly without announcing that they were the Danish Police. Rottbøll opened the door, dressed in pyjamas and with his right hand behind his back, and the police officer Øst, who seems to have been afraid that Rottbøll would shoot, closed with him – after saying that it was the Danish Police – and seized him by the arm, just as another police officer also entered the room. A shot from the revolver Rottbøll held in his hand went off, and hit Øst's buckel without wounding him, and this started a violent burst of fire from the two men and one more shot from Rottbøll's revolver. Twelve shots hit Rottbøll in all, and he was killed on the spot. Neither of the two policemen were injured.[44]

Thus Rottbøll shared the fates of Bruhn and Johannesen, losing his life for a cause which could not be carried through to victory until much later. His contribution was in the prepatory work. Others would harvest its fruits.

13. Hammer Returns

With Rottbøll's death, the SOE organisation was in reality brought to total collapse. There remained only Max Mikkelsen and the three new arrivals, Hans F. Hansen, Knud E. Petersen and Peter Nielsen. None of them were in a position to take on the leadership of the organisation. Their training had been especially directed at tasks which were now almost non-existent, and none of them had received the slightest instruction from London on the general lines of the work, so that they found themselves quite unprepared for a situation, the possibility of which – strangely enough – does not seem to have been foreseen. None of the four men had the ability to break through the difficulties, without authority and on their own initiative, and take over the leadership, and thus the team – for it still was a team – disintegrated.

One contributing factor was that the reconstruction after Johannesen's death had gathered all the threads in Rottbøll's hands, to a greater extent than would normally be the case. He alone possessed the necessary over-all perspective. When he was gone, his men were left, each in his hiding place, without contact with each other, without contact with the "Princes'" organisation, without contact with the existing Resistance organisation, or with leading personalities, without money and probably without hope. The last point seems to have been decisive. Technically speaking, Rottbøll had naturally not left them without the possibility of making the contacts, either with each other or, via one or two connecting links, with the existing Resistance organisations. We know that Mogens Fog made an unsuccessful attempt to get hold of Hans F. Hansen[1], and also that Max Mikkelsen still had his set and sending plans. However, the psychological factor in the situation, the feeling of hopelessness, the feeling of lack of authority, and the feeling of lack of a comprehensive view of things, resulted in each of them taking cover where he was, and waiting for an initiative from without. There now followed a nerve-racking time of waiting, filled with uncertainty, and filled with doubt. The accounts extant from three of the four men speak their own language on this situation:[2] "As we were without contact with the Headquarters in London, had no stuff, and did not know where we could get money or ration cards, it was especially difficult ... Our economic position got steadily worse ... It would be useless to go into the details of the many hours I have spent, wondering how we were to get things going."

The handful of Resistance men who had been in touch with the parachutists also suffered from a feeling that the organisation had been irreparably ditched,[3] and that after Rottbøll's death its position was hopeless. Duus Hansen states in his account[4] that the "British organisation was badly weakened", and in another place, even more definitely, that the Table organisation[5] had no importance. Mogens Fog states[6] of the remaining parachutists that "they could hardly be of much value in this country for the moment", and Kiilerich writes of the situation:[7] "Thus, in reality, the organisation collapsed." From abroad there was a similar assessment of the situation. The entry in Ebbe Munck's diary for 26 September 1942 reads in part:[8] "'Top' (Table),[9] as mentioned, has got into difficulties ... the whole organisation is compromised." And a day or two later, when he has discussed it with Borch-Johansen, who is still in Sweden:[10] "We must ... see that all the threads are connected up again, and it is my impression that there is a good contact between the "Liga" (the Intelligence Officers) and Orange (Mogens Fog). It is another matter that the whole of Top has collapsed for the moment."

At headquarters in London the news of Rottbøll's death came as a knockout blow. Not only was this a new disaster in a long chain of misfortunes, which up to then had prevented them from winning Denmark over to any decisive extent, but in addition, SOE was poorly equipped to take countermeasures. Apart from the fact that contact with the parachutists in Denmark was temporarily broken, the situation was that SOE had no idea who to send as a replacement for Rottbøll. Even on the long view it seemed difficult to find a substitute. In this crisis Hollingworth took a surprising decision. He asked Mogens Hammer, who had just arrived in England – without actually knowing of Rottbøll's death – to return as quickly as possible to Denmark and there act as a kind of temporary leader, until the final leader was chosen and trained. Mogens Hammer answered without hesitation, "Yes".

To illustrate this hazardous decision and its realisation, we have quite full information, partly in Hollingworth's, Spink's and Borch-Johansen's accounts, partly in a letter from Hollingworth of 1943 to Duus Hansen; and in addition, Ebbe Munck's diary casts some light on one point in the situation. Hammer had arrived in Stockholm on 23 or 24 September with Borch-Johansen, and they had reported to Turnbull. He seems to have continued to London immediately after. It appears, at least, from Ebbe Munck's diary[11] that the Danish Ambassador in Stockholm, the chamberlain, Kruse, tried to persuade the Swedish authorities to stop Borch-Johansen from continuing his journey to London, as it had been planned, so that he had to remain in Stockholm for some days, until the beginning of October, whereas no difficulties had been raised in the case of Hammer. Hammer must therefore have reached London at the end of September, to be met with the news of Rottbøll's death. According to Hollingworth's account, he was informed of Headquarters' wish that he return immediately to Denmark, at the same time:[12]

"I visited Hammer, therefore, as soon as he arrived in London, that is, the day of his arrival. I asked him to go back at once and carry on the work, and in spite of his astonishment at my request, and his strong impression that in the circumstances he would be in a very difficult position, he accepted, which shows what a brave man he was." Hollingworth adds, that he stood quite alone in this decision to send Hammer back.[13] The decision does not seem to have been taken quite so dramatically. It seems from both Spink's and Borch-Johansen's accounts that the decision was discussed at a staff meeting at Headquarters. Spink writes:[14] "Hollingworth had discussed the situation with me, and asked me what I thought of the possibility of sending Hammer back to Denmark. I remember that I had grave misgivings at such a step, but that since there seemed to be no other possibilities, I agreed with Hollingworth that such a procedure in those particular circumstances must be considered justifiable, and the lesser of two evils, at all events, since otherwise we were without any leader in the country."

Borch-Johansen's account[15] refers to discussions of the position between Hollingworth, Hammer and Borch-Johansen, who on his arrival in London on one of the first days of October, joined SOE's staff with the special duty of arranging coming deliveries of matériel to Denmark. It is also apparent from his account, that Borch-Johansen was with Hammer a good deal, after his arrival in London, and that he and Hollingworth saw Hammer off at the air field, on his new expedition to Denmark.

There can hardly be any doubt, therefore, that Hollingworth's account on this point is somewhat dramatized. He remembers the acute situation as even harder than it was, and it is clear that Hollingworth stressed the point that the responsibility for the decision was his. The fact that Hammer's return to Denmark later gave rise to a good deal of criticism,[16] and that in the face of this criticism Hollingworth took the full responsibility for the decision, can explain why his account on this point is in such uncompromising terms. But there is not the slightest doubt as to Hammer's unqualified, unhesitating acceptance of the proposal. Nor can there be any doubt that his motives were dictated by a strong sense of duty, and that it required all his strength of character to accept a proposal which must have been utterly contrary to his own wishes. The tension of the preceding months must have been fearful. Now, just at the moment when the tension was released, on his arrival in England, to throw himself again into new emergencies must have demanded more than ordinary robustness and strength of will. Borch-Johansen[17] states also, that Hammer appeared forced and out of balance when he and Hollingworth saw him off at the air field: "The last evening he gambled, and won the whole time, and his references to his luck were noticeably forced."

Hammer's courage and unselfishness at this moment ensure him an outstanding position in the history of the Danish Resistance struggle, regardless of the fact that his mission, generally speaking, failed – as it must fail – and regardless of the fact that he met justified criticism after he returned to Denmark. Hollingworth, who knows the details of his situation better than anyone, and his attitude to it, rightly underlines his bravery, both in the above quotation, and in a letter of 16 July 1943 to Duus Hansen,[18] in answer to criticism of Hammer from Denmark: "As for the Top (Hammer), he is a curious mixture of good and bad. All credit is due to him for courage. He went back purely as a stop-gap at a time when things were barely organized, we had just lost Rask (Rottbøll) and needed a man with 'guts' to pull the strings together again until we could find a new leader ... Top fulfilled a necessary function at that time and deserves praise for having accepted a job which most men would have refused."

In his account, Hollingworth also describes the train of thought which resulted in his decision to send Hammer back:[19] "My reason for choosing Hammer was that he knew the conditions in the country, and I calculated that the Germans, once he had left the country, would think that the last thing he would do would be to come back, and come back at once. They would, I thought, reckon that ... of all people, Hammer, who was known, would be the last man we should decide to send across again. It was contrary to rhyme and reason, and this was in fact why I did it. The unreasonable element in the idea would offer Hammer good security." This explanation, which Hollingworth gives in his account from 1947, is confirmed by the letter mentioned above, to Duus Hansen from 1943:[20] "It was a terrific risk we took – as he was 'wanted' by the police everywhere – but the audacity of the scheme carried it through. If it had not been for an unfortunate 'leakage' the Germans would not have realized so soon that the man who had escaped for his life had returned within three weeks. However, I hope no such further tricks will be necessary in future."

The fact that Hammer was wanted by the Germans, and both they and the Danish Police were in possession of a good deal of information about him, inevitably and naturally meant that Hammer had to proceed with the utmost caution – greater caution than must normally be observed. His situation became quite unique. This was reflected clearly in the unique instructions be received. He was ordered, first, to keep quiet and at all events not to do anything before receiving possible further instruction. "His task was really to be on the spot, for eventualities, and when the time came to prepare reception of the coming leader", writes Hollingworth.[21] It is understood, however, that on arrival in Denmark he should seek to pull the SOE organisation together in the crisis resulting from Rottbøll's death, but in the sense that it should not take any active steps but should keep itself intact until further orders were given. The task was not great, and it was extremely

159

thankless. It was not made easier by Hammer's receiving instructions not to get in direct contact with anyone but the parachutist Peter Nielsen, who was to be his only link with the others who belonged to or were in close touch with SOE. These were to know that a new leader had arrived, but not who this leader was. This peculiar part of Hammer's instructions is not mentioned in Hollingworth's account, but is reported in many of the other accounts. Fog, Kiilerich, Dedichen, Sv. E. Hammer, Hans F. Hansen and Knud E. Petersen all describe how, in the autumn, they suddenly receive mysterious messages from a man calling himself Lindberg, who states that he is the new leader of the parachutist organisation, and how they all unavoidably come to realise that this new man was Hammer.[22] The estate owner, Flemming Juncker, who knows the circumstances from conversations with Hammer himself, of about the same date, as well as with Hollingworth and Turnbull (Juncker escaped to England in 1944 and served in SOE Headquarters[23]) writes in his account:[24] "His instructions contained a very severe order that he was to keep his identity completely secret, and in no circumstances get into touch with the organisation's best helpers. He must neither visit them nor meet them, and they must not know who the temporary leader was, and he must only contact them through cut-outs.[25] He used "Ib" (Peter Nielsen) as cut-out, a parachutist who had been dropped in August near Trend, and he was the only man who knew the identity of the new leader. This shows, it seems to me, that Hollingworth, who had no one ready to replace Rottbøll, acted in a sort of desperation, when he sent over a man who was so thoroughly compromised in advance, and who, with such instructions, must be rather unsuitable as a leader."

It is also apparent from a letter from Hollingworth to Hammer from March 1943, that Hammer's instructions really did contain this extraordinarily rigorous order, and that SOE had believed that it could be upheld. Hollingworth writes on this question:[26] "I was very sorry to hear that there is a possibility that you will have to leave the country because your identity has become known in large circles. You agreed with us that your identity should be kept a strict secret."

One more security rule was laid down, to try to ensure absolute secrecy on Hammer's posting. There could naturally be no question, in the circumstances, of arranging for any form of reception for Hammer. The decision had to be taken to drop him "blind", and it was also decided to let Hammer carry out the "water jump" as it was called. This meant that he was dropped in the sea, near the coast, dressed in a specially constructed, watertight, inflatable rubber suit; he was then to swim ashore and submerge the rubber suit, so that he would land without trace, and even without the aircraft having to fly in over land: if it was reported, it would be presumed engaged in, for example, mine-laying operations. The decision involved the extremely hazardous factor for Hammer, that the special equipment which this form of water jump required had only just been constructed, and trials had not been completed. Hammer was therefore untrained in the use of the equipment, and had to manage with a theoretical explanation. Hollingworth mentions[27] that Hammer was the first man to use this equipment during an operation, and in the book already quoted, on the Parachute School in Ringway, there is an account of the start of special trials in water jumping in October 1942:[28]

"Late in October 1942 I received word that the War Office required experiments to be carried out to ascertain what particular difficulties existed in connection with parachuting into water at night. The trials were to be carried out with the utmost secrecy and as quickly as possible. By this time a fairly satisfactory waterproof suit had been produced which could be worn over ordinary clothing although it was of necessity rather bulky and uncomfortable. There was also the danger that if it became torn water could penetrate and by its weight might possibly force the wearer to the bottom." While Ringway was still experimenting, a Danish parachutist supplied the proof in practice that these remarks were correct.

Hammer jumped over the Kattegat, near the coast at Tisvilde,[29] North Zealand, and reached land safely, without being seen. The date of this second arrival in Denmark cannot be determined quite exactly, but it seems to have been in the middle, or possibly at the end of October. Borch-Johansen puts it at the end of October, but in the letter quoted above to Duus Hansen, Hollingworth writes[30] that Hammer has returned "within three weeks" after leaving Denmark, that is to say 16 October at the latest. Ole Kiilerich, Sv. E. Hansen and Max Mikkelsen all state that Hammer returned in October.

After arriving in Copenhagen, Hammer tried to get in touch with the members and helpers of the organisation. He seems to have achieved direct contact with Peter Nielsen quite quickly, and through him he tried to contact others. It soon proved hopeless, however, to get the organisation functioning even in the most rudimentary fashion, without removing his mask. All his attempts to carry out his instructions stranded on the suspicion which an anonymous approach met with, particularly at that time, and there was a demand from all sides that the new leader should come forward. "I then wrote back to Lindberg that I knew who he was, and that I did not wish to play blind man's buff," writes Kiilerich,[31] and Sv. E. Hammer, Dedichen, Otting and the parachutists[32] refused to co-operate under such conditions.[32]

Hammer was forced to get into direct touch with those whose co-operation he was seeking, first of all with Fog and Kiilerich. Fog's relations with SOE had become steadily closer during the spring and summer. He had helped Borch-Johansen in connexion with the reception of the Rottbøll team in April, and in May by undertaking a courier journey to Stockholm he had established contact with Ebbe Munck. At the beginning of June, when the news of Borch-Johansen's arrest came, he had been in Stockholm, ready to return to Denmark with information for the Intelligence officers, and in conversations between him and Ebbe Munck a closer relationship with SOE seems to have been arranged, or at least discussed, although the three sources on this subject – Fog's and Munck's accounts and Munck's diary – differ somewhat as to the character of the agreement. According to the diary, Fog agreed on about 1 June to help as liaison, after Borch-Johansen's imprisonment,[33] although there are no details as to what is intended. In Munck's account[34] he states that from this visit Fog entered into close co-operation with "the officers from the General Staff Intelligence Service and the other persons who were gradually attached to this nucleus of the original Danish Resistance Movement." This information agrees in the main with the facts in Fog's account, although the latter states[35] that during this visit in Stockholm both he and Ebbe Munck were still somewhat reserved towards each other, and he does not mention any arrangement having been agreed on future co-operation. Fog does state, however, that Munck mentioned that he had connexions in the British Legation, so Fog could hardly have been in doubt as to the situation, even though he still had to guess at some of it.

At all events, after this journey, Fog entered into closer contact with the Intelligence officers and the parachutists, and by definite agreement with Ebbe Munck he found and maintained contact with Borch-Johansen while he was underground, until in September he helped with the arrangements for Borch-Johansen's and Hammer's escape.[36] We have also seen how his connexion with Rottbøll grew stronger in the course of the summer, and how Rottbøll turned to Fog when Johannesen died in September.

When Rottbøll was killed on 26 September, it was therefore Fog who was closest to the SOE organisation. He and Kiilerich tried in every possible way to give help and to take things in hand. For example, the two men procured the bare necessities in money for the remaining parachutists. Fog had been in touch with Per Federspiel from June 1942, and was aware of the latter's position as a kind of paymaster, and "I[37] visited him again, now, and certain payments were made via me through Kiilerich to the three[38] ... Quite modest sums were paid out to the three, to the maintenance of sustenance." At the same time Fog made an unsuccessful attempt to get the parachutists into contact with the local Resistance groups and through his connexion with the Princes he had a message sent to England that he was prepared to help with the leadership of the parachutists in Denmark. "I received a photo-copied letter of thanks for this from a man who called himself the Earl (Turnbull) in Stockholm."[39]

It was therefore quite natural that Hammer turned first to Fog and Kiilerich when he returned. We have seen earlier how Hammer tried in vain to

162

establish an indirect contact with Kiilerich, and he also tried to do this with Fog, following his instructions. Fog writes:[40] ". . . in the mean time I received a letter one day from a person who claimed to have come to the country to lead the parachutists. He wanted to maintain indirect contact with me, and I answered this. Shortly after I received a letter, to the effect that although he was forbidden to contact anyone direct, he felt it was very important that we should have a talk, and we arranged a meeting in my office. It turned out, at this meeting, that it was Hammer who had come back again. From that time I maintained regular contact, with meetings at least once a week with Hammer, until he left the country in the early summer 1943."

As already pointed out, Hammer had not been given any real tasks, apart from remaining passively in the country and awaiting further orders, and the question naturally arose, whether the parachutists who had no missions should not be evacuated, since they could be a danger to the remnants of the organisation still in existence. Even before Hammer's return, Fog and Kiilerich seem to have discussed such an idea, and after his arrival it was definitely decided to evacuate all the SOE members except Hammer himself, and Peter Nielsen.[41] The three parachutists in question, Hans F. Hansen, Max Mikkelsen and Knud E. Petersen, and also Max Mikkelsen's wife, who was to be evacuated on grounds of security, were brought to Mrs. Emmy Valentin's flat in Høje Skodsborg, twelve miles north of Copenhagen, and the plan was that the three parachutists and Mrs. Mikkelsen should row to Sweden on the evening of 2 December, in a boat which was hung up in davits outside the Hotel Øresund. A wire cutter was procured, to cut the chain which fastened the boat, and Mrs. Valentin and Kiilerich were present in the flat to supervise the start.

The attempt at flight was hit, however, by a series of unforeseeable misfortunes,[42] so that it ended in disaster. First the start had to be postponed a day, because it was not possible to obtain the necessary oars in time, and the next day, when these had been procured and the attempt was made, bad luck hit again. During the walk from the flat down to the water, the party had to pass Strandvejen, and Max Mikkelsen and Knud Petersen, who were carrying the oars rolled up in rugs, were unlucky enough to meet the night watchman. His suspicions were aroused and he alarmed the Coast Guard bicycle patrol. In the mean time they tried to cut the chain with which the boat was fastened, but this failed completely, owing to the poor quality of the wire cutter, so that they had to return to Mrs. Valentin's flat to discuss what they should do. During this time, the Coast Guard patrol arrived and found fresh tracks in the snow down to the coast, as well as traces of the unsuccessful attempt to cut the chain, and they followed the tracks to the flat, where they kept watch until reinforcements of police, armed with sub-machineguns, arrived in force. Everyone who left

11*

the building had to account for themselves, and although Mrs. Valentin and Kiilerich succeeded in bluffing their way through the police cordon, the affair ended in imprisonment for the parachutists. On 12 December the three men were surrendered, on German demand, to the Gestapo, and later taken to Germany where they spent the rest of the war in German prisons and concentration camps.[43]

The German threats to sentence the three men to death met with violent protest from the Danish authorities, who referred to an agreement from April 1942 between General Lüdke and Eivind Larsen, the Permanent Under-Secretary of the Ministry of Justice, that Danish parachutists arrested with the help of the Danish Police would not be sentenced to death. When the German authorities expressed doubt whether in this instance the death sentence could be avoided, and stated generally that they found it necessary to cancel the agreement, Eivind Larsen, who led the negotiations on the Danish side, declared that in that case he would resign immediately, and that "he had good grounds for presuming that both the Public Prosecutor and Odmar, the Chief of Police, would take the same attitude." After this the Germans seem to have shrunk from carrying out the death sentence, and the three men's lives were saved, although they did not escape two and a half years of suffering in the German camps. The situation seems to have been that the local German authorities had given the promise in question, but it was afterwards repudiated from Berlin. The German authorities in Denmark realised the necessity of the Danish standpoint, that the minimum condition for co-operation with the Danish Police must be that in no case must the death penalty be used, and they seem to have been able to convince Berlin temporarily. Later the affair faded into the background. The Danish Police, however, followed the fate of the three men in Germany after they were deported, to assure themselves that the agreement was kept by the Germans.

The tragedy at Skodsborg ended the year of misfortunes for the Danish Section of SOE. It was the last in the long series of catastrophes with which that year was crowded, starting in December 1941, when Bruhn and Hammer had left England to begin SOE's work in Denmark. In contrast to the incalculable, unforeseeable and unavoidable misfortunes which had hitherto dogged their footsteps, the parachutists had to some extent brought this last disaster upon themselves, and it could perhaps be regarded with less bitterness. There was the redeeming feature, once the catastrophe was a fact, that the highest Danish authorities acted as forcefully as was possible in the circumstances. The three parachutists' bitterness at being handed over was natural, but this bitterness must be directed at the agreement from the spring 1942 and therefore against the whole political situation, and not against the authorities' attitude in this particular case. This time it seems rather as if the highest authorities were alone in not bungling the affair.

The imprisonment of the three parachutists brought consequences to others than themselves. It affected the purely Danish Resistance work. Kiilerich, who was editor of "Free Denmark", and Mrs. Valentin had to go underground and prepare an attempt to escape to Sweden. In Kiilerich's case, however, this saved him from being arrested, when the "Free Denmark" committee were taken a few days later,[44] and in his account Kiilerich emphasizes that the affair may also have saved Mogens Fog for the time being, when he writes:[45] "... Mogens Fog also avoided arrest, for one thing because my disappearance had made him even more careful, as he was the first person I visited, with Mrs. Valentin, on the morning of 4 December." In Fog's account, also, he implies that everyone was especially on guard in the days following the unsuccessful attempt at flight. He too reports that Mrs. Valentin and Kiilerich came to him on the morning of the 4th, and that they were brought into hiding successfully, first through Professor Chievitz, and continues:[46] "During those (first) days I also kept in touch with ... Captain Gyth, who was nervous about the whole situation. On the evening of 8 December, when I was with friends, I was rung up by Hammer, who told me that he had been informed through his police contact (I know now that it was Roland Olsen who had given the information to Duus Hansen, who had passed it on to Hammer) that a number of "Free Denmark" people, independently of the escape attempt, would be arrested the next morning, amongst others Professor Chievitz and I." The result of this was that Mogens Fog went underground, while Ole Chievitz preferred to let himself be arrested, because everyone could not disappear into illegal life.[47] If these are the bi-products of the Skodsborg affair, it was certainly not quite in vain. Only a few days after going underground, Fog published his first letter to his friends,[48] and this was the literary work which, more than any other, added fuel to the first flames of the Resistance beacon, and which at one stroke made Fog the central figure in the Danish Resistance struggle.

Contemporary assessment had no retrospective consideration for the affair. Its effect was further to undermine the reputation of SOE, which had already become extremely poor in Danish Resistance circles. SOE had now been established for a year in Denmark, and its work had not yet materialized in any important contribution to the home-grown Resistance work. It is easy to understand that a number of the Danish Resistance men who had been in contact with the organisation, and therefore believed themselves to be in a position to pass judgement on it, were by now pessimistic as to its possibilities. For them it could easily look as though the results of the year could be summed up in unmitigated disappointments, vain hopes, half promises which were not fulfilled, and confused and confusing decisions which ended in marking time. But it must be pointed out in this connexion, that none of the parachutists who had as yet been in Denmark had had any possibility of giving even an incomplete clarification of the future plans of the British organisation, or the British Resistance longterm policy, nor even of explaining the causes of the ineffectiveness that had characterised the work up to then. Mirages had perforce been used instead of realities, and no one could know that now that the necessary preparations had been made, the realities were just ahead. It is not strange, therefore, that SOE's share quotations, that winter 1942–43, were at rock bottom.

Among the critics of SOE, the Intelligence officers were in the front row. It had not been possible to get rid of the divergencies of opinion between them and SOE. On the contrary, the Intelligence officers insisted more strongly than ever on their standpoint, that the time had not come for activation in Denmark. For that reason, and also on grounds of security, the Intelligence officers kept SOE more or less at arm's length, as well as everyone who had become too much involved with the organisation. After Johannesen's and Rottbøll's deaths, when the slender thread of radio communication broke, the officers turned to Duus Hansen, and asked him to take over the work, and at the same time to cut off his connexions with SOE. Duus Hansen reports on this:[49]

"With Rottbøll's death, the British organisation was badly weakened for a time . . ., and the Army Intelligence officers approached me and asked me to work solely for that institution. It was thus agreed with London that I should be put at the exclusive disposal of the Intelligence Service. After a good deal of negotiation with London, I was equipped for this purpose with special signal plans and special codes,[50] and the British thus gave up their previous practice, not to equip people who were not trained in England with British codes . . . But I still kept the contact with the parachutists going, as Headquarters in London had after all directed me to send the Intelligence Service's correspondence but at the same time carry on the contact with SOE. A divergence of opinion arose between the Army Intelligence Service and SOE, as the Intelligence Service did not think I should have anything to do with SOE, when I was working for them." This information is confirmed in detail in a letter from Hollingworth to Duus Hansen from April 1943, in which he writes, in connexion with a number of technical instructions:[51] "As arranged with the Earl (Turnbull) we prefer you to send messages mainly for the other organisation, not for Table (SOE) (except in emergency). We must not run the risk of Table compromising our other friends."

The Intelligence officers' wish to keep SOE at a distance was therefore respected in principle by London, and Duus Hansen accepted it in principle. In reality, however, Duus Hansen stood in the centre of the SOE work and found it practically impossible to leave the work, and he certainly had not the slightest desire to do so. This is evident from all the work which he accomplished in 1943, in closest co-operation with the parachutists,[52] and it is also evident from the answer which Hollingworth received to his instructions:[53] "I have noted your wish that I should not be too much mixed up with Table. However, it is necessary for me to be in daily contact with Jam (Flemming Muus, who by then had become the parachutist leader) in order to ..." and here follows a list of a great many activities which made close daily contact necessary.

There is another point, on which we have information that the Intelligence officers were extremely cautious about having dealings with SOE men or those who were in close contact with them. When Kiilerich prepared his illegal crossing to Sweden in January 1943, to continue his journey to London from there, the Intelligence organisation was not prepared to give him any help. Ebbe Munck reports on this:[54] "The night of the 29th he got to Helsingborg from Stokkeby in a rubber boat ... There was fog and a strong current, but he managed the crossing by compass in three hours ... It was a shame that the Liga could not help him a bit more, but it was unfortunately necessary to give him the cold shoulder, as he was after all too irresponsible."

It appears from the various incidents described, that the Intelligence officers took no chances, or at least did not like to take chances. They made extremely severe demands as regards security. They could hardly do otherwise. They were playing a game of which the results did not only concern themselves. They occupied particularly responsible official positions, and if these were compromised, their fall could drag the whole Danish policy down with it. It was unavoidable that this should enforce special considerations upon the organisation, quite apart from the fact that they did not wish to spoil the Intelligence work which was now going so well. It was difficult, if not impossible for the SOE men to adjust themselves to these demands. Their psychological qualifications were of quite a different kind. Where circumstances required it, they took risks. Their activities in Denmark were one great risk, and they were recruited from among men who had made a covenant with daring. For them, different laws applied, and a different rhythm of life.

The foul wind which was blowing up against SOE in those winter months did not only come from the direction of the "Prince" organisation. After all the accidents, acute distrust seems to have spread among the people who were close to the organisation, and criticism was directed particularly against Hammer, and the danger which they considered his presence in Denmark involved. At this stage, Flemming Juncker, the estate owner, was becoming one of SOE's most important supporters in Denmark. His first contact with SOE had been when Stig Jensen had visited him at the beginning of 1942, to ask him to join in the work, and particularly to help to prepare the reception of weapons and explosives, which even then represented the promise of things to come.[55]

Juncker agreed to this, and during the summer 1942, various places in the neighbourhood of his manor, Overgaard, were reconnoitred. On a trip to Copenhagen Juncker also met Rottbøll, Duus Hansen, Kiilerich, Stig Jensen and several of the other initiates in the work.[56] In December 1942 Juncker was in Stockholm and met Turnbull for the first time. From that moment, at least, he was one of the organisation's most trusted members. In his account, amongst others, we can follow the growing displeasure with the state of things in Denmark:[57] "Around December (1942) I was in Stockholm, where I met Mr. Turnbull for the first time. I received a whole lot of admonitions, which I was to take home to Denmark: "table-top" (Hammer) was to stay passive, as the idea was that he was simply to keep the place until a new specially trained man finished his training. The result was, also, that great passivity characterized the enterprise at the same time. The whole thing looked rather hopeless at that period, no actions and very little possibility for any. People were extremely reserved, and the feeling in the country towards, for example, sabotage, was quite negative ... Inside the organisation, too, the winter was marked by a poor atmosphere. There was much dissatisfaction over 'table-top' being kept in the background so much, and that contact with him should be so difficult, and there was dissatisfaction with the consequent passivity ... At the end of February I was again in Stockholm, where I had a new conversation with Turnbull. I called his attention to the fact that we now knew who 'table-top' was ... I called Turnbull's attention to the fact that in Denmark we had absolutely no confidence in an arrangement whereby Hammer, who was compromised, was leader. I asked him to make representations in London so that we could get a better leader."

In Dedichen's and Duus Hansen's accounts also[58] there are expressions of distrust of Hammer, particularly with regard to his growing irresponsibility. Doubt is cast on his possibilities for rebuilding the organisation, and Fog writes:[59] "... I received the impression that Hammer did not get support from the British side as he had expected and wished, and it was therefore difficult for him to act as the actual leader in those functions he regarded as the right ones in this country ... what was carried out was very limited, as Hammer did not receive enough explosives from England,[60] and found it difficult to obtain access to military and other important circles."

As we have seen from Juncker's account, the demand was finally made that Hammer should be withdrawn from Denmark, and representations were made to Turnbull to this effect, with Duus Hansen as intermediary. This application reads in part:[61] "Regarding Lindberg (Hammer) it is found necessary to inform you that the situation in his case must be considered as being utterly untenable, as his identity is now known by a number of persons ... In several cases the identification has been made by persons, whom he has known earlier, noticing him, some in restaurants, some on the street, and in one case in the train, and the affair has been the subject of talk within the interested circles[62] ... It must therefore be seriously requested that Lindberg be recalled as quickly as possible, since his presence involves considerable danger to the safety of others and to the smooth progress of the work."

Hammer's mission ended as one could have foreseen it must, in failure. It would not be unreasonable to point out that to some extent this was his own fault, but it would be just as unreasonable to lay all the blame on him. Without any doubt he was guilty, particularly at the end of his time in Denmark, of a number of extremely incautious actions, which caused unrest among his assistants and distrust of his leadership, and without any doubt he badly lacked the qualifications, as Fog writes, for establishing the connexions and confidential co-operation with leading personalities which were essential for him. But could it have been otherwise? Hammer was trained as a ship's engineer, not a diplomat. His political views were uncomplicated, without light and shade,[63] and his actions direct and motivated more by fresh spontaneity than careful reflection. His courage was indisputable. Otherwise he would certainly not have pestered the Consulates in Dublin on 9 April, to get into the British Army. Otherwise he would certainly not, after these vain attempts, have continued with new applications a few days later in Liverpool.[64] Otherwise he would not have volunteered for the British Merchant Navy, and later have been among the first Danish volunteers in January 1941. Otherwise he would not have been selected to be the first radio-telegraphist in Denmark, and he would never have undertaken the heavy duty of returning in October 1942. That he was not able, in other respects, to fulfil the demands these duties involved, and that he failed, in education and personally, where the great majority would in no circumstances have made the attempt, cannot detract from his achievement. One can reproach him for rashness, as we have seen was done, and as we shall see would later be done in London. But it must then be emphasized that the psychological tension under which he lived must essentially influence any judgement passed upon his actions. He lived under a different law from ordinary people, and here it is of no importance whether others were capable of living normally under abnormal pressure.

Added to all this was his uniquely difficult situation, and his categorical instructions not to make direct contact with the people he was to work with. This could perhaps seem necessary, regarded from London. In Denmark it proved unworkable. It was intended to be a weapon against his pursuers, but at the same time tore the weapons out of his hands. Moreover, if he had obeyed his instructions literally, this would have isolated him so completely, that such a course must appear impracticable. Since it seems that Hammer did follow these instructions for weeks, this may provide one explanation for his later breaking out somewhat wildly from what may have been intolerable isolation. Furthermore, it seems as if his instructions were not clear on one important point, and perhaps could not be so. Several factors point to Hammer not having realised, himself, that his mission to Denmark was only temporary – that he was only expected to bluff his way through until the moment when another man would take over the post of leader, and that during his period of duty he could not expect support from England. It would have been correct to make this plain to him, but would it have been wise or even possible? With such an open declaration, would not his chiefs have undermined his self-confidence and authority, and would they not have laid bare the real situation, by laying the cards on the table. These were depressingly poor.

There is evidence from various sources that Hammer did not realise, at least fully, that his mission was only to tread water in Denmark. We have already seen that Fog had the impression that he did not receive enough support from London. Hammer certainly did not make it clear to Fog that there was nothing to be expected from that quarter, but mentioned definitely that his mission was[65] "to procure means for sabotage and then ... to receive more parachutists who can act both as operators and instructors ... and Hammer was at the same time politically interested ... and it was his opinion that a hard course ... could lead to the collapse of the Danish-German co-operation." Kiilerich,[66] also, states that the decision on the evacuation of the parachutists in December was probably due to Hammer having decided to reconstruct the organisation independently, from the bottom up. And finally, the request to London to send over a new leader implies that Hammer had not himself described his mission as temporary.

The situation appears most clearly, however, when one considers the circumstances in which Hammer was recalled. On 11 March 1943, Hollingworth wrote him a letter, which the new leader, Flemming Muus, brought with him when he came to Denmark on 12 March. In this[67] Hollingworth does not give a definite order to return, but reproaches Hammer for his lack of caution, and continues: "My own personal feeling is – and I am thinking of the safety of many valuable lives – that it might be better for you to come back, if you can get away without undue risk. You have had a long run in a most risky and exposed position and you could be of great value to us here. In the event of your leaving the country the following arrangement is proposed." There follows a series of points concerning the work in Denmark, and ends with an offer to Hammer to take over the leadership of the Table organisation in London, and adds: I just want you to know that you will be extremely welcome in London, and it is probable that the organization will greatly benefit if you are here and can advise us."

This offer to Hammer is confirmed later in a message to him through Muus, contained in a letter from Hollingworth to Muus:[68] "I got the message, re Top, coming home, and I hope he succeeds in getting out. On arrival here he will be regarded as the London representative of the Table organisation and will assist in future planning."

Hammer never became leader of the Table organisation. He escaped to Sweden, where he was interned for some months,[69] and then came to London; but there was no job for him at Headquarters. There had never been any intention of giving him such a leading administrative position, but it was considered so essential to get him out of Denmark, that the prospect of such a post had been held out in order to ensure that he agreed to leave. This is apparent from a letter from Hollingworth to Duus Hansen, in which, after praising Hammer's services, he gives the unvarnished facts:[70] "he will never again be sent back and will never be given a position of authority in London ... As far as Denmark is concerned Top (Hammer) is finished until the end of the war," and adds the explanation for offering him work at Headquarters.

Mogens Hammer served for the rest of the war as a Lieutenant in the Royal Army Service Corps[71] and died in Hamburg in 1945.[72] One of those who worked most closely with him in Denmark, Borch-Johansen, gives the following characterization of him, in his account:[73] "He was a big, tremendously strong man, an excellent sportsman, and had earlier won awards as a swimmer as well as in other sports. He possessed an unshakeable sang-froid, and this, combined with his technical skill, made him an outstanding man in the field. He burned with a primitive love of Denmark and an indomitable hatred of the enemy, and he regarded himself, first and last, as a soldier. His mentality was uncomplicated, just as his feelings were strong and clean. He was incapable of deceit, and his moral and physical courage were in a class by themselves. I remember, from a meeting ... where we discussed the situation with Hollingworth ... that he summed the situation up quite quietly and said: "There seems to be nothing else for it than that I go back and try and deal with things." ... That made an overwhelming impression on me, as I knew from experience how dead tired and spiritually exhausted we both were ... I think that among the many examples of personal courage I met in the war, this was the greatest." This is the appreciation of a friend. It agrees in the main with the impression that a study of his work must leave.

The British treatment of him was hard, and dictated by distrust of his "security". SOE was afraid of the consequences which his lack of caution could have; even after he returned to London there seems to have been some fear of his indiscretion, and he was kept away from Danish circles in London.[74] But when all is said and done, wars are won by hardness, and there is at all events little doubt that Hammer received summary treatment for the sake of the greater things which were at stake.

14. Change in British Policy

As the year 1942 drew to a close, there was an atmosphere of depression in Danish Resistance circles. A letter[1] from one of the Danish officers in the Intelligence Section to Ebbe Munck in November 1942 reads in part: "Darkness – darkness – that is the state of things in our little country, there is not much encouragement, but time passes – and all things come to an end some time."

One must admit that the autumn 1942 had been dark in several respects for those who hoped for progress in resistance against the Germans. We meet a similar summing-up from Erling Foss. In "the week" from 15 February 1943 to Christmas Møller he describes why he has tried to keep things quiet in the preceding period, and he gives a full explanation of the realistic, sceptical opinions he has expressed in the correspondence up to then. At one point in the long statement he writes:[2] "The main object of my letter was to give you an impression of the conditions we are subjected to. When you sum up the German results for the autumn you will see: 1) That the parachutists were either shot or taken prisoner. 2) Most of the men from the paper "The Free Danes" were taken. 3) The publishers of "Free Denmark" – first the printer and then Ole Chievitz and others – were taken. 4) Many Communists with Aksel Larsen were imprisoned. So the Germans thought they had made a clean sweep."

But now the hour was striking. Now the time was rapidly approaching, when events would take a decisive turn. On the battle front this had already occurred. One of the many strange features of the Second World War is the clearness and simplicity which characterize the curve of its course. Measured by the external military events, the period up to November 1942 marks up an almost constant advance for the Axis Powers. Then the curve turns. The Russian counter-offensive around Stalingrad and the great battles of the Western Allies in Africa[3] portend just as constant a retreat for the Axis Powers. From then on, the black clouds of defeat rise, relentlessly threatening, over horizons which were still far off in 1942, but now were closing in without pause, around Berlin, Rome and Tokio. Defeats followed each other in quick succession, and a psychological turn of the tide, in the warring and occupied countries, followed in the wake of the altered war situation.

In the case of Denmark this swing appears quite clearly. First and foremost, it is apparent in the illegal Press, which makes the final change-over in the winter to unconditional and unvarnished support of sabotage. The tone becomes steadily harder and more and more aggressive. It has been mentioned earlier that "Land and People", for example, subscribed to sabotage, and in its October number of that year, "Free Denmark" answers "Yes!" to Christmas Møller's sabotage speech.[4] At that stage, however, the illegal papers are suggesting sabotage with some caution, and take great pains with detailed arguments for its necessity. But from the spring 1943 they beat the drum for sabotage as a matter of course, and feel themselves in harmony with the new popular feeling. For example, we read in an article in "Free Denmark" from April 1943, with the title,[5] "Once more – Sabotage": "... When, last summer, Christmas Møller urged his fellow-countrymen in a radio speech from London to carry out sabotage ... there were many decent Danes who differed with his statements ... They forgot that we are standing in the midst of a fight ... Time has also shown that the call to sabotage has caught on among the population. From week to week, more and more Danish enterprises which work for the Germans are reported wrecked ... More sabotage, more blockage of deliveries of war material, more unreliable products will no doubt mean unpleasantness for the country for the moment – but it shortens the war and opens the way to our freedom in the future."

In "Land and People" for the same month, the tone is even more savage,[6] when the paper turns upon the sabotage guards: "The Danish people must ... repudiate the sabotage guards. They are helping the hangmen, and like the Frikorps, they are helping Hitler to recruit men for waging war ... The sabotage guards must be quite clear about this. They have joined the war on Hitler's side – and they have the Danish people against them."

The illegal Press felt sure of its assessment of the attitude of the population and gave less and less print, and finally none at all, to arguments for sabtage. Developments showed that this evaluation was correct, and it also harmonises with Erling Foss's analysis from the spring 1943, where, as already stated, he feels it his duty not to encourage over-optimistic statements. From a detailed account from February 1943 it appears that, in Foss's deliberately realistic judgement, developments have brought about a change in the psychological possibilities for sabotage. He writes:[7] "What good would it do, if I had written, contrary to the truth, *at that time* (the emphasis is Foss's) that an appeal for sabotage would have a good response ..., when afterwards the sabotage did not materialize? ... It was not possible to waken popular feeling for sabotage then ... A great change has gradually taken place, helped on by several factors: The Allies' advances. The decision, which is approaching. The danger of the Scavenius-Best velvet glove policy. Added to this, the bombing of B & W ... All this combined gives a different psychological atmosphere in Denmark today from that in October. If one wants to support and encourage this atmosphere, one must act wisely and use the right means." This assessment is certainly not far from the mark.[8]

The psychological swing-over was caused by political realities, and in this respect the autumn and winter 1942–43 brought considerable changes abroad as well as at home. In Denmark in the autumn 1942, people's attention had been concentrated on developments in the telegram crisis, intensified by the King's illness after a riding accident. The crisis resulted in the Scavenius Government, saddled with the newly appointed German plenipotentiary, Werner Best. Even though the composition of this government had quietened public feeling to some extent,[9] it was felt as the last stand for the policy of collaboration, and the population was therefore prepared for what seemed an inevitable rupture. After the long war of nerves during the telegram crisis, the people saw this approaching, calmly. On the German side, the long drawn-out tension, in which the Danish nation had been kept, was certainly a psychological blunder. Many had expected the worst and had reconciled themselves to the idea. Another astonishing German blunder was in allowing an election in March 1943. This election, held just after the military German defeats were obvious to everyone, clearly demonstrated the Danish solidarity, and gave rise to a feeling of optimism which was the best overture imaginable to the trials which were coming. Politically and psychologically therefore, the way was open for a termination of the policy of collaboration and a rupture with the Germans. In the winter 1942–43 Denmark, also, found herself at the intersection between the falling and rising curves of developments.

The main course of the war was naturally more important than the political developments inside Denmark. With Stalingrad, El Alamein, and Midway, and with the landing in North-West Africa, the German onslaught was halted, and the Allies took the offensive, supported by a growing war production which from now on permitted them to retain that offensive. Its effects were immediately apparent on all fronts, even the smallest. Also on the narrow front which we are considering, SOE's invisible front in Denmark, the stage was set for increased activity, and this time there were realities behind it. We follow developments in Ebbe Munck's diary.

In October 1942, at the conversation between Turnbull and Erling Foss, with Ebbe Munck as an interested observer,[10] Foss had declared that it was not yet time to strike, while Turnbull had begun to take the offensive and put forward the view that "even the least damage is of value".[11] In fact in September Turnbull had already started bombarding the Intelligence officers with arguments to get them to show in practice that the P plan would work. London had accepted it in April, but that acceptance was to prove extremely limited. From September onwards pressure was brought to bear on the officers. What was wanted was one or more sabotage actions, to begin with simply as proofs of the officers' ability and will to act. If

174

such a proof was not given, SOE would have to drop the agreement of April and go their own – that is SOE's – way. Turnbull's letters to Copenhagen in the autumn become more and more impatient, and finally, when there is no positive reaction from the officers, they become almost insulting. In September his impatience was already unmistakable:[12] "London is now impatient with the state of affairs in Denmark and insists with all respect to Danish patriots, that Denmark must fall in line with their comrades in other countries, and contribute something real now to breaking down the German system of communication and transport." The key word is "now". It was sabotage here and now that was wanted, not possibilities in an unknown future. In this connexion, political considerations, and consideration to the survival of the Army fell to the ground. Turnbull continues: "It is even possible that the Germans will take over in the near future without "Liga" ever having had the opportunity of proving whether or not the P plan will work. It would be tragic if the Germans were to take over this year without any sabotage or anything else having been done to harm them in Denmark, and therefore it seems to me personally that the best plan would be for 'Liga' to agree to put the P plan into operation this year, perhaps in November as 'Liga' suggested was possible when he was here in Stockholm ... I fear that London are absolutely determined to have some activity in Denmark in the nearest future since Denmark is the only country at present in which no organised sabotage activity against the Germans has been carried out ... I must say that for Denmark's future reputation it would be a very wise thing to make her contribution soon when it will really affect the result of the war, and not later when the war is already practically won ..."

Turnbull's pressure continued throughout the autumn[13] and was intensified, but it only met with vague answers, and this formed the background for the British decision, without breaking off communications with the officers, to give up the P plan and build instead upon SOE's connexions with the civilian Danish Resistance circles. This decision had crystallized by January 1943. In that month Turnbull went to London,[14] and when he returned it was evident that from now on the British aimed at a fighting struggle in Denmark and were prepared to support it. The diary records:[15] "Tb. (Turnbull) ... has come home after a quick trip which went according to plan ... London has evidently approved the viewpoint of the Liga (Intelligence officers) up to now, but are pressing for more activity."

Finally, in March, the British draw their swords. Colonel Nordentoft comes to Stockholm as representative for the Intelligence officers, to discuss the situation with Turnbull. Ebbe Munck has to hurry home from a winter holiday in the mountains, and the whole question of Great Britain's attitude to resistance developments in Denmark comes up for debate:[16] "Went up to the mountains on Monday 15 March ... expecting to have a ten days' holiday. Had five. The Proprietor (Jørgen Dahlhof) telephoned that Peter Nansen (Nordentoft) had come, and so there was nothing for it but to come down the mountain ... The character of the negotiations with Peter Nansen was rather painful. Opinion against opinion. Tb. says that it is no use explaining the special Danish conditions any longer, one is more interested in action now than in what may come later. It is a question of acting before the climax of the war is reached, after that, it is all settled, and there is not much value in what one can do. The others declare, to the contrary, that they know best what is to the country's advantage, and do not understand that a special action is demanded now, in the interests of confidence, since they laid their cards on the table long ago. They think that the important thing is to remain intact until the Day, and that all else is secondary in this connexion. Peter Nansen kept control of himself, but says later that he was on the point of leaving the meeting ... Had a couple of meetings with him later, and things were smoothed out a bit, but the whole thing seems to be rather in the air at the moment. He must talk to those concerned now, and then it will be decided whether each must go their own way, whether we can continue as hitherto, or whether there can be any co-operation in the form London wishes."

It could. The British answer came through Stockholm in April and was to the effect that London hoped for a continuation of the intelligence work, but that on the other hand they had now definitely decided to give the green light for SOE's work, without respect to the officers' worries. In reality the P plan was shelved. The answer was couched in friendly terms, but clearly negative in substance:[17] "However, we must emphasise again that, although we understand the Liga's attitude, we think that it does not necessarily coincide with the United Nations' strategy, which is that the Germans must be harmed now. Nor, incidentally, do we think that the Liga's attitude is based on a very clear grasp of the situation. Clearly the Germans are not going to leave a potentially revolting army in their midst. The first sign of the outbreak of a second front anywhere in Europe will bring the Germans down on the Liga forces." One feels that the answer has been drafted only a few months after the French Vichy Army had collapsed without any real struggle. From now on, it was not in military but in civilian Resistance circles that support was looked for in support of the Allied struggle.

London had now definitely chosen an active line in Denmark, partly because Great Britain was now ready for action. The time had come when SOE's policy could be realised. In February 1943 a team of four men landed north of Holte, and on 12 March 1943 the new leader, Flemming B. Muus landed with three more parachutists in Jutland. Realities in the form of explosives and weapons would soon follow, and it would soon prove that now indeed, there were possibilities for "a co-operation in the form

London wishes". The Danish Resistance Movement was home-grown and Danish, but it was naturally not self-governing in its decisions.

The prologue to the intensified British activity in Denmark was dramatic. On 27 January 1943, British bombers made a surprise attack on Burmeister & Wain. The purpose of the bombing was first of all psychological. In his thorough account of it in "Denmark under the Occupation",[18] Ebbe Munck calls it "psychological bombing". He relates what went before the bombing:[19] "After Christmas Møller's sabotage speech, we in Stockholm decided to approach the British High Command and ask for a demonstration bombing against a Copenhagen target, which was important to the conduct of the war. This was to remind Danish workers of the warlike character of the production, and the advantages it gave the Germans; next, to demonstrate for the Danish population, that Denmark was also on the war map, and that independent Danish sabotage was the task allotted to us, and as long as it was carried out effectively, it would protect us from further bombing. At first the Royal Air Force did not find it quite obvious, what the motives were for such bombing, but in the expectation of an increase in organised sabotage it was decided to carry out the desired demonstration flight during the shift pause in daylight on 27 January. The choice was between the Recoil Syndicate and B & W's machine workshop ... The question was debated, whether the workers could be informed, but this was not possible, as forewarning of the bombing would naturally prepare the German air defences."

The psychological effect of the bombing cannot, of course, be described with the same certainty as its preparation, but there is no doubt that the effect was enormous, even though one cannot, as does Ebbe Munck in his account in "Denmark under the Occupation" infer the immediate effect by referring to the actual increase in the number of sabotage actions which were carried out in the following months.[20] Other factors also contribute to this. However, the operation made it plain that British bombing of Danish targets was a reality which must be reckoned with, and the understanding of this would naturally speak for increased sabotage activity. In a contemporary analysis of public feeling Erling Foss gives his opinion: "The general reaction can be summed up as follows: General preoccupation with the fact that now things are beginning to happen ... It was also true that everyone had expected that this would have to happen one day. At first, feelings were generally mixed with some disappointment that ... B & W were not really hit. Knowledge of the real facts will soon spread, though ... The bombing did *not* arouse any general feeling against England. The Press also gives evidence of this, in that no attacks were made in that respect ... In a spot test on Nørrebro, there was only one of the ordinary people asked, out of about a hundred, who showed any disapproval."

The reports from Ebbe Munck to Christmas Møller emphasize the accuracy of this evaluation of the effect of the bombing.[21] In a letter of 15 February 1943 he writes: "Statements which corroborate each other, from new arrivals, confirm the reaction to the bombing which the Councillor (Erling Foss) described in his latest correspondance."[22]

In the period that this bombing was carried out, SOE's Headquarters in London were preparing to send over the parachutists who were now to come to Denmark to help the Danish Resistance in open fight. It was decided to send over eight men to begin with, divided into two teams, and Hollingworth decided to make Flemming B. Muus the leader. In his book "The Spark and the Flame", which in spite of its novelistic style must be regarded as documentary material for the history of the coming months,[23] Muus himself gives a vivid description of how he received the news of the appointment:[24] "One day at the end of January we were ... sent to London ... We were to report at Headquarters and receive our orders ... Hollingworth opened his briefing ... Then he turned directly to me: "The man, who at present is acting as the top leader in Denmark will shortly be recalled to London. I now have orders to ask you, Flemming Muus – will you be leader, England's representative in enemy-occupied Denmark, and take upon you the responsibility which attends this unusual mission?" This was in truth a surprise! Even though it must have been decided for some time, and even though at least ten people must have known of it, it had remained a well kept secret. There was a pause – at last I managed to break the silence and answer with a voice I did not recognize as my own: "YES, SIR!"

At the end of January 1943 Hollingworth had thus made his choice and had appointed the new leader, who would stamp the work within the SOE in Denmark in the epoch-making months, when this organisation, after so long and painfully groping its way, moved into action. Muus thus became the man who was to realize the British Resistance plans in Denmark. For decisive months he became one of the few links between Denmark and the free world. His appointment and the motives behind it demand more than a cursory interest.

On April 9 1940 Muus was living in Liberia, where he had worked for some years – from 1932 – as a branch manager in Sasstown.[25] Immediately after the Occupation he had volunteered, like so many other Danes abroad, for free Danish or British war service, but had been refused. Through one of the BBC broadcasts he heard Major Iversen's announcement that Danes could be enrolled in "The Buffs", and in February 1942, after volunteering for this regiment, he left Liberia to travel to London. His adventurous voyage ended on 1 April 1942 in Liverpool.[26]

In England he went via the Patriotic School into the SOE service,[27] after he had declared himself willing to perform whatever type of service might be desired of him. During the training with SOE he distinguished himself in such a way that he qualified for the leadership in Denmark. The British reports on his conduct are unanimous in mentioning his excellent bearing during the training. Hollingworth writes:[28] "I had picked out Flemming Muus as the coming leader. He was highly recommended and had passed through the school excellently ... There is no doubt in my mind that Flemming Muus was the best leader we ever had in Denmark. His arrival became the start of a very active period, where a great deal occurred, and a great deal that was essential. He was in my opinion a born organiser, intelligent, cultivated and in possession of decisive energy ... from our point of view, when we chose him, he seemed the obvious man for the job, and the enormous activity that developed after his arrival was a guarantee for us that he was the right man for the post." Spink gives a similar opinion,[29] and in Taylor's account, which is particularly interesting in this connexion, since Taylor followed the volunteers' affairs at the training schools, he writes:[30] "No one cognizant of the history of 1943 and 1944 will venture to deny that Muus displayed many touches of brilliance, but most of those who knew him well will admit just as readily that he was an adventurer, to be true a most charming and lovable adventurer, one whom I shall always regard as a good friend and comrade ... I should, however, like to place on record the British recognition of the magnificent work accomplished by him, a thing which should not be overlooked in passing judgement on him." Borch-Johansen, who at that period was serving in Baker Street and therefore came into close contact with Muus, expresses similar views.[31]

There was thus no doubt on the choice at Headquarters, and London's appreciation of the work Muus carried out after his arrival in Denmark is just as unanimous. All four members of the SOE Staff emphasize[32] that with Muus the work in Denmark really made progress, and give him the credit for this. The letters from Hollingworth to Muus in the spring and summer 1943 express again and again the warmest recognition of the splendid work that is being done.[33] The following exposition will show to what an extent this assessment is based upon irrefutable facts, which must have made a very great impression at Headquarters, where the man in the Field had to be judged according to the results he obtained. It should, however, be stressed, that the extremely high opinion of Muus in London is not only founded upon the purely personal impression he made during training, and the purely factual and surprisingly quick results which SOE could now show. Without doubt, it was also strengthened by the reports now received on him and his work, through various channels from Denmark.

Duus Hansen writes in a letter to Hollingworth:[34] "Since Jam's (Muus) arrival in Denmark there seems to be a completely different spirit in Table (SOE). There is order, punctuality, and discipline, and I can only say that I am glad to have met him and worked with him. It is my opinion that now at last Table has the conditions for being able to accomplish something. The suspicion of Table's choice of leader, felt previously from several quarters, is now well on the way to disappearing."

London must also have received favourable reports from Stockholm. The impression here harmonized with that of Duus Hansen. In a note from May in Ebbe Munck's diary he remarks that the organisation has acquired firmer form, and that the work can really get going now, and he adds that the Liga (Intelligence organisation) is now giving the Table people (the parachutists) increased support for their special tasks.[35] In June he underlines this opinion further:[36] "Generally speaking, there is more order in the work and it is in better shape. New people have come in at home without much difficulty, and others who were less suitable (Top etc.) have come out. The new Boss down there has won a good position at once, also in Peter's (the Intelligence organisation) opinion, and now they are more prepared to co-operate."

In the face of the harsh criticism of Muus which was later expressed in the court case against him regarding his financial transactions – a case which ended in a sentence – this unqualified positive assessment of him and his work still stands. For the very reason that the assessment put forward here as well as the reports which follow emphasize the effectiveness which SOE now acquired in such high degree, it will be only just to stress the fact that Muus's situation was quite different from that of his predecessors. The Allies were now on the offensive and had surplus resources with which to support smaller enterprises such as SOE's activity in Denmark; the German Front reeled back from the blows it received; the Danish Home Front, in step with this, was in tremendous development, and the harvest of dearly bought and bitter experience could be reaped. It was a favourable situation, which Muus was able to exploit, with great skill, but the light from his success should not cast any shadow behind it over the men who contributed to preparing the way for the victory SOE now harvested. In his book "The Spark and the Flame", Muus himself rightly advances this view, by calling attention to those who went before him.

The parachutists Einar Balling, Paul Jensen and Verner Johansen[37] were chosen to accompany Muus to Denmark, and besides these a further team of four men was picked to go to Denmark during the full moon period[38] preceding Muus's arrival, to start preparing the work. These forerunners consisted of Ole Geisler, Gunnar Christiansen, Adolf Larsen and Hans H. Larsen.[39] The very size of the teams sent show that Britain was now prepared to activize the work. The new policy was to be carried out in practice. Eight men were sent over in the course of a month, and more would soon follow.

As regards the forerunners, a further "blind" dropping was decided upon, this time just north of Furesøen. We do not know a great deal about this

180

dropping, in itself extremely interesting, which was made in the immediate neighbourhood of Copenhagen in February 1943. As there are no accounts from the four parachutists, we can have no details of the actual landing. The arrangements both for this and the following operations in the spring 1943 were made by Borch-Johansen. In his account he writes on the Furesø operation:[40] "Preparations were made for a series of droppings at the beginning of 1943, and in this connexion a number of landing places were chosen. The area around Madum Lake and west of Støvring, near Egtved, near Enebærodde, near Furesøen and near Gyldenløveshøj on Zealand were decided upon as suitable places. (The localities mentioned are spread over the whole of Denmark.) The investigations necessary were quickly carried out; the dropping at Furesøen soon followed. This plan was incidentally criticised by the British as being too audacious, whereas I found, on the contrary, that it was a good place which offered good chances for the team to get to Copenhagen by public transport, using the 'S' railway.[41] The plan included the possibility, if there was any suspicion of difficulty, for Gunnar Christiansen's radio being hidden in some cavities under the newspaper kiosk opposite the station in Holte, and I know that this particular operation was later spoken of as model, amongst other reasons because the team at that particular place could depend upon the very exact information on local conditions. The Geisler team which landed at Furesøen was sent over as assistants to Hammer, to get the radio service expanded."

Juncker,[42] who from now and up to the spring 1944 was the Danish leader of the reception work, mentions this dropping operation quite briefly in his account: "After making these arrangements[43] I returned to Denmark, and here four men had now arrived to supplement Hammer ... They had been dropped blind north of Furesøen." It appears from the police cross-examination of Adolf Larsen when he was imprisoned, later, that the arrival of the Geisler team took place on 13 February 1943 near Bistrup north of Furesøen.[44]

We may not know very much about the dropping operation at Furesøen, but we know a good deal about Muus's arrival in Denmark. Here we have accounts from all the four participants in the operation, and we have accounts from Borch-Johansen, Flemming Juncker and Robert Stærmose, who were all involved in the operation in various ways. Finally, conditions connected with the landing are mentioned in a report from Duus Hansen to Turnbull. There is general agreement between the accounts as regards the actual course of events, but there are considerable, and characteristic differences in the various participants' impressions of the details − differences which it would seem can be accounted for partly by the differences between the narrators' temperaments and situations.[45]

Only the main points in the dropping operation will be described here. This time it had been decided to carry out a partial reception, and to put this in Juncker's hand, after the recent contact with Stockholm had made such an arrangement possible. The arrangements were made at the end of February, and Juncker reports on this:[46] "At the end of February I was in Stockholm again, where I once more had a conversation with Turnbull ... he now informed me that he had just received a message from London that a new leader had completed his training and would arrive soon, and now asked me to prepare a couple of receptions. One would be of materiel, and we agreed that this should take place on Trinderup Heath near Mariager, and another would take place the same night, when four men were to be dropped blind in the neighbourhood of Støvring. In the morning they would come to the house of Stærmose, the Headmaster, where I was to get in touch with them. The idea that they should come there originated, I think, with Kiilerich, who was in London at that time." If Juncker is right in this opinion, one can see that the operation is based upon the experience from Rottbøll's reception at Farsø.

Thus the main framework was set up, though this had of necessity to be altered on several points. After his return from Stockholm Juncker visited Stærmose and put the plans before him, and although Stærmose promised his co-operation in principle, he had to point out that the high school was very much under observation following the reception at Farsø,[47] and that it would be very dangerous to house the men in the school. Stærmose had also to underline the fact that he would be on a tour of political meetings, because of the coming election,[48] during the days chosen for the reception. And he pointed out that the dropping point, east of the railway near Støvring was an unfortunate choice, because of the nature of the terrain and the regular guard on the railway line.[49] The two men were in agreement on these points, but it turned out to be impossible to get the arrangements changed – Juncker states that Hammer would not budge from the original arrangements and refused to countermand them. It was therefore arranged that Stærmose should carry out his tour as planned, so as not to arouse suspicion, and that when the parachutists arrived at the high school, his wife should send them on as quickly as possible by train to Aalborg, from where they should continue to a contact place in Terndrup, where Juncker would finally collect the team and bring them to their destinations. This modified plan was followed, with the exception that the dropping took place about five miles west of Støvring, owing to the pilot's error in orientation.

The team landed on the night of 11–12 March 1943 near Hornum Lake. The actual landing went well, except that Paul Jensen was considerably bruised, and only one of the bicycles they had brought could be found, in spite of a long search. The parachutes and other surplus equipment were thrown into the lake, and after a kilometre's march southwards, the last bicycle was also left behind. All the abandoned materiel was found the day after, by the Danish Police.[50]

At first the team had difficulty in finding their bearings, but they succeeded after a time, partly with the aid of road signs, probably on the Aalborg-Viborg road west of Støvring, and walked on, taking by-ways, to Støvring. On the way they noticed an energetic search being made by what they took to be German patrols with search lights,[51] so they took cover. By about 6 a.m. the team reached Støvring and after waiting there about an hour they went to the high school, and from there were directed to the train, which left for Aalborg soon after 7 a.m. There the team split up. Muus went to a cover address he had been given by Borch-Johansen,[52] and the three others went on to Terndrup, where they were fetched later in the day by Juncker, who took them on to the neighbourhood of Overgaard. They spent the night in a fir plantation, and were taken the following day to Randers. There they contacted the local Resistance group and Ole Geisler, who looked after them.[53]

The same night, containers with explosives were dropped on Trinderup Heath near Mariager, and a team of Resistance men from Randers whom Juncker had collected, with the help of two Randers residents, Henning Brøchner and Jørgen Bøje, brought the load to a temporary hiding place not far from the actual dropping point.[54]

The British planes had naturally not flown in unobserved, and the Danish Police started a search which resulted, on 12 March, in the discovery of the parachutists' equipment, so that both the Danish and the German authorities now knew of the arrival in Denmark of more parachutists. The search seems to have been begun the same night, 11–12 March, and it can have been the Danish Police whom the parachutists took to be German patrols. It is true that Juncker states in his account that an agreement had been made with the Danish Police in Aalborg that information that planes had been observed should not be passed on to the German authorities until after 8 a.m., so that a search would not be made until after 8 o'clock, when the team could be presumed in safety, but a report from Duus Hansen to Turnbull shortly after the landing underlines that a search by Danish Police in the course of the night was concentrated on exactly the area where the parachutists had come down, so their report on the night patrolling of the roads is possibly confirmed by this. Duus Hansen reports:[55] "... I can inform you here on the most recent landing, while pointing out that the greater part of the information has been given me by THE ELEPHANT (Juncker). Before the landing was to take place, the affair was discussed with various police authorities in Aalborg, who agreed that the search should be made casually, and as you had stated that the dropping would be 'due east of Støvring', the Superintendent had directed most of the emergency squad a good way out to the east of Støvring. Unfortunately there was an error, in that the dropping, instead of being as you informed us ... took place at exactly the same distance but 'due west'. It was unfortunately there that

183

the whole police squad was searching. In the whole landing operation I must say there was a good deal of luck ... All the men who were dropped are now in safety, two of them brought to ... until further notice, while GOSSIP (Muus) came into contact with THE ELEPHANT immediately after the dropping, and he looked after him the first couple of days and went with him to Copenhagen, where I have spoken with him."

Whatever the details may be, the four men were not caught, and the three droppings, at Furesø, Trinderup and Hornum had been successful. Eight new parachutists had arrived in Denmark, the stagnation, with a temporary leader without definite instructions, had ended, and for the first time explosives had now been received. This would soon have its effect.

The details of the dropping operation at Hornum Lake have a certain interest in that they illustrate how far the Resistance men had come, both in organisation and experience, as well as how far they still were from the efficiency which marked a later period, when the organisations were fully developed, and they were themselves thoroughly experienced. They had succeeded in getting the men down and in getting the materiel to cover, but, as Duus Hansen writes, they had had a certain amount of luck. The arrangement had rested on verbal agreements, which were a couple of weeks old, and which, when conditions turned out to be different from what had been foreseen, could not be altered by radio telegram. There had not been enough personnel to organise a real reception, with preliminary reconnaissance of the reception point and men stationed on the landing place itself, who could both guide the pilot in to the exact dropping point, and also look after the new arrivals on landing and bring them to safety immediately. It was not until the second day after landing that the four men reached permanent cover with helpers in Denmark.

Technically, therefore, the operation belongs rather to the earlier group of receptions, where it was necessary to manage with the thinnest organisation possible, and insufficiently developed channels of communication; but on the other hand, as we shall see, it represents the introduction to the well organised and epoch-making receptions at Hvidsten, which were the starting point of a new era in the history of the Resistance. The skimpy organisation which Juncker had hastily mustered after his return from Stockholm, to meet the demands of 11 March, developed in a few weeks to an efficient team, co-ordinated with the Jutland Resistance organisation, which was now built up under Juncker's leadership and with Ole Geisler as the direct local liaison with SOE. The distance from Hornum and Trinderup to Hvidsten can be measured, for example, by quoting what Muus was able to report few weeks later on 30 April, in his first fairly long report to London:[56] "The reception of Lamp (the parachutist Kaj Lund) as well as of Habit (the parachutist Lok Lindblad) went very well.[57] Immediately the men reached the ground trained personnel 'undressed' them, brought them to a waiting car and within 10 minutes of landing they were – in both cases – seated before a well laid table in a famous country inn.[58] The reception committee dealt most efficiently with 'chutes, containers, goods, etc." Here we have the earliest description we know of the Hvidsten group. Here we also have the earliest description of the Jutland Resistance organisation which would develop, first under Juncker and later under Toldstrup's leadership, into one of the most effective reception organisations in Europe.

15. The Parachutist Organisation Reorganised

In Aalborg Muus, as already described, had separated from his team and had made his way to a contact address. From there he got in touch with Juncker who fetched him to Overgaard. Here he went through the situation with Juncker, particularly the "Resistance political" situation, so that he was brought up to date as to conditions in Denmark. Stærmose[1] also took part in the discussions. Oddly enough, and quite by chance, Juncker and Muus, who were now to co-operate, knew each other from earlier days, but this did not prevent a good deal of mutual opposition from arising between them. In Juncker's account he makes no secret of this, and it is also apparent in Muus's reports to London,[2] but it also clear both from these sources and from events themselves, that this professional and personal conflict was not allowed to hinder the work of developing the active resistance which was just ahead.

We have few details of the instructions Muus must have received before leaving London. Neither Hollingworth nor Muus give any concrete information on them. But indirectly we know a good deal about the general directives London gave Muus, through a number of letters of instruction which Muus received in the course of the spring and summer from Headquarters in London.[3] From these letters it is evident that Muus's mission was the same as Bruhn and Rottbøll had been faced with earlier: to build up the internal SOE organisation to the greatest possible effectiveness; carry out receptions of weapons and explosives etc.; establish connexions with the Danish Resistance organisations, so as to give them the greatest possible help for the sabotage which had started, and should be urged forward; and contribute to the possible creation of such organisations and groups where these did not already exist. In addition there are special duties, such as making contact with the Intelligence officers, and co-ordinating the work of the two organisations.

So far there was nothing new, except the important difference that now there were resources behind the British instructions. We have more precise knowledge of the ideas of London for the build-up of the parachutist organisation through a letter Muus brought for Hammer. In this Hollingworth outlines this build-up. He writes, while at the same time asking Hammer, as mentioned previously, to return to London:[4]

". . . the following arrangement is proposed:

i) Field H.Q. should be moved from your part of the country[5] to the Elephant's (Juncker's) part[6] (because we have got to concentrate on that part for the time being).

ii) Table Gossip (Muus) should take over the local leadership in partnership with The Elephant. From the security point of view Table Gossip has the advantage of being known by very few people in your country. He could be what we always wanted you to be viz: *"the brains behind the scenes"*[7] and could operate *through* the Elephant and latter's connections.

iii) You should before leaving organize a *sub-H.Q.* in your part of the country to maintain communications with the Earl (Turnbull).

iv) Table Mat (Gunnar Christiansen) should remain attached to sub-H.Q. We can then send another of this kind called Table-Lamp (Kaj Lund) to Field H.Q. so that we can have direct communication with both Field H.Q. and sub-H.Q.

v) Table Lamp's skeds[8] will be co-ordinated with Table-Mat's. They can then communicate with each other via London H.Q. All messages received here from the one station for the other will be automatically repeated to the other station. Thus, if transport communications between Field H.Q. and sub-H.Q. should break down they can always get in touch with each other by W/T."

The instructions quoted, which one notices only take the form of a request, operate with the idea of placing the headquarters temporarily in Jutland with Muus as leader, working in close co-operation with Juncker, who should be in direct contact with the men in the field. At the same time another headquarters should be established in Copenhagen, to maintain communications with Sweden, and both the two branches should be supplied with their own radio service, so that they would be able to communicate quickly with each other via London.

The construction of the organisation which Muus now carried out looks very different, however. After the discussions at Overgaard, Muus went with Juncker to Copenhagen, after visiting his SOE comrades with Ole Geisler at their head, and various Resistance men in Randers.[9] In Copenhagen Juncker brought him into contact with, amongst others, Duus Hansen and Stig Jensen, and after this Muus was soon in touch with the leading Resistance men.[10] Here it was that the preparatory work from 1942 bore fruit. The threads of communication led from one Resistance group to another, and one had only to get hold of a loose end, to be able easily to find the way forward. After establishing himself and making the most necessary contacts, Muus now began his work as leader of SOE in Denmark. It will be relevant first to examine his reorganisation of SOE, and the first question which arises – what personnel there was at its disposal.

187

After the dropping operations at Furesøen and Hornum, the organisation consisted of ten men in all, and this number increased with new droppings in April and May. At the same time some men were for one reason or another lost to the work, so the number of parachutists varied a good deal. In the spring and summer 1943, however, the number went on increasing in spite of the reductions. In "The Spark and the Flame" Muus himself gives the number on 1 July as eighteen men,[11] and this corresponds roughly with what is implied in the existing reports from Muus to London.[12] In a letter of 30 April Muus mentions the reception of the parachutists Kaj Lund and Preben Lok Linblad; in the report of 21 May he mentions the reception of no less than five parachutists, divided into two teams – Poul Hansen, Peter Carlsen, Jakob Jensen, Vilfred Petersen and Hans Johansen; and finally in the report from July Muus refers to the arrival of three more men, Arne Boelskov, Aage Møller Christensen and Jens Peter Petersen. Most of these men are mentioned in "The Spark and the Flame", and details of their arrival in Denmark are contained in the accounts some of them have given.[13]

In all, in the period from February to July 1943, eighteen men came to Denmark. In addition there were the two who had been in the country since 1942 – Hammer and Peter Nielsen. As the number was reduced by four, as we shall see later, there were sixteen men in Denmark at the end of July. This number is quite close to that which Muus remembers.

It is improbable that more than those mentioned came over.[14] In a letter to Muus of 9 May 1943 Hollingworth mentions[15] that the RAF[16] have made difficulties as regards the May operations, and want them cancelled because of the light nights, which are particularly noticeable at the heights at which they fly in. The cancellations should be in force from 16 May to August. However, Hollingworth states that "the air boys" have been persuaded to carry out the operations planned for May, and to start again in the middle of July. The dropping of five men in the immediate future, in May, is announced. This corresponds exactly to the figures given above, according to which five men came over in May, and then there was a pause until the droppings were started again in July.[17]

Even if the reinforcements have only brought the total of personnel up to thirteen men, before the full light of the summer temporarily stops operations of this kind, and after this up to sixteen men in July – losses included – it seems as though this was more than Muus wished or had counted upon. In his report for April he asks for the additions to be limited:[18] "Regarding sending four instructors in May then I am afraid it will be too much. It is a fact that every additional member constitutes a danger – one way or another – and until such time as we are really well organised I much rather you limit the number of instructors to an absolute minimum hence I allowed me to send a WTmessage: SEND ONLY JENS JACOB JENSEN

AND PETER CARLSEN DURING MONTH OF MAY ... I hope very much indeed to be able to ask for twice four instructors during June[19] but I would like to build up slowly thus being enabled to take as much care as possible on the line of security."

In May Muus again emphasizes[20] that there is no lack of personnel, while he admits the possibility of loss, in which case one man, trained in radio transmission, would be welcome as a reserve. Muus also makes special requests as regards the choice of men to come to Denmark. He asks twice to have the parachutist Hecht Johansen to be sent over, but he was not sent until 1944.[21] In "The Spark and the Flame" he mentions[22] that he asked for Lok Linblad, and got him sent over, but otherwise it does not seem that his wishes were complied with, except in so far as those whom he did not wish to have were not sent. In a letter from May Hollingworth writes to him direct on this question:[23] "I am sorry we have not been able to comply exactly with your wishes in the matter of sending personnel. It is our principle to do our damnedest to give the field what it wants, but there are sometimes other considerations to be made which render it difficult."

The reinforcements in personnel Muus received are now accounted for. We have still to look at the loss of personnel. First there was the question of Hammer's and Peter Nielsen's situations. These did not give rise to difficulties. Muus met the two veterans in the work after he arrived in Copenhagen, and Hammer showed himself quite willing to hand over the leadership to Muus and return to England, and he also agreed to remain for a short time to help Muus in the first period. Muus mentions in his letter to Hollingworth of 30 April that he is in constant touch with Hammer and Peter Nielsen, and in "The Spark and the Flame" he mentions long conversations with Hammer.[24] With regard to Peter Nielsen, Muus decided to withdraw him from the work after a time. He writes on this to London:[25] "Am in touch with Alistair (Peter Nielsen) – in fact, I see him daily. As Top (Hammer) will be explaining to you he is badly in need of a holiday. He is now one of my cut-outs etc. etc. here and actually next in command – which is only natural he having been here such a long time. Alistair is also doing a good bit of instruction now, viewing landing spots etc. etc. Habit (Lok Linblad) is now being trained to take over his job in anticipation of his departure for yours. Please let me know by WT if you are agreeable that he gets leave." No confirmation of this can be found in the telegrams extant, but must presumably have been received. At least the two men left Denmark and returned via Sweden to England. Hammer left in April and Peter Nielsen somewhat later. Muus mentions June, in "The Spark and the Flame".[26]

Hammer's journey had a dramatic course, which is clearly reflected in some of the letters in existence. As the peculiar developments around this journey illustrate the conditions of the times, the difficulties and anxieties, it will be described here. Muus mentions that on Good Friday[27] he said Good-bye to Hammer, who was to try to get to Sweden in a kayak from Snekkersten, and on 30 April[28] he has already received a message by telegram that Hammer has got through to England. He writes the same day to Hollingworth:[29] "I congratulate Top (Hammer) on his safe arrival at yours, – it certainly was a record trip as far as speed is concerned. All his friends here send him loads of regards."

However, Hammer did not receive these greetings, as he had not arrived at all. On 9 May Hollingworth informs Muus in a letter:[30] "*Top*. Soon after we got your message that Top (Hammer) had left we heard from "Sugar" (Turnbull) that he had arrived there. That was why we wired you that he had arrived. Someone rang up from the town where "Sugar" (Turnbull) lives and said he was Top and would be coming round to the house in 10 minutes. He never turned up. We are having discreet enquiries made but as yet have not been able to trace him. He appears to have vanished into thin air. It is possible that it was a 'Stikker' (informer) who telephoned and it may be that Top (Hammer) never actually left your country. Would you therefore see whether it would be possible to have some discreet enquiries made. It is all very mysterious and worrying."

It was undeniably a mysterious and worrying situation, and it cannot have been less mysterious for Hollingworth when he received the following reply dated 21 May from Muus:[31] "*Top* (Hammer). It is distressing to hear that he has disappeared. He left here and I had a postcard from him sent from Helsingborg saying that everything went well across the Sound. I have started investigating but havn't got far yet. Shall, if necessary, let you know by WT when I find out something."

The riddle is solved by Ebbe Munck. In a note from June–July,[32] that is about two months after Hammer's departure: "Top (Hammer), who vanished for us after the first telephone call on his arrival, has come out again. He was taken at the central station on arrival in Stockholm and is impressed by how much the Swedish Police know." The episode shows how the special conditions of that time and of the secret work could give rise to unfounded suspicions. During the period of Hammer's disappearance, this – rather naturally – gave food, both in Denmark and England, for all kinds of suspicious speculations.

The anxiety over the Hammer mystery was not lessened by the fact that shortly before, there had been violent pressure in respect of two other affairs, the character of which could only animate to the utmost caution, and which both ended in tragedy. The two affairs were the cases of the parachutists Adolf Larsen and H. H. Larsen.

On 26 March 1943, Adolf Larsen was arrested in Frederikshavn.[33] After being dropped at Furesø he remained in Copenhagen for a few days, and then Geisler sent him to Frederikshavn. He was given illegal lodging in the home of the Director of the Frederikshavn Motor Factory, C. Hansen. After his arrival in Frederikshavn his conduct was quite incredible. He frequented the restaurants of the town, often drunk, and sought questionable female company. With one girl he met, he showed her his revolver and boasted and hinted at the secret and important character of his presence in the town. The result was that he and H. H. Hansen were arrested.

Worse was to come. After his arrest he talked unrestrainedly, and this set dangerous developments going. The information he gave led to the arrest of the couriers, the Divinity student Bang Olsen, and the Law student Erik Nyemann, and the investigations which followed brought the Støvring High School into the lime light, as Bang Olsen had notified the national register that he had moved from Copenhagen to the High School. The worst blow for the organisation, however, was that Bang Olsen was arrested on the main railway station in Copenhagen just after he arrived as courier, with a letter containing a great deal of information on the Table organisation (the parachutists) including a number of cover names. The letter was addressed to the Forest Superintendent Dalgas. However, the affair was not unravelled further.

One of the chief reasons why the affair did not end in disaster, apart from Larsen himself being handed over to the German authorities and being sent to Germany where he shared the fate of the three parachutists from the Skodsborg incident, seems to have been that the Danish Resistance men who were arrested in the affair, in contrast to Larsen, managed to hold back in their explanations and to co-ordinate these, and it was also a result of effective support from the Danish Police. At least Duus Hansen, who was SOE's most direct contact with the police, could send two detailed reports on the progress of the hearings to Hollingworth,[34] while they were still going on. The two reports[35] were given direct by the police and supplied detailed information on what was discovered during the handling of the affair. The information is very exact and agrees with what was later given in evidence to the Parliamentary Commission. In a third report there are personal comments on the affair, which clearly show the infiltration which had taken place within the Police Force. This reads in part as follows: "After the arrest of Table Tennis (Adolf Larsen) ... the situation for Table Manners (Geisler) in Jutland is not very clear ... Bang Olsen was caught on the railway station in Copenhagen ... He had a letter on him, written by the Elephant (Juncker)[36] ... he mentions nearly all the Table people's code names in the letter, e.g. Table-Top ... The whole question depends at the moment on whether those arrested are able to show enough steadfastness during cross-examination ... after there has been opportunity to influence the couriers, particularly, in the right direction,[37] it is probable that the explanations will hold ... One can only say, of Tennis's conduct

in this country, that from the first day it was marked by irresponsible carelessness ... His expenditure was beyond all reasonable limits and he was
often drunk ..."

There were no serious consequences from the Frederikshavn affair, but
there could have been. Geisler, for example, had been in Frederikshavn on
the day of Adolf Larsen's arrest, because information had been received
that Larsen's conduct called for serious intervention from his superiors, so
that Geisler found it necessary to investigate the situation himself. After
Larsen's arrest, serious anxiety continued as to what information he might
give, in addition to what he had already said, and the question was raised
as to whether a cyanide pill should be sent in to him in the prison. This
idea was given up as it was felt, and not without reason, that Larsen instead of taking the pill, would be able to give information on who had given
it to him.[38]

The other affair was no less likely to create a feeling of uncertainty
within the organisation. On 2 May 1943 a body was found near Sjælsø. The
man had been killed by a shot in the back of the head. The police investigation showed that the man was the parachutist H. H. Larsen, and it was
said that he had been very rash in his statements, and that he had presumably been killed by his own comrades.[39] The supposition was correct. On
instructions from London, it was decided to liquidate him, after which London Headquarters, as the higher command, took responsibility for what had
happened.[40]

The two affairs described were naturally extremely unfortunate for the
reputation of SOE, among all who knew of them. Serious criticism arose
once more, not least of the choice of personnel in London. In the comments
on the Frederikshavn events mentioned above, Duus Hansen states that the
letter which Bang Olsen was carrying when he was arrested contained criticism
by Juncker of the state of the organisation, and criticism must also have
been voiced from other quarters, such as the Intelligence officers.

Hollingworth refers in his letters to Muus and Duus Hansen to this criticism and defends the organisation, while he admits unreservedly how unfortunate these affairs have been. He puts it in unmistakable terms:[41] "The
reports we have received, re Tennis (Adolf Larsen) were extremely disturb-
ing. I cannot understand why he made such an idiot of himself. We regard
his indiscretion as criminal treachery ... Will you please tell the Elephant
(Juncker), if you are in touch with him, how much we regret the difficult
and dangerous position in which he has been placed ... We blame it on
ourselves for not picking the right material ... I can quite understand that
good people fight shy of having anything to do with us, when the boys we
send out make such fools of themselves." Three weeks later Hollingworth
returns to the criticism:[42] "I am sorry to see that there are people in
your country who regard our organization as being composed of irresponsible

192

rebels. Judging by the mistakes that have been made in the past one can hardly blame them. I should, however, be glad if you would rub it in to all concerned that this is a serious organization now stretching over all the world. We are not doing the job for love of adventure, but because we have got to beat the Hun ... Part of our trouble has been that we have had a ... great shortage of personnel from which to draw and we have paid for sending the wrong men to the Field. I would like the critics to know that London realises this." Finally, in a letter of the same date to Duus Hansen, with direct address to the Intelligence officers, he writes:[43] "We have been extremely unfortunate in having sent to the Field some boys who have acted as though the whole game were a great adventure and not a serious job. By their action they have brought the organization in great disrepute. My God, I can understand that X (Intelligence officers) wishes to have nothing to do with them. Nor would I if I were in X's shoes." Hollingworth goes on to stress the same points of explanation as those in his letter to Muus.

During the period we are considering, SOE was to suffer one more loss. On 25 August 1943 Arne Boelsskov was killed in his illegal flat in Copenhagen.[44] He was engaged in making packages containing explosives, fixed in such a way that the explosion took place when the package was opened. His assistant, the Falck rescue worker Teddy Petersen was killed with him, and when Muus did not succeed in obtaining a safe-conduct to remove the explosives, two more men were killed later in the day, a policeman and a rescue worker from the Zone rescue corps. During an examination of the flat on 2 September there was yet another explosion, and two men were wounded.

In the question of choice of personnel and in determining the pace at which they were sent over, it seems as if London reserved the right of decision, as a rule. On the other hand it was Muus who took the initiative as regards reorganisation in the field. Here he followed quite different lines from those we saw sketched out in Hollingworth's letter to Hammer. A study of this reorganisation will show that on this question he acted quite independently.

First of all, he decided to establish his headquarters in Copenhagen and not, as presumed in Hollingworth's directives, in Jutland. There he posted Geisler, with residence in Aarhus, as a kind of deputy chief, and let him take over the supervision of parachutists who were sent there.[45] This meant that the close co-operation between Muus and Juncker, which Hollingworth had presupposed, and which should have taken the form of Muus operating behind the scenes through Juncker's contacts, was not established. It was Geisler who came into direct touch with Juncker and with the extensive work which now started in Jutland under Juncker's leadership. Rapid communication between the two branches of the organisation was not achieved, as suggested in Hollingworth's letter, by establishing indirect radio contact between them via London. It is true that Kaj Lund, who was trained as a radio telegraphist in England, was sent to Jutland, but he did not succeed in establishing any contact with England, so that a connexion could be opened by this channel.[46] For a time, at least, the reason for this seems to have been that his radio set did not function, and when a new set was sent to Denmark in July, it finished up in the middle of Madum Lake, near where the reception took place.[47] After this the idea of letting Kaj Lund send telegrams was definitely abandoned.

Nor was it necessary that Kaj Lund should establish the two-way connexion Copenhagen-Jutland. It turned out to be possible to establish a much more effective and quick channel of communication, namely the private telephone line that led from Aarhus Privatbank to its Copenhagen branch. In the Copenhagen branch, Carl Larsen, the bank accountant, who had already been in touch with the work of the parachutists through Borch-Johansen, and at that time had already placed his flat at their disposal for illegal radio transmissions,[48] was the organisation's contact man. In Aarhus the bank assistant, Erik Bach Frederiksen became Geisler's contact man. In Bach Frederiksen's account is described, how this connection was established and how it functioned.[49] Bach Frederiksen reports that he had been working in the Copenhagen branch at the beginning of the war, and knew Carl Larsen well, from that period. Through their general political discussions Carl Larsen was aware of Bach Frederiksen's anti-German attitude. He mentions that the possibility of some day using the private telephone connexion for illegal purposes may have been discussed between the two men, before Bach Frederiksen left Copenhagen to work in the head office in Aarhus. He writes further: "Our conversations took place in connexion with Geisler, who would come to the counter in the bank at various times of the day, when he had any message he wanted to send to Copenhagen, or when he wanted any information. As a rule I could give him the answer, which the accountant Carl Larsen obtained in Copenhagen, after half an hour or an hour. To begin with this concerned financial questions[50] and questions in connexion with the Andy Larsen affair[51] ... However, it cannot have been long before the messages became ... fuller ... I remember, for example, that we discussed the details regarding receptions which started very soon under Geisler's leadership at Hvidsten, over this line. Gradually, it was not only these receptions, but all the receptions in Jutland, the localities, chosen as reception points, light signals, code words etc. that were arranged by the line. Aarhus Privatbank's line was very important for Geisler, as far as I know, because in contrast to the courier connexion it functioned extremely quickly ... This was also the case after the operator Kaj Lund was later sent to Jutland, as his results did not come up to our expectations." Bach Frederiksen states in conclusion that the connexion functioned up to December 1943.[52] Carl Larsen was then arrested by the Gestapo, and in April 1944 executed by a German firing squad. He had divulged nothing.

Such a rapid and reliable connexion was obviously preferable to indirect communications via London. One can perhaps infer a little of the tremendous value attributed to this connexion by noting that Muus refers to it in his otherwise quite frank reports to London, without mentioning how it works:[53] "I ... sent the sharpest instructions to the contrary both by telephone (Top (Hammer) will explain how that works) and by courier." As we know, it was a long time before Hammer reached London, and Hollingworth was not informed in the mean time on this connexion. Until it was explained, Hollingworth continued to urge Muus to get the radio connexion via London established. In May he writes to him:[54] "Lamp. (Kaj Lund). We are still waiting to hear him but no doubt there are reasons why he has not come up yet. It is rather important that we should have communications between Zealand and Jutland via London in case landcommunications break down."

The fact that Muus chose to place his headquarters in Copenhagen and let Geisler take over the closer contact with Juncker and with the actual work in the field, showed an essential difference between his concept of the work of the parachutist chief, and London's. According to the British concept, as it appears from Hollingworth's letter to Hammer, already quoted, Muus should only make direct contact with Danish Resistance men to the least possible extent, and should operate principally through Juncker's connexions. A decisive reason for this seems to have been the British fear that Muus ran unnecessarily great risks by contacting too many people. This view is drummed in again and again in Hollingworth's letters:[55] "I hope all your chaps will behave decently and for God's sake watch their security. They cannot be too careful. Keep Mat (Gunnar Christiansen) off the air when there are nothing urgent to send," or: "Be on your guards, however, against 'agents-provocateurs' ... If he is a Gestapo agent he *will* know a hell of a lot," or: "Don't take risks where risks can be avoided, and leave the riskiest jobs to specially chosen local people." In July there is a direct admonition:[56] "I am now going to deliver you a little raspberry! It is understood that in your position a certain amount of contacting is necessary. However, we feel that you are overdoing it and if you are not careful you will get caught. It is vitally necessary for you to keep in the background and work through others, even to the detriment of the work ... What can we think of a 'secret' organization, whose leader is known to everybody? This is intended to be a helpful criticism. Please accept it in the same spirit."

Unquestionably, Muus did not share the British concept of the duty of the parachutist leader, nor did he share the British anxiety. This is shown

13*

in all his work. In Copenhagen he had plenty of opportunity to obtain personal contacts on very many sides, and he made use of these possibilities, as we shall see, extensively. He was enough of a diplomat to accept the friendly reproach with an admission, as when he answers:[57] "The 'raspberries' were well deserved. I think it is great you are so exact and frank ... Obviously criticism is only of the good and I'd appreciate if you from time to time point out to me my mistakes;" but one finds more of his real standpoint in a later passage in the same letter: "On the other hand it is most difficult to obtain results without making contacts ..."

One can hardly doubt that when Muus chose Copenhagen as the seat of his headquarters, this represented more than the simple choice of residence. There is policy behind this choice. Perhaps there was also personal ambition to develop his position as Britain's representative in Denmark into something more than was implied in obtaining weapons and explosives for the Resistance groups. By placing himself here and extending contacts to all sides, Muus made himself the centre of events, and kept a hold on the most important of the strands which led out into the free world from fighting Denmark. It should be remembered that Muus dropped into a Resistance-political vacuum. The rapidly growing Resistance groups were not yet flocking to any united central authority. In these circumstances, Muus, with obvious assurance, gave his position as SOE's leader in Denmark a content which was neither presupposed nor foreseen from London, and which the corresponding positions hardly received in any other country.[58] London saw with wonder and enthusiasm how he increasingly infiltrated the home-grown Danish Resistance, and with growing success tried to make himself the Allied authority vis-à-vis fighting Denmark, and how he sought to intervene in the most varied domains in Resistance, national, and military politics.

In England there was lively applause for these developments, regardless of the fact that they must contribute to shifting the centre of gravity within SOE from London to Copenhagen. On 17 May – only two months after Muus arrived in Denmark – Hollingworth writes to him that he has been recommended for promotion, and that he can expect his majority before the end of the month, and adds:[59] "You are getting a good name and we are proud of you. A high-standing officer at H.Q. told me yesterday that one of the most surprising developments in our European organization was the success that has been obtained in Denmark since you boys went out. Let us keep it up."

Muus himself felt that he was in a strong position. There is an exultant, self-confident tone in his reports:[60] "With all good wishes to all good friends – tell them we all have the time of our life and that the spirit is very high indeed." He does not shrink from making sharp criticism of decisions in England. For example, he protests violently against Major Iversen

196

being replaced as chief of the recruiting office by Major Knauer.[61] He exploits the possibilities of the fair wind, with all sails set. When Hollingworth suggests that he put on the brakes a little, for a time, he turns down the proposal. Hollingworth writes:[62] "We have been pressing you pretty hard ever since your arrival and you have worked splendidly ... We therefore think that ... it is a good opportunity for you all to slacken off. Will you therefore *all of you* regard the second week in June as a period of *no activity* ... It will give you all an opportunity to relax." Muus does not even discuss the idea:[63] "It is awfully nice of you to think of giving us holidays but I am afraid Hitler won't agree. From a security and practical point of view it just won't be possible to 'lay off' for a week and I have, therefore, allowed me not to pass on your kind permission." Of course Muus and the rest of the SOE could have taken a week's leave. But Muus would not. He was in the process of expanding the central position he was creating for himself in the Danish Resistance world, and he intended to squeeze every advantage out of the favourable situation.

If there was any opposition to this expansion of the limits for the authority of the parachutist leader,[64] it came from Denmark. In the course of 1943 Juncker, at least, developed his critical view of him and gave expression to it both to Muus himself and to London. In his account he underlines that on his trips to Copenhagen he expressed his criticism and so entered a rather unfriendly relationship with Muus, and he adds that he also stressed his standpoints vis-à-vis Turnbull.[65] This corresponds exactly with the ill-feeling which Muus expressed towards Juncker in several of his letters to Hollingworth.[66] But all criticism was lost in the face of the developments in progress in Denmark. London gave these developments its applause, and credited most of them to Muus's account. In the autumn 1943 Turnbull could inform Juncker that London not only would not accept the criticism, but intended to increase Muus's powers further.[67]

As Muus thus saw his position and his mission, it was in Copenhagen that his work lay first of all, with important conferences with leading political, military and Resistance figures. In accordance with this point of view, he seems to have been somewhat reserved with regard to meeting the other parachutists, who took part in the individual action in the Field; they became bricks in a bigger game. It will be remembered that in Ålborg he separated himself from the team he had come over with. In "The Spark and the Flame" he mentions[68] that of the three comrades he landed with, he has not seen the one, since, and the second, only once. In a letter to Hollingworth he accounts for this as an actual principle:[69] "I do not meet all these boys personally as I consider it unwise, – Habit (Lok Linblad), who is my Chief-Cutout, keeps the connections. I fail to see why I should meet the boys, – it serves no purpose and you can rest assured that they get most concise instructions from me either by word of mouth or by letters.

Perhaps the boys do not like the idea of not meeting me – perhaps they cannot understand it – but that is a matter that can be discussed once the war is over."

With this the main framework for reorganisation was fixed. The various parachutists were now distributed around the country, where each of them – with varying success – tried to establish contact with the local groups, train them in sabotage and work at procuring the necessary weapons and explosives. The connexion between the individual members of the organisation was maintained through couriers. In the main, the distribution was as follows: In the Aarhus-Randers region, Ole Geisler acted with Verner Johansen as a kind of assistant. Paul Jensen acted in Aalborg, while Vilfred Petersen was posted to Viborg, Aage Møller Christensen to Fredericia with South Jutland as his working region, and Ejnar Balling to Esbjerg. Kaj Lund has already been mentioned as attached to the Jutland organisation. Peter Carlsen was posted to Fyn, and later Hans Johansen for a time, while the rest of the parachutists were occupied in Copenhagen. At the head was Muus himself with Lok Linblad as his assistant, then Gunnar Christiansen as telegraphist to the organisation, and first Poul Hansen, later Jens Peter Petersen as the direct liaisons with the various sabotage groups. Finally Arne Boelsskov was also posted here, while Jakob Jensen was sent to Lolland for a time, later to Jutland.

The personnel was constantly moving about, however, so that this framework only covers the original positions. A more detailed account of the shift in the distribution is without interest to the main subject. The results in the various places were extremely uneven, just as the circumstances were varied.[70]

16. Improving Communications with the free World

An examination of the development towards active resistance and the final break with the Germans, which was now making real headway and which will be followed from SOE's observation posts, can well start with a study of communications with England and thus with the free world – both direct telegraphic communication and communication by courier through Sweden. In this department Muus, on arriving in Denmark, was at once able to take advantage of the pioneer work already done in this field.

However incomplete the historical material may be in many respects, here it is abundant, and shows clearly that from the early spring of 1943, when Gunnar Christiansen was established as operator, and when almost simultaneously arrangements were agreed upon between Duus Hansen and London, there exists a fast and comparatively reliable line of direct communication between England and Denmark; and that this contact thereafter is quickly developed and consolidated. To illustrate this we have a more or less continuous correspondence between Duus Hansen and both Hollingworth and Turnbull, as well as several of the telegrams sent in increasing numbers by Duus Hansen, starting at the beginning of 1943.[1] Most of this correspondence naturally has a technical character[2] and contains discussions of transmission times and plans, codes, security, etc. A good deal of it, however, gives, directly and indirectly, valuable information of a more general character. Few of the technical sections of the correspondence are of historical interest, but they show quite clearly that from now on, steady, regular, fast communications are the accepted, routine conditions for the work. On this point, Muus escaped the worries which his predecessors had to face.

In his first report of 30 April he already stresses his pleasure at this state of things:[3] "Mat (Gunnar Christiansen) is doing exceedingly well – behaves exactly according to the Book of Words – only words of praise to be said here ... Napkin (Duus Hansen) is doing very well indeed. He certainly is a vital link in the organization and helps us no end not least through his connections with Richard and friends (Roland Olsen and other helpers in Police Corps)."

The altered situation in the telegraph service becomes even more evident from the remarks in Hollingworth's and Turnbull's letters to the men and women in the Field. In May Hollingworth writes to Muus:[4] "Will you please give Mat (Gunnar Christiansen) the following message: Thank you for your good work. Your operating is excellent," after which a long series of remarks follows on changes in transmission technique. In a following letter Hollingworth repeats his appreciation of Gunnar Christiansen's work:[5] "Mat (Gunnar Christiansen) has been doing extremely well – almost too well. I sincerely hope Lamp (Kaj Lund) will soon come up and relieve the traffic. When Lamp gets started successfully I suggest that as far as possible they each work *alternate weeks*. In the meantime, as it is possible that Lamp's operating is not so good as Mat's, I suggest that you start Lamp off on test messages ... You should not give him urgent operational messages to send until we have proved that the connection is O.K."

The work of Duus Hansen, also, was greatly appreciated in London. In April there are warm thanks for the information received and for suggestions for technical alterations which Duus Hansen has put forward,[6] and in July Hollingworth expresses his recognition direct, with the words:[7] "Your operating and coding is excellent in every way but there appears to be some misunderstanding with regard to call signs." He explains the misunderstanding and adds: "In the case of W/T operators who have been trained in our schools this point is covered in the instruction, but in your case we ought to have made it clear. Sorry!" There is a letter from Turnbull to Duus Hansen on exactly the same lines:[8] "Chop (Hollingworth) asks us to give you the following message which has been given to you verbally here. London greatly appreciates your valuable help ... Your W/T operating and coding excellent."

The reliable, effective service which telegraphic communication had now become, however, appears most strikingly in the following characterization from November 1943 in a letter from Hollingworth to Duus Hansen:[9] "When I knew that there would be an opportunity to send you a short message I asked our W/T H.Q. to let me have any criticisms on your operating that they could dig out. The reply I got read as follows: "Reference Napkin (Duus Hansen), Joseph (Fischer Holst)[10] and Mat (Gunnar Christiansen). We have no criticism to offer. All three operators are absolutely first-class and are the 3 best operators out of one group of 40, and amongst the best 10 out of several groups of operators running into hundreds.' I cannot add any appreciation to beat that." The Joseph mentioned in the letter is the Danish engineer Fischer Holst, who from September 1943 on Duus Hansen's appeal had undertaken to function as radio operator, and who from that moment carried the work through without a break to the end of the Occupation.[11] The letter quoted contains the following special mention of Fischer Holst: "We shall need as many good W/T operators as are obtainable and we hope you will be able to carry on your good work in this respect

200

for the future. You are obviously an excellent instructor. Joseph is doing splendidly, and it is a very rare feat to have such excellent communication with W/T operators who have never been trained in our special procedure in this country. Please try to get us some more like Joseph, they will be worth their weight in gold."

Even if one takes the possibility into account that the desire in London is naturally to encourage Resistance workers in their dangerous work as much as possible, the above quotations speak for themselves as London's indisputable appraisals of the work accomplished.

It is clear from the last remark referring to Fischer Holst that Duus Hansen's position in relation to SOE has completely altered during the summer and autumn of 1943. He is no longer regarded as simply or specially a telegraph operator, but primarily as an instructor. The implication in this change constitutes, perhaps, the clearest recognition of his service.

Normally, on grounds of security, SOE did not wish to have too intimate a co-operation with workers not trained in England, and of whom there was therefore no first-hand knowledge, but in Duus Hansen's case, experience had led to the conviction of the desirability of attaching him as closely as possible to the work, and making him head of the radio service, placed between London and the workers in the Field. He was thus responsible for providing transmission and receiving sets, finding suitable telegraphists in Denmark, and instructing them. Duus Hansen writes of this in his account:[12] "With this decision England had definitely abandoned the principle, that telegraph operators should be instructed and trained in England, and should use English equipment. The system worked satisfactorily for the English, and I was asked to extend it further and to hold more operators in reserve."

This alteration in Duus Hansen's position naturally did not take place at one stroke, but developed as a natural consequence of a co-operation which gradually became closer and closer, and more and more confidential. The correspondence reflects this development. After Muus's arrival it soon became clear to London, that Duus Hansen was co-operating so closely with him that he could be drawn into the work of planning without any important reservations.[13] "I take it that you see pretty well everything that goes through to Jam (Muus) and that he keeps you well informed without drawing you too far into the net. This is important because you are playing a most valuable part in coordinating the efforts of our boys in relationship with Bannock (the Intelligence officers)", writes Hollingworth, and a later letter is in the same tone:[14] "This is just a very short note to thank you for the splendid work you have been doing on our behalf. It is entirely due to you that our communications have been able to continue throughout some very difficult periods. Jam (Muus) will no doubt report to you in detail of the plans that have been discussed here in London."[15]

The fact that personal contact was now established with Duus Hansen contributed to his increased influence. Whereas he had hitherto been an anonymous operator, as far as London was concerned – "Mr. Ds.", Mr. Henry", "Mr. Napkin", whose telegraphic "hand-writing"[16] was familiar, and whose help was gradually understood to be reliable, he suddenly became flesh and blood to the British organisers when, in June 1943, he had the opportunity of visiting Stockholm. "Henry has paid us a visit here and has discussed many points. He is an excellent man and is of great value in his special field," writes Ebbe Munck[17] the same month, and in his letter of 16 July quoted above, Hollingworth writes to Duus Hansen:[18] "We were pleased to get a full report from Sugar (Turnbull) on the results of your visit and we regard you now as a very close friend." From June, London accepts the establishment of a daily contact with Duus Hansen.[19] A very marked strenthening in British confidence in him is finally evident after 29 August 1943, when the Intelligence officers, as explained later, decided to go to Sweden. Duus Hansen insisted here, that he would stay in Denmark and continue his work with SOE. He writes to Hollingworth:[20] "When Bannock (the Intelligence officers) left, we spoke of my following soon after, but I do not feel I can leave the country, as long as everything is not in order again, and all communications re-established. Besides, I should be ashamed to leave at a moment when there is pressing need for W/T communication." Thanks for this firm attitude are extremely warm and well deserved:[21] "Thanks for staying behind when you had the chance to leave. We needed your help badly at that particular stage, and we shall need it far more in the future. Thanks for everything."

Duus Hansen's position was thus gradually changed. In the spring he is telegraph operator. From July he is "a near friend", from September the recognized leader of the whole telegraph service to England. This service, already in marked development during the spring and summer, now expands rapidly. In September he can inform London that two new W/T operators are ready to start work:[22] "They are both trained men with twenty years' practical experience. They are willing to start as soon as possible. I am at present finishing building sets for them." Two months later, in November 1943, he can state in a longer report on the development of the telegraph service[23] that one of these operators, the engineer Fischer Holst mentioned above, is now working, and that three more operators are ready to start transmission, one of them being Duus Hansen's brother, a veterinary surgeon on Fyn, so that from that time there are in all six radio telegraphists available. The long report, which deals principally with technical problems, ends with the words: "Your request to 'stay off the air' will of course be complied with. There is no anxiety, either from Joseph's (Fischer Holst's) side or mine, and communication with London will be maintained in the quantity and to the extent of London's own wishes."

The telegraphic service was thus in rapid expansion. Muus did not need to worry seriously as to communications with England. These lay in such safe hands, that recognition from England and from Muus, unequivocal as it was, seems sparse compared to the merit. The establishment of a really reliable radio service, so expertly carried out, should not leave the impression that this important part of Resistance work was done quite easily, without risks, dangers and anxieties. On the contrary, this particular work was extremely dangerous and demanding. There were the unceasing work of adjustment to new codes, transmission plans, transmission times, the unavoidable misunderstandings in the daily work between outstations and the home station, and the everlasting struggle against the constantly expanding German security system, which demanded incessant watchfulness, imagination and courage from the operators, and in the course of time these, of necessity, claimed victims.[24] Nevertheless, these difficulties were overcome, and in 1943 arrests were avoided, even though it is clear from Duus Hansen's letter from November 1943 that the German direction finders are, from autumn 1943, becoming extremely effective.[25] We shall here touch only on the difficulties which arose during the work of establishing the W/T operator Kaj Lund, because these difficulties illustrate so well the value of finding men in Denmark, who both could and would undertake radio work, so that the troubles connected with dependence upon England for technical equipment and instruction of personnel were avoided.

As mentioned already, Kaj Lund came to Denmark in mid-April. During the first days after his arrival he went through with Duus Hansen some new plans for transmission which he had brought with him, and then was sent to Jutland to act as Ole Geisler's special telegraphist.[26] He did not succeed, however, in establishing radio contact, probably because the equipment broke down in the mean time, and a new set had to be sent from England. This set also had a sad fate, as it landed in the middle of Madum Lake. In Muus's report on this it is stated:[27] "On the 'Margarine'-'Tripe' reception (the reception of Aage Møller Christensen and Jens Peter Petersen) I have the following to say: ... It appears that 'Tripe' (Jens Peter Petersen) jumped 5 seconds before the command was actually given and 'Margarine' (Aage Møller Christensen) followed immediately. 'Tripe' landed alright but 'Margarine' went into the water of Madum Lake some 60 feet from the shore ... the wireless sets were despatched but the whole parcel fell right in the middle of the lake and disappeared – probably for good ... A terrible pity with the W.T. sets. Again 'Lamp' (Kaj Lund) is without means of communication ... I have now asked 'Napkin' to build him a set." This partly explains the many questions from London, as to when the new telegraphist can start work, and also provides the final solution to the whole problem of supplying radio sets: to have them made in Denmark.

The telegraphic service, however, was only one of the types of communication with the outside world. The other was the slower, but no less valuable courier route, which led to neutral Sweden and from there by various channels out into the free world. More detailed correspondence went this way, letters, reports, intelligence material which was not urgent, etc. This was the route taken by fugitives of the Resistance Movement, and other refugees, including, in the course of time, a not inconsiderable number of Allied pilots shot down over Denmark. This traffic gradually became organised by large refugee groups, and in the last years of the Occupation – particularly from the large-scale organisation of escape for Danish Jews in October 1943 – reached a quite astonishing size.[28]

It must, however, be stressed that in the spring and summer of 1943, this development still lay in the future. Regular escape routes were not yet established, and until the autumn of 1943, refugee transport, at least, was still in the experimental stages, where escape was a difficult and dangerous operation. In this survey we have seen how, as far back as 1940, the officers of the Intelligence Service had succeeded in maintaining a fairly dependable line of communication for letters, which was never entirely cut off, and how communication, with the use of all the possibilities for reliable courier routes which might present themselves, had become more and more frequent, but we have also had the opportunity, in short glimpses, to follow the extreme difficulties which those who had to escape to Sweden must face, from the beginning of the Occupation. We have seen how the dangerous crossing over the Øresund's ice had been the route for some, we have followed the difficulties in arranging a reliable and sufficiently camouflaged departure for Christmas Møller, we have heard of the tragedy at Skodsborg, and the long hours of trial for those who crossed to Sweden by kayak or rubber dinghy, such as Hammer, Borch-Johansen and Kiilerich. As the background for the eminent success with which the large refugee organisitions later solved this whole problem, it is valuable to stress how difficult conditions were, right up to the summer of 1943.

The despatch of letters gave the least difficulty, and as far as Muus was concerned, the channels established by the Intelligence officers were available. This is evident from the following remark in a letter to Hollingworth:[29] "Since the despatch of the last mail (Jam 8 and 9) the situation has altered appreciatively. After the departure of Bannock (the Intelligence officers) our mail connections have been cut but I have now been able reestablish the connection in such a way that we have two quite independent sources, one of which is hundred percent foolproof. It is this one I am using now and I shall greatly appreciate if you, immediately upon receipt of this, will w.t. me: 'Received Jam (Muus)10.'[30] The mail will reach 'the Skipper' (Ebbe Munck) within two days of despatch from here and I have all reasons to think that 'Sugar' (Turnbull), through 'the Skipper' can use the same link for mail addressed to me."

204

Up to 29 August, mail connexions with Stockholm via the Intelligence Section were available, but this channel broke down in the days following 29 August with the officers' decision to leave the country. This is clear also from a letter from that period from Duus Hansen to Hollingworth, sent through Turnbull, stating:[31] "This communiqué is being sent via Matros,[32] the only channel that is open at present. This channel is quite reliable, but unfortunately slow, as it takes 10–12 days before a message reaches Sugar (Turnbull) ... The few pieces of information which are enclosed have also been forwarded through another channel, and I enclose them only because it is possible that the other consignment can get lost."

Duus Hansen's letter is not quite clear, as he declares that after the Intelligence officers' departure to Sweden only one – slow – channel remains open,[32] while he also refers to a consignment forwarded by another route. This corresponds to Muus's information, that he has two mail routes available. The main point seems clear, however: up to 29 August it has been possible to send mail through the Intelligence organisation, and after that date a new channel of communication has had to be established. The problems involved in sending mail have not, then, presented decisive difficulties, but on the other hand, the problems of transport of persons have been acute. We meet them again and again in the letters. In Muus's first letter to London he already writes:[33] "There is a great shortage of folding boats for transport across the Sound. In fact: they are inprocurable now. I have been wondering whether you could send us some in containers or just dumped like a bicycle. (Top (Hammer) knows sizes etc.) It would be great if we could get just one in every consignment."

Seen in relation to a later period's targets, the possibilities envisaged for future transport are certainly modest. The problem has also been obvious on the other side of the Sound. In Ebbe Munck's diary he writes at that time, in connexion with a description of an escape from Denmark by rubber boat:[34] "The rubber boat was destroyed, following instructions. (We must have this stopped, it is not necessary and they can well be useful for us on this side.)" In July the problem is still unsolved, and Muus returns to the question in a letter to Hollingworth:[35] "You have been informed that half of the folding boat consignment fell into enemy hands.[36] We could very well have done with such a boat. – I am certainly glad to learn that you will repeat sending folding boats." In "The Spark and the Flame" Muus also gives a description of the trouble involved in building up what he calls an evacuation department:[37] "Jørgen Røjel, Ole Secher and Erik Kiersgaard worked very hard ... We had tremendous difficulty in getting hold of kayaks for the transport, and as we never got them back, it was an enormous problem ... we dreamt of fleets of kayaks – but we never managed to have even one in reserve." In the same account Muus points to the special refugee organisation, which was to solve the problem from the autumn onwards, in an organising achievement on far broader lines than those mentioned at this point: ". . . after 29 August, conditions altered to such a degree, that the kayak problem no longer existed."

Finally we hear of the difficulties of evacuation from Duus Hansen, who writes to Turnbull:[38] "As regards transport over the Sound of people who need to leave the country, the situation is now getting difficult. As you probably know, folding boats are nearly always used for these crossings – as they can always be brought to the point of embarkation without hindrance . . . There have been few instances . . . where ordinary boats were used. However, the coastal control is tightening more and more, and we shall have to rely exclusively on the use of folding boats, but unfortunately . . . these boats are almost unobtainable. Please give serious thought to sending us these boats, possibly with other material."

The fact that the problem of evacuation now arose with so much more urgency than hithergo was due to various causes. With increasing resistance there were of necessity more and more who were forced to go underground or to escape to Sweden. In addition, as mentioned before,[39] London wished suitable Resistance workers to be evacuated to Sweden, from where they could be brought to England for instruction in SOE; and finally London was extremely anxious that the utmost be done to help Allied pilots and crews who had been shot down, to get to Sweden. In a good many instances in the last years of the war, the Resistance succeeded in rescuing RAF men and bringing them to Sweden. In letters from Muus there are references to such cases,[40] and in Ebbe Munck's diary there is a short account of a single example:[41] "The latter (a Canadian pilot, Donald Smith) is a story on its own. He fell in the neighbourhood of Korsør after the raid on Stettin . . . He parachuted from a low height, and was the only one of a crew of eight who survived. The next night he walked by the main road towards 'Helsingør', as he put it, and kept going on the small iron ration which they all have in their flying suits. He slept in a stable, but was discovered in the morning by the farmer, who fortunately understood a little English. He had torn off his badges of rank. By a mistake he had been supplied with French, not Danish money, but the farmer looked after him well and gave him food and a little Danish money. He passed Copenhagen and drove direct to Helsingør, where he was lucky enough to get in touch with the Free Danes, amongst others Troen, who was preparing to leave in a rubber boat stolen from the Germans. Duus (?) Hansen in Bernstorffsvej helped, his wife delayed the police guard and they got well away, kept south of Hveen and reached Raa."

It did not always go so well as for the Canadian pilot. We have heard about his seven comrades, and we find the following sad lines in a letter from Muus:[42] "You will remember that we despatched Thalbitzer[43] and Wing-Commander Buckley, who, both, had escaped from a prisoncamp in

Germany, from here on March 28th. As we never heard anything from you or "Sugar" (Turnbull) about their safe arrival ... we took for granted they had been met with an accident during the crossing. This turns out to be correct. Thalbitzer's body was found near Hornbæk some time ago."

Thalbitzer's and Buckley's tragic deaths were part of the price that had to be paid in the efforts to solve the problem of evacuation in a primitive way, with kayaks, rubber boats, etc. A refugee service from Frederikshavn, more on the lines of what was coming, developed quite quietly, as far as can be seen during the spring of 1943. A fishing skipper whose name was Oluf Andersen, called "Wolle", undertook to sail refugees to Sweden, and as the venture was successful, it led to the organisation, under the leadership of A. Gylding Sabroe, a merchant in Frederikshavn, of what must be the first real refugee service in Denmark. Unfortunately there are no collected records describing the development of this service, but in an appendix to his account, Juncker mentions the route, with which he had fairly frequent contact. He writes, for example:[44] "The Deputy Chief of Police, Larsen, and Detective Inspector Mortensen, who later became a sort of Chief for Hjørring Shire, co-operated with Sabroe. The route came gradually to transport people to Sweden (including Allied pilots), and Nikolaysen became the Aalborg agent for the route. In this way the route gradually filled an important rôle in the Jutland Resistance organisation."[45]

From this it is clear that at its opening, the route was a valuable private initiative, and only after it was established was it coupled to the large Jutland Resistance organisation, which Juncker built up in the course of 1943. It seems that the connexion took place in the summer of 1943, and it can be traced in the documentary material available. On 15 July Turnbull writes to Duus Hansen:[46] "Two Danes have recently been helped to escape by the Captain of a fishing boat ... called the "Stanley" FN 101,[47] registered at Saeby or Laesø and owned by himself. He comes from Saeby. In both cases the Stanley brought the men close in shore at Varberg, so that they were able to wade ashore with all their kit. The escapes in question have been organised by a man called A GYLDING-SABROE ... you might like to make contact with this man and the Captain to see if we cannot develop this method, which seems to be a good one. We should like a report from you on this matter. It seems that the two men organise a regular weekly service and that the boat waits once a week in the neighbourhood of Saeby, not far from the island of Laesø. This method might be exceedingly useful to us in the future, especially as our communication with G (Göteborg) is so good. You may like to get MANDARIN (Juncker) interested in this, and if you decide to develop it please instruct the courier to call on our Vice-Consul, Ch. (Christensen) at G." Ten days later, the contact is in order. In a letter to Hollingworth, Muus mentions that he has had four men brought to Sweden by this route.[48]

This method was undeniably useful, and more useful than Turnbull certainly dreamt of. A few months later this route was to develop into the large organisation, the Danish Relief Organisation.[49] It is curious to see that as late as July 1943 – only three months before the great stream of refugees to Sweden is in full spate – no one dreams as yet, either in Sweden or in Denmark, of such a development. There are signs of a certain wondering astonishment, that it is possible to use boats of a larger type than folding boats and kayaks, and other safety precautions than to shelter in the darkness of the night. The planners' imigination halted with the possibilities which these conceptions offered. No wonder! The history of the Refugee Organisations is one of the strangest and most incredible in the history of Resistance, teeming with accounts of imagination and daring, of cheek and inventiveness, of ability to seize an opportunity with, often, a natural and logical solution. When bitter necessity demanded it, these and many other qualities showed themselves in abundance in the idealistic men and women, who created the great refugee organisations and raised the solution to a plane corresponding to the desperate situation and its merciless demands.

In so doing, they wrote their names indelibly in Danish history.

17. Contact with the Army and Police

One of the most important tasks which awaited Muus, when he came to Denmark, was to establish contact with the officers in the Intelligence Section, so that the two organizations could work side by side without friction. Muus seems to have accomplished this mission with considerable diplomatic skill. Irrespective of the fact that there still existed a basic divergence of opinion, a co-operation was now established, so that both parties informed the other on their work and tried to support each other. In his account in "The Spark and the Flame" Muus records[1] the relationship with the officers, and it is characteristic for his description that if anything, he emphasizes the difference of standpoint. It is as if he remembers this side of the picture most clearly, perhaps because he actually felt the distance between them rather acutely.

During his work in 1943, however, it seems as if he has refrained from pointing out the differences too sharply, and letters written at the time show rather that the two organizations have now found each other, and that there is little, if any, material friction. Here again, it should in justice be stressed that Muus's situation was easier than his predecessors', as he could feel that he had London behind him, in quite a different degree. London was, of course, full of gratitude and acknowledgement for the valuable intelligence received, then and for the previous three years, but in the question of potential or active resistance policy they had, as we have seen, made their decision, and now aimed at the quickest possible activisation – with or without the Intelligence officers. Muus was well aware of their standpoint, and this gave him an essentially stronger position than SOE had been able to give their earlier leaders in the field.

The British point of view, as mentioned, had been expounded vigorously to Nordentoft in March 1943 in Stockholm,[2] just at the period when Muus arrived in Denmark. On that occasion, no clarification had been reached. The officers' point of view had still been that strong activisation was undesirable. Turnbull had, however, insisted uncompromisingly on the British standpoint, and even though no really positive reply from the officers can be documented, it looks as though they tacitly accepted the change in the British position and adapted to it in the period following. In a note dated 7 April – 1 May 1943, Ebbe Munck writes[3] that he is waiting "impatiently for Peter's (the officers') reply in the great discussion", and in the following notes, while there is no mention that such a direct reply has arrived, he mentions twice[4] that relations between the Intelligence officers and SOE have improved considerably, and emphasizes that intelligence transmissions are good and regular.

From letters of the period one has the same impression, that the officers, though they did not adopt the British point of view directly, took note of it and continued the work in very good understanding with Muus. Muus refers to relations with the officers for the first time on 21 May:[5] "Napkin (Duus Hansen) is in close contact with me and is a most valuable man. It is true that he also is in contact with our friends but no objection is raised hereon from either side. In point of fact: our friends have, to a great extent, changed their former views on us and our activity and have let me know that whatever they can do to assist me they will do. Such I needed 10 gallons of petrol one night, – our friends got it for us in 8 minutes. Our friends have let me know that if I consider it necessary I can get into personal contact with them and vice versa. There is no reason for such a contact now but I am gratified knowing that it can be established should need be."

At that stage, it seems that while there is no personal contact as yet, a good mutual understanding has been established through Duus Hansen. Muus mentions in "The Spark and the Flame"[6] that personal contact was achieved later, and this also seems to be implied in a remark from one of his later letters to London, where he wrote:[7] "As far as 'Bannock' (the Intelligence officers) is concerned I fully realise of what great help they are to you, and the war-efforts in general and you can trust that I shall do all in my power to keep up the good relationship that now exists." In the following pages we shall see that Muus met at least one of the officers in the days around 29 August. As we have already seen, the co-operation between the two organisations led, amongst other things, to the establishment of SOE's Sweden mail.

This improvement in relations between the two organisations is naturally noted in London with real pleasure. The value placed in London on intelligence from Denmark appears now in the documents, for example in a letter to Duus Hansen:[8] "Will you please tell X (the officers) that London is deeply grateful for all services rendered; for the vast amounts of intelligence that has regularly come through and for the confidence X showed in us revealing some of their plans."

Serious efforts were evidently made to meet the special wishes of the Intelligence officers. Duus Hansen was thus assigned to them as their special operator,[9] and when, in May, they express the wish for more frequent contact, Hollingworth replies in the letter quoted above,[10] that there is complete willingness in London to make the necessary arrangements. It appears also in several of the letters, that every effort is made in SOE[11] to counteract and remove the not unfounded feeling of uncertainty among the Intelligence officers as to their co-operation with London – an uncertainty which must have been voiced at least in connexion with the accidents which had dogged a part of the work, and which were not always unavoidable. In connexion with the Frederikshavn[12] affair we read,[13] for example: "It is very difficult to judge how a man is going to turn out in the Field. However, we are learning by hard experience and I am glad to say that nothing that has happened up to date has dragged X into the mud ... I want to make it plain that NO DANES in this country ever get a glimpse of such matters (the intelligence material which is sent across), that we are carefully weighing up all sides of the various questions ... We mean business and we are dead serious."

It should also be stressed, that from the summer 1943 there is an actual alteration in the Intelligence officers' communication with England, in that they are informed that for the future, special intelligence material is to go direct to British Intelligence Headquarters, and that all messages to and from that organisation are to be marked in future with the name "Hannibal".[14] It is added that the object is for the officers in future to feel themselves in direct contact with the British Intelligence Service. As the new arrangement seems at first to have given rise to certain misunderstandings, it is defined, a months later, in a letter from Turnbull to the Intelligence organisation, where he writes:[15] "In your document ... you enclose a message to HANNIBAL in which you mention different telegrams about collaboration and coordination of plans. As a matter of fact these messages did not come from HANNIBAL which is our intelligence organisation, but from the operational people. I wonder how it was you thought these messages came from HANNIBAL, since the new intelligence questionnaires from HANNIBAL have always been prefixed by the name HANNIBAL and other communications about our operations from my headquarters which ... can still be referred to as 'London' ... My headquarters are prepared to guarantee absolute secrecy in the circulation of your special messages ... and I have been instructed to forward any such messages to my headquarters undeveloped. I entirely agree that such matters are so all-embracing and secret that it is necessary to take the strictest precautions."

The work of the Intelligence Service appears to have developed favourably under the new form, with long questionnaires from the British side on every possible military matter – location of German troops, German coastal defences, anti-aircraft batteries, defences of Danish and North German ports, the organisation of the German air observer service, the German research station at Peenemünde, etc.

Telegrams from England, for example, read in part:[16] "Can you telegraph report on activity at peenemuende repeat peenemuende near greifswald repeat greifswald where enemy are producing and experimenting with longe range rockets repeat rockets stop believe new radio repeat radio apparatus on bornholm repeat bornholm connected with these experiments stop we would like description of rocket and emplacement and scale of rocket and projector production at peenemuende repeat peenemuende." Or another Britich enquiry: "Please report if any heavy practise firing in baltic in rugen area or if any target practice being carried out with bornholm or its vicinity as target stop."[17]

Acknowledgements of the answers from Denmark take such forms as:[18] "Will you please tell Bannock (The Intelligence organisation) that Hannibal is delighted with the vast amount of intelligence material that they have been able to send through. It is greatly appreciated by all Service Departments concerned."

The events of 29 August, however, came to mean a temporary – but only temporary – halt in the intelligence service. As stated previously, the Intelligence officers decided, a few days after the violent German assumption of power, to go to Sweden. Irrespective of what weighty grounds officers may have had to take this step, their departure was naturally a hard blow for the leaders of SOE, perhaps especially because it seems to have been unexpected. In "The Spark and the Flame"[19] Muus describes his disappointment in pungent terms, and we can follow the reaction at their departure in contemporary documents, which are no less pungent in tone. A letter to Turnbull a few days later reads in part:[20] "It was a great disappointment to me that G. Bannock (G = Gyth. Bannock = the Intelligence organisation) left the country; I had lunch with him two or three days before he left and at that time he stated most emphatically that he intended to stay on and that his whole organisation as such still existed. I cannot see that ... he couldn't go on living under ground as for instance, Orange (Mogens Fog) has done for nearly a year. I have begun to set up an organisation similar to Bannock's ... Obviously it doesn't make it any easier that G. Bannock did'nt leave a word of information for me prior to his departure. As you will gather from above I am rather bitter ... but it may be due to lack of correct information." To this Muus adds his bitterness at the officers having asked Duus Hansen to follow them to Sweden, a proposal which, as we know, he rejected.[21]

Within a few days Duus Hansen also writes to Turnbull, and describes his feeling of being left in the air, after the officers' departure:[22] "Before Bannock (the Intelligence officers) crossed to you, we spoke of the organization being able to go on functioning and still supply you with intelligence. Unfortunately Bannock gave me no information on where I could address messages, and I therefore counted on receiving an enquiry from someone or other, but this has not yet occurred. It is possible that Bannock expected me to leave immediately after, and has therefore done nothing. But I have no intention of leaving, as long as there is any possibility of remaining here, and I would therefore appreciate it, if you would put me in contact, through Bannock, with the remaining members here at home, so that the Intelligence Service can be re-established as before."[23]

It is clear, from the remarks quoted, that after the officers' departure, SOE's leaders were not briefed on the plans which were later decided for continuing intelligence work, and that they were considering building up an intelligence net themselves. No briefing was received from London, either. This seems to have been the situation well into the autumn of 1943. On 24 November Duus Hansen is still reporting that he has succeeded in getting some connexions within the police force and among officers, but that he does not know for certain whether London wishes him to try to obtain information and forward it. "Since 29 August I have not heard a word from you," he writes to Hollingworth.[24]

The officers did, however, arrange for the intelligence work to be carried on, as it was put in the hands of Svend Truelsen, Secretary of the Agricultural Union. After the necessary re-organization, he took up the work where the officers had left it.[25] Plans for the future included the idea of establishing a radio service between Denmark and the officers in Sweden, but this does not seem to have been carried out.[26]

Muus was thus right in his supposition, that his bitterness could be accounted for by a lack of exact information. Nevertheless, it is strange that he and Duus Hansen were kept in ignorance for many weeks of these important arrangements. The reason may have been, amongst others, that London now wished to separate the intelligence work completely from the growing operational work, and therefore refrained from confiding the plans to SOE; also Duus Hansen may have been regarded as so closely involved with the men of SOE that it was best to exclude him, in case he did not separate himself from SOE and follow the officers to Sweden. That was the last thing Duus Hansen wished to do. His loyalty to the work in SOE ruled this out – a loyalty which, right from 1941, had been the fundamental motive in his illegal work, and after Muus's arrival in Denmark was stronger than ever. Behind this whole development one again feels the opposition between the two Resistance organisations, which were harnessed together in the common struggle, but which, throughout their career, found it extremely difficult to pull together.

It should be mentioned briefly that Muus was also in contact with officers of the Navy. In July 1943 he informs Hollingworth,[27] that he has had some conversations with Commander Bahnsen, and that on one occasion he underlined the bad impression which the surrender of the torpedo boats in 1941 had made in the free world. Duus Hansen also refers to such conversations in his account[28] and adds, that his statement had made a great impression on the Naval Command. We know, however, that the information cannot have come as much of a shock. The Naval Command had already been thoroughly informed, in 1941, of this fact.[29]

In connexion with the account of SOE's contact with the Army it will be natural also to consider the close connexion which existed with individuals in the Danish Police. A close contact with members of the Army and Police were among the foundation stones in the construction of SOE's organization, and from both quarters invaluable services were rendered to the members of SOE.

Co-operation between parachutists and Danish policemen were of no new date. They went back, as we have seen, to the spring of 1942, when Detective Inspector Roland Olsen had been able and willing to give Sneum, Gyberg and Duus Hansen indispensable support in a critical situation, and the confidential and sympathetic co-operation had not been interrupted in the following period, but through all the hardships had developed and strengthened; and now – in spring 1943 – the full value of the co-operation showed itself and became a fundamental reason for the relative security in which SOE could now work. This basic point of view should be maintained and emphasized, even while one keeps the unreasonable, grim episodes from the autumn of 1942 in mind. Even though it is true, that at Johannesen's and Rottbøll's deaths and to some extent at the capture of the three parachutists at Skodsborg, as well as in other instances, Danish police actions against their compatriots completely lacked the sympathy and flexibility which these difficult situations demanded; and even though it is true, that co-operation with individual members of the Police proved fruitless in some cases, in the face of the collective Police machinery, it is no less true that contact with many warm-hearted, sterling Danish policemen both then and not least in 1943 proved extremely valuable and contributed in no small degree to the Resistance work which was gradually developing.

After the Occupation ended, the Danish Police were often judged with prejudice, because of the situations where they undeniably acted wrongly in the administration of a policy which assigned a desperate duty to them; and in the same way, a great many of the accounts upon which this exposition is partly founded express an essentially critical view of the Police and its work, just as Resistance literature teems with accusations against the Police. Complaints against the Police and its zeal in combatting members of the Resistance are frequent in these reports, and the attitude toward the Police is negative to a marked degree, even from narrators who received much direct help in their work from individual policemen. There is nothing strange in this. The tragic consequences in those cases, where the Police or individual members of the Police Force acted without sufficient understanding of the demands of the situation were so glaring, that a reaction was unavoidable, and many of the narrators could only, in the nature of things, regard the

Police as an enemy – as the most dangerous of all enemies. From these quarters a graduated, just impression of the conditions cannot be expected.

On this background, particularly, it seems right here, where the documentary material tells a somewhat different story, to stress the bright sides of the picture. The object is not to settle accounts and weigh assets against liabilities – such a balance sheet would be irrelevant, if only because the values in question are so different – but simply to underline that the assets are enormous, and are all too often forgotten. When a Roland Olsen released Gyberg on the Town Hall Square, and turned away and fed the pigeons; when an Østergaard-Nielsen, when cross-examining Erling Foss, put the words into his mouth; when a Weiss suggested to the Police Commissioner Odmar that he be allowed to make a lenient arrest of Rottbøll; when a Haakon Lauritzen telephoned to Støvring and gave warning of a police raid on Farsø – in these as in hundreds of other cases the spirit of the Danish Police showed itself. The hundreds of cases must be stressed here, for the very reason that this is a part of the truth which is most easily overlooked.

As mentioned, Muus's connexion with the Police, effected chiefly through Duus Hansen, was an asset he inherited from 1942. The connexion is evident, for example from references in his letters to London to information he had received through the Police in cases concerning SOE and its work. In connexion with the Frederikshavn affair[30] and various sabotage cases, mentioned in a long list of sabotage actions dated 21 May 1943, he states:[31] "Above report is an extract from the official Police-report." The fact that the contact with the Police was Duus Hansen is clear from another sentence in the same letter, where it is stated of him that he has "excellent connexions with the 'Yard'".

We have already had the opportunity of noting Duus Hansen's close contact with the Police, and it also appears in his own letters to Hollingworth and Turnbull. In both archives there are a number of reports, based on information which Duus Hansen has received direct from the Danish Police – several of them have already been mentioned in these pages[32] – and in his collection of sabotage reports and miscellaneous intelligence, which was sent to England in a number of photo copies, made on the copying paper used at the Police Headquarters.[33] In August 1943 it even seems to have been a routine matter to supply Duus Hansen and through him SOE with the information which the Police received. In Roland Olsen's account, at least, it is stated:[34] "A type-writer stood ready for use day and night with paper and carbon copies, on which the situation reports were taken down hour for hour ... Copies were sent both to the Government and to the Germans, and the extra copy to London was naturally not forgotten in this case either."

The value of a quick and reliable connexion with the Police was obviously very great, particularly in the period up to 29 August, when the Police still had the official duty of taking part in investigations in cases which were particularly interesting for SOE. In a great many critical situations this contact made it possible to take counter-measures, prepare evidence, suppress information etc., or in other serious cases it made flight possible, where this was a necessity.[35] One particularly clear example of the value of the direct co-operation with the Police is given in a report to the special archive for the Fyn region, where it is stated:[36] "To create the best possible security for the members of the organization,[37] contact with the Police was sought, and found in Police-Sergeant Vogelius Andersen and Detective-Inspector Troelsen both in the Technical Police Department. As members of the technical department they had special qualifications for being able to give protection to members of the organization, first in that they obtained information on the knowledge received by the Security Police on the sabotage which was carried out, and secondly because they had the possibility of removing evidence of sabotage on the spot, as they always received advance information as to where and when sabotage would take place ... In addition one was able through them to follow the effectiveness of sabotage carried out."

Co-operation with the Police in the spring of 1943 was thus not only close but also extremely comprehensive. Furthermore, it seems as if it was meeting increasing sympathy within the ranks of the Police, partly owing to the general growing opposition to the Germans, and partly no doubt because the episodes which had taken place in an earlier period between police and parachutists were such as to expose the nationally untenable position of the Police. The logical development was that in the degree that the parachutists extended their work and merged into the growing Resistance, the Police had to draw back from agreements on co-operation with the German authorities, or take up a hopeless conflict with the population – a conflict just as unacceptable to the majority of policemen as for their officers. Here was the Occupation's grim question of balance, again. And events were inevitably tilting the scales to the side of the will to resist. The process was in full swing.

We hear of it in an optimistic letter from Roland Olsen to Hollingworth from this period.[38] Roland Olsen analyses the situation in Denmark as a whole and comes to the conclusion that in general, it is developing in the "right" direction, and the morale of the population is good; that German attempts to win them over are rejected, and also that good anti-German work is carried out in spite of every difficulty. Regarding special conditions in the Police he writes: "A few days ago we were informed at Police Headqquarters that there is satisfaction in the highest places ... with the work carried out by the staff of the political departments of the Police. This message was brought to the personnel by the Permanent Secretary, Eivind Larsen, direct from His Majesty the King ... In the rest of the country by

216

the way, opinions are divided on these departments' work, and especially the Communists have threatened more than once with severe measures after the war, but developments are bringing more and more members of the Police to realise that also in this sphere there is something called 'Danish work'. Arrests are still made, however, but I suppose it is necessary to keep the fiction alive, and in spite of everything there are also police who are more policemen than Danes."

Work which was directly friendly to the Resistance, which was done by a growing number of police, naturally met with the warmest recognition in England. In a letter from Turnbull to Roland Olsen this is unequivocally expressed:[39] "... I express my thanks and appreciation for all you do to help our efforts ... although I regard your very valuable contribution as a Danish contribution, I would like to express our deepest appreciation, as strongly as possible, for everything you are doing ... I have heard of ... the countless ways in which you have helped our people ... We know the risks you have run, and continue to run ... Once more, – Thank you for all you have done." A long and extremely appreciative letter also came from Hollingworth, who expresses his thanks in the warmest terms for the services rendered to the work.[40]

The events of 29 August were naturally of the greatest importance to all the work described here. In the first place, an alteration took place in the whole field of police activity, and hereafter the Danish Police withdrew from all the special cases which up to then had been dealt with under the Special Public Prosecutor – principally cases concerning sabotage, espionage and "Zersetzung".[41] The new practice – for no actual agreement was reached – relieved the Police greatly in its relations with the population. For the work of the Resistance, the change in the police position was a decided advantage, even though, in connexion with the special work described here it also meant that access to glimpses of the German cards was now reduced. Temporarily it also meant that several of the Police had to escape to Sweden, such as, immediately after 29 August, Roland Olsen and Max Weiss.[42]

Contact with the Police was quickly re-established, however. In September 1943 Duus Hansen can write to Hollingworth,[43] that "connexion is again established with the 'Yard'. It is not so good as before, but we can at least follow the Germans' work in broad outline." Eight days later he touches on the same subject in a letter to Turnbull:[44] "Unfortunately it is becoming more difficult to get good information from 'the Yard', as many of our friends are gone now, but we have already got a couple of substitutes,[45] who can give us the news, but on broad lines only, as the Danish Police must not deal with cases of sabotage, espionage or illegal activities any longer."

The same day Duus Hansen is able to forward Hollingworth detailed accounts of developments in Denmark in a report with the heading, "Various

217

Communications received from Friends at the 'Yard'".[46] The interruption after 29 August was thus of short duration, and Duus Hansen's fear, that it would be more difficult in future to obtain what information the police might have, proved unfounded. Frequent police reports in Duus Hansen's archive, also after 29 August, make this clear. Here as everywhere in the history of Danish Resistance, it is evident that behind the movement were reserves of such dimensions that they never at any point ran out – no un-essential feature of the movement's character.

18. Hvidsten

Up to now this book has had to deal primarily with the work of planning. The path has been long and hard, toward the final goal for these plans, for all these theories, counsels, agreements and experiments, and it is not to be wondered at, if the reader, after patient perusal, is beginning impatiently to ask for the results which came out of all the planning. But now we have finished our wanderings, and can move out on to the reception fields in Jutland, there to listen for the buzz of the planes, see the parachutes open, and later follow the material farther on its way to the sabotage points.

One could have shortened the journey and made the path, which was painful and seemingly unending to those who followed it, with all its dangers, its disappointments, and all its trivialities, easy and comfortable for the reader. This would have done violence to one of the decisive truths behind the Resistance Movement: That its final victory rested on a mountain of endless preparations, carried out by thousands of people, in thousands of different ways and in thousands of different places. Therefore was it, that the first part of the saga must be long, and must often march time. The impatient – and most Resistance workers were impatient – had in those days too to arm themselves with patience and persistence in their endeavours to make the road passable. If the best of them had failed on this point, there would have been no Resistance. Now Resistance was a fact, and we can turn our attention to the outward struggle.

Our first station is in Jutland – in the Randers district, where Juncker, co-operating with Geisler from March 1943, was occupied in building up the Resistance machinery which in the coming months was to pump out supplies and potential into the whole of the Danish Resistance corps, as well as turn to account a long series of possibilities in Jutland, densely occupied as it was by German troops. We thus take up the thread again where we dropped it, when we followed Muus to Copenhagen for an orientation on the work of organization which he started there. Parallel with this – quiet as it had to be – ran the brilliant operations in the field, which we have seen London headquarters praise in the letters to Muus. Let us try and investigate, as accurately as possible what happened. Let us, in accordance with the plan for this thesis, now follow the parachutists and so the Resistance work which expanded around them. We accompany Ole Geisler into the area where he came to exert such efforts.

Geisler parachuted down near Fureso Lake in February 1943[1] and immediately tried to contact Hammer. At about the same time Juncker returned from Stockholm, where he had discussed plans with Turnbull for the parachute droppings on 11–12 March. In Copenhagen he now arranged with Hammer that Geisler and Adolf Larsen should go to Jutland to lead the proposed reception programme on SOE's behalf, in preparation for the intense sabotage which was now their aim.[2] Hammer then directed the two men to Jutland. We have heard of Adolf Larsen's fate. Here we are considering Geisler's. That was certainly rather different.

Unfortunately there is no written account from Geisler of the extensive work accomplished while he was in Denmark – a period of a little over two years. I wrote to him in 1947 and again in 1948, asking him to write a report, and he answered from South Africa, where he was staying, in very favourable terms. But his health was already so undermined, partly as the result of the pressure he had lived under during the Occupation, that he was not equal to completing the report before he died, on 4 October 1948. A description of him must therefore needs be the description of the deeds in which he played such a decisive rôle. It is only in glimpses that we see the outline of his tall, lanky figure, behind the events. It is only through his comrades' and collaborators' testimony that, now and then, he comes alive for us.[3]

Precisely when he went to Jutland, it is not possible to determine, but it seems to have been immediately after Juncker's return from Stockholm and his conversations with Hammer, probably just at the beginning of March. We know that Muus met him in Randers, well established and in full activity, a few days after his arrival in Denmark on 12 March,[4] and we shall see that Geisler took part in the reception on Trinderup heath, the night of the twelfth. In Henning Brøchner's report we read:[5]

"At the end of February or the beginning of March 1943 I was rung up by ... the furrier Jørgen Boje, who asked me to come over to him at once ... at first he made some vague remarks about whether I would be willing to bicycle out and take reception of something from a plane. I asked him to speak freely, and he told me then that four or five men were needed, and together we made out the following list ...: Svend Aage Frederiksen, Peter Jensen, Eigil Thornsberg and ourselves. The next evening we met in the flat of Boje's widowed mother ..." Here, in addition to those mentioned, were Juncker, Geisler and Adolf Larsen, and the account continues: "Geisler and Juncker now explained what the task was – to find a suitable place for dropping. In fact Juncker had already found a place ... The same evening we were to listen to the radio ... The next evening we got the message, and Geisler, Andy Larsen, Thornsberg, Svend Aage Frederiksen and Peter Jensen left. They managed to get contact, and took reception of weapons and explosives ... Early next morning I was in touch with Ole Geisler and Boje, and we discussed what we should do with the stuff, which lay, covered up, out in the plantation."

In a historical account one should hardly drift too far from the naked facts. And yet the temptation can sometimes be too strong. The Resistance struggle was, after, far more than naked facts. Its elements constantly seize the imagination. Imagine that meeting in Mrs. Boje's flat, one evening in March 1943. Out of it developed the famous Hvidsten receptions, with all they included – the violently expanding sabotage of the spring and summer, which led on to the great general strike in August, and to the 29th of August. Even though one cannot say to what degree that meeting came to be decisive for this development, one can certainly establish the fact that we are present at a council of war of greater importance than the participants could possibly conceive. Truly it was a strange council of war, where the civilian elements were dominant. The place: the living-room in an elderly widow's flat. Those present: a Danish land-owner; a Danish engineer who, after service in the Hong Kong Police, was trained as a pilot in a Norwegian camp in Canada and later as parachutist in England; a Danish cowboy from the Argentine, trained as a parachutist in England; Brøchner, a gentlemen's outfitter; Jørgen Boje, furrier and Scoutmaster; and three or four of their personal friends, ordinary Danes, who were now suddenly whirled into one of the most dramatic chapters in Danish history. The story of the Resistance is full of similar situations and perspectives. Is it not part of the historian's task now and then to make a halt, and cast his eye over these perspectives, and, without this, would not the story be less true?

March 10, at the latest, Geisler was in Randers, then, and in contact with Juncker and the little group that was hastily collected for the first in the series of receptions that were to follow. After completing this reception and preparing for the next, Geisler went to Aarhus, where he settled for a number of months, as his work came to lie mostly in the Randers district and the neighbourhood of Aarhus. Whilst Muus became leader of staff work, Geisler became leader of the work in the field. We can follow his establishment in the Aarhus headquarters of those days. In the editor Aage Schoch's record he writes[6] that he came into contact with Geisler immediately after the latter's arrival in Denmark, and that before Geisler left for Jutland, he gave him the address of the dental surgeons, the Misses Jøker in Aarhus. Geisler seems already to have visited them and spent the night before he came to Randers on 10 or 11 March. Brøchner mentions, at least, that he came to Randers from Aarhus, where he "spent the night at the Misses Jøkers' in Aarhus."[7] After the Trinderup reception, when he returned to Aarhus to get established, he stayed first with the Misses Jøker again, and it seems that without this help it would have been difficult for him to settle in the town. Juncker and Dr. Baastrup Thomsen, who quickly became his most important contact in the town, both describe his difficulies in finding a place to live.

Juncker's account reads:[8] "Geisler was to settle permanently in Aarhus, where, however, it was very difficult to get him placed. There was no one who would take on the responsibility, and I had to run from pillar to post before finally succeeding with Miss Jøker, the doctor, whose address we had been given by Schoch. Generally speaking, there was a very poor spirit in Aarhus at that period of the Occupation." Baastrup Thomsen supplements:[9] "One of the last days of February 1943 I was rung up by the Economics M.A., Aksel Voigt ... there was something important he wanted to discuss ... I was to meet him and Miss Jøker at the latter's flat ... Here sat a tall, lanky, charming man, who called himself Aksel Nielsen, and who asked whether I could and would house him ... I said, Yes, of course, to this, and he moved ... over to my flat. He had landed by parachute a few days earlier, so he told me a little later ... and after Schoch, the editor, had given him the Jøkers' address ... he had come to Jutland. He was originally accompanied by another parachutist ... who had been betrayed ... and Geisler's cover address at the Jøkers' was compromised; he had to get away as there was fear of a razzia in the Jøkers' flat ... It was important to find several practicable lodgings in the Aarhus area. But it turned out to be extremely difficult, as the atmosphere was very little in favour of active work. I combed ... my ... circle of acquaintances, and succeeded, in co-operation with the bank clerk Bach Frederiksen, ... in finding three or four flats."

After several weeks had passed, it was thus still a problem for Geisler to get a roof over his head in the strange town. During the attempts to find lodging he came into contact with Bach Frederiksen, and then the way opened for the solution of one of his main problems, the telephone connexion through Aarhus Privatbank with Copenhagen and so with London. This side of Geisler's establishment has already been described.[10] With this connexion behind him and supported by the parachutists who now came under his leadership, he could turn to co-operation with Juncker and to the contacts he obtained almost everywhere in Jutland, thanks to Juncker's energetic work.[11] Now the first priority was to organise reception and so procure material.

With the Trinderup dropping, for the first time, British explosives and other sabotage materiel were obtained. The small, hastily improvised reception team had not managed to remove the materiel during the night, however, and it seems as though the important question of getting the materiel away and into storage had not yet reached a considered solution. On the morning of 12 March, as we have heard, the materiel lay, covered, out in the plantation near Skrødstrup. The question of its coming fate must be solved immediately, and the solution of this question brings us straight into the heart of the reception work which now started at Hvidsten.

During the discussions on the morning of 12 March[12] Brøchner proposed mentioning the problem to his doctor, Thorup Petersen, to see if he would put his car at their disposal for transport. Thorup Petersen agreed to this, and also mentioned the innkeeper Marius Fiil in Hvidsten as a man who would surely be willing to give assistance. Geisler and Thorup Petersen then went to Hvidsten and immediately obtained Fiil's promise of help. In the course of the next two days Fiil transported the materiel by horse cart to Hvidsten, from where it was conveyed on to Randers in Thorup Petersen's car. In Randers it was stowed temporarily in Jørgen Boje's store-rooms.

This store, however, was quickly abandoned, as it was regarded as unsuitable and the materiel was then removed to Brøchner's business storage-rooms. Brøchner himself writes:[13] "... the stuff was brought in small packages and suitcases up into my store-rooms ... There the materiel was unpacked, and from there it was distributed during the next three or four months, together with stuff from all the following receptions." The removal must have been carried out almost immediately. At least it was at Brøchner's about a week after the dropping, when Muus passed through Randers[14] and went through the materiel with Geisler. Later it was moved to other more suitable storage.[15] The details of this are not important, but it should be stressed that in the spring of 1943, until receptions started elsewhere, Randers was the main centre from which sabotage materiel was distributed, by courier or in other ways, to the rest of the country.[16] Even the reception point was soon changed. Marius Fiil had succeeded in forming a local reception team, the famous Hvidsten Group, which constituted the core of the team who took part in the various receptions, but who were supplemented alternately with parachutists under Geisler's leadership, and with men from Randers. After this it was obviously unreasonable to use a reception point as far away as Trinderup – the distance from there to Hvidsten is about ten kilometres as the crow flies – and Fiil therefore proposed moving the point[17] to a spot near the inn, from where materiel as well as parachutists could quickly be brought to relative safety. In the following period new receptions were carried out there, and went surprisingly well. Brøchner who, as we shall see, had first-hand knowledge of developments, writes:[18] "In the following period new receptions followed each other in quick succession. On various occasions I was there myself, but I cannot quite keep all the receptions separate in my mind. I do, however, remember that a series of parachutists passed through our home, after the receptions,[19] and were supplied with money, instructions on general conditions in Denmark, clothes, etc. The money was received at intervals from Ole Geisler."

The new reception point was quickly accepted in London, and was already functioning in the full moon period in April, where reception was evidently carried out on the night of 17 April, when Kaj Lund came over, and on 21 April, when Lok Linblad came over. Both report on the reception at Hvidsten, where they were received by members of the Hvidsten Group, as well as by Ole Geisler and Verner Johansen. As an illustration, Lok Linblad's account is given here:[20] "I crossed over on 21 April and came down at Hvidsten together with four containers. I had with me compass, revolver, 2000 Kr., crystals, undeveloped films for Geisler, map of the area, and contact addresses in Mariager with code name (the address was given by Bork-Johansen) ... In Hvidsten I was received by the inn-keeper and his son and son-in-law, the veterinary surgeon Iversen and Anders Stenz (the famous Hvidsten Group)[21] as well as Ole Geisler and Verner Johansen. I was driven to the son-in-law's house and spent the night there. The next morning I was driven to Randers by Torup Pedersen."[22]

We seem now to be familiar with the arena for events. We know the most important of the actors as well as the scenery. On the basis of Lok Linblad's matter-of-fact words and of the seeming simplicity and ease with which the reception work was now accomplished, one might get the impression that this work was already running on a simple, easy routine, which contained no problems. Nothing could be further from the truth. Every one of these operations was, as long as the Occupation lasted, a deadly dangerous and extremely difficult affair, where human lives were always at stake, and where the smallest accident could lead to catastrophe, for the plane crew, for the parachutists, and for the men on the ground. No one has given more clear-cut or finer expression for this than Stig Jensen, who – certainly at a much later period of the Occupation when he acted as reception chief for Sjælland – in a detailed report to Hollingworth, after analysing the difficulties in reception work, ends with the words:[23] "I am afraid these lines will make you think we take these things lightly.[24] This is a misunderstanding. We take them with deadly seriousness, and think out and carry through the work with the most meticulous care. We know what is accomplished from your side, and we especially admire the RAF's daring pilots, who again and again find the way through the pitch-dark night to the poor little points, where we have fixed our rendez-vous and wait for them with patience, but impatiently. We are longing to see their mugs and shake their fists and say "Thank you". While I sit writing these lines, four well-known names are sounding through the ether.[25] In five minutes, 200 men will start preparing what we hope will be a happy event and a desired arrival. Lights are checked, weapons are brought out of their hiding-places. Lorries with MGs[26] mounted on the driver's cabin roll out after the cycle patrols. The area of the point, the packing place, the depot is reconnoitred once more for the last time. The guards mount their posts, and then we all listen, out in the night, for the angry, egging buzz. If he comes, he can find us."

As mentioned, these words come from a later period, where infinitely more experience had been gained, and where the organisation was infinitely better constructed. Nevertheless, they contain such a fine characterization of Resistance work as such – regardless of the period – that they should be quoted here as accompaniment to the description of the Hvidsten Group's pioneer work. As a further corrective to Lok Linblad's sober account, and as testimony that even the luckiest and least eventful reception had its problems, Muus's report to Hollingworth can be quoted, also a propos Kaj Lund's and Lok Linblad's reception:[27] »... we should like to point out that in both cases, but particularly in the last case when Habit (Lok Linblad) landed, the aircraft flew far too high probably between 1000 to 1100 feet – and the despatch could very well have been observed for miles, – fortunately this was not the case but we would like to have the aircraft to go down between 300 and 400 feet. Furthermore it is dangerous to have the plane fly straight to the spot, despatch the cargo, and return in a beeline. This was very much the case when Lamp (Kaj Lund) arrived whilst Habit's plane spent far too much time over the spot making huge circles, despatching containers firstly and only 5 to 6 minutes afterwards did Habit appear. As a matter of fact, the ground staff was of the opinion that only the containers were being landed and the lights had been removed when the 'plane appeared again landing habit.''

Muus touches here on a couple of the multitudinous technical problems involved in the completion of every dropping operation, and which in some respects became more marked, as the number of droppings increased. On the other hand, the thousands of dropping operations which SOE in conjunction with the RAF came to carry out all over the world, brought with them the development of enormously expert technique and the harvest of countless valuable lessons. Before we go any further in describing the dropping work, which followed on the heels of the first Hvidsten receptions, it will be useful to draw up the main lines of the work involved in every single dropping. We shall therefore examine closely the basic instructions which Hollingworth sends to Muus in May, regarding organisation of reception preparations, and so get a glimpse of the special technique which was now being developed in this domain.[28]

A primary condition for a methodical and fairly certain performance in such operations was the establishment of the radio service. This condition was now a fact in Denmark, and we can leave this side of the work for the moment. The next difficulty was connected with purely astronomic conditions. Since it was necessary to be able to see, the light nights around full moon were preferred for these operations, and here at once we have a limiting factor. In the case of Denmark, the short, light summer nights were the next limiting factor, as the RAF – in 1943 – flatly refused to have anything to do with droppings during this period. Hollingworth writes:[29] "Owing to the short nights we are unable to do any dropping during the month of June. After the middle of July, however, this disadvantage will turn in our favour in that for some considerable time we shall be able to conduct *non-moon* operations." Apart from the critical period, and in favourable light conditions, it was thus possible to carry out dropping operations.

The initiative came from England. Several weeks in advance it would be calculated from there, to what extent it was possible, in view of general strategic demands, to count on an allowance of materiel and machines for operations over Denmark; and in accordance with this London asked the Resistance men in Denmark to give particulars of possible suitable reception points. The likelihood of allocation of materiel and machines depended upon London's assessment of the importance of the work in the country in question, and here Denmark was working its way up, and its position was gradually improving.[30] In the instructions to Muus, Hollingworth defines the situation with the words:[31] "When the 'balloon goes up' which, now the whole of Tunisia is ours,[32] may happen sooner than we imagined, the RAF will be so busy on other jobs that it will be difficult for us to obtain the aircraft we shall ... So between now and then it is up to us to make the best use of our opportunities ... To make the most of this on a wholesale scale will require sound and careful consideration and the following paragraphs give you an idea of what we can deliver and how we suggest reception should be organized at your end."

In accordance with the demands in the instructions, a systematic reconnaissance of suitable points[33] now begins in Denmark, and they are then proposed to London. In this work there are naturally a long series of conditions to take into consideration: the situation of the place, the approaches, dwellings in the neighbourhood, the situation of German defences, etc., as well as possible landmarks in the area, which can make it possible for the pilot to find the place, even in unfavourable conditions. Hollingworth specifies the requirements as follows:[34] "1. There must be good landmarks in the neighbourhood. 2. Lights must be well away from trees, which cause them appear to be 'flashing'. 3. The points must be well away from ack-ack posts and fighters." Then follows a list of detailed demands regarding the position of the reception points in relation to each other, which have a bearing on the work described below.

When reconnaissance is complete, the place is proposed to London,[35] after which the RAF decides whether, in view of the state of the approaches and possible enemy installations near the flight course, etc., they can accept it. A long list of proposed points was rejected – for instance, for fairly long periods the RAF turned down proposals for operations on Zealand and in South Jutland[36] – and many more places had to be reconnoitred and proposed than the number required. Added to this, London wished each point to have another place in reserve nearby, so that the dropping could

226

be attempted at the second point, if contact failed at the first; also, every aircraft carrying fifteen containers was to deliver these at three different places, five at each point or its reserve. The three points, with corresponding reserve points, were to form a group, according to the British proposal, and London asked for three such groups, in all, for the period 18 July to 25 September, with eighteen points altogether, to be reconnoitred and accepted. The three points were to be used in succession, with two droppings at those of each group, before changing over to the second or third group, presuming, of course, that none of the places in question became compromised.

Such a detailed system as that specified in Hollingworth's proposal does not seem to have been put into effect, and it is mentioned here to illustrate the extent of the reconnaissance work required for a dropping programme "according to the book". Even with the adaptations accepted in the end, the work to find suitable places and getting them approved was very considerable.

Once the point was approved, a "kettle" was agreed for each place, i.e. a code word or phrase, which when given on the BBC would announce that a dropping would be carried out at that place on that night; and a time table would be given of the approximate hour for droppings in the different phases of the moon that month. The necessary light signals were also fixed, for exchange between the plane crew and the men on the ground immediately before the dropping. This was partly for the pilot to be sure that no hindrance for the completion of the operation had for any reason arisen, and partly to lead him to the precise spot. After this it was up to the RAF crew to make such an accurate dropping of the material that it landed on the reception point – a task which had to be carried out according to the height of the plane, the speed, the wind force, etc. It can be mentioned in conclusion that a so-called "crack" signal – a radio signal, usually a short group of numbers – was fixed to make sure that the radio service could quickly confirm that last minute arrangements for the dropping had been received and understood, or the contrary. For example, the radio service in Denmark could thus, by sending an agreed group of numbers – 9-3-8 or the like – confirm at the last minute that the reception was prepared and ready, or show that one wished it to be cancelled. These detailed arrangements are given or referred to in the instructions from Hollingworth mentioned previously.

If all this was in order, it remained for the men in the Field to place the reception teams at each point, to organise the alarm system, to provide guards, to make arrangements for light signals, to organise transport and storage, as well as to work out the further distribution of the materiel after reception. Then the dropping could take place in theory and often in practice according to the agreed scheme, but naturally often altered by new difficulties caused by the weather, German intervention, or unforeseen accidents of every kind.

To illustrate how great the difficulties could be for the completion of such a dropping, the following collection of English telegrams can be quoted. They were received by the operator, the veterinary surgeon Duus Hansen, at a later stage of the Occupation:[37]

The question had been put from Odense, whether weapons could be dropped at a given spot on the estate of Rugaard, on North-West Fyn. The following reply was received:

"We can deliver to rugaard rpt rugaard funen stop our eight stop can you receive twelve containers stop will send recognition signals and kettle."

The reply was then given in the affirmative. The next telegram from England said: *"we will deliver twelve containers h.e. (explosives) and stens and pistols rugaard from monday tenth stop groundflashes r for red plainflashes b for beer stop kettle greetings to stefan stop reception times twenty three hundred to nought three hundred ours g.m.t. stop crack nine three eight means you are ready to receive."*

The crack signal was then given, and the following message: *"stand by from to-morrow tuesday stop twelve containers and 1 package stop our fourth listen for greetings to stefan rpt stefan stop good luck."*

The operator now listened for "Greetings to Stefan" and then came the following telegram: *"regret air operation stefan rpt stefan postponed stop our thirteenth stop our thirteenth stop confirm same reception arrangements next moon april 27 until may tenth stop first four rpt four nights most suitable."*

A later telegram announced: *"confirm with crack nine four nine you can recerve twelve containers one package rugaard rpt rugaard from twenty seventh april to tenth may stop our fourteenth stop reception times twentytwo thirty to nought one thirty g.m.t."*

The crack signal was sent, and the following received: *"we will deliver twelve containers one package rugaard from april twentyseventh stop kettle greetings to stefan rpt stefan stop our fifteenth stop plainflashes b for beer ground r for red stop."*

However, there were no "Greetings for Stefan", but the following telegram was received: *"not possible deliver twelve containers stop listen for stefan from tomorrow friday stop our seventeenth stop report general situation funen rpt funen."*

The next day there was a little more: *"stand by saturday twentyninth stop our eighteenth stop will deliver one extra package nine millimetre sten ammunition suitable german arms stop good luck."*

Still no "Greetings to Stefan" — but two days later came the following telegram: *"will deliver first opportunity stop keep listening for stefan rpt stefan stop our fifth stop good luck."*

And again two days later: *"we will deliver rugaard rpt rugaard to-night saturday stop twelve containers two packages stop our sixth stop listen for stefan stop good luck."*

Now at last, "Greetings to Stefan" followed, and the dropping was carried out as planned, but the following day the message came: *"we delivered to stefan saturday night sixth but aircraft has not rpt not returned stop our twenty report immediately stop give every assistance to crew rpt crew."*

The information was given from Denmark that the plane had been shot down on the return flight.

The difficulties might not always be so great, and the majority of droppings did not end so tragically, but these episodes suffice to show that to carry through the whole of this important side of the Resistance struggle was very far from being a simple, straightforward routine matter. On the contrary it was an exceedingly complicated, difficult process, where the work was done with a minimum safety margin, and under intense pressure. It should be added, that in all we have considered, there has been no mention of the difficulties and dangers which met the plane crews. The situation is seen almost entirely from the viewpoint of the reception teams.

It must then be clear that the work carried out in Hvidsten in the spring of 1943, with so little previous experience, must take an outstanding place in the history of the Resistance. These men had every right to the words from England:[38] "First of all we all send you and the boys our hearty thanks and congratulations ... your receptions have been first-class and the air boys wish me to convey a special word of thanks."

On this background one can understand the intense satisfaction and expectation with which the men of Hvidsten received an important piece of equipment for improving reception work, the so-called "S-phone", an instrument which enabled the reception group to get wireless contact with the crew in the approaching plane. This gave them the possibility of directing the aircraft to the exact point, informing the pilot of any special conditions on the landing place, wind force, etc., just as the pilot could inform them precisely what he was dropping and in what order. Finally, the S-phone enabled the men on the ground to tell the pilot the result of the dropping.

The first S-phone was brought over by Peter Carlsen and Poul Hansen, when they landed on 10 May 1943 at Hvidsten, and it was taken into use a week later, on 17 May, at the reception of the three parachutists, Hans Johansen, Vilfred Petersen and Jakob Jensen.[39] In a letter which Peter Carlsen had with him from Hollingworth, there is an appendix[40] with technical instructions for the use of the instrument. In this letter Hollingworth emphasises the importance of using the set as soon as possible, preferably

– and this took place – for the dropping on 17 May:[41] "We would like to conduct the mid-May operation by S-phone, as if it is used successfully in this operation ... it will be invaluable for later operations. The lads who are bringing this message are fully trained in its use ... They should ... teach a member of the reception committee how to work the set for the future ... For the actual operation instead of the call sign "Tommy" the ground will be called "Hitler", and instead of "Albert" the pilot will be called "Mussolini" ... It is possible that you will not be able to use the S-phone for the mid-May operation ... However, we would, if possible, like to make the attempt this time because it will mean so much to the success of future operations when the personnel are thoroughly au fait with the procedure."

There certainly seems to have been certain technical and personal difficulties to overcome. A smile lurks behind the dry reports, in a letter from Muus to Hollingworth:[42] "The 'S' phones were received with delight and everyone was looking forward to use them. However, when the Mustard (Jakob Jensen) Party was about to arrive the 'S' phones were operated by us without result. We have evidence that the pilot HEARD 'HITLER' but had decided, prior to departure from the aerodrome, NOT to answer. 'I don't want to have anything to do with that damn thing' is alleged to have been said by the pilot." Or on 25 July:[43] "Further on 'Sandwich' (Boelsskov) reception: The S-phones were in use and functioned perfectly alright. One draw-back, though. The pilot, operating the 'Mussolini'-end, refused to speak anything but Polish and although we are quite willing to operate the S-phones in Danish, Swedish, Norwegian, German, French, English and two or three African dialects none of us understand Polish which we regret."

The latter situation is also described in Baastrup Thomsen's record; he apparently overheard the conversation that night. His account also gives a picture of Geisler:[44] "Geisler led all these receptions personally ... Both during the receptions and in the other active operations he was himself in the line of fire, calm and firm, and he possessed a charming quiet mastery which made everyone willing to work for him. At one of these receptions we got a so-called S-phone. Geisler operated this as a rule. I well remember the first evening[45] it was to be used. Geisler stood carefully called for the code: "Hitler calling Mussolini." However, it was Poles who were flying the plane, and as I stood beside the S-phone I could clearly hear the Poles discussing in Polish, whereas they made no answer at all to our repeated questions on the S-phone. On the other hand, the Poles were always very reliable pilots and always, with great skill, found the appointed places."

19. Dropping Operations Expanded

In the last chapter we had an opportunity of following the first phase of the important dropping operations at Hvidsten, and of looking fairly closely at the technique of dropping and reception – both in what was aimed at and what, in practice, were its limits in the spring 1943.

We have still to investigate the extent of these dropping operations and their details. We shall confine ourselves to the period up to the middle of August. Whatever was dropped before then could play a rôle in the developments which led to 29 August. After this date, the primary objective of the Resistance – the break with the policy of collaboration – was achieved, and the developments which followed were based upon revised plans. These gradually led to such an expansion of dropping operations and of the work involved, that their volume was totally altered. It would seem, therefore, that there are reasonable grounds for examining the work of dropping and reception in the spring and summer 1943, when the foundation was laid for their later development. This period must be further divided into two phases: from 11 March to the middle of May, and from mid-July to mid-August. As far as the first of these periods is concerned, the historical material permits quite an exact record of the dropping operations, whereas there is some uncertainty as regards the second period.

We have already seen how Hollingworth on 9 May has to inform Muus that the RAF have refused to fly materiel over Denmark after 16 May and up to August, and how, nevertheless, he has succeeded in getting an operation, already arranged for just after 16 May, carried out according to plan, and in having operations started again in the middle of July. We have further seen how Hollingworth on 17 May emphasizes the necessity for accepting this enforced pause, and presses Muus during the interval to work out a considerably increased programme for receptions after mid-July, possibly by preparing for droppings also during periods with less moonlight than believed necessary hitherto.[1]

In the first period there seem to have been six droppings in all: those described, near Trinderup Heath and Hornum Lake on 11–12 March; the four droppings near Hvidsten (on 17 and 21 April and 10 and 17 May). The first two operations have been recounted, and the last four are described in Muus's correspondence with Hollingworth and in the accounts for the archives.[2] We know the men involved. In addition to the four at Hornum, these were Kaj Lund (17 April), Lok Lindblad (21 April), Peter Carlsen and Poul Hansen (10 May) and Hans Johansen, Vilfred Petersen and Jakob Jensen (17 May).

It is more difficult to determine how much materiel was dropped.[3] Most of it must have been dropped on Trinderup Heath, where materiel only was delivered, whereas at Hornum only men were landed. At the four Hvidsten receptions both men and materiel came down. Muus's remark, that the group at Hvidsten quickly coped with the containers received, goods, etc., points to this, as does the complaint that when Lok Linblad landed, the containers were dropped several minutes before he jumped.[4] In his account Lok Linblad mentions that he had four containers with him.[5] Brøchner, in his account, states that it took two days to transport the stuff received from Trinderup to Hvidsten. Fiil must have made at least two more trips after this. Lastly Brøchner, who supplied the storage room for the material, speaks of "stuff from all the following receptions".[6] This is the last piece of concrete information in this interesting point.

One can, however, make certain calculations which may be of assistance for an approximate estimate. In the letter to Muus of 17 May, in which Hollingworth outlines the plans for the dropping programme for the summer,[7] he calculates with a maximum of fifteen containers per plane, on condition that no personnel is to be dropped. It should therefore be possible at least to estimate the absolute maximum for the deliveries in question. At Hornum, four men came down, but no materiel. If we calculate roughly one man as equalling four containers, and take these figures as a starting point, we arrive at the following absolute maxima:

Hornum	4 men	0 containers
Trinderup	0 men	15 containers
Hvidsten 1.	1 man	11 containers
Hvidsten 2.	1 man	11 containers
Hvidsten 3.	2 men	7 containers
Hvidsten 4.	3 men	3 containers
In all	11 men	47 containers

It must be stated at once, that the estimated figures are probably far too high. For example, according to Lok Linblad's information in his account, only four containers were dropped with him (Hvidsten 2.); in the above table we calculated with eleven containers, to be on the safe side, and have presumed that Lok Linblad may not have remembered the correct quantity. This is not important, however. What is essential is that it is quite evident that at best, there can only be a question of very limited quantities and the following examination of the period July-August, as we shall see, will confirm this main conclusion.

The dropping operations in question took place, generally speaking, according to plan and without serious accidents. It seems that now a little of the luck which SOE had hitherto lacked, and which was sorely needed for the work, made its appearance at last. It was only in the last of the droppings that the operation trembled on the brink of disaster. Muus relates:[8] "Mustard, Pudding and Brawn (Jakob Jensen, Vilfred Petersen and Hans Johansen) landed according to plan – everything went alright. The Huns were exercising on OUR field all afternoon up till 20 minutes before the aircraft was expected.[9] When they had 'won' their exercise they, the Huns, cleared out and we entered the field." Seen from Copenhagen, the episode did not look overwhelmingly dramatic. Seen from Hvidsten inn, the evening's work was decidedly more colourful. In Peter Carlsen's account we read:[10] "Out at Hvidsten I went in to Tulle. Here we sat and chatted for a little while, listened to the radio at 6 o'clock, which confirmed that the plane was coming ... while we sat there comfortably chatting, someone suddenly looked out of the window and noticed that a whole lot of German soldiers were walking about, carrying apparatus which looked like radio sets ... As the Germans went on walking and snooping out there, Fiil suddenly said he was going to go out and see what was the matter ... A little while later he came in again and reassured us in his sober way, that it was all all right. It was just some soldiers on an exercise. He had gone over to them and started chatting with them, and had invited them to coffee and Danish pastries ... and they had then told him they were on an exercise, and would be going back to their barracks before long." The whole thing illustrates Fiil's quiet, steady way of behaving in such a situation.[11]

Soon after the middle of July, the dropping operations were resumed. The request to find new reception points for an expanded programme had now borne fruit. At least from now on and up to the middle of August, droppings were made in various places. On the basis of Muus's report to Hollingworth of 25 July 1943,[12] droppings can be noted at Enebærodde on Fyn in two instances, at Hvidsten once and at Madum Lake once, but other dropping operations were also carried out beside these. At Madum Lake there were at least two droppings, that mentioned in Muus's report,[13] where the parachutists Aage Møller Christensen and Jens Peter Petersen landed, and the well known dropping incident of 17 August, when one of the reception team, Erik Vangsted was killed, and another, Kjær Sørensen, was taken prisoner and later executed.[14] The receptions at Madum Lake were organised by the parachutist Paul Jensen, who was posted permanently in Aalborg. He had originally had his sabotage materiel delivered from the depot in Randers, but during May he had three reception points reconnoitred and approved, amongst them the place at Madum Lake, after which independent reception work was started from Aalborg. Paul Jensen mentions three receptions at Madum, but puts one of them in June, where we have seen that no operations took place.[15] Lapses of memory as regards exact dates are not uncommon in the accounts.

Dropping activities now spread to Zealand also, after the RAF agreed to carry out a dropping operation on Gyldenløveshøj in mid-August.[16] In addition, Geisler's nearest colleagues, Flemming Juncker and Baastrup Thomsen both state[17] that receptions were now carried out at places which had been reconnoitred and approved in the course of the summer, and Jørgen Diemer worked with Juncker at finding new places and getting them approved.[18] Exact details of this work do not come to light in the accounts. Juncker mentions Djursland, but without giving the period in question, and Baastrup Thomsen records, a little more precisely, on the work in Djursland:[19] "... I found a place in Djursland near Langesø. And after it had been approved in London we had two receptions there in the course of the summer. Afterwards this place was compromised ... I then found a place in Rosenholm Forest, working with the scoutmaster Orla Andersen from Hornslet, who was later executed by the Germans. The explosives and somewhat scanty weapons which were received were transported via Hvidsten to Randers."

Curiously enough, a somewhat later document casts light back upon these events, and confirms that receptions did actually take place in Djursland before the end of July. In a letter from Muus to Turnbull[20] from the end of September 1943, Muus proposes four reception points for the period 6–16 October, as follows:

Point 1. JUT. HH – Book 2. Page 15. D 1. South-east of "Høj" in "Skodsborg Høj".
Point 2. JUT. B – Book 1. Page 26. B 3. North of "mm" in "Gammelstrup Hede".
Point 3. Mustard Point.
Point 4. JUT. O. Book 1. Page 38 (used in July).

The references are from the Geodetic Institute map of Denmark in the three-volume edition, and the last of the four points, which according to this was used in July, does actually lie in Djursland.

Muus's letter also clears up some confusion in the historical material regarding the continued dropping at Hvidsten. We know that the parachutist Arne Boelsskov came down here on 23 July. Muus reports on this to London:[21] "... Your Broadcasting-Signal was duly received at 1629 hours GMT on the 22nd inst. and, accordingly, we stood by at all agreed points.[22] At 0028 hours GMT July 23rd, 'Sandwich' (Boelsskov) was dropped at the Mustard Point (Hvidsten. Jakob Jensen = Mustard) ... The signal 'Low flying aircraft approaching, look out for parachutists' was broadcast by the Huns at 0012 hours GMT (16 minutes before 'Sandwich' descended) and they were certainly on their look-out. Unfortunately the 'Mustard Point' has been compromised and we cannot use it anymore. 'Sandwich' and the reception-party had, in fact, a narrow escape."

According to this report, the Hvidsten point was cancelled after this event. Baastrup also mentions that the place was compromised, but adds that Fiil, in spite of warnings through the Danish Police, was willing to continue, and that after this, two more receptions were carried out on the old reception point.[23] Also Doctor Jørgen Røjel, who was doing his hospital service in Randers from the summer of 1943, and became one of the leaders of illegal work there, mentions that the place was cancelled for a time, but was later taken into use again.[24] The letter quoted, from Muus to Turnbull of 21 September 1943, confirms that the place was used again, as the third point proposed, "Mustard Point", is in fact Hvidsten.

It is apparent, therefore, that for the short period we are considering here – from 15 July to approximately 15 August – there is some difficulty in determining the exact volume of the dropping operations. Seven receptions can be established as certain: two at Enebærodde at the end of July;[25] three at Madum Lake, one of them on about 25 July, the others on 2 and 17 August; one at Hvidsten on 23 July; at least one in Djursland before the end of July; and one dropping near Gyldenløveshøj in August.

The list is not quite complete. There may have been other droppings, but enough have been mentioned to illustrate the fact that the pace has been stepped up. In under four weeks, from 22 July to the middle of August, there are at least two more operations than in the nine-week period from 12 March to 17 May. Furthermore, on the basis of those mentioned, it seems reasonable to suppose that considerably more materiel has been dropped than during the period in the spring. Only three parachutists are sent over during the summer period: Boelsskov at Hvidsten on 23 July, and Aage Møller Christensen and Jens Peter Petersen at Madum Lake a day or two later.[26] On both these occasions containers were dropped, and the operations at Enebærodde, Gyldenløveshøj, in Djursland and at Madum Lake on 17 August consisted of material deliveries alone. Possible droppings in addition to these were of materiel only. Nothing further can be deduced from the existing records.

Although the volume of materiel cannot be determined quite precisely for this period, we can, by using another historical source, form an estimate of the absolute maximum of materiel dropped. This is by examining Hollingworth's instructions to Muus of 17 August 1943. These read in part:[27] "When dropping operations recommence in July it is our duty to get as many assorted standard containers to the Field as possible. The next stage after that is to send over specially made up containers for specific jobs ... *Theoretically* it is possible to deliver 200 containers between July 18th and September 25th. Allowing for delays, however, we will set the target at *100 containers*. This sounds a high figure but it can be done if properly organized."

Two hundred containers theoretically possible, and one hundred containers as the target for the whole period up to 25 September – this gives one hundred, and fifty, respectively, for the half period up to the middle of August, to which we have confined ourselves in this instance. These figures, which are announced on the same day as the deliveries of the spring period finish, also cast a light on previous events. After the successful dropping operations in March, April and May, Hollingworth considers one hundred containers a large number. It is clear, at all events, that the above calculation is not set unreasonably low. In this case it is hardly possible to repeat the calculation made for the spring period, since we cannot ascertain the number of droppings with complete certitude, but it is most probable that the droppings during the period from July to August did not much exceed the fifty containers Hollingworth had reckoned in May as a practical possibility, and it should also be remembered that all the materiel at Madum Lake on 17 August fell into the hands of the Germans.

On this basis, the result of the spring and summer deliveries must have amounted to comparatively modest quantities, even though, on the background of the earlier vacuum, they have been felt to be large. In all, the RAF dropped 4,862 containers and 383 parcels over Denmark during the whole of the Occupation.[28] Even if we disregard the parcels and reckon with the maximum number suggested here, the deliveries of British materiel before the middle of August 1943 only total 2–3 % – probably under 2 % – of the entire British deliveries during the whole Occupation. The figure is surprisingly small, compared with the importance of these particular early deliveries, of which it will be our next task to give an account.

However, before turing to look at the materiel received, on its wandering course out into the Danish Resistance organisation, we shall mention briefly a few episodes connected with the dropping operations of the summer. Of the two droppings at Enebærodde, one seems to have gone according to plan. The other, on 22 July, was flavoured with a minor, partly comical episode, from which arose a good deal of scribbling in the Danish-British correspondence. During their training in England the Danish volunteers were strictly enjoined on no account to engage in illegal journalism. We have seen how Hammer was blamed earlier for disregarding this order. In the summer 1943, however, SOE changed their minds on this point, and decided to take on propaganda work in Denmark, with the aid of propaganda material printed in England and sent illegally to Denmark.[29] The editor Sven Seehusen was asked by the British to undertake this, in co-operation with Major Rantzau, and during conversations in Stockholm with Turnbull he agreed to do so.[30]

Muus, who was not originally informed of these negotiations, was very much annoyed when he received news of them, and expressed his irritation in a letter to Turnbull. Turnbull's reply was a fairly long letter, in which he disagrees emphatically and explains the position.[31] He underlines, not without a certain sharpness of tone, that Muus and the "Table" organisation (the parachutists) are to have no part in the propaganda drive – "we have kept you and the Table *entirely* separate from it *and will continue* to do so" (the italics are Turnbull's) – that there is full confidence in Seehusen and Rantzau, and that the decisions have been taken "at a high level"; this implies that no interference will be allowed from Muus on this question. The letter ends with a repetition of the general instruction to Muus to keep clear of all propaganda work, while he is instructed, at the same time, to forward the propaganda material which may be dropped in containers, direct and quickly through an intermediary – Diemer is suggested – to Seehusen, who will be responsible for its distribution in Denmark. The order is somewhat self-contradictory, and Turnbull can hardly have been satisfied with his own position in the affair. At the end he tries to smoothe things over a little: "Please do not misunderstand the tone of this message. If it is a little sharp it is because I am worried for your sake."

There is quite a considerable correspondence to throw light on this affair. As it only touches the perimetre of our subject, the question will only be summed up briefly, as it appears from this correspondence.[32] Seehusen was to receive propaganda material from England (books, periodicals, films, etc.) and arrange for its distribution, partly forwarding the material received direct, where there was a question of "mass deliveries", partly by independent duplication at his own discretion. It also appears that London wanted tips and suggestions as to the type and form of propaganda. The original plan was for Rantzau to organise reception of the deliveries of material, parallel with the receptions for which SOE was responsible. It was this condition that gave rise to Muus's protests, and the idea was dropped. It was finally decided to send over the propaganda material with the ordinary droppings, and it was this course of action which resulted in the accident at Enebærodde.

It was here that a considerable delivery of propaganda material was dropped, in addition to the expected containers with sabotage materiel, and Peter Carlsen acted according to his directives, and "drowned" the whole delivery of propaganda material summarily in the Kattegat. It was not until after the accident that Rantzau came to Odense – in vain. He writes to Turnbull on this:[33] "On 25 instant I was informed through Jam (Muus) that they would try, probably on the 26th ... to send me some material, which I was *very* glad of (Rantzau's italics), as the various cancellations[34] however understandable they were, have naturally been a great disappointment ... I went to the place in question ... but the affair took a more than sad turn ... because ... it had *not* (Rantzau's italics) been sent on the 26th, but earlier, on the 22nd, and also because Jam's local man had acted very strictly according to his instructions ... and had therefore drowned the delivery in the water nearby." In his letter dated 25 July[35] – but in which the lines in question are not written until the 27th – Muus puts the blame for what had happened on London, and states that he had not received any information that the delivery would come until it was too late. He adds that he has now given a general order that such deliveries are to be withdrawn, in future, and given to him to deal with.

It is, however, evident that Muus was irritated at all this work. He gives this unmistakable expression in "The Spark and the Flame"[35] and in the letter of 25 July he waves the accident aside with the words, "Well, this is, of course most unfortunate, but shall we cry over spilt milk." It is also characteristic for his attitude that when he gets the parachutist Hecht Johansen to Denmark in 1944, as a special trainee in propaganda work, he puts him to operational work and disregards direct orders.[37] His opinion on this point is very likely inspired by the suspicion of propaganda which was not unusual in British military circles. In "The Spark and the Flame", when he mentions the propaganda material from Enebærodde as being "of the sort which would let us win the war quicker than you can spell Pro-pa-gan-da-de-part-ment" it sounds rather like a British soldiers' joke. After the Enebærodde dropping, another way was found for sending the propaganda across. In August Turnbull writes to Duus Hansen and informs him that in future the material will be sent through the Consul in Gøteborg, Albert Christensen, and the "Matros" connexion with which we are already familiar.[38]

In the period we are considering, the British propaganda came thus to a watery end. Later, considerable deliveries came through, consisting, for example, of periodicals such as the British "Free Denmark", leaflets, often in German for German soldiers, miniature editions of "The Times" printed on rice paper, films such as "Desert Victory", etc. etc.

The worst disaster, however, during the droppings of the summer, was at Madum Lake. There had already been some bad luck in connexion with this in July: first, the dropping had had to be given up because of thick fog, then the dropping succeeded but a radio set landed in the lake.[39] But the dropping of 17 August ended in tragedy. The leader of these receptions, Paul Jensen, relates:[40] "At a reception on 17 August we were surprised by a German motor patrol. How far this may have been due to an informer, or to the fact that the pilot circled four times before the dropping, was never cleared up. It developed into a shooting battle until our car was wrecked north of Skørping, and we had to abandon it and the materiel. Erik Vangsted was killed and Kjær Sørensen was taken prisoner and later executed.[41] The rest, ten men in all, got away."

It only remains, now, as regards this account of the dropping operations, to look at the contents of the containers. The exercise is not complicated. It was essentially a question of explosives and other sabotage materiel, whereas only a few weapons were dropped. We have already heard this last point mentioned in Baastrup Thomsen's account,[42] and it is also commented on in other records. The explanation is two-fold. First, the sole aim was still sabotage and the idea of military groups had not been taken up as yet, and secondly, available weapons were sent mainly elsewhere in 1943, first of all to France and Yugoslavia, where underground armies were now being built up. Weapons were therefore scarce and it was very difficult to supply even the barest requirements in weapons for the groups. One or two quotations can illustrate this situation. In Børge Brandt's and Kaj Christiansen's book, "Sabotage" we read:[43] "In spite of all the talk of arming 'the Communist underworld', all the weaponry we could scrape together for the first action was an old army pistol. Later we found that it did not work. After a while, we did get hold of a couple of revolvers, but the fact was, that for a long time most of the participants in an action could not be armed at all."

The Communist groups were not alone in suffering from this scarcity. In July 1943, Rantzau writes to Turnbull: "It is more and more clear to me, however, that I ... must have the possibility of arming my groups of helpers, and as this will be difficult for me otherwise, I again remind you about pistols."[44]

A few weapons did arrive, but even where we can establish that there was a delivery of weapons, it is apparent that Denmark received what was left over. In a letter to Hollingworth, Muus passes on some criticism from Peter Carlsen of the weapons just received:[45] "He has received 24 pistols out of which 6 were not in working order ... That they were all old models is just bye the bye. Is it not possible to get Colts only. These old models are most inconvinient to carry about and hide."

Most of the materiel dropped was thus sabotage materiel, explosives, magnetic bombs, detonators, fuses, insulating tape, etc. In addition to this there were naturally special deliveries of all kinds, the folding boats already mentioned, radio material, etc. Two types of explosives were sent over, the "808" and the "PE" explosives which would later become the principal means of sabotage.[46] The "808" had considerable disadvantages as compared with the PE material. It required more careful treatment, it was more difficult to detonate, it could only be shaped after long and careful warming up, and in addition it had a particularly penetrating smell, which was naturally unfortunate for its special purpose. Lastly, it gave the men who worked with it annoying headaches, partly owing to the smell and partly when they touched it. This was why Muus asks for more PE in April:[47] "If you could send PE only and exclude 808 we'd be obliged. I suppose there will be some difficulties, though." In the same letter Muus makes other requests regarding the materiel, and he asks insistently for magnetic bombs: "We need loads of magnets." This corresponds exactly with a remark from

Hollingworth that at first one had had to make a point of sending standard equipment to Denmark. Later the question could be considered of meeting special requirements.[48]

Finally, a little humourous feature is included, because humour was after all a part of the Danish Resistance struggle, and because it illustrates everyday life, and how, in the midst of great events, time had to be found for solving the small, grey, everyday problems. The little feature can be told with two quotations. On 30 April Muus writes to Hollingworth: "Please do not send chocolates, tea, coffee, cigarettes, etc. in the containers any more. It is awfully nice of you, but ..." This was the triumph of spirit. In July follows that of matter: "Some 2 or 3 months ago I asked you to stop sending, by containers, such things as cigarettes, coffee, tea, whisky, etc. ... The matter of cigarettes has, however, grown rather serious and as you will realise all our boys use to smoke rather heavily ... I should, therefore, be obliged if ..." It is hardly necessary to complete the quotation. The generation which experienced the Occupation will hardly restrain a smile of sympathy on a question for which later generations may perhaps have less understanding.

20. Sabotage Groups

Simultaneously with the escalation of dropping operations, there was a tremendous rise in sabotage. Month after month up to the hectic days at the end of August 1943 showed increases in numbers and effectiveness. While 29 sabotage actions had been the maximum for a single month in 1942, no less than 198 sabotage actions figure in the records for August 1943.[1] Sabotage was no longer simply a means of demonstration, it was a weapon. The change was registered abroad. In May Hollingworth can write to Muus with a certain tone of triumph:[2] "At last Denmark is really in the news and is on the front page of our newspapers."

It would, however, be quite wrong to draw a parallel, without further comment, between the pace of the dropping operations and the pace of sabotage, as though it was a simple fact that sabotage depended entirely upon SOE's work. Before we turn to an examination of sabotage it should be emphasized that it would also have come without SOE. In the survey of sabotage in "Facts of the Occupation" the number of sabotage operations all over the country is given as 194 in all, from 9 April 1940 to 1 March 1943,[3] that is to say before the first British explosives were available; and an organisation of the size of "Bopa" was set up and in full activity with serious sabotage as far back as 1942.[4] It should also be remembered that sabotage was carried out practically exclusively by Danish Resistance men, who, in by far the majority of cases, had no direct connexion with the men of SOE.

At this point, where in accordance with the plan for this thesis and with the character of the records, we are to penetrate the Resistance Movement by the paths which were laid from SOE's headquarters in to this home-grown organism, and where the men in and around SOE came to play a dominant rôle, these facts cannot be stressed too strongly. We have chosen to look at things from a particular angle, the angle which probably gives the best over-all view. *But it is a particular angle*, and this must be *quite clear* throughout.

On the other hand, it is obvious that the SOE droppings became a principal part of the basis for sabotage. It is naturally impossible to say what would have happened in this direction, if the contribution which Denmark could make in the common struggle had been ignored by the Allies. It is possible, but not very probable, that quite serious sabotage would still have been developed on the basis of the resources which could be produced within the country's own borders. In the work on sabotage already quoted, in which Børge Brandt and Kaj Christiansen[5] treat the sabotage carried out by "Bopa", and which is a leading work in the elucidation of sabotage, they give a thorough account of the efforts made to build up sabotage with local resources − home-made incendiary bombs and explosive bombs, or whatever it was possible to obtain in various ways, such as trotyl and aerolite etc. The description seems, however, to fade out in the difficulties which this form of sabotage had met, and it is stated definitely:[6] "Towards the end of the war we worked so to speak exclusively with the ready-made explosives and special accessories, which made the knowledge of chemistry and mechanics which one can acquire from the book unnecessary." (This was a text book on home production of means of sabotage.)"

Long-winded speculations are, however, superfluous. As it turned out, SOE's dropping points became the hotbeds for sabotage, and the helping hand which Great Britain and later the USA − also in their own interest − gave the Danish Resistance Movement became the principal determining factor for the strength of sabotage. In the summary survey in "Facts of the Occupation" it is expressed as follows:[7] "In the course of the spring and summer 1943 the droppings speeded up, and from now on became more and more numerous, and gave the increasingly strong sabotage groups more and more striking power, by supplying them with modern materiel, so that sabotage explosions now replaced what had earlier been almost exclusively sabotage fires."

What is true of the material side of Resistance is also true of the psychological. The attitude of the Danish population towards the Germans was decided primarily by Danish conditions. Fury against the occupying power lay as a latent possibility right from 9 April 1940. It grew slowly, fed by general irritation at the Occupation, as it was gradually prolonged and more and more of a burden, fed too by constant German violations and a weak and clumsy Danish foreign policy. But public feeling received increased impetus and strength to a great degree from without, from the general reminders of the war situation, from the interest shown in the Danish stand, from the BBC. It is useless to wonder how feeling would have developed without these incitements. As it was, influence from abroad became a decisive stimulant. The appearance of the parachutists, also, had a stimulating effect. Their importance was due as much to the materiel they brought as to the feeling of fellowship with the free world of which they were the incarnation. It is not possible to appraise Danish and British influences separately. It was a question of interchange, where the final result depended upon reciprocity. Let us here describe an interchange from the angle we have chosen, and then let every man judge from the facts laid before him.

We must return to March 1943. The materiel from Trinderup Heath lay in Randers, recently moved to Brøchner's storage rooms: Where did it go?

How was it used? What part did it come to play in the development of the Resistance struggle now beginning? Can its path out to the groups be established at all? Before we answer these and similar questions, we must look at the creation of local groups which was now under weigh all over the country.

First, it must be stated definitely that here where it is a case of an examination of local conditions throughout the country, there can be no question of a complete exposition, within the framework of this thesis.[8] One or two main features can be pointed out, one or two tendencies can be suggested, but conditions varied so much that an exception here will often be truer than a possible rule. It is very likely that no collective generalisation can apply to the concrete example.

It has been shown already, that the earliest signs that the groups were forming appeared during the first years of the Occupation.[9] Personal intercourse in people's homes, at their places of work and in clubs and organisations made people notice signs, and these were used. The Occupation made the Danes very observant and sharpened their memories, and although people often knew less about each others doings in those days, on the other hand they sensed so much the more of each others thoughts and feelings, when 1943 began. People sorted themselves out, man to man, during those years – a process which was essential for the rapid, immediate creation of groups, when this became necessary. By far the greatest number of groups can be traced back to private friendships, tested – consciously or unconsciously – with this in view. We can take as an example the rapid rallying which led to the creation of the Hvidsten group.[10] This is a characteristic feature. Another is the formation of groups arising from the hectic activity of the meetings within the sporting and political organisations in 1940–41. The circles which met here on a perfectly legal, but clearly anti-German basis, crystallized in many instances at a later stage, in illegal groups. It is true of many of those who took part in these meetings that they joined in the activity in a general urge for action, but without any definite objective. Toldstrup's book, "No Victory without a Fight",[11] gives some examples of this development. The illegal Press certainly came to mean a great deal for the formation of groups. The reference here is not to the illegal groups which directly created the illegal Press, but to the fact that the distribution and exchange of illegal newspapers became the entry, for many, to more serious illegal activity. "In the early period of the Occupation I had exchanged illegal papers and books with N.N." "The first signs that I noticed of the beginnings of the Resistance Movement was that I ... began to receive illegal papers ... that naturally led to our ... being drawn directly into the work." Such remarks[12] are examples, chosen at random, which occur again and again in the records.

One gets the general impression that the formation of groups, when this became necessary, was carried out quickly, and was to some extent already in the making before the concrete demand arose. The forms and make-up of the groups was often determined accidentally, and in 1943 the existing possibilities for setting up groups were seldom if ever exhausted. The great mass of the people came to stand outside the active movement, and as time went on, formed a reserve which was more and more favourably disposed.

There were only very limited numbers of real sabotage groups in the spring 1943. "Bopa" was an exception. This organisation was peculiar in that it was purely a sabotage organisation from the start. Elsewhere in the country, conditions were such that the groups were still all-round organisations, in 1943, where members generally took part in all the illegal work that cropped up, primarily newspaper work. What sabotage was carried out at that time cannot be traced to organisations working systematically at sabotage, apart from "Bopa".

One might ask whether the parachutists had no contact with sabotage groups before the spring 1943. They had come to Denmark for the very purpose of carrying out sabotage, and would therefore eagerly seek contact with such groups, if they existed. It can be stated here, that Rottbøll, during his conversations with Fog, had discussed establishing contact with the Communist sabotage groups,[13] but that the discussions had not led to concrete results, owing to Rottbøll's death; and in view of SOE's whole attitude at that time, they could only have been exploratory. In the months following Rottbøll's death, a tendency to form groups can be traced. Both Knud E. Petersen and Hans F. Hansen[14] report that they, as well as Peter Nielsen, carried out instruction in sabotage for some small groups, and Lok Linblad states[15] that Peter Nielsen, on his arrival in Denmark in April 1943, "worked at training a group of four men, which was the remnant of the minor organisation, which he had created together with Hammer". Muus also[16] mentions Peter Nielsen's work as instructor.

None of this left any traces in the nature of active sabotage, and any instruction must certainly have been theoretical, and any organisation hypothetical, before March 1943. This leaves "Bopa" alone.

But now, Flemming Juncker took up work in Jutland. It is left to him, in co-operation with the parachutists under Geisler's leadership to organise Resistance groups throughout the whole of Jutland, and the groups seem to have sprung up with almost explosive momentum, so that Jutland was activised in the course of a few months. Activist groups, some already at work, can be pointed out in the summer 1943, for example in Frederikshavn, Aalborg, Randers, Aarhus, Viborg, Fredericia, Varde, Esbjerg, Aabenraa and Tønder,[17] and the formation of groups was in preparation in many other places. This was not solely a result of Juncker's activity. In Aalborg, most of the credit must be attributed to the parachutist Paul Jensen, and in South Jutland, Aage Møller Christensen held many strings in his hands.

But the main part of the work was done by Juncker, and the preparatory work, in the great majority of cases, was also his.

The formation of the groups was only the introduction to the work. Co-ordination was just as important and far more difficult. The groups had to be welded together into a whole. The conditions of communication between them had to be agreed and maintained; money, instructions, weapons and explosives had to be brought out to the groups, and this involved the development of an extensive courier service; and the organisations had to be linked up to the head organisation in Copenhagen. All this lay in Juncker's and Geisler's hands and resulted in their having to travel extensively, while at the same time the dropping operations continued in the Randers district and inspired rapid organisation. In his record, Juncker himself describes this work with great modesty, decidedly more modesty than can be accepted from a historical point of view:[18] "The work now began on the formation of groups and sabotage, and there was a great deal of difference in what was achieved in the various places ... I was at that time a sort of consulting grandfather for the organisation and worked at giving assistance where it was needed. For example, I got hold of couriers, to travel with messages and explosives." Juncker then describes the Frederikshavn affair, the main lines of the reception work, the distribution of the parachutists and his growing opposition to Muus, and continues: "... I often had to go to Copenhagen to demand the absolute necessities from him (Muus) so that in this way I came to play a rôle as a sort of liaison officer between headquarters and the Jutland section. At the same time as I made these journeys, I worked to expand the organisations' field of activity, particularly in southern Jutland and down the west coast: In this work I had the assistance of Jørgen Diemer, who acted as my assistant for some months, and travelled all over West and South Jutland. Here he established contacts, for example in the Varde district ... Tønder ... The procedure was for Diemer to establish contact with the local people, and for me to pass on these contacts to Geisler, who took them up."

Diemer gives the following information on this work:[19] "(I) travelled to Jutland with Juncker. My work here was to produce dropping points. With Juncker I discussed the possible points on the map, which we might consider, and when we had found a place which seemed suitable, it was my job, in practice, to try to get the local Danish Unity Party people to take on the work of reception,[20] as from my work in the Danish Unity Party I knew the people who could be trusted, if need be, in the districts in question. Contact was established with Aalborg, Struer, Varde, Esbjerg, South Jutland, Viborg and generally speaking with a number of areas in Jutland ... During the travel which this work involved, I had the opportunity of doing a good deal of courier service, partly in Jutland, partly between Jutland and Copenhagen, and also acted as a sort of secretary for Juncker."

There is a more personal slant in the picture of the organiser, Juncker, which Toldstrup gives. He became Juncker's assistant and successor, after first Diemer, later Chr. Ulrik Hansen had acted as assistants.[21] Toldstrup writes:[22] "That night ... I met Faber (Juncker). I had heard his name earlier, but had no knowledge of what his position was or what he looked like. When I saw him, I was in no doubt as to his position. That man could only be one thing, namely chief. His impressive figure, his wise face, the balance of mind which shone from him – everything was there which must make him leader." And in another place:[23] "Faber's most important mission was to go out and find the leaders or talk with those who were already there in some of the towns. He was a master in this domain. The confidence which radiated from his appearance and character resulted in his never having difficulty in getting on the right speaking terms with people, and when he had been out preparing the way, he returned to Aarhus ... where the new connexions were passed on to me."

These quotations also give us a glimpse of Juncker as the great rallying figure in the work of construction. Always on the move, full of inspiring vitality and remorseless energy, he travelled all over Jutland and forced his way through to the individuals and small groups who were capable of and willing to take up the duties of 1943. After opening up the path, he would pass on the contacts to Diemer, to Geisler, and later to Chr. Ulrik Hansen and Toldstrup. They then followed in his footsteps. We hear of this from Bach Frederiksen: "The actual work began, as far as I could follow it, with Geisler travelling round to a number of Jutland towns and contacting various people[24] ... After a time he would pass on these addresses to me, so that I was always able to get in touch with Geisler, when I received a telephone call from Carl Larsen ... This was quite important, because Geisler travelled a good deal, not only at the beginning, but also later, as the work developed."

The incessant travel, which served from now on to hold the various links in the organisation together, was in full progress. Juncker travelled, Diemer travelled, Geisler travelled, most of the parachutists travelled, delivered money, explosives, orders; couriers appeared and disappeared again. This is the monotonous theme of the work, forever repeating itself. We know a number of the couriers. Sometimes we hear that the parachutists are used as couriers,[25] and we have heard previously of Bang Olsen and Nyemann, whom Juncker had met at Støvring High School.[26] A courier who was used a great deal, a man who came to play an important rôle in the work of construction, was George Quistgaard. We meet his name and that of his wife, Ellen Quistgaard, in the records, sometimes as couriers, sometimes as participants in receptions.[27] Lok Linblad mentions that it was Quistgaard who, besides taking part in the work in Jutland, together with Stig Jensen led the earliest receptions on Zealand.[28]

A detailed description of the Jutland group work which now started lies outside the framework of this book. We must confine ourselves to the characteristic features of the group construction, and here the strong element of chance wil be mentioned first. The movement spread from man to man, by quite fortuitous paths, which were determined by personal acquaintanceship, and these paths were often crossed by others. We are faced with a chaos of initiatives, which can often be unravelled as regards individual instances, but where a unified survey cannot be worked out, and is unimportant if the main point – the chaos – is clear. This applies to the work of organisation, where one chance connexion led to others just as incidental; and it applies to the work of organisation, which aimed at a specific line to begin with, but where the aim soon had to yield to the actual possibilities. For example, we have seen the fortuitous character of developments in Randers or the work started by the parachutist Paul Jensen in Aalborg, where the groups were recruited partly according to the principle of casual contacts, and partly as a result of co-operation with a group previously organised by "Free Denmark".[29] From Diemer's account quoted above, it appears that he and Juncker followed, to some extent, the contacts already existing with people in the Danish Unity Party, and in many cases it was men from this party who joined in the work, but the contacts often led on to people from quite different circles. An excellent example of this is the Varde-Esbjerg district.[30]

In Varde, Diemer approached the Assistant Chief Constable, Schlanbusch, who had been the Varde candidate of the Danish Unity Party in the election in March 1943, and asked him to help in the arrangements for receptions. Schlanbusch was already Chairman for "The Free North" and a member of a newly established local group within "Free Denmark", set up through quite a different initiative. Schlanbusch now came into contact, partly through his work and partly through personal acquaintances, with a Communist sabotage group, which then, under the leadership of the parachutist Aage Møller Christensen, assisted at the first reception in the area.[31] This group was also connected with the Communist group in Esbjerg, which again was linked with the head organisation through the parachutist Balling, who had contacted it through one of Diemer's/Juncker's Danish Unity Party contacts. Curiously enough, Balling had stayed with the Chief Constable, Simony, Varde, on his way to Esbjerg, without Simony's Assistant Chief Constable, Schlanbusch, having had the slightest idea of this. The fact that Simony had been in communication previously with Hammer, and that Balling's contact with Simony went through Hammer/Geisler, are only mentioned to confuse the picture even more. Communist groups, Danish Unity Party groups, Free Denmark groups, chance acquaintances – all the stops are pulled out and give a multiple tone which is typical for the group formation we are considering.

While SOE was making contact with the Resistance groups thus established in Jutland, a corresponding result was achieved on Fyn. In May Peter Carlsen was sent to Odense[32] and in the course of a few weeks an active group was collected, largely consisting of serving officers. Here too, the element of chance is noticeable in the formation of the groups. Carlsen brought two introductions with him from Muus, one to a personal acquaintance, which was not used, and one to a lawyer, Rud, who came to play a corresponding rôle in building up the Resistance in Odense to that of Juncker in Jutland. Through his personal acquaintances a group was quickly put together, characterized by the serving officers who joined in the work. Later, connexion was established with the local Communist organisations, and in the summer the creation of groups spread from Odense out to the Funen towns on the coast. The Funen organisation which resulted from the formation of these groups became quite an independent organisation, linked for the time being to the groups in the rest of the country through Carlsen and the parachutist Hans Johansen, who took part in the work on Fyn during the summer 1943.[33]

On Zealand, no SOE men were posted outside Copenhagen in the period we are studying. Here Copenhagen drew all the personnel. Here it was Muus himself who established the necessary contacts to the active groups, with Lok Linblad. As pointed out earlier, SOE had as yet no real contact with the sabotage groups when Muus arrived in Copenhagen. Now the connexion was established. On the one hand some few groups were now set up, with Peter Nielsen and later Paul Hansen and Jens Peter Petersen as instructors in sabotage,[34] and on the other hand – and especially important – contact was now established between "Bopa" and the parachutists.

The channel here was through Mogens Fog. Fog writes on this subject:[35] "In March 1943 Stig Jensen asked to have a talk with me. He told me that Hammer would be replaced by a new leader ... when we met, Hammer was with him. Muus informed me that he was the new leader, but that Hammer would stay in the country for a time to brief him on the existing organisation. He found this very incomplete and asked for my help, on the basis of the groups I had contact with, in creating a more comprehensive organisation, both for reception of stuff and parachutist agents, and introduction to the Danish Resistance Movement as a whole ... One of the first things we did was to establish connexion between Muus's organisation and the sabotage groups, especially those which were later called BOPA. I arranged this connexion through Børge Houmann and did not follow it in detail later. He kept me informed that he obtained contact at the same time with Holger Danske,[36] and together we discussed (the forms)[37] of co-operation and the distribution of explosives to the two groups."

In fact Børge Houmann's account confirms this information:[38] "In March 1943 Muus arrived in the country and I met him the first time through Fog in the Hermitage Deer Park. He wanted to have men available for carrying out sabotage, and we never really agreed on this question, as he wanted to have his own little private group, to which we should deliver the men, but they should act on his orders. He got six men put at his disposal ... At the same time we got men for him in the provinces, as we contacted his people in Odense, Esbjerg, Aarhus and Aalborg with some of our local groups.[39] The direct contact in the daily work between the parachutist organisation and us was arranged through Tuesday meetings between Muus and myself, where we discussed the "political" directives for the Resistance work and the actions which were to be carried out. The constant difficulty for me was to get Muus to deliver the quantity of explosives which our people considered necessary. He wanted exact information on what was used in each action, and did not recognize 'misses'. He felt suspicious, I think, that we were trying to build up a private store."

In his version of the co-operation in "The Spark and the Flame"[40] Muus does not mention the difficulties recorded by Houmann. On the other hand there is a passage in one of his letters to Hollingworth from the summer 1943, which corresponds to Houmann's remark, that he wanted to keep a check on the Communist sabotage. Muus writes in July:[41] "I have made "Jelly" (Poul Hansen) Sabotagechief for Copenhagen and he has under him various groups. Some groups, (Communists) which I do not want "Jelly" to get mixed up into, are attended by yours truly with "Orange" (Fog) as a most efficient helper – not least as far as contacts are concerned. It is my aim to get all sabotage-groups collected under one hat and I am a long way towards that goal." This seems to agree better with Houmann's account than with Muus's own:[42] "Børge Houmann was an extremely pleasant man to hold conferences with, and we reached an understanding quite quickly. After a couple more meetings we entered into a fruitful co-operation."

It can hardly be doubted that Muus was eager to co-operate with the Communists and glad of their decisive efforts in the Resistance work, even though on the Communists' side the impression seems to have been that he held back in the distribution of explosives. The quite natural explanation may be that Muus did not actually have large quantities[43] at his disposal, but that he would hardly divulge this fact, out of consideration for the prestige of the whole parachutist organisation. The reverse would be more like his usual policy. Muus's desire for co-operation with the Communists is also apparent from one of the records. Carlsen relates, in his account,[44] that his co-operation with the Odense Communists – known as the Walther Group[45] – collapsed for a time but later started up again, when Carlsen received direct orders from Muus to start co-operation with the group again.

The connexion between Muus and "Bopa" seems to have been established quite soon after his arrival. His meeting with Fog, before Hammer's departure, took place at the end of April, and on 30 April he writes to Hollingworth:[46] "We are now well on our way to get the full cooperation of the Communists and other groups." At that stage the preliminary conversations with Houmann must presumably have been in progress.[47]

The contact with the other large sabotage group, "Holger Danske", which Mogens Fog mentions in the quotation above, came a good deal later. "Holger Danske" goes back to a sabotage group which was founded on the initiative of Josef Søndergaard in the spring 1943.[48] At the beginning of the group's existence they had to struggle with the same materiel difficulties as we have heard that "Bopa" suffered from,[49] but some time in the summer of 1943 SOE also made contact with this organisation, which then received a share of the British materiel.[50] It cannot be determined precisely when the connexion was made. Muus does not mention the group directly in the correspondence with England. It seems, however, to have been rather late. According to the description in Josef Petersen's and "Bob" Jarset's book on "Holger Danske", the link-up with SOE did not occur until after Josef Søndergaard, who had been arrested in the summer, was liberated by two comrades on 5 August. He then met a representative of SOE, whom the group only knew as "P.H."[51] It is clear that this must have been a meeting between Søndergaard and the parachutist Poul Hansen, whom we have just heard that Muus made his direct liaison with the sabotage groups.

The last pages concerning the formation of the groups may well seem both confused and confusing. They should rightly leave an impression of incalculability. The situation all over the country was confused, jumbled, disparate, and characterized by chance connexions. In one place we see the groups spring up from the Free Denmark organisation, and in another it is the Danish Unity Party which dominates the scene, in a third place people from the local cross-country club form the nucleus of the organisation, and in a fourth place our investigations lead us into circles of serving officers or of the Police. We find the Communist groups almost everywhere, and the picture is everywhere confused by circles or individual contacts which are brought into the mosaic through the chance acquaintanceships, which determined recruitment first of all. The variegated picture is further coloured when one looks at the people who fill it. If one casts ones thoughts down through the country, wandering after the law of chance associations, into the groups which are to be met in the records, documents and books forming the background for knowledge of these groups, we pass the fisherman and the bank clerk, the policeman and the insurance agent, the estate owner and the draper, the innkeeper and the veterinary surgeon, the doctor and the mechanic, the officer and the game keeper, the farmer and the paint dealer, the editor, the professor and the student. It will be difficult to mention a group in society which is not represented.

This breadth was the strength of the Resistance Movement, and was the condition for the political collapse which was rapidly approaching, and which was brought about by causes which were not determined by locality or class.

250

21. Sabotage

The two decisive conditions for a real sabotage offensive, materiel and personnel, were now present. Not in any great amounts nor numbers, but, as we shall see, sufficiently. Developments were now pressed into a crescendo, which left the sober-minded breathless and surprised the daring, until the 29th August set its irredeemable "fermata".

In this development, SOE's activity was of decisive importance. The materiel now provided became a determining factor in the sabotage activity of the summer. It is not possible to decide in detail and with certainty, to what extent the British materiel influenced the situation, and how soon it can be traced in earnest in the sabotage, but important sides of this question can be exposed successfully in various ways, and we shall try to do this in the following pages.

Through the various accounts already quoted, we have heard how the materiel was brought out by couriers to the eagerly waiting groups. This seems to have been the only practicable method as regards the transport of materiel to the Jutland groups. As regards the transport of materiel to Copenhagen, both Brøchner and Bach Frederiksen mention in their accounts that ordinary delivery was also effected besides the courier service. Brøchner states[1] that in one case materiel was sent by the DFDS steamer on the route Randers-Copenhagen, and Bach Frederiksen mentions[2] railway deliveries of suitcases sent as express goods. Important quantities of explosives and other sabotage materiel certainly reached Copenhagen, as we shall see later.

This summary information does not give a satisfactory picture of the extent and times of the deliveries – and their use. We do not find detailed information in Muus's or others correspondence with London, although we do get a hint of it. As already mentioned,[3] Hollingworth had asked Muus[4] in a letter to send consecutive reports on all the sabotage actions on which he could get information. The reports were to be marked in a special way, so that it would be possible to decide in London to what extent the sabotage actions in question had been due to SOE's efforts.

Had such lists existed, we should to some extent have had the answer to the question we are asking ourselves. But on the one side one must remember that such lists would suffer from the weakness that Muus would naturally – and not only in SOE's interest – be tempted to claim sabotage actions with which he either had no connexion, or where the connexion was very slight, simply because his possibilities for getting supplies must improve, in the same degree as the sabotage in which SOE had a hand was seen to increase. One becomes doubly uncertain of information of this kind, when one sees that Hollingworth practically whispers in Muus's ear the advice not to be too modest.[5]

However, only one single list of this kind exists, and the hint of an answer to this problem which it supplies is given with all the reserve implied above. The list[6] includes 22 sabotage actions. Of these, seven are marked "Jam" (the sabotage carried out by groups with which SOE is in direct contact), thirteen marked "Plum Jam" (sabotage carried out by groups with which SOE is in indirect contact), and two marked "Jam Tart" (sabotage actions with no connexion with SOE). All the sabotage operations are from Copenhagen. According to this, SOE's men should already be well integrated in the sabotage groups at the end of May, but as stated, the material quoted for the assessment of this is as uncertain as it is flimsy.

Another hint can be deduced from Duus Hansen's papers. There is a bunch of sabotage reports, apparently drawn up by the individual groups, and in a number of cases countersigned by the parachutist "Jelly" (Poul Hansen) whom Muus had posted to maintain contact with the individual sabotage groups in Copenhagen.[7] The reports have apparently been sent in for Muus's orientation, and several of them are marked with his "book mark", a hand-written easily recognizable "M", which he used during the war on notes he had seen.[8] There are in all twenty reports of this kind from Copenhagen in the period up to 29 August, and here the connexion from SOE out to the groups seems to be established by the fact that Muus has received the reports. How important a part SOE has played in these twenty incidental sabotage actions, does not transpire from the reports, however. In some cases the reports mention[9] that British explosives were used, in some trotyl is mentioned, and in some the type of explosives is not given. Here again we must content ourselves with a hint.

On one or two single points, the account can fill in the picture to some extent. It appears from several accounts[10] that in the case of Aalborg, Esbjerg and Odense, there has been energetic sabotage activity in the summer 1943, brought about directly by the deliveries of British materiel. Here SOE's activity has been decisive for developments. But even here the information on local events, although fairly detailed, is not satisfactory when the object is to get an impression of the situation in the country as a whole.

We are thus able to follow SOE's activity out in the groups, although to a very limited extent, and give a long delayed answer to the question of SOE's importance for sabotage. This was a question which Hollingworth asked himself and Muus, in those spring and summer months, hoping to be confirmed in his most daring hopes; and it was without doubt a question which the German Commanding General von Hanneken was asking himself and his Intelligence officers in the same period, and with growing anxiety. But there exists other documentary material, which gives a decidedly more satisfactory answer to this question. The Danish Police were called in at that time in cases of sabotage, and carried out an investigation of the damage. In connexion with these investigations, a statement was normally required from the Technical Department of the Police, and the statements in question give a useful basis for assessing to what extent and at how early a stage the British materiel appeared as an essential factor in sabotage. As far as Copenhagen is concerned, the statements on the technical side of sabotage were issued by the Naval Research Institute.

In the following pages the results of an investigation will be given on the basis of a number of these statements. There is a question of a total of 336 statements from the period 1 April 1943 to 29 August 1943, made by the technical departments in Aalborg, Aarhus and Odense and from the Naval Research Institute. In addition there are 44 statements from the months of September and October, a period where there are only very few statements from the Police and none from the Naval Research Institute.

One or two comments should be added as to the treatment of the materiel. After a perusal of the statements, these have been divided into two groups: 1. Sabotage actions where the technical investigations have shown evidence of the use of British sabotage materiel; 2. Sabotage actions where such evidence has not been found or where the use of Danish (including home-made) or German materiel is proved. The fact that a sabotage action is included in the first group, on this basis, means thus that the action has, for example, depended solely upon the use of British materiel. In fact there are several sabotage actions in which Danish, German and British materiel are all used in various variations. The actual figures will therefore give the impression that the British materiel constituted a disproportionately broader basis for sabotage than it may have done. On the other hand, one should bear in mind that the sabotage actions in which British materiel appears, are generally larger and more serious, where the damage is considerable, whereas in the group where there is no evidence of British materiel, in many instances actions are quite unimportant, right down to painting on walls, hoardings, etc., or cutting down telephone poles, etc. Further, in this group there are probably various instances where British materiel is used, and where, for different reasons, this is not proved. In several cases it has been possible to point to British materiel because it has been used incorrectly, and has completely or partly failed to work. If this had not happened, it is probable that the damage would have been so extensive that no proof of the origin of the materiel would have been possible. It is stated in the police report in question that particularly in the earlier sabotage actions there can be instances where British materiel is not proved, simply

253

because the Police did not realise that there was a possibility of finding such materiel.[11]

All in all, it can probably be stated definitely, that if the number possibly gives some disproportion in favour of the use of British materiel, on the other hand it is certain that the British materiel has played a considerably greater part than the actual figures show, when an assessment is to be made of the effectiveness of the sabotage, and the extent of the damage.

	Aalborg			Aarhus			København			Odense			Ialt		
	Brit.	Not Brit.	in all	Brit.	Not Brit.	in all	Brit.	Not Brit.	in all	Brit.	Not Brit.	in all	Brit.	Not Brit.	in all
April	0	8	8	0	6	6	0	26	26	0	12	12	0	52	52
March	2	6	8	5	0	5	6	13	19	0	16	16	13	35	48
June	4	5	9	4	3	7	0	12	12	0	4	4	8	24	32
July	5	5	10	8	5	13	17	15	32	5	11	16	35	36	71
August	10	10	20	24	21	45	18	22	40	13	15	28	65	68	133
In all	21	34	55	41	35	76	41	88	129	18	58	76	121	215	336
Sept.	8	3	11	8	8	16	No statement			6	3	9	22	14	36
October	2	1	3				extant			0	5	5	2	6	8

It has been proved earlier that the need for sabotage materiel could not nearly be covered in the period up to 29 August, and it may be added that right up to 5 May 1945, the shout for materiel would never stop for a moment. In 1943, where the number of sabotage actions suddenly rose[12] it was especially vociferous. The infusion of modern materiel which SOE now dropped, was all the more decisive. It did not only contribute – as far as can be judged, to a decisive degree – to making sabotage more effective, and therefore helped to change the attitude of the public towards it. The appearance of British materiel also had psychological consequences, in two respects.

It certainly acted as a strong stimulant in Resistance circles, and gave many of the Resistance men the feeling that they were now in contact with the free world, and their fight thereby gained perspective. The very feeling that Denmark was not forgotten, but that now, after the years of silence people in circles outside Denmark hoped for and expected an active Resistance in Denmark, became an inspiration for many, confirming some in the stand they took, decisive in helping others to take a stand. We have already described[13] how the dropping operations, and the feeling of direct contact with the free world which they brought, released a strong emotion, a deeply moving feeling of belonging to a fellowship which at one stroke broke down the sensation of loneliness and impotence, which could be difficult or even impossible for the single Resistance man to shake off.

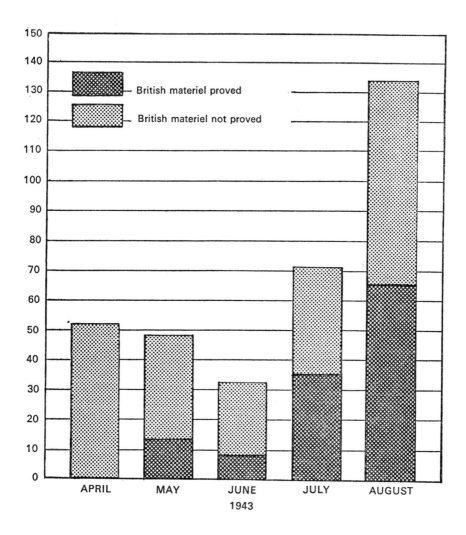

150
140
130 — British materiel proved
120 — British materiel not proved
110
100
90
80
70
60
50
40
30
20
10
0

APRIL   MAY   JUNE   JULY   AUGUST
1943

It is not a question of post-war romanticism, when Toldstrup, in his book[14] writes of his first reception: "Only those who have experienced such a moment can understand the feelings which streamed through the men on the field. Before the aircraft arrives, one stands in the dark with a feeling of being surrounded by enemies on all sides. Every tree that creaks, every twig that snaps, every sound that comes out of the night must be taken in advance as coming from someone who is after one's life. But then suddenly one gets the claps of a hand from someone who comes as a friend. At such a moment one feels oneself an ally." The feeling described here is the common property of hundreds of Danish Resistance people. The description has the mark of firsthand experience in and between the lines, and it is confirmed by many others.[15]

The psychological effect of the British deliveries was hardly confined to the men and women of the Resistance. It seems reasonable to suppose that it must also have affected the German authorities, and made them somewhat thoughtful as to the military developments in general. For the German military authorities, especially, each realisation that British infestation was increasing in Denmark must also involve a corresponding, extremely unpleasant realisation that the North Sea Front was being perforated. Even if the holes were still few and small, and the stream still thin and militarily unimportant, the stream was there, and it was becoming constant. German nervousness was evident and was allowed expression. We hear of it from Werner Best:[16] "In the beginning of 1943, sabotage increased, however, and, according to the opinion of the witness (Best), organised ... This took place, in the opinion of the witness, because one wished to 'explode' his policy, baiting the German Army's and Headquarters' nervousness and sense of prestige ... The witness was, however, during the whole period of the opinion that sabotage played no actual rôle as regards the German conduct of the war, and all his reports were also to this effect ... However, General von Hanneken was more and more dissatisfied with developments, and he was apparently also nervous about them." One may add that Ebbe Munck, in a letter to Christmas Møller from July 1943[17] speaks of "the nervous atmosphere among the officers and men of the occupying power."

German sensitiveness on the subject of the growing sabotage was naturally no secret. Erling Foss mentions it several times in his correspondence,[18] and Muus notes it with satisfaction in one of his letters to London:[19] "As you probably know, Dr. Best has prohibited all mentioning of sabotage in the newspapers. He thinks, probably rightly, that it gives 'a taste of blood' if people hear too much about it." Foss also mentions the ban, but gives another explanation, namely that Best did not wish that[20] "Berlin should read in the Danish papers about sabotage operations in the Denmark he was governing."

For the SOE people, the German sensitiveness fell as manna from heaven. If Denmark was forced into a battle situation vis-à-vis the Germans, not only would the psychological background for popular feeling be completely changed, but SOE would be in a very much stronger position as to their efforts to wrest increased awareness of the work in Denmark from the British authorities. The vicious circle from 1940 would truly be changed to a beneficent circle, where an ever more tense situation in Denmark would bring with it rising interest in the work here. The SOE were not alone in their desire to provoke a break with the Germans. They shared this desire with a growing number of Danish Resistance men.[21] But for the men of SOE, consideration of the reaction in London was naturally more telling; they had a weighty, if secondary motive. It would of course be a mistake to believe that the SOE people – Danes as well as Britons – agitated for sabotage solely in order to bring about a more acute situation in Denmark and thus put themselves in a more favourable position. Their primary interest and their orders were to cause as much damage as possible to the German conduct of the war; but their secondary motive was there, and it inevitably played a rôle in their reasoning. For example, it meant that SOE was not held back by the fear of "Norwegian conditions", which might be the consequence. Rather they desired them, or at least had an important motive for desiring them.

For Muus the secondary motive was surely decisive. In the first place he certainly saw sabotage as a weapon against the policy of collaboration. In this connexion, it was less important to what extent it damaged the German war effort, in the face of which it could only be a pin prick, at that stage. One of Muus's nearest colleagues, the parachutist Peter Carlsen, mentions in his account[22] that the objective was to disrupt the policy of collaboration, and Dedichen emphasizes the same point in his account.[23] Duus Hansen also mentions[24] Muus's opinion to the same effect. Muus himself comments on his attitude in his book "The Spark and the Flame", where he relates[25] how on 3 August he sends a telegram to London[26] – not extant in the archives – in which he takes stock of the position, concluding that by urging sabotage on, it will be possible to force the Germans to take "drastic measures", and in which he asks directly whether London wishes to "force a result". The reply from London is short and to the point: "GO RIGHT AHEAD". Then "the biggest wave of sabotage was released which had yet swept over the country." Operations are here mentioned in which the Forum was blown up on 24 August, and the railway network in Jutland was extensively damaged in the night between 25 and 26 August. Muus continues: "It made the Germans absolutely furious. The reaction came everywhere ... it led directly to the Germans demanding that the Government bring in the death penalty for sabotage, it led directly to the Government crisis ... led to the night between 28 and 29 August, when Denmark won a victory over the indolence which had marked the country, generally speaking, for nearly 3½ years."

This exposition is directly incorrect, and is one of the book's most serious blots. Apart from the fact that the concluding remark is unfair and unreasonable, and can only seem comprehensible because it is made by a man who has come from outside, and who has not been through the 3½ years with his countrymen, the dramatised account, describing the sabotage actions of 24–26 August as decisive for the German demands, is not correct. The German decision had already been taken after the violent wave of General Strikes, which swept across the country in August, starting in Esbjerg and Odense.[27] On 24 August, Best was called to Berlin, where he received drastic German demands to the Danish Government for, amongst other things, the death penalty for sabotage. Nevertheless, Muus's exposition does contain an important truth: that with sabotage as a weapon, he wished to provoke a situation which made the policy of collaboration impossible.

From a contemporary note in Ebbe Munck's diary it is evident that Muus did push on with sabotage energetically – more energetically than was desired in many quarters. In the days leading up to 29 August he writes:[28] "It is possible that things are getting a bit out of control, and it is a fact that Jam (Muus), who tries to fan the flames, must hold back. It is not up to him to decide the moment to let off the fireworks." It is a fact that Muus did not have the authority to decide the moment. But it is an open question whether, in spite of this, it was not SOE who decided it in the end. At least from that quarter everything was done which could be done to speed up developments.

On this background, an examination of the objectives which the various parties had for sabotage is of minor interest, but nevertheless, to conclude this account of sabotage up to 29 August, we shall deal with this as far as the historical material allows. In some places, in letters extant in the archives from Hollingworth to Muus,[29] Hollingworth names a few targets – mostly industrial – which the British wish attacked. The targets mentioned are, however, quite few in number and apparently chosen rather at random; seen in comparison with the existing possibilities for sabotage, and the intimate knowledge which SOE had or could obtain through the Intelligence officers on Danish conditions, the remarks on this seem rather to be stamped by their diffusion and scarcity than by their precise statement of British wishes that this or that production should be stopped or retarded. General directives are not given in the letters.

It is perhaps rash, but tempting, to conclude from this that SOE's headquarters at least did not wish for anything more or other than a violent intensification of sabotage generally, that is they aimed for the time being more at political results than at defined military results. A primary desire from the British point of view must be to disturb the Germans as much as possible, but for this it was not necessary to attack special targets. Hollingworth's remark, quoted earlier, that Muus should take the credit for the optimal amount of sabotage, corresponds with this suggestion. Whereas at a later stage of the Occupation, targets were attacked mostly according to the wishes expressed from abroad – this applies of course especially to railway sabotage, which had its particular strategic importance – in 1943 this seems only occasionally to have been the case. It would be incorrect to suppose that sabotage before 29 August was decided from a centralized leadership at all. In by far the greatest number of instances, the decision as to what should be hit was taken out in the groups. As far as the great Copenhagen sabotage organisations were concerned, a central leading authority was established at a later stage in the Occupation, consisting of a committee[30] appointed by the Freedom Council, but before the creation of the Freedom Council, such an authority did not exist, either for Copenhagen or out in the provinces.

"Bopa" as the oldest organised association had its own leaders, and in the other groups, which were still very small, and where discussions mostly took place man to man, they tried to find their way[31] to reasonable targets – sometimes also unreasonable – based on general directives and knowledge of local conditions. To the extent that the parachutists were connected with the sabotage actions, there are signs that there was an effort to have plans for sabotage approved, in Jutland usually by Geisler, on Fyn by Peter Carlsen. Paul Jensen mentions[32] that "conferences were held regularly, where Ole Geisler and I discussed targets and means with our other men in Jutland. Now and again conferences were also held in Copenhagen with Muus." On the same lines, the parachutist Aage Møller Christensen[33] states that he received orders at least once for a particular action from Geisler, but that later – again through Geisler – the orders were countermanded. Lastly, Peter Carlsen mentions that discussions took place with Muus on the desirability of individual actions.[34]

Information in somewhat greater detail can be found in Lok Linblad's and Dedichen's accounts. Lok Linblad writes:[35] "Partly with him (Muus) and partly on my own, I went through the list of firms which worked for the Germans, which we obtained from industrial circles. The list included the extent and type of work, and from this, sometimes with Muus, sometimes with Jens Erik (Peter) Petersen, I picked out the firms we considered had the greatest value for the Germans ... In addition I had contact with the people in Jutland and on Fyn, and often had discussions with them when Muus was not there." Dedichen's account also mentions lists of industrial sabotage targets:[36] "We organised sabotage at about this time (1943) with the help of Gunnar Seidenfaden, who was at the Foreign Ministry. On Monday mornings I received a type-written list of the total German orders to Danish factories ... We could thus ascertain very easily which factories we could crack down on most effectively."

In SOE's inner circle in Copenhagen, its members had their own ideas as to which targets it was most desirable to hit. This appears from Houmann's account, in which he writes on this question:[37] "There was often considerable divergence of opinion between Muus and myself as to which plants should be sabotaged. It happened again and again that I believed I could prove, with remarks and figures from the staff of a firm, that it was carrying out a great deal of work for the Germans, while Muus declared to this that he was in possession of information which showed that the firm only delivered very small quantities to the Germans, and he opposed sabotaging it. Where he got his information I was never told, but as far as I understood, he got it from the engineer Dedichen, who in turn got it from Gunnar Seidenfaden."

Lastly it must be stated that Erling Foss also made great efforts at that time, to obtain information which could be valuable for reasonable decisions as to which targets should be hit, and to pass on this information to SOE and the sabotage organisations through the editor Schoch.[38] It is characteristic of Foss's argument that the wrong firms must not be hit, so as not to damage the prestige of sabotage in Danish circles. The argument is psychological and not strategic.

All in all, the picture is somewhat fragmentary. It is apparent that as yet there was no central direction of sabotage, but that from several sides attempts were being made to solve the question of co-ordinating efforts and planning sabotage in a reasonable way. The Freedom Council would eventually solve this problem, as so many others.

To conclude this account of sabotage up to the 29th August, we shall quote an interesting passage in one of Hollingworth's letters to Muus. It may give the real answer to the question of the British attitude to sabotage in Denmark at that stage, which is interesting, particularly considering the developments to come. On 17 May 1943 he writes:[39]

"At the moment you are engaged entirely on day to day sabotage, but the time will shortly come when you have to undertake synchronized operations as a part of a general offensive. When that time comes it will be necessary to be able to give you urgent instructions in the form of a crack signal.[40] Plans are being drawn up now for the part you are going to play in this great final battle for liberation, and we hope soon to be able to send you full instructions. These will probably comprise in the first instance directions for widescale reconnaissance. Later you will probably receive by special direct messenger a number of sealed plans ... Similar plans will be sent to other organizations in your country, who will have just as important a part to play but each in a different way. Each plan will give instructions for action in given circumstances, which will be controlled by the military situation of the moment. Having received these sealed instructions, which will be sent by a special devised secret method ... you will then be told how and when to expect your crack-signals ... On receipt of such a message your scattered groups, wherever they may be, will immediately open the ... plan in their possession and go in action. In this connection we are considering the legal aspect of supplying you with armbands or some form of uniform, which will give you a military status and grant protection for those of you who are taken prisoners. I am telling you all this now so that you can see what possibilities lie ahead. Press on with the arrangements for receiving stores, but for God's sake keep in the background at this stage so that you will still be battleworthy on zero day."

The plans Hollingworth here refers to, on the creation of military formations, is the first sign of what would be realised nearly a year later, in the spring 1944, and the situation he refers to did not arise until two years had passed, nearly to a day. In connexion with the perspectives which are hinted at here, the choice of individual Danish factories as suitable targets for sabotage is unimportant.

There is a new ring of optimism in the tone from London. Is it the victories in Russia and Africa – Hollingworth's letter is written a few days after the final collapse in Tunisia – and expectation of great results from the imminent expedition against Italy, that sounds in the letter? At least the possibility is not ruled out in London that rapid developments may arise in the near future, and that long-term plans could suddenly become immediate. For that very reason, it is an urgent matter that political collapse should be brought about in Denmark. Later the task would be to expand the Resistance Movement's organisation and build it into the great Allied fighting machine, which alone could, and finally did, give it military importance.

Political collapse came on 29 August, when the Danish Government finally answered, "No", to the German demands, and the German authorities took over control in Denmark, at the same time as small Army units were disarmed in all the barracks, and the Danish Fleet was sunk by its officers and men. The day itself and its events will not be described here.[41]

Here it will only be placed on record that the honour of the day and the responsibility for the day belonged to the Resistance Movement. In a phrase from a letter of the time, from Frode Jakobsen to Christmas Møller:[42] "It was a good Sunday."

22. Denmarks Freedom Council

SOE's missions in Denmark were solely military. The organisation had no political mandate, and normally its members had no political duties to fulfil. Until Muus came to Denmark in March 1943, there are no signs of any tendency for SOE's representatives to try to cross this boundary. Muus, however, did not keep himself scrupulously within the limits which his orders covered. It has already been pointed out that he interpreted his mission with considerably more elasticity than was foreseen as a condition in London, and in a peculiar situation, where he actually became the growing Resistance Movement's nearest contact with London and thereby with the free world, he tried occasionally also to enter the political domain. A description of SOE's activities in the summer 1943 will be incomplete without an account of this side of his activities.

Quite soon after his arrival in Denmark, he came into contact with Herman Dedichen. He himself states[1] that the first meeting with him took place at the beginning of April, and this corresponds quite well with Dedichen's account, in which he writes that it was Hammer who introduced Muus to him.[2] As Muus came to Copenhagen on about 20 March and said goodbye to Hammer on 23 April,[3] the time seems to be established correctly. Dedichen was closely connected with the daily newspaper "Politiken", and had considerable political connexions, and quite close relations soon developed between the two men. This was important in that Muus was introduced through Dedichen to some of the country's leading politicians. It is difficult to determine the extent and content of the conversations which now followed, on the basis of the relatively slight material to their elucidation, as the latter consists solely of post war accounts by Muus, Dedichen and Fog. In Muus's contemporary letters to London, one obviously looks in vain for information on these contacts, which lay far outside the framework London had set for his activities, and which undeniably did not harmonize at least with SOE's official attitude to conditions in Denmark. Perhaps for the very reason that there could only be a question of sounding the feeling between the two parties, and this did not lead to concrete results, the accounts in question are noticeably vague in decribing the content of these talks; and Fog's mention of them, in his account and in the chapter on the Danish Freedom Council in "Denmark under the Occupation"[4] is extremely brief. Nor is there complete agreement as to details between the accounts. As regards essentials, however, there seems to be no doubt as to what took place.

Muus and Dedichen both state that the idea of seeking contact with leading politicians arose in the summer 1943. Muus uses the expression "early in the summer",[5] while Dedichen mentions May or June.[6] On the question as to who it was who took the initiative, there is some uncertainty. Muus mentions that "Dedichen had long preached to me how wrong it was that I had no contact with leading politicians", while Dedichen states that Muus took the initiative: "He, however, expressed ... a strong desire to make the acquaintance of certain politicians." Without further evidence, it seems reasonable to suppose that it was Dedichen who was father to the thought. Dedichen was politically orientated towards the Radicals,[7] and with the unqualified, positive attitude he had taken from the start, to the Resistance struggle, he must have had a strong desire that the cleft between the politicians and the Resistance people should not be widened further during the climax of events which was now approaching. In his account[8] he himself speaks of his and Muus's common desire "to unify the whole nation to fight against the Germans". It was also Dedichen who had the personal contacts both with the politicians and with SOE, and this must have made the thought of arranging a contact very obvious. Muus's political position, when he came to Denmark, was probably quite uncomplicated. After several years in Liberia he can only have had a limited knowledge of internal Danish political conditions. It is hardly reasonable to suppose that the special abundance of shades, which characterized the political spectrum in Denmark more and more, as the Occupation went on, was fully understood in England, especially in the categorical atmosphere which was typical for the training camps for Danish parachutist volunteers. In a report to Christmas Møller from Ebbe Munck,[9] the latter refers directly to the parachutists' lack of political qualifications. He writes: "It has been stated repeatedly by our colleagues in Denmark that the parachutists who are sent into the country lack political education to a remarkable degree ... They ask, therefore, whether it is not possible to a greater extent to give them some knowledge of the picture of the struggle as a whole, and of the special conditions which are ruling in Denmark."

Nevertheless we see Muus, a few weeks after arriving in Denmark, and at a time when he is standing in the midst of the battle to torpedo the policy of collaboration, quite prepared and apparently very eager to obtain contact with the politicians, who in spite of severe scruples had remained loyal toward the policy of collaboration. Dedichen mentions on one occasion, after the publication of Alsing Andersen's circular of 2 September,[10] how it came to "a violent scene between Muus and the politicians".[11] But even after this Muus was eager to maintain contact, so Dedichen reports: "We managed to bring them together again, so that the Freedom Council[12] and the politicians, at the end of 1943, were again on speaking terms with each other." This corresponds with a letter from Muus to Hollingworth from a later period, when the connexion was well known in London:[13] "For a long time I have been the liaison between the various bodies (this refers to the Freedom Council and the politicians). I believe you will agree when I say that this solution is much more satisfactory." One must admit that Muus did not lack flexibility.

It has been mentioned that the atmosphere in Britain was hardly such as to make any comprehension of political work in Denmark easier, during the Occupation. From there it must have been easy and very tempting to wave aside the honest and well-motivated considerations which were the basis for many politicians' support of the collaboration policy, even when it became politically doubtful and dangerous. At a distance, things took on all too easily a different perspective, and one of Christmas Møller's most valuable services was that, with his intimate knowledge of conditions and persons, he kept himself free from such a simplification.[14] Obviously the atmosphere in SOE was particularly unsuited to sympathy with the finer shades of the Danish presentation of the problems. Here – between the British officers and the Danish volunteers – the attitude to Danish problems easily became oversimplified. It is therefore, in connexion with an examination of Muus's attitude to political Danish questions, extremely interesting to register that he himself, in these surroundings, seems to have met the idea that it would be of value, if the Resistance Movement did not shut itself in, but sought contact with the political circles to which it was in tactical opposition.

Ideas of this kind came from Spink. Before the war he had lived for several years in Denmark, and had contacts from that period among Social Democrat circles here.[15] His acquaintanceships from that time allowed him, to a greater extent than most Englishmen, to assess political developments during the Occupation; and his personal conviction of the clear anti-Nazi attitude of the leading Social Democrat politicians was quite unshaken by their support of the policy of collaboration, the motives of which he fully understood, although he may not have approved of them. He now passed on his opinion and knowledge to Muus, before he joined in sending him to Denmark. Spink writes on this point:[16] ". . . quite shortly before his arrival in Denmark (I) discussed . . . with him that it would be of value, if he visited Hedtoft and through him obtained contact with the great Social Democratic Party. I have later heard from Hedtoft that he made an approach of this kind. My incentive was that it was politically unfortunate that the largest Danish political party was not in touch with the Resistance Movement, which we in London were trying to create . . . I also pointed out to Muus that it would be of value for a coming Resistance Movement in Denmark that it should have a broad political background in a great existing party, to the greatest extent possible." The idea of obtaining contact with political circles was therefore not altogether foreign to Muus when he came to Denmark. Now it was realised through Dedichen.

Muus mentions[17] that at the first meeting he met the Social Democrats Hedtoft, H. C. Hansen and Alsing Andersen, and that the ex-Prime Minister Buhl, who had resigned in 1942, later took part in the meetings. Dedichen on the other hand states[18] that it was Buhl and Hedtoft who were present at the first meeting, and that the meetings later included the Conservatives Ole Bjørn Kraft, Aksel Møller and Poul Sørensen. The statements are certainly somewhat different, but they correspond with each other as to the meetings having continued with a certain regularity, but with different people, so the lapse of memory as to who were present originally is really very understandable, and not particularly important. The conversations did not lead to any concrete results, and for both parties they seem primarily to have brought an orientation on viewpoints and developments, which could be of value in the coming period. Mogens Fog was informed of the contact which was established,[19] and took part himself in regular meetings with Muus and Dedichen during the summer. In "Denmark under the Occupation" he refers briefly to these political conversations and also mentions his knowledge of them in his account:[20] "As regards his (Muus's) political views, there was no doubt that he stood on the Resistance Movement's lines and wished for a break between the Danish and German Governments. At the same time he saw it as his mission, particularly after 29 August, as far as possible to form a connexion both with the Army and with a number of political personalities, whom he later had the opportunity of meeting through the engineer Dedekind (Dedichen). He attached importance to this, not only, I think, in consideration of the movement, but also because it flattered him to have as wide-spread and influential connexions as at all possible. During his first period[21] here he did not say much about the wider political perspectives for what happened, but seemed to concentrate on the work within the framework in which it had been planned up to then." Houmann was also informed of Muus's connexion with political circles and mentions in his account[22] that Muus claimed to have instructions to create the closest possible co-operation with the politicians, and that his view was that the "politicians were forced out in the situation where they found themselves, that one understood their position abroad."

It can hardly be doubted that it was a disappointment for Muus that he did not manage, through the contacts he had achieved, to contrive that leading politicians joined the inner circle of leaders in the Resistance Movement directly. Both he and Dedichen agree that this was the main object of the conversations. When the Freedom Council was formed in September, and Muus joined this, he was very much in favour of getting leading politicians on the Council, and he describes in "The Spark and the Flame"[23] what a disappointment it was for him that this did not occur, because the politicians turned the proposal down.

Muus's desire for this is also emphasized in Dedichen's account, which reads in part:[24] "In June 1943, Muus told me that he had a meeting with Chievitz and Fog in the Deer Park, as usual. They agreed there that an illegal government should really be formed; and they had for some time tried to find a name for this government, and in the end they arrived at the name "The Danish Liberation Council or Denmark's Liberation Council ... the first thing Muus said to me when he comes and enthusiastically tells me about half an hour after the conversation took place is, 'now we must have Hedtoft and Ole Bjørn Kraft with us on the council.' In this I quite agree with him."

This description of the creation of the council does not correspond with what one hears on the subject from other sources. No definite decision to set up the council was taken as early as June 1943, and negotiations on its formation bypassed Muus, who did not take part in the first meeting of the council, even though it appears from the proclamation which was sent out after the meeting,[25] that Muus is regarded as a member. However, there is nothing against Muus having discussed the idea with Chievitz and Fog in June 1943, or his having been informed of the idea by them. One of the characteristic features of the formation of the council was that the idea was ventilated several months before its realisation, and it will appear from the following account that Fog did take part in the earliest discussions.

A throrough exposition of the formation of the Freedom Council will appear in the next volume.[26] Several descriptions are contained in works published in the years just after 1945.[27] Here we shall only give a short outline.

It was natural to wish to create a co-ordinating organ for the various, by now somewhat complicated Resistance organisations, which gave rise to the idea. The election in March 1943 had disclosed the lack of such co-ordination, and the increasing sabotage, carried out by independent groups, underlined further the desirability of some form of common leadership. Foss entertained such thoughts, and so did Fog, but the decisive factor was that the leader of the "Study Ring", Frode Jakobsen, took up the idea of centralized direction of Danish Resistance, and after some difficulty obtained contact with these two Resistance men, and argued for the necessity of creating a centralized leadership of this kind. A preparatory meeting took place in the early summer of 1943, and at this meeting[28] Frode Jakobsen developed the idea of a "Liberation Committee", an idea which differed somewhat from what Foss and Fog had thought of. However, there was complete agreement as to carrying the idea further, and it was decided that Aage Schoch should join the discussions, representing the connexion with SOE.[29] At a new meeting, at the beginning of August, the decision was taken to invite the Danish Unity Party and the Communists to take part in the formation of the council, and their acceptance was obtained.[30] Negotiations had reached this point when the 29th August dawned. Events now made the formation of the council urgent, and the day itself high-lighted the necessity of setting up a central authority. There were different opinions as to how the German violations should be answered. The Communists wanted a general strike to be proclaimed, while for example "Free Denmark" hesitated in such a step.[31]

The decisive meeting was then fixed for 16 September 1943, and took place at the home of the language teacher, Harild, Nørrebrogade 156.

It will be apparent from the above account, that the Freedom Council in the form it was given, was essentially a result of Frode Jakobsen's efforts for the idea, but that others had had similar ideas, such as Foss and Fog. Since the election in March, the Communists had also considered it necessary that the Resistance Movement's forces should be unified.[32] Such ideas of unity were therefore in the air. This is also illustrated by the fact that while the discussions on the formation of the Freedom Council were taking place, other circles were also considering plans which ran more or less parallel with them.

Werner Gyberg writes in his account:[33] "In 1943 Roland (Olsen) urged me to help create a council, called "The Danish Joint Council", and a meeting was called on 15 July 1943. Among those present were Roland, Chr. Andersen, Weiss, Mikkelsen, Kaj Holbæk, Svend Sehusen, Robert Jensen, Duus-Hansen, Flemming Muus, Peter Petersen and myself. The idea was to form a joint organisation for the Resistance struggle, and after the war to carry out an effective clean-up." A detailed description of the history of this joint council is given in Roland Olsen's account.[34] He dates its origin as early as May 1943, and mentions that "one" (he is thinking of the resistance-minded members of the Police) found it unfortunate that the illegal papers did not appear unanimous, that the saboteurs did not agree as to the treatment of the sabotage guards, and that a possible German collapse would bring a number of duties which there was no one to take up. On the basis of such considerations he called a constituent meeting on 5 June 1943. Roland Olsen's list of those present is somewhat different from Gyberg's. It also includes, in addition to those mentioned in Gyberg's account, Major Gyth, but adds that Gyth, Muus and Duus-Hansen had sent their excuses, as they found the meeting unfortunate on security grounds.

At the meeting, according to Roland Olsen's account, it was particularly Holbæk who agitated for the idea, and proposed that the meeting constituted itself as the Resistance Movement Joint Council. A resolution was passed with the following wording: "At a meeting on Constitution Day, 5 June, somewhere in Copenhagen,[35] representatives for the illegal national circles in Denmark met, and discussed future directives, and agreed to continue jointly to counter all un-Danish tendencies in the country during the Occupation. It was agreed to remain a unit after the war, and on a non-political Danish basis to promote national feeling in the Danish population. Further it would be considered a duty to demand that those who have worked against Danish interests during the Occupation should be made responsible for their actions." The resolution[36] was signed "The Danish Joint Council".

The Joint Council's lifetime was short. No new complete meeting could be called before the circle was split by the events of 29 August, when a number of the members went to Sweden. The council's work was therefore without importance, but it is interesting as a symptom. The idea of a united leadership of the Resistance struggle was ripening.

On 16 September 1943 this idea was realised with the formation of Denmarks Freedom Council.[27] and with this was created one of the strangest organisations in the history of Denmark: a self-appointed, loosely formed and linked comradeship of men who, in a crisis where the desire for leadership was latent in the nation, were capable of perceiving the currents of feeling among their countrymen, and who therefore succeeded in speaking to these countrymen so that their speech was heard and their instructions followed. The fact that they were self-appointed, that they were unknown, and that without mandate they took serious decisions which became binding, and weighty with serious consequences for the whole nation – all these objections faded before the right which the people – the only possible opposition – gave them in every situation, again and again, by asking the question: What does the Freedom Council say? – and then following its reply with a unanimity which again and again confirmed the Council's mandate. Few Danish Governments have spoken with such authority. None have spoken in more serious circumstances.

A week after the creation of the Council, Foss writes to Ebbe Munck:[38] "This is Jam (Muus) post. You will also get the Council's statement at the start ... For your information and London's, the Council consists of representatives for the organisations Free Denmark, the Circles (the now officially dissolved Study Circle) and Free Danes and the Communists. In addition a representative for the Danish Unity Party and for the Communists. I represent both the connexion and Free Danes with whom I have contact. There is a man who should represent the Home Front, and has some student connexions. Jam represents the Free Danes abroad. That is in all seven, who meet every week."

The six who met on 16 September and set up the Freedom Council were Fog, Foss, Houmann, Frode Jakobsen, Schoch and Jørgen Staffeldt.[39] Muus joined the Freedom Council as representative for the free Danes abroad. In the first proclamation of the Council, paragraph 2 reads:[40] "The Council has admitted a representative for free Danes abroad whose important work for the cause of Denmark we acknowledge in high degree." It was not, therefore, as representative for SOE that Muus was welcomed to the Freedom Council, but as representative for the tens of thousands of Danes who had volunteered, out in the free world, to fight against violence and tyranny. Nevertheless, SOE obtained direct contact through Muus with the work the Council began, to gather its forces in the common struggle.

Thus SOE also obtained a reasonable position in the Resistance struggle, a position which had been intended for the organisation all along: as supporting organisation – as an indispensable supporting organisation – for the struggle, with weapons which the Resistance Movement had chosen for the country. The secondary duty which SOE had taken upon itself up to now, to animate to resistance or directly to try to call forth resistance, was now fulfilled. Not primarily by SOE but by the thousands of Danish initiatives all over the country; on the other hand, also by SOE men. From now on it was a question of a more specific, but at the same time a more satisfactory mission: to give the Resistance Movement, which now rallied to the leaders of the Freedom Council, all possible technical support. The change must inevitably reduce SOE's importance. While up to now an important part of the leadership of Resistance had had to lie within SOE, where there were possibilities for creating some co-ordination, at least partially, future developments would involve the organisation now subordinating itself, and turning its attention to technical work.

The new situation after the events of 29 August and of the weeks which followed, and the alterations in the conditions of the work which the events involved, must make it desirable both for Headquarters in London and for Muus, to meet for fundamental negotiations on future work. Shortly after 29 August Muus therefore received orders to go to London.[41] Muus himself dates the order to "some days after the 29 August", and to judge from two of his letters, to Turnbull and Hollingworth respectively, the order seems to have been definite in the days around 16–18 September. On 16 September, to Turnbull, he refers to the journey as a possibility,[42] while on 18 September, in the letter to Hollingworth,[43] it appears as a certainty.

According to his letter to Hollingworth, Muus seems to have realised that the main subject for the coming discussions would be the creation of the underground army, which Hollingworth had already hinted at in May. He left Lok Linblad to supervise the current business,[44] and on 7 October Stig Jensen followed him to Skovshoved, from where he crossed to Sweden in a fishing boat.[45] As the boat chugged out of Skovshoved harbour, and Stig Jensen turned back into the darkness of the land, the curtain fell silently on one of the great acts in the Occupation drama.

Notes

1. The 9th of April – Seen from Without

1. The news in "The Times" for April 10th describes events in Denmark and Norway as thoroughly as the information available permits. But the following days Denmark recedes totally into the background and once the news about Denmark's capitulation and the spasmodic resistance offered has been published, all attention as far as Denmark is concerned is focussed on the importance for Germany of Danish foodstuffs and of Danish stocks of oil-products. News about Denmark is fast dwindling down, whereas events in Norway day after day are given more attention and are commented on with increasing admiration for Norway. The difference in the treatment of the two countries can also be traced in the editorial articles of the paper: "Denmark, with an army and navy that amount to little more than police forces and patrol vessels, could do nothing in reply ... Norway is courageously resisting the invader." "Le Temps" deals with Denmark in a short and scanty way and without sympathy for Denmark's conduct. On April 10th the paper notes in its "Bulletin du jour" that "... toutes les informations de source privée que l'on possède s'accordent á constater l'occupation du Danemark et la non-résistance des Danois." This short and pointed resumé can be compared with the item about Norway, starting: "Les Norvégiens ont résisté avec tous leurs moyens, et le gouvernement de la Norvège a repoussé couragement la mise en demeure du Reich de n'avoir pas a s'opposer à l'invasion du pays." The papers "Bulletin du jour" for April 11th is titled "Le Drame Scandinave". In an article of 132 lines there are 3 lines about Denmark. In the closing remarks of the article only Norway is mentioned: "L'impression produite dans le monde entier par le coup de force allemand contre la Norvège est profonde."

2. Derry: "The Campaign in Norway" pag. 18. Hubatsch: "Die deutsche Besetzung von Dänemark und Norwegen" pag. 25–26 and 37 –38.

3. The mentioned works by Hubatsch and Derry. Cf. Winston Churchill: "The Second World War" I. Pag. 420 ff.

4. Ibid. pag. 466.

5. Scavenius: "Forhandlingspolitikken under besættelsen", pag. 21. In his book, "Danmark besat og befriet", Hartvig Frisch has a slightly different version of Churchill's statement. He quotes Churchill for saying that "Denmark would helplessly come between the claws of the tiger" and that England "had written off Denmark". None of the two authors

state their source of information. The two authors date the meeting differently. Scavenius has the precise date, February 2, while Frisch has January. The date, February 2, has been confirmed to me by chiefeditor Terkel M. Terkelsen, who attended the meeting.

6. C.M. solved this task through a series of articles in the English "Frit Danmark", edited 1945 under the title: "Danmark under den anden Verdenskrig".

7. "Parl. Komm. Betænkning" V, pag. 196 ff.

8. See f.i. business manager Børge Møllers description of feelings in England after April 9th in "Danmark under besættelsen" III, pag. 677 and editor Blytgen Petersens statement ibid. pag. 540 Cf. Robert Jørgensen: "London kalder" pag. 23.

9. "Besættelsestidens Fakta" II, pag. 1254.

10. Munch: "Danmark under verdenskrig og besættelse" I, pag. 127. Cf. "Frit Danmarks hvidbog" II, pag. 140.

11. Hollingworths's account pag. 1.

12. The journey and discussions here (see below) are described in accounts of Hollingworth, Spink, Stagg and Taylor.

13. Hollingworth's account, pag. 2.

14. Bogen om Christmas Møller", pag. 216.

15. Spink's account, pag. 11 Cf. below pag. 77 and 264–65.

16. Tillge-Rasmussens obituary of Gallop. "Politiken", 27/9–1948.

17. Robert Jørgensen: "London kalder" pag. 29 and 90–91. concerning the impressions Gallop received in Denmark after April 9th, cf. the following.

18. The personel of the legation was from April 10th placed under German guard. "Parl. Komm." XIII, pag. 967.

19. It seems to be this conversation, to which Gallop referred in his speech in BBC on April 9th, 1942, quoted above.

20. Federspiels account, pag. 1–2.

21. Later on member of the central committee of resistance in Funen.

22. Stated by Hans Muus.

23. "Frit Danmarks hvidbog" II, pag. 140–41. This information comes from editor Ebbe Munck, who, as we shall see, was the Danish resistance-man who got closest connection with the Danish intelligence-officers on one hand and with English officials on the other.

24. Op. cit., pag. 140 and 474–75. Cf. Spink's account, pag. 9.

25. Cited account, pag. 1. Cf. the above quoted statement by Per Federspiel

26. Robert Jørgensen: "London kalder" pag. 21, cf. pag. 26. Cf. also Leif Gundel: "Her er London", pag. 8 and Niels Grunnet in "Danmark under besættelsen" III, pag. 738.

27. See below pag. 76–77.

28. Sten Gudme's account pag. 3.

29. The special military intelligence, which to some extent will be treated in this exposition, is left out of account.

30. See below, chapters 9, 10 and 12.

31. Cited account, pag. 4.

32. Hollingworth's account, pag 5. Hollingworth's remark here is a little summary. As we shall see below there was at the time a contact through Ebbe Munck. But undeniably the contact was still rather loose, so that the general picture, given in the remark, is correct.

33. As regards the discussions mentioned see in general the accounts

given by Hollingworth, Spink, pag. 1, Stagg, pag. 1 and Taylor, pag. 1–2.

34. Hollingworth's account, pag. 2.
35. Cited account, pag. 1. Cf. Tillge-Rasmussen's obituary of Gallop, cf. note 16.
36. Robert Jørgensen: "London kalder". pag. 34.
37. E. Holm-Petersen & A. Rosendahl: "Fra sejl til diesel" III, pag. 68–91. Cf. Børge Møller in "Danmark under besættelsen" III, pag. 671–710. Altogether about ⅔ of the Danish merchant marine with ca. 1.066.000 DWT was cut off from the shipping companies at home. Ca. 60 % of all ships overseas were lost and ca. 570 Danish seamen lost their lives in allied service. The total number of Danish seamen in allied service is estimated by Børge Møller at ca. 5000.
38. Robert Jørgensen: "London kalder", pag. 20.
39. "Parliamentary debates" vol. 360, column 1199–1200.
40. Robert Jørgensen: "London kalder", pag. 20.
41. Hollingworth's account, pag. 2.
42. Spink's account, pag. 1.
43. Stagg's account, pag. 1.

2. Among Danes in London

1. Cf. a long series of accounts, given by Danish seamen, sailing during the war, in J. Hjort: "Den danske sømand under de to verdenskrige 1914–18 og 1939–45", pag. 77–213. Some of the accounts which have been given by Danish SOE-agents to Rigsarkivet, also contain personal descriptions of the circumstances under which Danish seamen took part in the allied struggle.
2. Hans F. Hansen's account, pag. 1.
3. Engineer Eisenhardt in Hjort: "Den danske sømand under to verdenskrige", pag. 143.
4. W. M. Iversen's account, pag. 1.
5. Fl. B. Muus: "Ingen tænder et lys", pag. 5.
6. Chr. Vibe: "Ene ligger Grønland", pag. 24.
7. Iversen's archives, folder 1.
8. Iversen's account, pag. 2–3.
9. See about this application and following applications on similar occasions Iversen's archive, folder 1.
10. "Danmark under besættelsen" III, pag. 540. Cf. Robert Jørgensen: "London kalder", pag. 31.
11. The following exposition of developments in Danish circles in London, apart from printed material, is built mainly upon Iversen's contemporary documents. As Iversen himself took part in the discussions, we are going to follow, his documents do not give an objective, but a strongly subjective, partly a passionately coloured picture of the general development. Regarding the Danish voluntary movement – the main task of this description – and regarding the development before the creation of The Danish Council 30 September 1940 – the minutes of the working committee of the Council starts on this day – the description must, however, mainly lean on these documents. It was Iversen, who pushed the voluntary movement forward and had to do with it, and his contemporary documents give a picture of the enthusiasm with which he identified himself with this cause, and they are the main source – partly the only source – which can illuminate the start of the Danish voluntary movement. When "The

Danish Council" took over in 1941, recruiting through Iversen was already in full swing. See the following chapters, especially the chapter about recruiting.

12. Op. cit. I, pag. 127.

13. See about these negotiations and about the general attitude and circumstances of the ambassadors P. Munch: "Danmark under verdenskrig og besættelse" I, pag. 127–32.

14. Ibid, pag. 128.

15. "Parlamentarisk kommissions betænkning" V, pag. 175. Cf. volume XIII, pag. 1004 ff.

16. "Danmark under besættelsen" III, pag. 522.

17. P. Munch in "Danmark under verdenskrig og besættelse" I, pag. 127.

18. A short account of Kauffmann's attitude during the war is given by Kiilerich in "Danmark under besættelsen" III, pag. 516–22. Cf. Bodelsen's exposition in "Frit Danmarks hvidbog" II, pag. 128–35. A detailed exposition of Kauffmann's negotiations and decisions is given in Finn Løkkegaard: "Det danske gesandtskab i Washington, 1940–42."

19. Cf. Kiilerich's description in "Danmark under besættelsen" III, pag. 523.

21. Cf. Iversen's account, pag. 3.

22. Blytgen Petersen's description in "Danmark under besættelsen" III, pag. 539–94.

23. Iversen's account, pag. 3.

24. Iversen's archive, folder 2. The plan dated 20 June 1940.

25. Iversen's archive, folder 2.

26. Iversen's account, pag. 4.

27. Shortly after the capitulation Børge Møller became the leader of the Danish section of "National Union of Seamen" (NUS) and looked after the interests of Danish seamen in so far as they sailed under English contracts. Cf. "Danmark under besættelsen" III, pag. 674 ff.

28. "Danmark under besættelsen" III, pag. 678.

29. Churchill: "The Second World War" II, pag. 192. That de Gaulle's conduct had an influence upon Danish feelings seems evident from the fact that both Blytgen Petersen, Robert Jørgensen and Mich. Iversen mention his influence: "Danmark under besættelsen" III, pag. 540, Robert Jørgensen: "London kalder", pag. 25–26 and 31 and Iversen's account, pag. 7.

30. The meeting is shortly recorded in Robert Jørgensen: "London kalder", pag. 32.

31. Olaf Francis Poulsen was born 25-5-1911 as a son of the Danish shipowner Hans Poulsen, settled in Belgium. After the German attack upon Belgium he fled to England to enlist in English service. After the war he was in November 1948 appointed Danish consul in Gent and died in April 1950.

32. Cf. Muus: "Ingen tænder et lys", pag. 16 and Peter Carlsens account pag. 1. Muus's book has been published in English under the title "The Spark and the Flame" but will appear in the notes under the Danish title.

33. Iversen's archive, folder 2.

34. If the list is arranged isolating the pros and cons the following succession will appear: Pros – cons – pros – pros – cons – cons – pros – cons – pros – cons – pros – pros – pros – pros – pros – pros. This order seems to indicate that the frame of mind during the meeting has moved into an attitude in favour of a voluntary movement. To make matters clear it must be emphasized, that

Poulsen's "pros" and "cons" only indicate, whether the persons concerned at the moment were for or against a Danish voluntary movement. As far as a creation of a Danish movement was concerned there was unity in spite of divergencies as to immediate ways and means.

35. In his short reference to the meeting Robert Jørgensen makes no precise comment on the aim of the meeting. His short information corresponds, however, to the information given in Poulsen's and Iversen's accounts. That some sort of recruiting amongst Danes had already been ventilated during this provisional meeting, is evident from both Poulsen's and Iversen's statements and it will be seen in the following that Iversen immediately after the meeting goes ahead working along these lines.

36. Memorandum, dated Sussex (Iversen's home) 7. August. Iversen's archive, folder 2.

37. Secretary in "The Danish Merchat Navy Welfare Committee". Cf. "Danmark under besættelsen" III, pag. 679 ff.

38. The two quoted accounts. Robert Jørgensen: "London kalder" pag. 32. A note in Olaf Poulsen's account, written in Iversen's handwriting, to the effect that the Danish minister to Seamen, K. Jensen, should have been a member, seems not confirmed anywhere. Dohm was a business man and represented the "Nilfisk"-firm in Great Britain, Holdthusen was a long-standing local London-director of "Det Forenede Dampskibsselskab", and Ivar Lunn represented "I. C. Hempel's Skibsfarvefabrik" in Great Britain.

39. See Iversen's accounts of the meetings in the committee, Iversen's archive, folder 2.

40. In his book: "London kalder", pag. 31, R.J. mentions the approach to Gallop, but he does not mention Kenny, and he states that a condition for a co-operation with official circles in England was a consent from the majority of Danes in England that the movement be economically selfsupporting and that no attempt be made to form any "National Council" or "Government". R. J. records furthermore, that these views were accepted by Secretary of State, lord Halifax. R.J. dates the informative application to *before* the meeting of the 26th. His book is, however, written after the war and a lapse of memory in this respect is easily understandable. Most probably it has been a question of several "feelers" in the matter. From July 1940 R.J. had regular contact with Gallop as the latter for the first time talked over BBC to Denmark in July, incidentally after a proposal from Turnbull. (See Robert Jørgensen: "London kalder" pag. 29).

41. Reports in Iversen's archive, folder 2.

42. Copy of this letter from 18/8–1940 is to be found in Iversen's archive, folder 2.

43. Iversen's archive, folder 2.

44. Memorandum, titled "Personal notes and impressions", 7. August 1940. Iversen's archive, folder 2.

45. The idea of a Danish Spitfire-fund to be implemented later on is f.i. discussed already here. About this fund cf. article by Palmér in "Danmark under besættelsen" III, pag. 717–20.

46. "Proposal for the formation of a Danish voluntary organisation", 11

August 1940. Iversen's archive, folder 2.

47. Also this thought should later on become a reality. Cf. Palmér's article in "Danmark under besættelsen" III, pag. 728.

48. "Memorandum on procedure in the Danish Question" pag. 1, undated but from the contents without doubt from that time.

49. "Memorandum on Danish sentiments in England" 1/11–1940, Iversen's archive, folder 2.

50. "they" refer in general to Iversen's opponents in the question of a volontary movement.

51. Iversen's account, pag. 6.

52. Report in Iversen's archive, folder 2.

53. The inquiry mentioned was in a somewhat different form adressed to the government in Question Time in Parliament 14 August 1940. Undersecretary of State, mr. Butler, answered on behalf of the government. The wording was:

Mr. G. Strauss asked ... whether any steps are being taken to contact, and organize, the services of the Danes in this country who are anxious to help Great Britain in the prosecution of the war?

Mr. Butler: The value of the hon. Member's suggestion is realized, but I can say no more than that the government welcomes assistance from all quarters in the prosecution of the war.

Mr. Strauss: Is the Minister aware that a responsible committee consisting of Danes has been set up for this purpose, and will he give that committee such help as he can?

Mr. Butler: I have given an answer to the hon. Member's question. I am aware of the organisation to which he refers and the work which it is doing. (Parliamentary Debates, volume 364, column 755).

54. The word is presumably "corroborated".

55. It goes without saying, that Stagg was unable to elucidate on just that point, whereas Stagg, as will be clear in the following, was well informed about the development towards English plans of a Danish military organisation.

56. Churchill refers to this organisation in a letter of 22 July 1940 to Minister of War, Anthony Eden. Churchill: "The Second World War" II, pag. 572.

57. Hollingworth's account pag. 4.

58. Cf. Derry: "The Campaign in Norway" pag. 279.

59. Letter from Hambro to Iversen 2/9 1940, Iversen's archive, folder 2.

60. See below pag. 46–51.

61. Quoted letter of 18/8 1940, Iversen's archive, folder 2.

62. Iversen's archive, folder 42.

63. Iversen's archive, folder 43. Rf. Iversen's account pag. 5–6.

64. Iversen's archive, folder 4.

65. Iversen's account, pag. 5.

66. Iversen's account, pag. 6.

67. The original proclamation in the collections of Frihedsmuseet in Copenhagen. Text published in Hartvig Frisch: "Danmark besat og befriet" I, pag. 368–69.

68. Iversen's archive, folder 3.

69. "Danmark under besættelsen" III, pag. 524. Rf. "Frit Danmarks hvidbog" II, pag. 112–13 and Robert Jørgensen: "London kalder" pag. 38–39.

70. Iversen's account, pag. 6.

71. Op. cit. pag. 368. Frisch incorrectly dates the foundation of the Council to 6 October.

72. Rf. Robert Jørgensen: "London kalder", pag. 31.
73. In his proclamation Iversen had polemically turned against the work of the committee with the words: "Much time has been wasted upon the formation of committees, so we will act first and sit in committee later on."

3. The Start of the Danish Section of SOE

1. Churchill: "Into Battle".
2. Churchill: "The Second World War" II, pag. 172.
3. Ibid. II, pag. 174.
4. Ibid. II, pag. 229–30.
5. Ibid. II, pag. 230–31.
6. Op. cit. II, pag. 223.
7. Op. cit. II, pag. 217–19.
8. Op. cit. II, pag. 223.
9. Bruce Lockhart: "Comes the Reckoning", pag. 159. Cf. Robert Sherwood: "Roosevelt and Hopkins" pag. 273 and 459. It appears from Sherwood's book, that the mentioned strategic programme was established through secret English-American staff-conversations already in February 1941. Cf. William Hardy McNeill: "America, Britain & Russia 1941–46", pag. 5 ff.
10. Churchill: "The Second World War" II, pag. 217–18. In a letter of 23 July 1940 to Anthony Eden Churchill again touches on the subject. Cited work II, pag. 572.
11. In connection with the remarks made about the English interest in support of subversive action in the occupied countries we shall quote the following remarks from professor W. J. M. Mackenzie, who after the war worked out an exposition to the War Office about SOE's activities: "The British began to think of subversive operations very soon after the fall of France. They were determined to fight, and had to find some plan which would give them a hope of ultimate victory. The formula was blockade, bombing, subversion ... there was, until the German attack on Russia, no other plan. SOE was set up on paper as early as July 1940. In fact it had no men and no resources, and was not in a position to do much in the winter season of 1940/41" (Remarks put forward in a private letter as an answer to a question from me).
12. Bruce Lockhart: "Comes the Reckoning", pag. 159.
13. Ibid. pag. 150.
14. As already mentioned Churchill refers to it in a letter 23 July to Minister of War, Anthony Eden, as "the new organisation under Ministry of Economic Warfare", The wording in the letter is: "It is of course urgent and indispensable that every effort should be made to obtain secretly the best possible information about the German forces in the various countries overrun, and to establish intimate contacts with local people, and to plant agents. This, I hope, is being done on the largest scale ... by the new organization." "The Second World War" II, pag. 572.
15. See for instance pag. 83–85.
16. In an appendix to his account Hollingworth, who became chief of the Danish section expresses his evaluation: "In my opinion activity in Danish circles in the summer of 1940 had no effect whatsoever on developments. Certain Danes were very helpful, but Security was such in those days that few London Danes were allowed to know what was being planned, so

it would be unfair to criticise." Hollingworth was, however, in Iceland during the summer 1940 (see below pag. 52) and his evaluation only alludes to the Danish activity in London, not to the activity we in the following shall see unfolding itself in Stockholm. It is of course possible that Hollingworth is right in his opinion, but it will follow from the total of this exposition, that the English circles mentioned were at least extremely attentive to developments in Danish circles, in London as well as in Stockholm.

17. Prime-Minister Chamberlain 5 April 1940 to "The Central Council of the National Union of Conservative and Unionist Association". Churchill: "The Second World War" I, pag. 461.

18. Speech in the House of Commons 13 May 1940.

19. Munck's account, pag. 1. Cf. his book: "Døren til den frie verden".

20. Ebbe Munck took part in the Scoresbysound-expedition 1924, Charcot-expedition 1926 and Courtauld-expedition 1935. He was one of the leaders of the Danish expedition to Northeast Greenland 1938–40 and the Danish Pearyland-expedition 1947.

21. See Ebbe Munck in "Danmark under besættelsen" III, pag. 475–76 and Munck's account, pag. 2.

22. Munck's account pag. 2.

23. Primarily involved were the following officers, mentioned in the order in which they were connected to the work and with the rank, they had during the war: Captain V. Gyth, captain H. Lunding, Lt-Colonel E. Nordentoft, captain (of the navy) P. Mørch and captain P. Winkel. Under the just mentioned was a staff of younger officers. Af-

ter the transfer of the staff to Stockholm in September 1943 the work was reorganised by captain of the reserve – later major in the British army – Svend Truelsen. (See below pag. 213 and next volume, chapter 5). The intelligence-material sent to England via Stockholm exists in copies in the official archives in question, now transferred to Rigsarkivet. For the exposition of the Danish resistance the technical part of the material has no direct importance. There exist no accounts from the officers in the intelligence-service and considering the nature of the case such accounts could not be expected. As it will appear from the following exposition, their work is exclusively elucidated through contemporary documents and through information from the civilians with whom they worked.

24. Munck's account, pag. 2. Cf. "Frit Danmarks hvidbog" II, pag 140–42.

25. Munck's account, pag. 1–2.

26. Foss: "Fra passiv til aktiv modstand", pag. 23.

27. Munck's account, pag. 2. Cf. Seidenfadens account, pag. 3.

28. Borch-Johansen's account, pag. 1–2. Fog's account, pag. 4–5. Federspiel's account, pag. 7. Foss: "From passiv til aktiv modstand", pag. 62. The arrival of couriers is also mentioned several times in Munck's diary, which exists from November 1941. See e.g. pag. 1, 12, 32 and 48. (The diary often uses a code language easily seen through, as when the wording f.i. on page 48 is: "Visit by the doctor who was kind enough to bring a little soap". In the following page it becomes clear that it is a question of in-

telligence-material and that the "doctor" is professor Mogens Fog, leading resistance-figure. Cf. Fog's account, pag. 4–5). Munck's archive, diary.

29. Borch-Johansen's account, pag. 1–2. See below pag. 79.
30. Erling Foss: "Fra passiv til aktiv modstand", pag. 62–63, October 1941.
31. Op. cit. II, pag. 142–43.
32. Munck's account, pag. 2–3.
33. III, pag. 476.
34. See below pag. 52.
35. Munck's account, pag. 2–3.
36. Cited account, pag. 1.
37. In Sir Charles's account pag. 1–2: "Thus was started what was to be one of the most important and successful Resistance Movements in Occupied Europe." As to the English evaluation of the special intelligence-work see next volume, chapter 5.
38. Munck's account, pag. 4.
39. "Danmark under besættelsen" III, pag. 477. Cf. Hollingworth's account, pag. 3–4. Cf. Munck's diary, pag. 5, Munck's archive.
40. Cited account, pag. 3.
41. According to Munck's information in "Danmark under besættelsen" III, pag. 477. Cf. "Frit Danmarks hvidbog" II, pag. 142.
42. Sten Gudme's account, pag. 2 with appendix. See below pag. 76–77.
43. Gudme's account, pag. 1.
44. Concerning the following see Hollingworth's account, pag. 2–4.
45. Muus: "Ingen tænder et lys", pag. 19, cf. Lok Linblad's account, pag. 1–2. On the other hand it seems a coincidence, albeit a funny coincidence, that the headquarters of the organisation were placed in Baker Street, the street of Sherlock Holmes.

46. Cited account, pag. 3.
47. Hollingworth, who in this case is the only source, gives the information, that the training comprised telegraphy, knowledge of illegal printing, security-measures, handling of explosives etc. It seems furthermore not unreasonable to guess that the first and primary aim was to impress upon the two Englishmen the atmosphere behind the work, which was its basis. Admittedly the staging was effectful.

4. Teething troubles

1. A description of the development of the work in headquarters in Baker Street is given by Hollingworth in his account, pag. 4 and 12–17, as well as in an appendix to his account, pag. 1–2. The following description is mainly taken from his information. Cf. Spink's account pag. 1–2. The general nature of work in SOE in M. R. D. Foot: "SOE in France" and Bickham Sweet-Escott: "Baker Street Irregular".
2. Churchill: "The Second World War" IV, pag. 77.
3. Ibid. I, pag. 332.
4. Until then Colin Gubbins had directed training within the organisation. Information from Hollingworth.
5. Bruce Lockhart: "Comes the Reckoning".
6. Op. cit., pag. 2.
7. Robert Jørgensen: "London kalder". See e.g. pag. 19–20 and 35. Cf. Leif Gundel: "Her er London", pag. 6. Cf. also critical remarks, put forward by Erling Foss in several of his letters to England. Foss: "Fra passiv til aktiv modstand", pag. 67–68, 73–74 and 84.

8. Churchill: "The Second World War" II, pag. 218.
9. Ibid. II, pag. 413.
10. Maurice Newnham: "Prelude to Glory", pag. 5.
11. As mentioned below, pag. 70–71 the training of SOE-personel took place at "schools" round about in England.
12. Maurice Newnham: "Prelude to Glory". Cf. Descriptions of training in Ringway in R. N. Gale: "With the 6th Airborne Division in Normandy". Cf. Muus: "Ingen tænder et lys", pag. 33–39.
13. It is impossible to give a reference in detail. The whole book is about difficulties and their gradual surmounting. See however chapter 4.
14. Newnham: "Prelude to Glory", pag 28.
15. A detailed description of this operation in Hilary St. George Saunders: "The Story of the Parachute Regiment 1940–45", pag. 17–26.
16. Newnham: "Prelude to Glory", pag. 25.
17. Ibid, pag. 25.
18. Ibid, pag. 30.
19. Hollingworth's account, pag. 5.
20. The negotiations are known partly through Ebbe Munck's contemporary diary (notes of 16, 21, 24 and 27 April 1944, Munck's archive), partly through Hollingworth's account, pag. 21–22, and finally through Frode Jakobsens description in "Danmark under besættelsen" II, pag. 729–32. The exact time as to date and hour for the meetings is possible on the basis of Munck's diary.
21. Foss is not directly mentioned in Munck's diary, but the diary states that in the meeting on 16 April "all present members of the Freedom Council" took part, which expression written at that time must include Foss.
22. John Ray became Turnbull's assistant in the Danish work, when this work had assumed such dimensions, that one man no longer could cope with it. (See Hollingworth's account, pag. 13).
23. "Danmark under besættelsen" II, pag. 729–32. The description here is ascertained by the statement in Munck's rather brief diary as well as in Hollingworth's account. Cf. e.g. Munck: ""Magisteren" (Frode Jakobsen), who is the central figure thinks that the Danes could actually take on more than intended by the English". (Diary, note of 21 April).
24. Hollingworth's account, pag. 19.
25. Letters from Hollingworth to Muus 9/5–43, pag. 1 and 17/5–43, pag. 2. Duus Hansen's archive, folder 2.
26. Letter of 17/5–43, pag. 2. Duus Hansen's archive, folder 2.
27. See below pag. 252.
28. Hollingworth's account, pag. 23.
29. Hollingworth's account, pag. 4–5.
30. Ibid, pag. 4.
31. Cf. Taylors account, pag. 17 and Hollingworth's account, pag. 13. Neither Taylor nor Hollingworth mention precisely when Taylor entered the work, but it appears from the two accounts that all through the training Taylor had the work mentioned, and the Danish training schools were actually established in the beginning of 1941. See below, pag 70 ff.
32. Hollingworth's account, pag. 5.

5. The Problem of Recruiting

1. See below pag. 67. Difficulties are still considerable in 1943. In letters from Ebbe Munck to Christmas Møller, Munck even in 1943 is still complaining over the difficulty of

getting volunteers to England, and he finally gives up the thought of getting them over in considerable numbers. (See letters of 6/4, 18/7, 25/8 and 17/9 1943. Munck's archive, parcel I, folder mrk. "Rapporter from London I").

2. Letter from Hollingworth to Duus Hansen 9/5–43 pag. 2. Duus Hansen's archive, folder 9.

3. Letter from Muus to Hollingworth 21/5–43, pag. 3. Duus Hansen's archive, folder 3.

4. Letter from Muus to Hollingworth 25/7–43, Duus Hansen's archive, folder 3.

5. In 1944, nevertheless, six Danish officers were brought to England to be trained in SOE as liaison-officers to the "underground army". Accounts from 4 of these, J. V. Helk, E. Fl. von Holck, V. P. Kofod and F. Vang in Rigsarkivet.

6. Philippe Barrès: "Charles de Gaulle". A formal agreement between the English government and de Gaulle was signed 1. July 1940.

7. Iversen's account, pag. 8–9.

8. Letter from Stagg to Iversen 17/12 –1940, Iversen's archive, folder 26.

9. Muster rolls over this first batch of volunteers are to be found in Iversen's archive, folder 18. See below pag. 66–67. cf. Hollingworth's account, pag. 7.

10. Hollingworth's account, pag. 6.

11. For reference to these circumstances in general see the copious source material in Iversen's archive. The number of volunteers in "The Buffs" was never very great. In 1943 Iversen in a letter to Christmas Møller gives a total of 245 men. (Iversen's archive, folder 39).

12. Hollingworth's account, appendix, pag. 2 and Iversen's account, pag. 16.

13. Iversen's archive, folder 16. Concerning the correspondence about this case cf. this folder. The letters cited here are: 27/3, 5/5, 26/5, 3/6 and 19/7, all in 1941.

14. Hollingworth's account, pag. 11.

15. Hollingworth has: "... it (the official recruiting) provided a "cover" for our recruiting for secret work. Furthermore, it provided a "pool" of men, from whom we might subsequently select for our work. It was, however, obvious to the Germans that the Danes would be doing something active over on our side. In these days, when we did not want the Germans to know how interested we were in Denmark, it was a good thing to focus attention on entries into the Buffs regiment and to let Captain Iversen campaign for separate Danish Bren Gun Carrier Units etc. (Hollingworth's account, appendix, page 2).

16. A sharp discussion between the parties about the two conceptions is carried on in 1942. (Letter and memorandum 21/5–42 from "The Danish Council"'s working-committee to Iversen and answering letter from him 4/6–42. Iversen's archive, folder 15).

17. Already 24 July 1941, five days after the new arrangement, Dohm complains to Iversen about the fact that the Council has been withheld information regarding the volunteers, and Iversen replies that he is unable to give the information wanted. (Letter from Dohm to Iversen 24/7–41 and letter from Iversen to Dohm 25/7–41, Iversen's archive, folder 36). From Iversen's correspondence with Christmas Møller is seen that the situation did not improve during 1942 or 1943. (Iversen's archive, folder 39).

18. Iversen's account, pag. 21–24 and his archive, folder 30.
19. Hollingworth's account, pag. 6.
20. Ibid. pag. 7.
21. Here Hollingworth is mistaken at a few points. Thus the stated number of volunteers at this recruiting must be far too high. Muster rolls and pay rolls of this first contingent prove that it consisted of only fifteen men whereof at least Iversen and Carl Johan Bruhn came from London. (Iversen's archive, folder 18). Among the fifteen were Hammer and Lassen, while Lok Linblad did not enlist until later and started his training in the second batch of volunteers. (Iversen's archive, folder 18. Cf. Lok Linblad's account, pag. 1).
22. Iversen's account, pag. 10.
23. Lok Linblad's account, pag. 1–2.
24. When Lok Linblad mentions that the original idea was that he was to join "The Buffs" it must be a lapse of memory. According to his own account (pag. 1, cf. Iversen's archive, folder 18) he was recruited by Iversen in February 1941. Iversen can hardly have mentioned "The Buffs" as no arrangement with this regiment was yet made. That Iversen has spoken about the recruiting to a regular military unit is without doubt.
25. "Danmark under besættelsen" III, pag. 683–84.
26. Iversen's archive, folder 27. Cf. Aage Møller Christensen's account, pag. 1 and Hans F. Hansen's account, pag. 2–3. The correspondence is too slender to allow a fixation of exact numbers, but it appears that the volunteers were referred one by one or two at a time at the most and at several weeks' interval.
27. Letter from Heel to Iversen 17/1–42. Iversen's archive, folder 27.
28. Hollingworth's account, appendix, pag. 2.
29. Ragna Siden: "Chr. Mich. Rottbøll", pag. 46–47.
30. Ebbe Munck's diary, pag 27, Munck's archive. Boelsskov was to have been off to England in the same aircraft as the one that took Christmas Møller to England on May 5th 1942. Both he and Rottbøll had to wait several weeks until there was room in the planes, which illustrates the earlier mentioned fact that for a long time the connection between England and Sweden was very difficult. (Munck's diary, pag. 38).
31. In a note to Hollingworth, November 1942, Iversen sums up his complaints against SOE. The most important are: 1) The actual aim of the recruiting had not been given from the start. 2) Iversen was given an English promise that he might guarantee the volunteers that the work was to be strictly military, which was not the case always. 3) The recruiting took place behind his back. 4) He was kept in ignorance as to the plans and without instructions. 5) This fact had resulted in his discussing the conditions of the volunteers with them under misapprehensions, which had sapped the morale among them, a circumstance for which he was blamed. 6) SOE had failed to support him in front of the volunteers and "The Danish Council". 7) Applications from him to SOE had been unanswered. 8) In several cases men who had been picked for parachute work were unfit for the work and got inadequate information as to the job. 9) Iver-

sen had been refused admittance to the training schools. (Iversen's archive, folder 24).

32. In the letter cited above from Iversen to Hollingworth reference is made to these difficulties. Cf. Lok Linblad's account, pag. 2–3 and Anne Connan's account, pag. 3. (dr. Anne Connan was married to Carl Johan Bruhn and happened to get a strong impression of the tension among the volunteers). Hollingworth's account, pag. 6.

33. Iversen's archive, folder 24.

34. During all difficulties the "official" recruiting progressed normally, but as mentioned without great quantitative results. In 1941 recruiting was extended to Canada and USA by a delegation, sent by "The Danish Council" and headed by K. G. Anker--Petersen. ("Danmark under besættelsen" III, pag. 551 and 717. Cf. Peter Carlsen's account, pag. 1).

6. Training

1. Mention is made only of the special schools belonging under SOE. The Danish volunteers joining "The Buffs" were quartered in Canterbury and the training there was the normal English military training. (Iversen's archive, folder 16–22).

2. The British officers conducting the training during the war were: Colonel I. V. Spooner, Colonel O. Browne, Major A. M. Goal. (Taylor's account, pag. 17 and Hollingworth's account, pag. 13). Hollingworth also mentions a certain major Grayson as the first commanding officer of the training. The latter is not mentioned in Taylor's account, neither is he mentioned in the accounts of the various parachutists, whereas Spooner is mentioned several times.

3. Taylor's account, pag. 12–13. Taylor mentions "a somewhat strained relationship between trainees and the various British officers."

4. Cited account, pag. 13–14.

5. See accounts from Peter Carlsen, Hans F. Hansen, Verner Johansen, Lok Linblad and Knud E. Petersen.

6. Op. cit., pag. 29–57.

7. Taylor's account, pag. 10–12.

8. Hollingworth's account, pag. 13.

9. Cited account, pag. 17.

10. The following survey is from Taylor's account.

11. Lok Linblad's account has it that in this school the high explosives technique was the main subject.

12. The number of the school is not given in Taylor's account.

13. About this training cf. the quoted book, Newnham: "Prelude to Glory".

14. See below pag. 229 f.

15. First of all it was decisive when there was an opportunity to send the person to Denmark. Often a qualified man might wait for a long time before being sent over. The training time for a random number of volunteers is like this, counting from the beginning of the training until the sending to Denmark: Boelsskov: ca. 14 months. Hans F. Hansen ca. 13 months. Lok Linblad ca. 26 months. Muus ca. 9 months. Rottbøll ca. 8 months.

16. Taylor's account, pag. 7–8. Cf. Hollingworth's account, pag. 13.

17. Hollingworth's account, pag. 8, 9–10 and 20. Cf. Spink's account, pag. 11.

18. See next passage.

19. Taylor's account, pag. 3.

20. "Anders Lassen, sømand og soldat". Jørgen Halck: "En dansk soldat".

21. Cf. Lok Linblad's account, pag. 2.
22. Spink's account, pag. 5. Taylor emphasizes the courage shown by the Danish volunteers, while otherwise criticizing the majority of them. Cited account, pag. 16.
23. Muus: "Ingen tænder et lys", pag. 32.
24. Hollingworth's account, pag. 7.
25. Newnham: "Prelude to Glory", pag. 151.
26. Taylor's account, pag. 14. Cf. Roland Olsen's account, pag. 51.
27. Taylor's account, pag. 3.
28. The appointment was in force the moment he left the aircraft by parachute. In several cases parachutists had to return to base and did not in such a case return as officers after a futile flight over Denmark.
29. "Parl. Komm. Betænkn." VII, volume 2, pag. 1237–1263.
30. See below, pag. 164 and pag. 191.

7. The First Actions

1. Spink's account, pag. 2–3.
2. Churchill: "The Second World War" III, pag. 643. Cf. Spink's account, pag. 3.
3. Stagg's account, pag. 3–4.
4. Spink's account, pag. 6–7.
5. See below, pag. 81–82.
6. Re Gudme's travel to England cf. his account, pag. 1–3.
7. Re "Patriotic School", e.g. Muus: "Ingen tænder et lys", pag. 14–16.
8. Defined thus by Bruce Lockhart, who in the summer of 1941 was made head of the British propaganda. Lockhart: "Comes the Reckoning", pag. 125. This book gives an exhaustive description of all British propaganda work. Cf. Gudme's account, pag. 3.
9. Munck's account, pag. 5 Cf. "Danmark under besættelsen" III, pag. 477–78.
10. The whole case was not cleared up until 1943 through Munck's and Christmas Møller's correspondence. Apart from Munck's account see letter from Munck to C.M. 28/3–43, pag. 2 and letter from C.M. to Munck 16/4–43, Munck's archive, folder mrk. "Rapporter London I". In Stagg's account is stated that the telegram on this case was already sent January 1941. (Stagg's account, pag. 3).
11. For this second invitation see Jørgen Hæstrup: "Christmas Møllers Londonbreve", pag. 18–23.
12. Gudme's account, pag. 2. Cf. Erik Seidenfaden's introduction to Blædel: "Forbrydelse og Dumhed", pag. 18.
13. Spink's account, pag. 9–10.
14. Hartvig Frisch: "Danmark besat og befriet" I, pag. 237. Cf. Foss: "Fra passiv til aktiv modstand", pag. 266. Dalton's letter to Hedtoft Hansen is published in Jørgen Hæstrup: "Christmas Møllers Londonbreve", pag. 17.
15. See above pag. 48 f.
16. The idea that Denmark herself should finance the support of the allied countries was one of Munck's leading ideas. In a letter to Christmas Møller of 3/6–43 he writes: "Speaking about the rather considerable crowd of volunteers we have in Sweden and whereof several draw funds from the English legation here, I should like to put forward a question of principle: Has it ever been brought home to the British authorities that the money paid out to Danes or tasks in Denmark are loans? There can be no doubt about this – or can there, ... There

can be no doubt whatever that the nation will desire to return such money as Britain may lay out." Munck's archive, folder mrk. "Rapporter London I".

17. Munck's account, pag. 4.
18. Code word for the financing plan.
19. Federspiel's account, pag. 7. Both Munck's and Federspiel's accounts mention the meeting but Federspiel is the only one to date it. Strangely enough Munck's diary does not mention the meeting but mentions that Hemmer Gudme was in Stockholm in December 1941 (cited diary, pag. 6–8) which agrees with Federspiel's information that before going to Stockholm he received a preliminary instruction through Hemmer Gudme. It may also be mentioned that after having reported conversations with Hemmer Gudme Munck ends the diary-note with an enigmatic parenthesis: "Plan V-Charlie-money-Instruction at church." The mysterious words may refer to the possibility that Hemmer Gudme at a meeting near "the church" was briefed about the principal lines of the plan.
20. Federspiel account, pag. 6–9. Munck's account, pag. 4.
21. Federspiel's account, pag. 9–12. Cf. Foss: "Fra passiv til aktiv modstand", pag. 268–69.
22. Munck's account, pag. 6.
23. These analyses were by Foss titled "Ugen". Essential parts of these analyses are published in his book: "Fra passiv til aktiv modstand".
24. Munck's account, pag. 7. In Munck's archive the correspondence with Washington is only kept after 1. November 1942. (Munck's archive, folder mrk. "Rapporter Washington"), but according to Munck's account the contact with Washington was established from USA's participation in the war. In his account, pag. 7, Munck states that he 11/4–1940 had telegraphed to Kauffmann, offering his service, but that Kauffmann had asked him to stay in Stockholm. Cf. "Skipperen, en bog om Ebbe Munck" (ed. Jørgen Hæstrup), pag. 160.
25. Munck's diary, pag. 11–12, Munck's archive.
26. Rf. the fact that the German espionage in Stockholm would of course not fail to notice any possible journey of Munck's to England. Munck tried as long as possible to avoid German or Swedish authorities getting any evidence of his illegal work. As late as 1943 he rejects the thought of going to London (letter to Christmas Møller 3/2–43. Munck's archive, I, folder "Rapporter London I") and only in March 1943 in another letter to Christmas Møller (28/3–43) did he touch on the idea of ignoring any exposure to the Germans. "This (viz. going to London) means of course to show our hand to the Germans, as the journey inevitably would be observed, but it is possible ... that this fact could be ignored" (Munck's archive, cited folder).
27. Gudme's account, pag. 4.
28. The leader of propaganda to Scandinavian countries, Tom Barman.
29. Churchill: "The Second World War" III, pag. 582–83.
30. As will be seen from the following the decision to send off the first parachute group was taken in the late summer 1941. Before their departure in December 1941 the situation in Denmark had undergone a considerable change. Within this period violent demonstrations in

November 1941 against the accession to the Anti-Comintern Pact had taken place.

31. Bruhn was born in Copenhagen 1904, matriculated in 1923, was apprenticed to a merchant and later on became a ranger student, three years at Bregentved and then in Stenderup forest near Kolding. 1931 he went to Malacca, married an English physician, dr. Anne Connan, and after a few years' stay in Denmark where he ran a sawmill in Vordingborg, he went to England in 1934 to qualify as a doctor. His idea was to return to Malacca to work as a doctor together with his wife.

32. Cf. the following: dr. Anne Connan's account.

33. Ibid.

34. Hollingworth's account, pag. 8.

35. Iversen's archive, folder 18.

36. Hollingworth's account, pag. 8.

37. Hollingworth is mistaken here. Bruhn passed his examination in September and not in December. Cf. dr. Connan: "All the time while he was in training he was continuing ... studies and in September he qualified as a doctor."

38. Hans F. Hansen's account, pag. 3.

39. About Mogens Hammer, see the following. Cf. Svend Erik Hammer's account.

40. See below pag. 75 f. Cf. Hollingworth's account, pag. 8–9.

41. Cf. about this regional division "Danmark under besættelsen" II, pag. 727.

42. Hollingworth's account, pag. 9.

43. Spink's account, pag. 8.

44. Hans F. Hansen's account, pag. 5.

45. During autumn 1941 and winter 1941–42 England's supply difficulties were increasing on account of the materiel deliveries to Russia and the demands of the war in the Far East.

46. Hollingworth's account, pag. 11. Spink's account, pag. 8.

47. See below, pag. 87–88.

48. Iversen's archive, folder 4.

49. Anne Connan's account, pag. 1. Dr. Connan mentions that Bruhn was given a receipt for this letter.

50. Hollingworth's account, pag. 9.

51. Cited diary, pag. 14. As we know Munck at this time was still of the opinion that Christmas Møller had received a request already in March. Cf. above, pag. 77.

52. See Robert Jørgensen: "London kalder", pag. 74 ff.

53. Cf. Ebbe Munck's account, pag. 4–5, where he states: "In continued negotiations during the years it was difficult for the British to forget this episode which must be marked as the nadir of the curve we had to pass from ... 9 April to ... 5 May."

54. Cf. P. Munch: "Danmark under verdenskrig og besættelse" I, pag. 215–16 and Scavenius: "Forhandlingspolitikken under besættelsen", pag. 107–09.

55. Federspiel's account, pag. 3–4.

56. Munck's account, pag. 4–5.

57. During the negotiations the number of torpedo boats was lowered from twelve to six.

58. Appendix to Ebbe Munck's diary, pag. 1 and 2.

59. Foss: "Fra passiv til aktiv modstand", pag. 48.

60. The affair was again drawn attention to in 1943 in a conversation between the then leader of the SOE in Denmark, Fl. B. Muus and commander Bahnsen. It does not appear whether Muus had any mandate from England to emphasize again the seriousness with which

this affair was regarded in England, but as a leader of the SOE he of course spoke with some authority. Letter from Muus to Hollingworth 25/7–43, pag. 13. Duus Hansen's archive, folder 3. Cf. Muus: "Ingen tænder et lys", pag. 99–100.

61. Hollingworth's account, pag. 9.
62. Anne Connan's account, pag. 2.
63. Munck's diary, pag. 9–10. Note from 6 January 1942.
64. The intelligence officer's organisation.
65. Hollingworth's account, pag. 8–9.
66. See note 31 about Bruhn's connection with Bregentved and Vordingborg. That there was no reception but that it was a blind dropping is also seen from the fact that Christmas Møller who some days after the dropping got into connection with Hammer, in 1942 reproached Iversen that no preparations had been made to receive the two men, and that there was no organisation ready to receive them in Denmark as promised. (Iversen's account, pag. 20). Bruhn's decision thus resulted in the misconception on the part of Christmas Møller and others that the work in Denmark was started in a haphazard way.
67. Gudme's account, pag. 3–4.
68. This description is ascertained in the essential points – the stating of Seidenfaden's name and the agreement about the advertisement – in Hollingworth's account, pag. 9.
69. Hollingworth's account, pag. 9.
70. Taylor's account, pag. 4. Hollingworth's account, pag. 10, where a similar explanation is given.
71. Newnham: "Prelude to Glory", pag. 109.
72. Hollingworth's account, pag. 10.

73. See the newspaper "Politiken" 1. January, 1942. It was agreed in London that the advertisement was to refer to a handbag. The lock was Bruhn, the handle Hammer. "Missing" meant "killed", "broken" meant wounded. Hollingworth's account, pag. 10.
74. Spink's account, pag. 7.

8. Two Fronts Meet

1. Cited account, pag. 1. Cf. Hollingworth's account, pag. 10. The information in the two accounts is confirmed in a great many points by the Danish police report about the discovery of Bruhn's body and the materiel dropped. The dropping took place at Torpeskov near Haslev, (Danske Politiefterretninger, nr. 5).
2. Dedichen's account, pag. 4.
3. Parl. Komm. Betænkn. VII, volume 2, pag. 1238.
4. Sv. E. Hammer's account, pag. 1.
5. Hollingworth's account, pag. 11. The English reproaches against Hammer for bad "security" (see below pag. 168 and pag. 170 f) also refer to this first connection with members of the family.
6. Sv. E. Hammer's account, pag. 1–2.
7. Hollingworth's account, pag. 17–18. Hollingworth's account differs from that of Sv. E. Hammer in the way that it was about an information in an acute situation, while it appears from Sv. E. Hammer's account that it was about an information for permanent use.
8. Seidenfaden's account, pag. 5.
9. Dedichen's account, pag. 3. Dedichen dates the meeting 28 December. It may, however, be more reasonable to assume that it was a few days later. In the first place Sv. E. Hammer, as mentioned, is

able to state exactly how Mogens Hammer first went to see members of his family. In the second place Dedichen mentions that he arranged the said advertisement in "Politiken", which was not published until January 1.

10. Hollingworth's account, pag. 10–11.
11. It does not appear directly from the accounts how Hammer got in touch with Christmas Møller and Blædel, but it is not difficult to guess. Seidenfaden had connections with both these men. Dedichen was in touch with Blædel. See below, pag. 105–107.
12. 40.893.
13. About three hundred persons were eventually arrested amongst whom was the member of the Danish Parliament (Folketinget) Martin Nielsen, but several of the leading men of the party escaped arrestation, thus two other members of the Danish Parliament, Aksel Larsen and Alfred Jensen, as well as Børge Houmann, business manager of the communist paper, "Arbejderbladet". As for Aksel Larsen, however, only for a time. ("Parl. Komm. Betænkn. VII, 2 volume, pag. 847–912).
14. Houmann's account, pag. 1. Houmann's information here is verified in an account of a resistance man in Varde, Jens Godske Pedersen.
15. 255,236 votes.
16. Foss: "Fra passiv til aktiv modstand", pag. 74. The analysis here is intended to be guiding for the BBC broadcasting.
17. "Besættelsestidens fakta" II, pag. 1297. According to the information here the paper was issued in 10,000 numbers rising to 130,000 numbers printed. The final figures correspond on the whole to those given in "Frit Danmarks hvidbog" II, pag. 297, whereas the figure of the initial numbers seems to be far too high.
18. Re "Politiske maanedsbreve" see "Frit Danmarks hvidbog" II, pag. 297, cf. Houmann's account, pag. 2. Later on the paper was merged in "Land og folk".
19. "Frit Danmarks hvidbog" II, pag. 296–97. Cf. Houmann's account pag. 2, where the number of copies printed is estimated at four thousand, and it is added that with great difficulties the pamphlet was distributed all over the country on the same day. Even if Houmann emphasized the difficulties it appears, however, that this is an efficient organisation.
20. Cf. Houmann's account, pag. 3: "In December 1941 we published Steinbeck's: "The Moon is Down" together with the communist students."
21. Before the organized sabotage were little attempts by single persons starting right after 9th April 1942. (Cf. "Besættelsestidens fakta" II, pag. 1203).
22. Houmann's account, pag. 3.
23. "Besættelsestidens fakta" II, pag. 1203. "Frit Danmarks hvidbog" II, pag. 326–27. Brandt & Christiansen: "Sabotage", pag. 10–11.
24. This hardly needs further documentation. Refer in general to Foss's analyses in "Fra passiv til aktiv modstand". See f.i. pag. 105 and 110–12. In his account pag. 3 Houmann – in accordance with Brandt & Christiansen: "Sabotage", pag. 9–10 – states that the organized sabotage was initiated 9/4 1942 and that the population in general was unappreciative.
25. The figures of sabotage during the

years 1940–42 are totalled as 10-19–122. ("Besættelsestidens fakta" II, pag. 1206). Not until 1943 does the figure soar to 969.

26. A member and later on a leader of "Bopa", see "Danmark under besættelsen" III, pag. 176. Thing is identical with "Børge Brandt", co-editor of the cited book "Sabotage".

27. Op. cit. II, pag. 326–28.

28. In "Nationaltidende" of 22/2 1946 was reported the German notes of the interrogations of Aksel Larsen after his imprisonment in autumn 1942. Even if these notes must be repudiated as a reliable source (see Karl V. Jensen in "Frit Danmark" 1/3 1946, pag. 11) some statements of Aksel Larsen's especially such as he had no reason to hide, may elucidate the matter, when they can be ascertained from elsewhere. Aksel Larsen's contemporary information about the beginning of the communistic sabotage coincides with what has already been stated here. An extract of the article in "Nationaltidende" is quoted in Frisch: "Danmark besat og befriet" I, pag. 385–88.

29. See below, pag. 98.

30. In his account pag. 1 Houmann dates these decisions as far back as 1940.

31. This only happened gradually. The communists had no co-operation with Hammer as he refused to have any contact with them. Houmann's account, pag. 3–4.

32. The Russian radio broadcastings to Denmark were not initiated until 1943 ("Besættelsestidens fakta" II, pag. 1288).

33. Letter from Døssing to Ebbe Munck 11/12–43, Munck's archive, I, folder mrk. "Rapporter Moskva".

34. Madame Kollontay the Sovjet am-bassador to Sweden denied to Erik Seidenfaden that this article be the expression of an official Russian conception. The article is quoted in "Frit Danmarks hvidbog" II, pag. 467–70.

35. See about the Danish-Sovjet relations volume II and III of this work, especially volume II, chapter 7–9 and volume III, chapter 2 and 10. A considerable material to the whole of this question exist in Thomas Døssing's, Erik Seidenfaden's and Ebbe Munck's archives.

36. To illustrate the scope of these meeting activities some figures may be given from Egil Barfod's account regarding the number of Danish Unity Party's meetings during a period chosen at random. The figures are from the last half of May 1942 where DUP arranged 76 meetings. At 23 of these meetings where the number of the audience is known, the latter totalled 3.555. In June the same year DUP held 160 meetings totalling 10.400 participants. Even if we suppose that DUP was leading in this work, the figures are both striking and elucidating. Cited account, pag. 3.

37. Wichmann Ryefelt and Erling Nielsen: "Peter de Hemmer Gudme", pag. 72–78. Cf. Barfod's account, pag. 1. The importance of these confidential meetings is emphasized in several accounts, written shortly after 1945 by clergymen in the diocese of Aarhus.

38. Foss: "Fra passiv til aktiv modstand", pag. 63.

39. Bruce Lockhart: "Comes the Reckoning", pag. 143–44.

40. "Besættelsestidens fakta" II, pag. 1297. The printed copies of "De frie danske": 200 rising to 20.000 and "Frihedsstøtten" (from Febru-

ary 1943 "Dansk Maanedspost"): 300 rising to 15.000.

41. About "De frie danske" see "Danmark under besættelsen" III, pag. 16–22, "Frit Danmarks hvidbog" II, pag. 299–305 together with a thorough account of this circle in "Parl. Komm. Betænkn." VII, volume I, pag, 244–251 and pag. 641–45. The passage quoted here is from Sv. E. Hammer's account, pag. 2 f.

42. According to "Danmark under besættelsen" III, pag. 16 f., cf. "Besættelsestidens fakta" II, pag. 1297 the starting of the group was as early as 1940.

43. Cf. Sonny Nielsen's account, pag. 1.

44. In his book, "Danmark besat og befriet" I, pag. 207, Frisch, however, points out that this unity had already shown itself during the students' demonstrations against the Anti-Comintern Pact in November 1941.

45. See about these negotiations "Danmark under besættelsen" III, pag. 22 ff. "Frit Danmarks hvidbog" II, pag. 284–89. Cf. Supplementary information in Fog's and Houmann's accounts.

46. "Frit Danmarks hvidbog" II, pag. 284. Cf. Houmann's account, pag. 1–2 and Fog's account pag. 1.

47. La Cour: "Danmarks historie 1900–1945" II, pag. 354. Cf. same author: "For dansk domstol under besættelsen".

48. About the earliest activity of Danish Unity Party see Arne Sørensen in Chr. Refslund: "Fem aar" II, pag. 216–18. Accounts from Barfod, Diemer and Stærmose, pag. 1–3, 1–2 and 1–3.

49. La Cour: "Danmarks historie 1900–1945" I, pag. 350–55. It concerned the pamphlets "Om at sige ja – og nej" (January 1941, 14.000), "Ord til os i dag" (March 1941, 21.400), "Kender De Graabonden?" (September 1941, 15.000) and "Med lov skal land bygges" (February 1942, 22.000). ("Besættelsestidens fakta" II, pag. 1350.

50. Barfod's account, pag. 2. Diemer's account, pag. 2.

51. The quotation taken from Arthur Hansen's article about "Ringen" in "Frit Danmarks hvidbog" II, pag. 289.

52. Cited article pag. 290.

53. "Frit Danmark" 25/1 1946, pag. 1–2 and 14.

54. Ibid. where Hal Koch gives an account of an application he received in the winter 1941–42 from Aksel Larsen asking him to enter "Frit Danmark" and motivates why he had to refuse the application.

55. Cited account, pag. 1–2. The account is supplemented by information from Ødum's assistants in the organisation work, Carl Aude-Hansen and H. Engberg Pedersen. Statements from the two assistants verifie Ødum's account and emphasizes the resistance to the idea of preparing illegality.

56. See f.i. 15/1–41, 6/10–41, 8/11–41 and 5/2–42.

57. See about these tendencies Knud Pedersen: "Churchill-klubben", "Danmark under besættelsen" III, pag. 142, appendix to Sv. E. Hammer's account.

58. Op. cit., pag. 19–20.

59. "Frit Danmark" and not "Land og folk" or "De frie danske" has been chosen because the former may be said to approach a moderate line of resistance, as it arose from a co-operation with various sides.

60. See f.i. "Frit Danmarks hvidbog" II, pag. 284.

61. "Det illegale Frit Danmark", pag. 17–19.
62. The address is quoted in "Frit Danmark", May 1942. ("Det illegale Frit Danmark", pag. 29–30.
63. "Det illegale Frit Danmark", pag. 30–31. The spokesman at the presentation of this address was the barrister, Ernst Petersen, who together with bishop Hans Øllgaard, rector Løgstrup and director Scheibel were the promoters of a meeting of citizens where the adress was adopted. The address was caused by the stir after the Anti-Comintern Pact, the date November 1941. The address was followed by corresponding addresses in Funen. (Stated by Ernst Petersen).
64. Foss: "Fra passiv til aktiv modstand", pag. 67. (December 1941).
65. "Frit Danmark", June 1942. ("Det illegale Frit Danmark", pag. 43–44).
66. Foss: "Fra passiv til aktiv modstand", pag. 63 ff. I consider Foss's analyses to be of great value in elucidating conditions in occupied Denmark. In the first place they are contemporary, secondly Foss, as will appear from his book, had contacts to many sides, thirdly he deliberately set himself the task to study the atmosphere of the country and lastly he apparently endeavoured to render his information in a cautious form, independant of his own very marked standpoints.

9. The First Contacts with England

1. Christmas Møller resigned as Minister of Trade 30 October 1940 and in January 1941 he resigned his seat in the Parliament (Folketing) at the same time resigning in the party organization ("Danmark under verdenskrig og besættelse" I, pag. 188–89 and pag. 208).
2. See Foss: "Fra passiv til aktiv modstand", pag. 36–37.
3. "Bogen om Christmas Møller" pag. 177.
4. Ibid. pag. 178.
5. Foss: "Fra passiv til aktiv modstand", pag. 78, report from 19/3 1942.
6. La Cour: "For dansk domstol under besættelsen", pag. 60 and 90. Cf. Foss: "Fra passiv til aktiv modstand", pag. 78, where it says about the influence of C.M.: "If X had not been behind, inspiring and guiding one and all, the whole thing might have slipped as another yielding to the violent pressure."
7. See above pag. 100 f.
8. Christmas Møller's illegal departure will be treated as a whole below. See pag. 132 f.
9. Seidenfaden's account, pag. 6.
10. "Bogen om Christmas Møller", pag. 183. Cf. Borch-Johansen's account, pag. 3.
11. "Danmark under besættelsen" III, pag. 10.
12. Seidenfaden's account, pag. 4.
13. Before leaving for England Gudme consulted Blædel. Cf. Gudme's account.
14. Federspiel's account, pag. 2.
15. "Frit Danmarks hvidbog" II, pag. 300.
16. Seidenfaden's account, pag. 6.
17. This is verified by a report from Kai Otting to Turnbull, dated 7/10 –43. (Ebbe Munck's archive, IV, folder mrk. "Marken"). According to this report Otting, who was employed at the paper, "Berlingske Tidende", had got contact with Hammer a few days after his arrival in Denmark, and Hammer paid a daily visit to his office. Otting re-

cords about the connection through Hammer with "De frie danske": "... I, for my part, also joined the work with "De frie danske", of which Hammer's brother was a co-founder. The co-operation, however, was not direct, as I had no confidence in the young people. But I provided manuscripts from Blædel and from myself. Arthur (Hammer) passed them on ..."

18. Hollingworth's account, pag. II. Cf. below, pag. 236–38. The English attitude to this changed later on, and parachutists were trained to take direct part in illegal press work. See Hecht Johansen's account pag. 2.

19. Spink's account, pag. 7.

20. This seems hardly probable. From both Hollingworth's, Taylor's and Spink's accounts it appears that only very little contact was obtained with Hammer, and Ebbe Munck's diary does not mention any information from Hammer. For all that, it may be true that Hammer, through the intelligence officers with whom the SOE people soon came into contact (see below, pag. 120 ff.) had an occasional message sent over.

21. Cited account, pag. 3–4.

22. "Parl. Komm. Betænkn." VII, volume 1, pag. 641–44. At one point Sv. E. Hammer's otherwise sober and precise account seems rather incomprehensible. Thirty armed men is above what normally could be mustered those days.

23. As will be remembered, Borch-Johansen was one of the most frequently used couriers in the intelligence service via Stockholm.

24. Turnbull was married to a daughter of the Brazilian envoy to Denmark.

25. Borch-Johansen's account, pag. 4.

26. Cited diary, pag. 36.

27. Hollingworth's account, pag. 10. Spink's account, pag. 7–8. Taylor's account pag. 4–5.

28. Borch-ohansen's account, pag. 4.

29. Ibid.

30. Ibid, pag. 10.

31. About the Schmidt case see below, pag. 135 f.

32. Below will be given a survey of Duus Hansen's importance for the radio work. Essential parts of the correspondence regarding the radio work is preserved in Duus Hansen's archive.

34. The contact may have been obtained through Kaj Otting. It appears from the above mentioned report to Turnbull, that as early as 1940 he had had illegal co-operation with Stig Jensen and the above mentioned Frits Drescher. (Munck's archive, IV, folder mrk. "Marken").

34. Duus Hansen's account, pag. 5. Cf. Juncker's account, pag. 1–2.

35. Duus Hansen's account, pag. 4.

36. Ragna Siden: "Chr. Mich. Rottbøll", pag. 44–45.

37. Information given to the author by inspector Andersen, owner of the plane. Cf. "Danmark under besættelsen" III, pag. 480.

38. Stagg's account, pag. 3.

39. Sneum did not arrive in Denmark by submarine but by parachute, which will appear from the following.

40. Because of various misunderstandings Sneum was in prison for quite a while.

41. The Danish volunteers who escaped to England and declared themselves willing to do a job in Denmark were normally attached to SOE. Sneum is the exception that proves the rule. It may be

mentioned, however, that Fl. B. Muus very nearly got "roped in" by SIS. See Spink's account, pag. 5. Cf. Muus: "Ingen tænder et lys", pag. 19–22.

42. Cf. Roland Olsen's account, pag. 29–30. A survey of Roland Olsen's resistance work will be given later. At this time he served in the special affairs department of the Public Prosecutor. It says in the account after Sneum had returned to Denmark: "In department AS (department for special affairs) they were well aware that it was Sneum who had participated in stealing the aircraft at Odense. Now he was again mentioned in this new case . . ."

43. Re the Sneum-case cf. "Parl. Komm. Betænkn." VII, volume 1, pag. 252.

44. As the reason of the disagreements is of no importance there is no documentation here.

45. Gyberg's account, pag. 2–3 and Duus Hansen's account, pag. 2–3.

46. Ibid. pag. 1–2.

47. Ibid.

48. See below, pag. 205.

49. About Robert Jensen see "Danmark under besættelsen" III, pag. 305. Cf. "Den aabne dør til den frie verden" about the activity of "Dansk-Svensk flygtningetjeneste" in Malmø. Cf. Ib Larsen's account, pag. 17–18, which brings a character sketch from one of his closest collaborators.

50. Roland Olsen's account, pag. 30. Cf. Gyberg's account, pag. 5.

51. Cited account, pag. 5.

52. In his account Roland Olsen says that he stated his concern to his superior, Superintendant Odmar, that the situation might lead to arrest of Sneum. He declared that he refused to arrest Sneum. It says after this: "We might be able to concoct some sort of a fairy tale to hand out to the "Herrenvolk" who followed the examinations step by step. We talked about it, whereupon Odmar said that he saw my points" (Cited account, pag. 31).

53. Cited account, pag. 31–32. Cf. Gyberg's account, pag. 5.

54. Gyberg's account, pag. 5–6. Roland Olsen's account, pag. 32–33. Duus Hansen's account, pag. 5.

55. Duus Hansen's account, pag. 5–6.

56. No contact was made with Hammer until after the meeting in Gyberg's home, mentioned above. Roland Olsen states that Sneum at this meeting was eager to hear what was known about the Haslev case. At that time, the last days of March, there was consequently no contact. (Cited account, pag. 33).

57. See below, pag. 117 f.

58. Duus Hansen's account, pag. 6. Cf. Spink's account, pag. 8, which parallel to Duus Hansen dates the first radio transmissions to that time. Both are right. The first transmission took place on April 17th. (See Jørgen Hæstrup: "Table Top", article in "Jyske Samlinger" from 1961).

59. See below, pag. 169, note 63.

60. See f.i. Sv. E. Hammer's account, pag. 4–5 and Dedichen's account, pag. 3–5.

61. Rottbøll was born in 1917. (Ragna Siden: "Chr. Mich. Rottbøll", pag. 7). When he was requested to go to Denmark Rottbøll was only twenty-four years old. However, both his actions as well as his letters (quoted in Ragna Siden's book) betray a mature and conscientious man, committing himself to every

problem with which he was confronted with great independance.

62. Hollingworth's account, pag. 11.
63. Hollingworth must refer to Hammer.
64. Spink's account, pag. 9. Cf. Hollingworth's account, pag. 12.

10. The Rottbøll Team and Their Working Conditions

1. Ragna Siden: "Chr. Mich. Rottbøll", pag. 23.
2. Ibid. pag. 27. Written in Finland, after Rottbøll had volunteered in the Russian-Finnish war.
3. Ibid. pag. 22.
4. Ibid. pag. 23. Cf. Stærmose's account, pag. 3.
5. See above pag. 67.
6. Detailed information about the two men's term as seamen during the war is to be found in Ragna Siden "Chr. Mich. Rottbøll", pag. 52–56. Cf. Max Mikkelsen's account.
7. Ebbe Munck's account, pag. 7.
8. Max Mikkelsen's account, pag. 3
9. Borch-Johansen's account, pag. 6–7.
10. Ebbe Munck's diary 26/3-43, pag. 28, Munck's archive.
11. Ibid. pag. 36.
12. It does not appear who "we" is, but as will be remembered, Borch-Johansen had organised his own intelligence group. On the other hand the reference is probably to the attempt Ebbe Munck mentions in his diary March 26th, where "Hertugen" (the Duke) swerved into the ditch". We know from Max Mikkelsen that one of the returns to base was made because there were no signals on the reception field. At that time the car might be lying in the ditch near Roskilde?
13. Borch-Johansen's account, pag. 7. Cf. Fog's account, pag. 2–3.
14. Seidenfaden's account, pag. 7. Max

Mikkelsen's account, pag. 4.
15. Bruce Lockhart: "Comes the Reckoning", pag. 182.
16. General Dallas Brooks, head of the military wing of the department for enemy propaganda.
17. Field-Marchal, Sir Alanbrooke, chief of the Imperial General Staff.
18. Reference is made to SOE.
19. Bruce Lockhart: "Comes the Reckoning", pag. 184.
20. Cf. Leif Gundel' "Her er London", pag. 72–73. Cf. Foss: "Fra passiv til aktiv modstand", pag. 105.
21. Spink's account, pag. 8.
22. Gudme's account, pag. 4.
23. Munck's diary 14/2-1942, Diary, pag. 24. Munck's archive.
24. 11 May 1940 Clement R. Attlee had entered the English Cabinet as Lord Privy Seal and 3 October Sir Andrew Duncan had been appointed Minister of Supply. (Winston Churchill: "The Second World War" II, pag. 13 and 438). In a note in pencil Ebbe Munck, however, has corrected Duncan into Dalton. In this case he refers to the Minister of Economic Warfare, the above pag. 54 mentioned Hugh Dalton. The information that "he is the one who points out the bombing targets" points, albeit incorrectly, to Dalton.
25. The above (note 17) mentioned Sir Alanbrooke.
26. Munck's diary, pag. 26. Munck's archive.
27. At this time Captain Lunding was on a visit to Stockholm.
28. Letter from Turnbull to "Ligaen" (the officers), see Jørgen Hæstrup: "Table Top", dissertation in "Jyske samlinger", Ny række V, 1961, pag. 376.
29. Ibid. 376 ff. where an account of the letter is given in detail. The

letters mentioned in note 28 and 29 exist in "Munck's supplements-arkiv", which contains an important stream of letters, exchanged between the officers in Copenhagen and Turnbull/Ebbe Munck during 1942–43, partly intelligence material, partly operational and political correspondence.

30. As to the P-plan see "Besættelsens hvem hvad hvor", pag. 302 f.
31. An agreement which right from the beginning in 1940 had been Munck's and the officer's wish.
32. This fact stands out most clearly in Borch-Johansen's account, which contains a direct controversy against the conception of the intelligence officers (see f.i. pag. 17) and in Duus Hansen's account, Duus Hansen being the one to have the closest connection with the intelligence officers. (See below pag. 166 f.). Cf. Fog's account, pag. 6.
33. Cited account, pag. 9–10.
34. Borch-Johansen's account, pag. 8, 9–10, 11–12. Cf. Sv. E. Hammer's account, pag. 5. Cf. Fog's account, pag. 5–6. Cf. Otting's report to Turnbull 7/10–43, Munck's archive, IV, folder mrk. "Marken").
35. Duus Hansen's account, pag. 8. About Duus Hansen's special position as telegraphist for the intelligence officers, see below pag. 166 f.
36. Op. cit., pag. 98–99.
37. Muus refers to the P-plan.
38. See below pag. 155 f.
39. Munck's diary, pag. 58–59, Munck's archive.
40. Christmas Møller had been recognized by several people on his way to the Liim Fiord from where he sailed to Sweden (Cf. Frisch: "Danmark besat og befriet", I, pag. 237. Cf. Roland Olsen's account, pag. 48. Cf. below pag. 135 f.

41. Reference is here made to the fact that Mogens Fog, who just now happened to be in Sweden, agreed to take over after Borch-Johansen. See below pag. 137 f.
42. Munck's diary, pag. 65, Munck's archive.
43. Foss refers to the meeting in his book: "Fra passiv til aktiv modstand", pag. 109–110.
44. English policy is once more swinging back to an active line. The alteration is described at some length in Jørgen Hæstrup: "Table Top" (see note 28) pag. 398 ff. It must be remembered that the conversation took place just before the battle of El-Alamein which was launched 23 October 1942 and the landing in French Northwest Africa November 8th.
45. Ebbe Munck must have had the few parachutists in mind.
46. Letter from Ebbe Munck to Christmas Møller 16/10–42, appendix to Munck's diary, pag. 68–73. Munck's archive.
47. In the same days Erling Foss writes to Christmas Møller from Stockholm – Foss's letter is dated 12/10 –42 – and he expresses a similar view. (Foss: "Fra passiv til aktiv modstand", pag. 110–12).
48. The intelligence-organisation.
49. Hollingworth's account, pag. 11. My view that Rottbøll's instructions were vague is verified in the following piece of information received from Hollingworth, 1 July 1953. He writes: "You mentioned that Rottbøll was under some disadvantage owing to the lack of full instructions ... it was undoubtedly the dispute that was going on in connection with the P-plan, which delayed some of our policy decisions. His brief was that more de-

tailed instructions would follow in the light of the situationreports, he sent back to H.Q." Cf. also Jørgen Hæstrup: "Table Top" (see note 28), pag. 387 ff.

50. Hollingworth's account, pag. 18–19.

51. Borch-Johansen's account, pag. 9–10. Stig Jensen, in whose home Rottbøll lived for a time, and who was one of the Danish resistance people to whom he was most closely connected gives the following character sketch of him: "Rottbøll was a wonderful man. Tall, slim with a marvellous constitution, calm and controlled, but lightning quick in an emergency ... Ras (Rottbøll) was an excellent sportsman". ("Danmarks frihedskamp" II, pag. 640).

52. Borch-Johansen was imprisoned and escaped at the end of May. See below, pag. 136.

53. Borch-Johansen's account, pag. 10, Dedichen's account, pag. 7, Knud E. Petersen's account, pag. 5. Cf. Ragna Siden: "Chr. Mich. Rottbøll", pag. 51, where one of his fellow trainees in England gives a fine character sketch of him.

54. Dedichen's account, pag. 10, Sv. E. Hammer's account, pag. 4, Knud E. Petersen's account, pag. 5–6. The latter who arrived in Denmark in August, says that only then was a message sent from London to the effect that Rottbøll was to be chief It appears from Hollingworth's statements, however, that he all the time had considered Rottbøll to be chief. But for all that the said friction may have instituted new instructions which emphasized this fact. That such instructions were sent is documented in Jørgen Hæstrup: "Table Top".

55. The letters between SOE-headquarters in London and the people in the field, which are mentioned in the following, are all recorded and debated in Jørgen Hæstrup: "Table Top", pag. 388 ff. This dissertation, published in "Jyske samlinger", 1961, is mainly based upon an extensive correspondence exchanged via Stockholm. The collection of letters is available in the so-called "Ebbe Munck's suppleringsarkiv" in the National Archives in Copenhagen.

11. Towards Sabotage

1. See above pag. 106.

2. Both Munck and Christmas Møller agree in this dating of the application, after the first application (mentioned above pag. 77) had failed to reach Christmas Møller. Letter from Munck to Christmas Møller 28/3–43 and from Christmas Møller to Munck 16/4–43, Munck's archive, I, folder mrk. "Rapporter London I". Besides it appears from Munck's above mentioned letter of 16/10–42 to Christmas Møller that the two men already in 1940, December 29th, had had connection with each other in Copenhagen. Munck's diary, pag. 69. Cf. Jørgen Hæstrup: "Christmas Møllers Londonbreve", pag. 10 f.

3. Foss: "Fra passiv til aktiv modstand", pag. 77.

4. Ibid.

5. Ibid.

6. Reference is made to Hedtoft Hansen.

7. Borch-Johansen's account, pag. 6.

8. Munck's diary, note from 2 December 1941. Cf. Munck's account, pag. 5. According to Munck the

meeting took place in a cottage in Djursholmen, belonging to mr. Urch, a correspondent to "The Times". One characteristic divergence deserves mentioning. While Borch-Johansen remembers the talk as being very long, Munck's contemporary diary states, that the meeting was brief.

9. That Christmas Møller deliberated the matter very carefully is evident from the fact, that the people in Stockholm on November 6th received a letter from C.M., in which he expresses certain doubts. Munck's diary, pag. 1.

10. "Bogen om Christmas Møller", pag. 171 ff. in which mrs. Gertrud Møller, partly based upon contemporary diary notes, gives a detailed description of the journey. Cf. Borch-Johansen's account, pag. 5–6.

11. In December 1947 Christmas Møller promised to work out an account about his brief contact with the parachutists before his journey to England in 1942. Unfortunately his sudden death 30/4–48 prevented this.

12. About the German reaction and the attitude of the Danish government see "Parl. Komm. Betænkn." XIII, pag. 617–29. Cf. Scavenius: "Forhandlingspolitikken under besættelsen", pag. 99–100. Foss: "Fra passiv til aktiv modstand", pag. 88–93. P. Munch: "Danmark under verdenskrig og besættelse" II, pag. 86–87 and Frisch: "Danmark besat og befriet" I, pag. 237–38.

13. Foss: "Fra passiv til aktiv modstand", pag. 88–91.

14. Ibid., pag. 91–93.

15. See f.i. Martinsen: "Kampen for Danmark", pag. 135. Cf. "Danmark under besættelsen" I, pag. 568.

16. Ebbe Munck's diary, note from

28/5–42, pag. 48.

17. Ibid. note from 26/4 1942, pag. 36.

18. Ibid. Note from 4/5–1942, pag. 37.

19. Ibid.

20. Ibid., pag. 48–49 and 52.

21. Ibid. Note from 8/6 1942, pag. 52.

22. "Danmark under besættelsen" I, pag. 559. Cf. "Skipperen, en bog om Ebbe Munck" (ed. Jørgen Hæstrup), pag. 204 f.

23. Foss: "Fra passiv til aktiv modstand", pag. 95–96.

24. To return if such a request should come.

25. Ebbe Munck's diary, note from 8/6, pag. 50. Munch's archive.

26. Kammerherre J. C. W. Kruse, Denmark's envoy in Stockholm.

27. Roland Olsen's account, pag. 48.

28. See about the following Foss: "Fra passiv til aktiv modstand", pag. 90–93.

29. Borch-Johansen was arrested 29/5 –42 and escaped the next day.

30. Borch-Johansen's account, pag. 10–11. Cf. Nikolaysen's account, pag. 1.

31. Borch-Johansen's account, pag. 11. Cf. Roland Olsen's account, pag. 49.

32. Borch-Johansen's account, pag. 11–12.

33. Ebbe Munck's diary, note from 1/6 –43, pag. 48–49. Munck's archive. The note in question covers several days. The following note is dated 4/6.

34. La Cour: "For dansk domstol under besættelsen", pag. 61–62.

35. Roland Olsen's account, pag. 49.

36. Kiilerich's account, pag. 5.

37. The words refer to Rottbøll and Johannesen. Max Mikkelsen joined later, as we have seen.

38. As mentioned above this did not prevent some friction between

Rottbøll and Hammer as to their sphere of competence.

39. Cited account, pag. 5. Cf. Dedichen's account, pag. 7.
40. In Otting's report to Turnbull 7/10 –43 (Munck's archive, IV, folder mrk. "Marken") there is also a reference to the meeting, and it appears from his report that also later there was some talk about a meeting.
41. Sv. E. Hammer's account, pag. 5.
42. Fog's account, pag. 5–6.
43. The word seems to be "counteractions". This account was dictated with use of a tape-recorder and later typed by a secretary, hence the misunderstanding of the word. The two words are very similar in Danish.
44. Cited account, pag. 6.
45. Fog mentions that he received the message during his summer-holiday.
46. Cited account, pag. 11.
47. Cf. that Gyth during the meeting is quoted for having mentioned the German possibilities to reach the Urals. The German summer offensive in 1942 was started on June 28th. Kiilerich's earlier date seems explained by the fact, that the desirability of the meeting must have been discussed ever since Rottbøll's arrival in April.
48. See above pag. 128 Borch Johansen's remarks about Rottbøll's impatience.
49. See Houmann's account, pag. 4, where it is mentioned, that Rottbøll got contact with "the communist (sabotage) groups". Correspondingly Fog mentions that he and Rottbøll discussed the connection between communist groups and the parachutists and that they made the agreement that the parachutists were to provide for explosives and give instructions. (Ac-

count, pag. 8).
50. Cited account, pag. 6–7.
51. Cited account, pag. 6–7.
52. Cited account, pag. 3.
53. Cited account, pag. 4.
54. Buhl's speech is published in "Besættelsestidens fakta" I, pag. 205. Buhl condemned sabotage and asked the population to help the authorities to stop it. Cf. about the reactions to the speech Foss's evaluation in "Fra passiv til aktiv modstand", pag. 111.
55. See f.i. Frisch: "Danmark besat og befriet" I, pag. 240–41.
56. "Besættelsestidens fakta" I, pag. 50 –52.
57. Ibid., pag. 696.
58. "Det illegale Frit Danmark", pag. 62–63.
59. Ibid., pag. 43.
60. "Besættelsestidens fakta" II, pag. 1310.
61. See above pag. 100 f.
62. As to the wording of the speech see "Besættelsestidens fakta" II, pag. 1260 f. C.M. asked strongly for sabotage and condemned any idea of neutrality.
63. This is completely in accordance with the above stated moderate line in the English directives for the spring and summer of 1942. See pag. 122 ff.
64. "Bogen om Christmas Møller", pag. 201–02 and Leif Gundel: "Her er London", pag. 72–73.
65. Cited account, pag. 4.
66. The moderate policy.
67. Se above, pag. 80.
68. Wavendon Park Farm, where the "black" propaganda was produced.
69. See above pag. 80.
70. See above, pag. 58–59 and pag. 111 ff.
71. Munck's diary, note dated ultimo August 1942, pag. 53, Munck's ar-

chive.

72. Ibid. Note dated 10–16/9–1942, pag. 55.

73. The diary refers to an English appeal over BBC to people in Helsingør.

74. Cited account, pag. 7.

75. Cited account, pag. 3.

86. Kiilerich's account, pag. 7. Cf. Juncker's account, pag. 1 where it is mentioned, that Stig Jensen who was Rottbøll's illegal host for part of the time, he spent in Denmark, had approached Juncker and got his sanction.

77. Diemer's account, pag. 4.

78. Cited account, pag. 4.

79. Both of them that summer had taken their school-leaving certificate and were staying as students at the high school in Støvring. Both were eager members of the "Danish Unity Party" and after the occupation both had been ardent organizers of meetings in and around Viborg as pupils in a senior school. This is especially true of Chr. U. Hansen. Se "Chr. Ulrik Hansen" (ed. Elith Olesen & Inge Theut), pag. 7–17. Cf. Stærmose's account, pag. 4. Cf. Toldstrup: "Uden kamp ingen sejr", pag. 21–22.

80. Rottbøll's father was a landowner in Northern Jutland, Børglum kloster.

81. Stærmose's account, pag. 4.

82. Sonne's account, pag. 2.

83. This was made possible because Stærmose who took an active part in the direction of "Frivillig dansk arbejdstjeneste" which just at the time had a camp going on an island, every day had a telephone talk with Kiilerich who frequently wrote articles about the camp. In these routine talks codemessages could be inserted without danger.

84. Sonne's account, pag. 2–3.

85. Hans F. Hansen mentions in his account that a heavy mist swept over the field during the search.

86. This first, loosely organized reception in Denmark is in great detail elucidated through accounts from many participating persons, Diemer, Børge Eriksen, Stærmose, Kiilerich, Sonne, Hans F. Hansen, Knud E. Petersen and Haakon Lauritzen. Later in the summer one of the reception-team, Erik Nymann, who was executed in 1944, confided the event to Toldstrup, who later on became the reception-leader for all Jutland, and he mentions his recollection of Nymann's confidence in his book: "Uden kamp ingen sejr". (pag. 21–22). It seems reasonable to pay attention to the fact, that this accumulation of accounts illustrate exceptionally well the value of accounts. There is an amazing identity not only in the main feature of events but also in details, even chronological ones, an identity which of course can not be normative for all accounts. It seems reasonable to assume that the tension of the experience connected with the fact, that this tension, especially for the participants on the ground, was stretched over a long time and consequently of a latent character, made it possible for the narrators to form exceptionally sharp and correct pictures in their memories of what took place.

12. SOE Hit by New Misfortunes

1. The mentioned "Possone" plus a W/T-set, Johannesen had with him. Max Mikkelsen's set seems to have been lost at Jyderup. (Max Mikkelsen's account, pag. 5. Duus Han-

sen's account, pag. 7).

2. Hollingworth's account, pag. 16.
3. Taylor's account, pag. 5.
4. "Parl. Komm. Betænkn." II, volume 1, pag. 254 ff.
5. Kiilerich's account, pag. 4.
6. Max Mikkelsen's account, pag. 4–5.
7. Cf. Dedichen's account, pag. 7.
8. See about Borch-Johansen's information above, pag. 108. Cf. Max Mikkelsen's account, pag. 5.
9. Se above, pag. 108. Cf. Max Mikkelsen's account, pag. 5.
10. Sonne's account, pag. 2. Cf. Stærmose's account, pag. 5.
11. Cited account, pag. 6. Cf. Letter from Duus Hansen to Hollingworth 26/11–43. Duus Hansen's archive, folder 10.
12. This appears f.i. from a piece of information in Max Mikkelsen's account concerning the transfer of messages of non-urgent character. Later on such messages took the slower but not less dangerous way via Sweden.
13. Can one help wondering how resistance could have been carried out at a later stage when it had attained great dimensions, if the Germans had not driven thousands under ground, thus relieving them from normal daily commitments.
14. Duus Hansen's account, pag. 7.
15. Max Mikkelsen's account, pag. 5–6.
16. Cited account, pag. 6.
17. See about this demand and about the following police action "Parl. Komm. Betænkn." VII, volume 1, pag. 254–56.
18. Ragna Siden: "Chr. Mich. Rottbøll", pag. 93–94. Cf. Diemer's account, pag. 3–4 and Knud E. Petersen's account, pag. 6. The latter mentions that Johannesen had had difficulty in obtaining contact so that his transmission periods had become too long.
19. Cf. "Parl. Komm. Betænkn.", cited in note 17.
20. In Ragna Siden: "Chr. Mich. Rottbøll", pag. 57–58 is quoted a letter from Johannesen which in a moving way expresses his warm, patriotic way of thinking. He writes: "Let us face what will come ... if only those, who are now children ... might be spared the same thing when one day they are launched into the world to work. If only they might find a world with all nations living in friendship ... But if our children must face the same thing ... then I would wish that we had never had our little boy ... then he shall learn that he is a Dane. He shall learn to love Denmark as his mother and if the country be in peril he shall learn to help her." At the time J. was sailing on the Thames under frequent bombardement. He saw East-London on fire during the "blitz".
21. Foss: "Fra passiv til aktiv modstand", pag. 87–88.
22. Hans F. Hansen and Knud E. Petersen both mention that they had been on guard during transmissions (Cited accounts pag. 11 and 6).
23. Duus Hansen's account, pag. 7.
24. Fog's account, pag. 7–8.
25. Hans F. Hansen and Knud E. Petersen who otherwise mention their being on guard during transmissions do not specify whether they "covered" the transmission that day. From the context it rather looks, as if they did not "cover" on that day.
26. That a warning-system was in function already before September

5th appears from the fact, that a planned razzia against a transmission place on Christianshavn Torv was cancelled as the transmitting from here stopped. "Parl. Komm. Betænkn." VII, volume 1, pag. 254–56. Cf. Roland Olsen's account, pag. 45–46.

27. Juncker's account, pag. 2.

28. It seems quite likely that in Juncker's account is hidden a piece of second-hand information, somewhat misunderstood on his part, which he must have received. Roland Olsen – not Duus Hansen, as mentioned by Juncker – was away in the days around 5–9 September. (Roland Olsen's account, pag. 46). Was this the explanation, why Rottbøll did not want any transmission?

29. A description of this action in "Parl. Komm. Betænkn.", VII, volume 1, pag. 244 ff. Supplementary information concerning the infiltration in this group in appendix to Sv. E. Hammer's account, pag. 8–11 as well as in Kiilerich's account, pag. 7.

30. Dedichen's account, pag. 6–7. Cf. Ebbe Munck's diary, where a critical tone is heard in the following: "Arthur (Hammer) has got mixed up with the illegal press and has on the whole not followed instructions". (Munck's archive, IV, folder mrk. "Marken").

31. "Parl. Komm. Betænkn." VII, volume I, pag. 246.

32. Fog's account, pag. 7.

33. Borch-Johansen's account, pag. 12.

34. Fog's account, pag. 7. Cf. Otting's report to Turnbull 7/10–43. (Munck's archive, IV, folder mrk. "Marken").

35. Munck's diary, pag. 57. Cf. Otting's report (note 34), which in a few points confirms the information given.

36. Borch-Johansen's account, pag. 12–13.

37. Cited account, pag. 8.

38. The localization of the apartment was due to German work. On September 25th Abwehrstelle reported to the Danish police that a parachutist, presumably Mogens Hammer, now and then stayed in the apartment Øresundsgade 19, V floor. ("Parl. Komm. Betænkn. VII, volume 1, pag. 257).

39. Duus Hansen's account, pag. 7. In the trial which the Public Prosecutor opened in 1950 against Ragna Siden, Kate Fleron and Børge Houmann the private agreements were thoroughly documented. Hearings of the witnesses Max Weiss, Roland Olsen, Borch Johansen, Stig Jensen, Duus Hansen, Jørgen Diemer and others all verify the decision taken not to shoot at the Danish police and the announcement of this decision along at least two ways of communication to the police executive, superintendant Odmar. Cf. Letter from Hollingworth to Duus Hansen 9/5–43 pag. 2. Duus Hansen's archive, folder 9.

40. Duus Hansen's expression is not precise. According to the description in his account he must exclusively point to the parachute organisation.

41. "Parl. Komm. Betænkn." VII, volume 3, shorthand record, pag. 420.

42. The shooting in Vinkelager.

43. Concerning the following, see explanation during the trial in March 1950. Cf. note 39.

44. The so-called Øst-case in March 1950 (caused by Ragna Siden's book and reviews by Kate Fleron and Børge Houmann) turned on the

decisive question, whether Rott-bøll's first shot went off as a con-sequence of Øst's grasp of Rottbøll's arm and therefore had to be char-acterized as an accidental shot, or whether the shot was a deliberate act on Rottbøll's part. The difficulty in the clearing up of this question lay mainly in the fact, that only two policemen, who were parties to the drama, had witnessed the se-quence of events, and that the strong affect, which the violent events must have meant for them – the post mortem certificate of Rott-bøll's body definitely indicates that the affect had been violent – with-out much doubt must have influ-enced their ability to perceive and remember the course of events with any certainty. Lapses of memory under such circumstances are ex-tremely frequent, indeed normal. No wonder, that while Øst in a talk with Rottbøll's father a few days after the affair assumed that the shot was accidental, in 1950 during the trial he maintained a quite dif-ferent explanation. It seems to be more important for a clarification of the tragic event to emphasize, as the judge in 1950 pointed out, that the police patrol was not informed of the assurance given that the pa-rachutists would not fire. This, at least, could have contributed to give the arrest the flexible, tolerant and quiet character, which might have prevented the catastrophe.

13. Hammer Returns

1. See below, pag. 162.
2. Hans F. Hansen's account, pag. 13 –14.
3. Hans F. Hansen's account, pag. 12 –14. Cf. Knud E. Petersen's account

pag. 7. According to this account it looks as if the connection was temporarily lost.
4. Cited account, pag. 8 and 9.
5. "Table" was a code name used within the Danish section of SOE. Every one of the members of the organisation had a cover name in some way or other connected to the word "table". "Table-Napkin", "Table-Manners", "Table-Tennis" etc.
6. Fog's account, pag. 9.
7. Kiilerich's account, pag. 8.
8. Ebbe Munck's diary, pag. 57. Munck's archive.
9. Table Top was Hammer's cover name (later on also used for Rott-bøll). Munck must here mean "table" as indicated in the paren-thesis.
10. Munck's diary, note 28/9 1942. Diary, pag. 60, Munck's archive.
11. Ibid., note 25–30 September. Diary, pag. 57–61.
12. Hollingworth's account, pag. 19.
13. Ibid., pag. 20.
14. Spink's account, pag. 11.
15. Borch-Johansen's account, pag. 15.
16. See below, pag. 168 ff.
17. Borch-Johansen's account, pag. 15.
18. Letter from Hollingworth to Duus Hansen 16/7–43, pag. 4. Duus Hansen's archive, folder 9.
19. Hollingworth's account, pag. 19–20.
20. Letter from Hollingworth to Duus Hansen 16/7–43, pag. 4. Duus Hansen's archive, folder 9.
21. Hollingworth's account, pag. 20.
22. In his report to Turnbull 7/10–43 Otting mentions that he got a letter from "Lindberg", who proposed co-operation, but in such a way that all communication should be in writ-ing. Like most of the others Ham-mer approached in this way, Ot-

ting refused the idea of such a co-operation, and a few days later he had cleared up the mystery of "Lindberg"'s identity having learnt that Hammer had been seen in the restaurant, "Lorry". (Cited report, pag. 5. Munck's archive, parcel IV, folder mrk. "Marken").

23. Juncker's account, pag. 18.
24. Ibid., pag. 3–4.
25. The English word "cut-out" was taken up in illegal Danish language.
26. Letter from Hollingworth to Hammer 11/3–43. Duus Hansen's archive, folder 1.
27. Hollingworth's account, pag. 20.
28. Newnham: "Prelude to Glory", pag. 153.
29. At least somewhere on the coast of Zealand. Juncker in his account has the place as Tisvilde, while Otting in his report to Turnbull, mentioned in note 22 has it "near my summer-house".
30. Letter from Hollingworth to Duus Hansen 16/7–43, pag. 4. Duus Hansen's archive, folder 9.
31. Kiilerich's account, pag. 9.
32. Cf. these accounts as well as Otting's cited report.
33. See above pag. 137.
34. Cited account, pag. 6.
35. Fog's account, pag. 4–5. The connections between Munck and the intelligence officers must have been quite clear to Fog as on his journey he brought along a mysterious tube of toothpaste, containing a film of intelligence material.
36. See Fog's account, pag. 4–7.
37. Fog's account, pag. 9. Both Hans F. Hansen and Knud E. Petersen mention that they had connection with Kiilerich, but Knud E. Petersen maintains that Kiilerich was unable to provide money, and both

agree, that they received money through casual connections (Cited accounts pag. 12 and 7–8). The question is unessential. All four narrators are in agreement as to their miserable situation, but the practical difficulties must have strengthened the two parachutists' impression of a complete breakdown of the organisation.

38. Shall be four.
39. Fog's account, pag. 8–9. Hans F. Hansen's account, pag. 13 and Kiilerich's account, pag. 8.
40. Fog's account, pag. 9.
41. Fog's account, pag. 8. Kiilerich's account, pag. 9.
42. The attempt of escape and the following negotiations with the German authorities is thoroughly treated in "Parl. Komm. Betænkn." VII, volume 1, pag. 259–60 with notes. See cited work. Cf. Accounts from Kiilerich, Hans F. Hansen and Knud E. Petersen, which give supplementary details. Best's report of the case in "Parl. Komm. Betænkn." XIII, pag. 1331.
43. Their experiences here, especially their experiences in connection with their liberation in May 1945 were the most extraordinary any Dane had experienced during the war and give a tragic, shocking and at the same time grotesque picture of the dissolution of Germany in 1945. Cf. the three men's accounts and a pamphlet, issued 1946 by "Landesstelle für Südtyrol": "Liberation in the South Tyrolese Dolomites".
44. "Frit Danmarks hvidbog" II, pag. 285. Cf. Kiilerich's account, pag. 9.
45. Kiilerich's account, pag. 9.
46. Fog's account, pag. 11.
47. In a letter to Christmas Møller 11/5–43 Chievitz writes: "I hap-

pened to get a "tip" the day before, but chose arrest for three reasons, firstly because the whole thing would be too "thick" if both Fog and I were gone and our "connection", who warned us, would most likely be neutralized, and secondly I believe it created a stir and made people think and thirdly I know better than anybody else how difficult it can be to get out of the country, and that possibility must be reserved the younger and more compromised." (Letter from Christmas Møller's archive, published in Jørgen Hæstrup: "Christmas Møllers Londonbreve", pag. 68 ff.).

48. An extract of the letter in "Det illegale Frit Danmark", pag. 119–20.

49. Duus Hansen's account, pag. 8–9.

50. Duus Hansen does not indicate precisely, when or where these negotiations took place. It will appear from the following that the negotiations were carried on via Stockholm.

51. Letter from Hollingworth to Duus Hansen 19/4–43, pag. 1. Duus Hansen's archive, folder 9.

52. In the following it will not always be possible to refer to particular pages.

53. Letter from Duus Hansen to Hollingworth 23/5–43, pag. 1. Duus Hansen's archive, folder 10.

54. Munck's diary, note 14 January–10 February 1943. Diary, page 89. Munck's archive.

55. See above pag. 144.

56. Juncker's account, pag. 1. Kiilerich's account, pag. 7.

57. Juncker's account, pag. 4–5.

58. Cited accounts, pag. 10–11 and 9.

59. Fog's account, pag. 10–11.

60. Actually, Hammer got nothing.

There were, as has been seen, no droppings during the winter months, in which Hammer had orders to hold the fort, and Hammer was fully informed, that no droppings were planned. For all that Hammer may well have pretended, that he worked with plans of the kind. It would have been in accordance with his instructions, if he had tried to fill the vacuum with bluff, if only for psychological reasons. Hans F. Hansen and Knud E. Petersen both mention that they got the impression, that he prepared for reception in Zealand.

61. Letter from Duus Hansen to Turnbull, pag. 2. Duus Hansen's archive, folder 12. The letter is undated, but as Duus Hansen's code name in the English correspondence is first Ds., later Henry and from 19/4–43 Table Napkin there is here a certain clue for a date, in so far as Duus Hansen signs Ds. It is not unreasonable to assume, that the letter is from about February, so that the application coincides with the application from Juncker, mentioned earlier.

62. It appears from the letter, that it was a general view that Hammer was too careless in his activities.

63. Borch-Johansen's account, pag. 4–5. Cf. Hammer's articles in "De frie Danske". According to information from Sv. E. Hammer, Mogens Hammer wrote the articles: "Vær opmærksom, brug øjnene" (April 1942). "Udenrigsministerielle farcer" (April 1942). "Christmas Møllers rejse til England" (June 1942).

64. Sv. E. Hammer's account, pag. 1.

65. Fog's account, pag. 9–10.

66. Kiilerich's account, pag. 9.

67. Letter from Hollingworth to Ham-

mer 11/3–43, pag. 1–2. Duus Hansen's archive, folder 1.
68. Letter from Hollingworth to Muus 19/4–43. Duus Hansen's archive, folder 2.
69. See below, pag. 189–90. Borch-Johansen's account, pag. 15.
70. Letter from Hollingworth to Duus Hansen 16/7–43, pag. 4. Duus Hansen's archive, folder 9.
71. Borch-Johansen's account, pag. 5.
72. "Danmark under besættelsen" III, pag. 480.
73. Borch-Johansen gives this characterization of him in his account, which also mentions several sporadic episodes typical of Hammer's bravery.
74. Letter from Hollingworth to Duus Hansen 16/7–43, pag. 4. Duus Hansen's archive, folder 9.

14. Change in British Policy

1. Letter, dated 22/11–42. Enclosed in Munck's diary between pag. 79 and 80, Munck's archive.
2. Foss: "Fra passiv til aktiv modstand", pag. 148.
3. The Allied offensives started 23 October from Egypt and 8 November with landings in French Northwest Africa. The Russian offensive around Stalingrad started 19 November.
4. "Det illegale Frit Danmark", pag. 89 ff.
5. Ibid., pag. 165 ff.
6. "Besættelsestidens fakta" II, pag. 1316.
7. Foss: "Fra passiv til aktiv modstand", pag. 146–49.
8. In the formerly quoted letter from Chievitz to Christmas Møller 11/5–43 Chievitz expresses himself along the same line. Munck's archive, I, folder mrk. "Rapporter London I".

9. See Foss: "Fra passiv til aktiv modstand", pag. 133–34.
10. See above, pag. 121.
11. Munck's diary, pag. 65. Munck's archive.
12. Jørgen Hæstrup: "Table Top" ("Jyske Samlinger", 1961), pag. 407. Turnbull's letters during the autumn are quoted here.
13. Ibid. pag. 408 ff.
14. Munck's diary, pag. 84, Munck's archive.
15. Ibid. note dated 14/1–10/2 1943, diary, pag. 89, Munck's archive.
16. Ibid. note dated 1/3–1/4 1943, Diary, pag. 94–95. Munck's archive.
17. Jørgen Hæstrup: "Table Top" (see note 12), pag. 412 ff.
18. "Danmark under besættelsen" III, pag. 487–88.
19. Munck's account, pag. 7–8.
20. Sabotage figures for the first 6 months of 1943 are estimated in "Besættelsestidens fakta" as 14-29: 60-70-62-44. Cited work II, pag. 1206. See below, chapter 21.
21. Letters from Ebbe Munck to Christmas Møller 3/2–43 and 15/2–43. Munck's archive, IV, folder mrk. "Rapporter London I".
22. Cf. about reactions in Copenhagen, Frisch: "Danmark besat og befriet" I, pag. 291–92.
23. Muus's book, published in 1950, is based upon an earlier version, as Muus, who in 1946 was sentenced to imprisonment for embezzlement (cf. his book "Ingen tænder et lys", pag. 206–07) worked out in prison a rough draught of an exposition of his activity in Denmark during the Occupation. It is this copy which in an adapted form has been published as "Ingen tænder et lys". The adaptation is mostly of a formal character and is based upon the copy mentioned,

which is four years closer to the events described. This must be considered of importance in an evaluation of the book as a source. The original copy exists in Rigsarkivet in "Muus's archive". The book must, however, be treated with some caution. In details it may be incorrect. Cf. critical remarks below. In all essentials it is confirmed by the collected documentary material.

24. Muus: "Ingen tænder et lys", pag. 59–60.

25. About Muus's stay in Liberia see his book: "Det begyndte under sydkorset."

26. Further information in Muus: "Ingen tænder et lys", pag. 5–11.

27. Muus was very nearly attached to SIS – just like Thomas Sneum – when SOE intervened and demanded his service.

28. Hollingworth's account, pag. 20.

29. Spink's account, pag. 11.

30. Taylor's account, pag. 5–6.

31. Borch-Johansen's account, pag. 16 and 18.

32. Cited accounts.

33. An appreciative tone pervades all the letters. Cf. following chapters.

34. Letter from Duus Hansen to Hollingworth 23/5–43, pag. 1. Duus Hansen's archive, folder 10.

35. Munck's diary, pag. 102, Munck's archive.

36. Munck's diary, note dated June–July 1943. Diary pag. 104. Munck's archive.

37. Accounts from these three men in Rigsarkivet. About their way to SOE, see their accounts.

38. Droppings were timed to the periods, where moonlight made a precise orientation as easy as possible.

39. From these four no accounts exist.

About Geisler, see "Salmonsens leksikontidsskrift", 1949, sp. 402–03. About Adolf Larsen and H. H. Larsen see "Parl. Komm. Betænkn." VII, volume 1, pag. 261 and 263–64. H. H. Larsen's name is here wrongly given as K. Larsen.

40. Borch-Johansen's account, pag. 16.

41. The team came to Copenhagen by the last S-train from Holte. Cf. Roland Olsen's account, pag. 44.

22. Cited account, pag. 6.

43. In February 1943 Juncker was in Stockholm, where he settled the future droppings with Turnbull. Cf. the following.

42. "Parl. Komm. Betænkn." VII, volume 1, pag. 261.

45. It is thus a characteristic trait, that the parachutists' accounts all emphasize the dramatic element of the situations.

46. Juncker's account, pag. 5.

47. The Farsø-droppings had led to thorough interrogations of Stærmose and Sonne, as the police seriously suspected the possible involvement of the two men in the reception. (Stærmose's account, pag. 5–6, Sonne's account, pag. 4–5).

48. The election took place 23 March 1943.

49. Cf. about the negotiations of the two men: Juncker's account, pag. 6–7. Stærmose's account, pag. 5–6. Sonne's account, pag. 4–5).

50. "Parl. Komm. Betænkn." VII, volume 1, pag. 260.

51. Verner Johansen's account, pag. 4–5. Muus: "Ingen tænder et lys", pag. 70–71.

52. The man in question was insurance agent Nikolaysen. Muus: "Ingen tænder et lys", pag. 70–71.

53. A thorough, but in the geographic matter inaccurate description of

these events is given by Muus in "Ingen tænder et lys", pag. 67–73. This description is supplemented through the accounts of his companions. Generally speaking there is agreement as to the course of events.

54. Juncker's account, pag. 6. Brøchners account, pag. 1. Cf. below pag. 223.
55. Letter from Duus Hansen to Turnbull, undated. Duus Hansen's archive, folder 12.
56. Letter from Muus to Hollingworth 30/4–43, pag. 2. Duus Hansen's archive, folder 3.
57. The two men came down at Hvidsten 17 and 21 April 1943. Cf. their accounts pag. 2 and 3.
58. The inn at Hvidsten.

15. The Parachutist Organisation Reorganised

1. Muus: "Ingen tænder et lys", pag. 75–76. Juncker's account, pag. 8–9. Stærmose's account, pag. 7.
2. Juncker's account, pag. 10–11. Letter from Muus to Hollingworth 30/4–43. Duus Hansen's archive, folder 3.
3. These letters are in Duus Hansen's archive, folder 2.
4. Letter from Hollingworth to Hammer 11/3–43; pag. 1 Duus Hansen's archive, folder 1.
5. Copenhagen.
6. Jutland.
7. Hollingworth's italics.
8. Signalplans.
9. Muus: "Ingen tænder et lys", pag. 76.
10. Ibid. pag. 75–79. Juncker's account, pag. 8–9.
11. Muus: Ingen tænder et lys", pag. 102.
12. From 1943 the following reports

are preserved: Nr. 1 30/4–43, nr. 2. 21/5–43, nr. 7 25/7–43 and nr. 10 18/9–43. The reports are in the form of letters and are fairly long – from 5 to 13 typed pages in folio, partly with appendices – and contain a lot of detailed information concerning the work in Denmark.

13. Accounts exist from Aage Møller Christensen, Peter Carlsen, Lok Linblad and Kaj Lund.
14. A thorough reading of reports and accounts gives no basis for any such supposition. Muus: "Ingen tænder et lys" mentions no names, which are not included in the chapters in this exposition. Neither has Juncker, who mentions the placing of individual parachutists in his account, any further names.
15. Letter from Hollingworth to Muus 9/5–43, pag. 1. Duus Hansen's archive, folder 2.
16. Royal Air Force, which had the responsibility for the dropping operations.
17. Cf. below about dropping operations, chapter 18 and 19. After July 1943 no new parachutists were dropped in the period, which we are dealing with here.
18. Letter from Muus to Hollingworth 30/4–43, pag. 1–2. Duus Hansen's archive, folder 2.
19. At that time Muus had not yet received the information that operations were cancelled from ca. 15 May to the middle of July.
20. Letter from Muus to Hollingworth 21/5–43, pag. 2. Duus Hansen's archive, folder 3.
21. Hecht Johansen's account, pag. 2. Cf. the mentioned letters from Muus.
22. Muus: "Ingen tænder et lys", pag. 90. Cf. Lok Linblad's account, pag.

3:" Muus had asked for me, and I went over on April 21th."

23. Letter from Hollingworth to Muus 9/5–43. Duus Hansen's archive, folder 2.

24. Muus: "Ingen tænder et lys", pag. 82–87.

25. Letter from Muus to Hollingworth 30/4–43, pag. 3. Duus Hansen's archive, folder 3.

26. Muus: "Ingen tænder et lys", pag. 87.

27. Good Friday in 1943 was on April 23th.

28. Muus: "Ingen tænder et lys", pag. 90. The date seems confirmed by Kaj Lund's account, pag. 2.

29. Letter from Muus to Hollingworth 30/4–43. Duus Hansen's archive, folder 3. Concerning the telegraphic message see the following letter from Hollingworth.

30. Letter from Hollingworth to Muus 9/5–43, pag. 4. Duus Hansen's archive, folder 2.

31. Letter from Muus to Hollingworth 21/5–43, pag. 2. Duus Hansen's archive, folder 3.

32. Ebbe Munck's diary, pag. 106, Munck's archive.

33. A thorough description of the Adolf Larsen-case in "Parl. Komm. Betænkn." VII, volume 1, pag. 260 –63. Cf. Account from Verner Jensen, pag. 2–3.

34. Cf. Roland Olsen's account, pag. 61–63, which confirms and is confirmed by information in Duus Hansen's reports.

35. Reports in Duus Hansen's archive, folder 10.

36. "Parl. Komm. Betænkn." has here the peculiar – and incorrect – information that the letter-writer, a certain Eliasen (Juncker's cover-name), was later on identified as dead in hospital in Kolding on May 17th 1943.

37. Roland Olsen has it that the two couriers were taken to the German police in Aarhus, and that it was possible to arrange a joint explanation with them during the journey to Aarhus.

38. Muus's letter to Hollingworth 30/4 –43, pag. 2. Duus Hansen's archive, folder 3. Cf. Bach Frederiksen's account, pag. 1–2.

39. "Parl. Komm. Betænkn." VII, volume 1, pag. 263–64.

40. Muus briefly mentions the case in "Ingen tænder et lys", pag. 93 Cf. Letters from Hollingworth to Muus 19/4–43 and 9/5–43 as well as letter from Muus to Hollingworth 30/4–43. Duus Hansen's archive, folder 2 and 3. Cf. Lok Linblad's account, pag. 3.

41. Letter from Hollingworth to Muus 19/4–43. Duus Hansen's archive, folder 2.

42. Letter from Hollingworth to Muus 9/5–43, pag. 4–5. Duus Hansen's archive, folder 2.

43. Ibid.

44. A thorough description of the disaster on Thielesvej is given in the newspaper, "Information", 29. August 1953.

45. Muus: "Ingen tænder et lys", pag. 102. Cf. Lok Linblad's account, pag. 3. Cf. Muus's letters to Hollingworth, where he in the sections, marked "personnel", states the changing placing of the people in the field.

46. Re the attempts to establish a radio service in Jutland se below pag. 195 and 203.

47. Letter from Muus to Hollingworth 25/7–43, pag. 11. Duus Hansen's archive, folder 3.

48. Borch-Johansen's account, pag. 4.

49. Cited account, pag. 2–3.

50. Carl Larsen acted as a sort of paymaster for SOE with connection to Per Federspiel. Cf. Muus: "Ingen tænder et lys", pag. 111–12.

51. Within the organisation Adolf Larsen's name was "Andy".

52. Cf. about this connection Kaj Lund's account, pag. 3. Also Juncker mentions the connection in his account.

53. Letter from Muus to Hollingworth 30/4–43, pag. 3. Duus Hansen's archive, folder 3. It appears that the telephone connection was established already in April. Kaj Lund came to Denmark 17/4 and the connection had been active before the difficulties in his sending became apparent, which explains that these difficulties were taken rather lightly in Denmark.

54. Letter from Hollingworth to Muus 9/5–43. Duus Hansen's archive, folder 2.

55. Hollingworth's letters to Muus 9/5 –43 and 17/5–43, pages 2 and 8. Duus Hansen's archive, folder 2.

56. Letter from Hollingworth to Muus 26/7–43. Duus Hansen's archive, folder 2.

57. Letter from Muus to Hollingworth 25/7–43, pag. 13. Duus Hansen's archive, folder 3. The letter is from 25/7–43 but has not been sent until Muus's reception of Hollingworth's letter of 26/7, thus containing brief answers to Hollingworth's questions in the said letter.

58. Most of the European countries, occupied by the Germans, had governments in exile in London, which kept an eye on developments. A certain parallel to conditions in Denmark may be found almost anywhere in the occupied countries. An analysis of the European Resistance Movements is given in Jørgen Hæstrup: "Den 4. våbenart. Hovedtræk af de europæiske modstandsbevægelsers historie, 1939–45" and in Henri Michel: "La Guerre de l'Ombre".

59. Letter from Hollingworth to Muus 17/5–43. Duus Hansen's archive, folder 2.

60. Letter from Muus to Hollingworth 21/5–43. Duus Hansen's archive, folder 3.

61. Letter from Muus to Hollingworth 25/7–43. Duus Hansen's archive, folder 3.

62. Letter from Hollingworth to Muus 9/5–43. Duus Hansen's archive, folder 2.

63. Letter from Muus to Hollingworth 21/5–43. Duus Hansen's archive, folder 3.

64. See generally the following description.

65. Juncker's account, pag. 10–11.

66. Letters from Muus to Hollingworth 30/4–43 and 25/7–43, pag. 3 and 13. Duus Hansen's archive, folder 3.

67. Juncker's account, pag. 11. Cf. Federspiel's account, pag. 8–9.

68. Op. cit., pag. 73.

69. Letter from Muus to Hollingworth 21/5–43. Duus Hansen's archive, folder 3.

70. The placing and shifting of the parachutists may be ascertained through many sources. Muus's letters to Hollingworth in the sections marked "personnel" state the changing placing. In "Ingen tænder et lys", especially pages 88 and 102 –06 Muus has an incomplete survey, and corresponding surveys exist in Juncker's and Lok Linblad's accounts. Cf. the existing accounts of the individual parachutists. It is fair to point to the work, which Paul Jensen and Peter Carl-

sen carried out in Aalborg and Odense. Here the representatives of SOE were to play a special part in the resistance work. Both parachutists have given accounts, which in detail expound their share in the development. As for Odense cf. the special archive for the Funen-region, which after May 5th 1945 was collected by the former regional committee of Funen, as for Aalborg cf. account by Haakon Lauritzen and Arne Nielsen.

16. Improving Communications with the Free World

1. See in general Duus Hansen's archive, folder 9, 10, 11 and 12 and the folders with telegrams.
2. A description of the illegal radio service is given by Duus Hansen in the periodical "Danmark", 6 volume, nr. 23–24, pag. 543–48.
3. Letter from Muus to Hollingworth 30/4–43, pag. 3–4. Duus Hansen's archive, folder 3.
4. Letter from Hollingworth to Muus 9/5–43, pag. 2. Duus Hansen's archive, folder 2.
5. Letter from Hollingworth to Muus 17/5–43, pag. 1. Duus Hansen's archive, folder 2.
6. Letter from Hollingworth to Duus Hansen 19/4–43, Duus Hansen's archive, folder 9.
7. Letter from Hollingworth to Duus Hansen 16/7–43, pag. 1. Duus Hansen's archive, folder 9.
8. Letter from Turnbull to Duus Hansen 22/6–43. Duus Hansen's archive, folder 11.
9. Letter from Hollingworth to Duus Hansen 6/11–43, pag. 1. Duus Hansen's archive, folder 9.
10. Cf. the following.
11. About the work of Fischer Holst,

see his archive.
12. Duus Hansen's account, pag. 13.
13. Letter from Hollingworth to Duus Hansen 16/7–43, pag. 2. Duus Hansen's archive, folder 9.
14. Letter from Hollingworth to Duus Hansen 6/11–43. Duus Hansen's archive, folder 9.
15. At that time Muus was in London to discuss the organization of future work. Cf. Muus: "Ingen tænder et lys", pag. 135 ff.
16. London was able to identify the "telegraph writing" of each telegraphist, thus being able to make sure that set and codes were not used by others than just the man they counted on.
17. Ebbe Munck's diary, note dated June–July 1943, pag. 105. Munck's archive.
18. Cited letter pag. 3.
19. Letter from Turnbull to Duus Hansen 23/6–43, pag. 1. Duus Hansen's archive, folder 11.
20. Letter from Duus Hansen to Hollingworth 11/9–43, pag. 1. Duus Hansen's archive, folder 10.
21. Letter from Hollingworth to Duus Hansen 6/11–43. Duus Hansen's archive, folder 9.
22. Letter from Duus Hansen to Hollingworth 24/11–43, pag. 3. Duus Hansen's archive, folder 10.
23. Letter from Duus Hansen to Hollingworth 24/11–43. Duus Hansen's archive, folder 10.
24. During the Occupation one telegraphist was killed under arrest, one was executed, four were arrested and deported and one had to flee to Sweden.
25. Letter from Duus Hansen to Hollingworth 24/11–43. Duus Hansen's archive, folder 10.
26. Letter from Muus to Hollingworth 30/4–43, pag. 4. Duus Hansen's

archive, folder 3. Cf. Kaj Lund's account, pag. 2–3.

27. Letter from Muus to Hollingworth 25/7–43. Duus Hansen's archive, folder 3.

28. Cf. for instance "Danmark under besættelsen" II, pag. 381–406. Erling Kjær: "Med Gestapo i kølvandet". "Den aabne dør til den frie verden". A very great amount of material about the history of these refugee organisations exist. Immediately after the liberation Leif B. Hendil handed over the archive for Dansk-Svensk Flygtningetjeneste to Rigsarkivet, and in the archives, collected by the author, there is plenty of material about the refugee organisations, thus in archives from Ebbe Munck, Werner Gyberg and Verner Jensen.

29. Letter from Muus to Hollingworth 18/9–43. Duus Hansen's archive, folder 3.

30. Muus's letter of 18/9–43 is marked "Filmsmessage nr. 10".

31. Letter from Duus Hansen to Hollingworth 11/9–43. Duus Hansen's archive, folder 10.

32. The "matros", formerly mentioned in Gyberg's account. See above pag. 111 f.

33. Letter from Muus to Hollingworth 30/4–43, pag. 5. Duus Hansen's archive, folder 3.

34. Ebbe Munck's diary. Note dated May 1943. Diary, pag. 101. Munck's archive.

35. Letter from Muus to Hollingworth 30/4–43, pag. 11. Duus Hansen's archive, folder 3.

36. Reference is made to a dropping at Hvidsten, where the reception-group failed to collect all the equipment.

37. Muus: "Ingen tænder et lys", pag. 96. Cf. "Den hvide brigade", pag. 51. Cf. Knud E. Petersen's account, pag. 8.

38. Undated letter, but after its contents seemingly from the beginning of June 1943. Duus Hansen's archive, folder 12.

39. See above pag. 67.

40. Letters from Muus to Hollingworth 30/4–43, pag. 5, 25/7–43, pag. 10 and 18/9–43, pag. 2. Duus Hansen's archive, folder 3.

41. Ebbe Munck's diary, note dated May 1943, pag. 100, Munck's archive.

42. Letter from Muus to Hollingworth 25/7–43. Duus Hansen's archive, folder 3.

43. Billy Thalbitzer: "Med R.A.F. for Danmark. Historien om Jørgen Thalbitzer". Cf. "Danmark under besættelsen" III, pag. 717.

44. Cited account, appendix.

45. Cf. Einar Balling's account pag. 6, stating that Balling was evacuated through this route together with a Canadian pilot.

46. Letter from Turnbull to Duus Hansen 15/7–43, pag. 1. Duus Hansen's archive, folder 11.

47. Sign for boats from the Frederikshavndistrict.

48. Letter from Muus to Hollingworth 25/7–43. Duus Hansen's archive, folder 3.

49. A short survey about this route in "Danmark under besættelsen" III, pag. 399–402. Cf. Gyberg's and Verner Jensen's accounts. A copious material allowing a detailed description of the history of the route exists in Gyberg's, Verner Jensen's and Ebbe Munck's archives.

17. Contact with the Army and Police

1. Op. cit., pag. 98–99.
2. See above pag. 176.
3. Ebbe Munck's diary, pag. 97.

Munck's archive.

4. Ibid. Notes dated May 1943 and June–July 1943, diary pag. 102 and 104, Munck's archive.

5. Letter from Muus to Hollingworth 21/5–43, pag. 3. Duus Hansen's archive, folder 3.

6. Op. cit., pag. 98–99.

7. Letter from Muus to Hollingworth 25/7–43, pag. 11, Duus Hansen's archive, folder 3.

8. Letter from Hollingworth to Duus Hansen 9/5–43, pag. 2, Duus Hansen's archive, folder 9.

9. See above, pag. 166.

10. Hollingworth's letter 9/5–43 to Duus Hansen, see note 8.

11. E.g. above, pag. 166–67. cf. pag. 192–93.

12. See above, pag. 190 f.

13. Letter from Hollingworth to Duus Hansen 9/5–43, pag. 1–2. Duus Hansen's archive, folder 9.

14. Letter from Hollingworth to Duus Hansen 16/7–43, pag. 1. Duus Hansen's archive, folder 9.

15. Letter from Turnbull to the Intelligence-officers 27/8–43, pag. 1. Duus Hansen's archive, folder 15.

16. Telegrams received by Duus Hansen. Duus Hansen's archive, folder 27.

17. Cf. that a V-1 bomb in 1943 landed undamaged in Bornholm after test-shooting. On that occasion captain Hassager Christiansen managed to measure and photograph the bomb and to get his results forwarded to England (through the officers' intelligence-net) before he was arrested by the Germans. See detailed description in Jørgen H. Barfoed: "Et Centrum i periferien. Modstandsbevægelsen på Bornholm", chapter IV.

18. Letter from Hollingworth to Duus Hansen 16/7–43, pag. 3. Duus

19. Hansen's archive, folder 9.

19. Op. cit., pag. 124–25.

20. Letter from Muus to Turnbull 16/9 –43, pag. 1–2. Duus Hansen's archive, folder 5.

21. See above pag. 202.

22. Letter from Duus Hansen to Turnbull 20/9–43, Duus Hansen's archive, folder 12.

23. Cf. about Duus Hansen's attitude his account, pag. 12.

24. Letter from Duus Hansen to Hollingworth 24/11–43 pag. 1. Duus Hansen's archive, folder 10.

25. Cf. Federspiel's account, pag. 13–14. Officers from the intelligence-service worked after their arrival in Stockholm in close co-operation with Munck. (Munck's account, pag. 8). Cf. Volume II, chapter 5.

26. Letter from Duus Hansen to Hollingworth 24/11–43. Cf. note 24.

27. Letter from Muus to Hollingworth 25/7–43, pag. 13. Duus Hansen's archive, pag. 3. Cf. Muus: "Ingen tænder et lys" pag. 99–100.

28. Duus Hansen's account, pag. 12.

29. Cf. above, pag. 84–86. In his account Egil Barfod mentions, that he arranged for Muus's contact with Bahnsen. The reason was that the English wanted the Danish minesweepers to be sabotaged. (Barfod's account, pag. 4–5). No direct order of that kind exists in Muus's correspondence with London, but from earnest inquiries in Hollingworth's letters to Muus it is obvious that London was strongly interested in the Danish mine-sweepers.

30. See above pag. 190 f.

31. Letter from Muus to Hollingworth 21/5–43, pag. 6. Duus Hansen's archive, folder 3.

32. See above pag. 191.

33. Examples are abundant throughout Duus Hansen's archive, especially

in folder 24.

34. Roland Olsen's account, pag. 79.

35. Cf. Roland Olsen's account, pag. 62 –64, where some examples are given. Similar examples appear time and again in the general literature about resistance or in the collection of accounts in the National Archives in Copenhagen. To take just one example, see Carlo Christensen: "Under jorden i Borgergade". The book is full of examples.

36. "Beretning om dannelse af den første faldskærmsgruppe i Odense". Archive for the Funen-region.

37. The sabotage group gathered around the parachutist Peter Carlsen.

38. Letter from Roland Olsen to Hollingworth, mrk. "Filmsmessage nr. 10". Duus Hansen's archive, folder 10.

39. Letter from Turnbull to Roland Olsen 26/6–43. Duus Hansen's archive, folder 15.

40. Letter quoted in Roland Olsen's account, pag. 65–66.

41. A clear survey of the prolonged negotiations, which laid down the framework agreement of future police-activity in "Danmark under verdenskrig og besættelse" III, pag. 154 ff. A thorough exposition in Jørgen Hæstrup: "Til landets bedste" I, chapter 14 and II, pag. 12–14.

42. Roland Olsen's account, pag. 82–85.

43. Letter from Duus Hansen to Hollingworth 11/9–43, pag. 1. Duus Hansen's archive, folder 10.

44. Letter from Duus Hansen to Turnbull 20/9–43, pag. 1. Duus Hansen's archive, folder 12.

45. Duus Hansen's main contact became police-officer Ib Larsen, who before August 29th had been Roland Olsen's closest assistant in the department. When the connection on August 29th broke down, Ib Larsen succeeded in getting a new connection with Duus Hansen through professor Chievitz. (Ib Larsen's account pag. 16).

46. Duus Hansen's archive, folder 10.

18. Hvidsten

1. See above pag. 180 f.

2. Junckers account, pag. 6.

3. A lonely remark in a letter from Geisler to me four months before his death must be quoted here. In a short description of the work in spring 1943 he writes: "When I think back to that period . . . February-March 1943 and the rest of the year, the results, we obtained, seem so small and unessential as compared with the great events later on in the war, where the little crowd, which then worked so well against much greater odds, were sitting hidden and forgotten round about in German prisons, in Sweden or, so many of them, under the obligatory six feet earth . . . I consider that period as one of the richest in my life, where I got my best friends and in too many cases lost them again."

4. See above pag. 187.

5. Cited account pag. 1.

6. Schoch's account.

7. Brøchner's account pag. 1.

8. Juncker's account pag. 9.

9. Baastrup Thomsen's account pag. 2 –3. It appears, that the question is about the situation at the end of March 1943 after Adolf Larsen's arrest and not, as Baastrup Thomsen remembers, in the last days of February. Cf. Georg Andresen: "Aarhus under besættelsen", pag.

263–65.

10. See above pag. 194 f.

11. See below chapter 19.

12. Concerning the following see Juncker's account pag. 9 and Brøchner's account pag. 1. Cf. Axel Holm: "Hvidstengruppen". This book is obviously based upon interviews with people around the Hvidsten-group, but it does not mention any source. Both as to the events told here and as to the following description of receptions at Hvidsten the reader will recognize essential traits in the book regardless of the fact that the book is very inaccurate.

13. Brøchner's account pag. 2.

14. Muus: "Ingen tænder et lys", pag. 76.

15. Brøchner's account pag. 2.

16. See below pag. 251.

17. About the organisation of reception-work at Hvidsten see: Juncker's account pag. 6. "Danmark under besættelsen" III, pag. 217–19 and 453–61. Muus: "Ingen tænder et lys" pag. 88–89. Supplementary information in accounts from: Einar Balling, Peter Carlsen, Verner Johansen, Preben Lok Linblad and Kaj Lund. Rf. Brøchner's account.

18. Brøchner's account pag. 2.

19. Cf. accounts of Einar Balling pag. 3 and Peter Carlsen pag. 2–3.

20. Cited account pag. 3.

21. Lok Linblad does not mention all the members of the group. It comprised several more. Eight members were court-martialled and sentenced to death on June 26th 1944, three – among them Marius Fiil's wife – were sentenced to lifelong prison. Cf. Frisch: "Danmark besat og befriet" III, pag. 149.

22. See above pag. 184 f where Muus mentions that the two men were taken to a famous inn few minutes after landing.

23. Report of 26/2–45 from Stig Jensen til Hollingworth, Stig Jensen's archive.

24. The report is sprinkled with little illustrative and humorous details.

25. Dropping over a reception-place was advertised over BBC through a special greeting to the "name" of the place in question.

26. Machine-gun.

27. Letter from Muus to Hollingworth 30/4–43, pag. 2. Duus Hansen's archive, folder 3.

28. The instruction is found in Hollingworth's letter to Muus 17/5–43, Duus Hansen's archive, folder 2. The instruction illustrates the technique of dropping as that technique had developped in spring 1943. Extensive descriptions of dropping-operations are given in "Frit Danmarks hvidbog" II, pag. 345–51 and in Toldstrup: "Uden kamp ingen sejr", especially pag. 132 ff.

29. Cited letter of 17/5–43, pag. 4. Here Hollingworth only mentions his misgivings as to the short nights. In a formerly quoted letter of 9/5–43 he also mentions, that the nights are too light and gives the information, that R.A.F. originally had decided to cancel operations from May 16th to the middle of August, a limitation which he succeeded to reduce to 17 May–18 July.

30. Hollingworth's account pag. 19, cf. Muus: "Ingen tænder et lys" pag. 101 ff. Cf. above pag. 196 f.

31. Cited letter pag. 4.

32. Fighting in Tunisia ended 13 May 1943.

33. Cf. Peter Carlsen's account pag. 4.

Diemer's account pag. 5. Juncker's account pag. 10 and Baastrup Thomsen's account pag. 5.

34. Cited letter 17/5–43, pag. 6.
35. See f.i. Muus: "Ingen tænder et lys", pag. 88–89, 106, 109–10.
36. Cf. Aage Møller Christensen's account pag. 3, Diemer's account pag. 6. Muus: "Ingen tænder et lys", pag. 109–10. In Southern Jutland R.A.F. never accepted droppings. Cf. "Frit Danmarks hvidbog" II, pag. 348.
37. The column of telegrams provided by the veterinarian and W/T-operator, H. Kj. Duus Hansen.
38. Letter from Hollingworth to Muus 9/5–43. Duus Hansen's archive, folder 2.
39. Peter Carlsen's account, pag. 3.
40. Appendix in letter from Hollingworth to Muus 9/5–43, Duus Hansen's archive, folder 2.
41. Cited letter 17/5–43 pag. 2.
42. Letter from Muus to Hollingworth 21/5–43, pag. 1. Duus Hansen's archive, folder 3.
43. Letter from Muus to Hollingworth 21/5–43, pag. 1. Duus Hansen's archive, folder 3.
44. Baastrup Thomsen's account, pag. 4.
45. Baastrup Thomsen does not know that the set already had been used 17 May.

19. Dropping Operations Expanded

1. See above pag. 188 and pag. 225 f.
2. Muus's letters to Hollingworth 30/4–43 and 21/5–43 and Hollingworth's letters to Muus 9/5–43 and 17/5–43. Duus Hansen's archive, folder 2 and 3. Cf. accounts from Kaj Lund, Preben Lok Linblad and Peter Carlsen pag. 2, 3, 2.
3. Both the letters exchanged as well as the accounts give few or no pre-

cise information.
4. See above pag. 225.
5. Lok Linblad's account pag. 3.
6. Brøchner's account pag. 2.
7. See chapter 18, note 28.
8. Letter from Muus to Hollingworth 21/5–43 pag. 11. Duus Hansen's archive, folder 3.
9. Cf. Peter Carlsen's account pag. 4, which gives the hour at 22 p.m.
10. Peter Carlsen's account pag. 3–4.
11. The incident can also be found in Gerda Fiil's version. ("Danmark under besættelsen" III, pag. 457). The sequence of events: German soldiers on exercise, unrest in the inn and Fiil's steady handing out of food and drink is the same, whereas statements as to hour vary considerably in the two accounts.
12. Cited letter to Hollingworth pag. 1, 7, 8 and 11. Duus Hansen's archive, folder 3.
13. See besides Muus's letter to Hollingworth Aage Møller Christensen's account pag. 2. The date for this dropping was about July 25th.
14. Paul Jensen's account pag. 8. "Parl. Komm. Betænkning" VI, pag. 264 f. Cf. Arboe-Rasmussen: "Den første".
15. Paul Jensen's account pag. 4–8. The police-office in Aalborg has informed that three droppings took place near Madum, medio July and August 2th and 17th.
16. Muus: "Ingen tænder et lys" pag. 109–11. Ottings report to Turnbull 7/10–43 (Ebbe Munck's archive, parcel IV, folder marked "Marken"). Cf. "Danmark under besættelsen" III, pag. 100. Here the author, Stig Jensen, who himself was one of the reception-leaders erroneously dates the event to the Rottbøll-days, August 1942.
17. Juncker's account pag. 10. Baastrup

Thomsen's account pag. 5.

18. Diemer's account pag. 5–6.
19. Cited account pag. 5.
20. Letter from Muus to Turnbull 21/9 –43 pag. 1. Duus Hansen's archive, folder 5.
21. Letter from Muus to Hollingworth 25/7–43 pag. 1. Duus Hansen's archive, folder 3.
22. It appears from Møller Christensen's account that one of these "points" was Madum-lake. Hollingworth's request for reserveplaces seems to have been met.
23. Baastrup Thomsen's account pag. 4–5.
24. "Den hvide brigade" pag. 54–55.
25. Two contemporary letters, Muus's letter to Hollingworth 25/7–43 pag. 7 and 9, and captain Rantzau's letter to Turnbull 28/7–43 (Duus Hansen's archive, folder 3 and 19) have corresponding dates for these two droppings: July 22th and 26th. Cf. "Rapport om dannelsen af den første faldskærmsgruppe i Odense" (archive for the Funenregion), which also mentions two droppings but erroneously place them at the latter part of June. Cf. also Peter Carlsen's account, which curiously enough only mentions one dropping.
26. The two men were to have been dropped the same night as Boelsskov (23 July) but had to return to base as the night proved to be misty over the Madum-region so that orientation was impossible. Few days later they were dropped after a new flight. (Møller Christensen's account pag. 2. Cf. letter from Muus to Hollingworth 25/7–43 pag. 11. Duus Hansen's archive, folder 3).
27. Cited letter pag. 4 and 5. Duus Hansen's archive, folder 2.

28. Cf. "Danmark under besættelsen" III, pag. 104 in a chapter about R.A.F.-help to Denmark with the British "Air-Ministry" as author. In "Frit Danmarks hvidbog" II, pag. 340–51 the number is estimated at ca. 6300 containers. No source is, however, given of this information, just as several errors in the columns can be pointed out, e.g. deliveries in June 1943.
29. Cf. Sten Gudme's account pag. 4–5.
30. Ebbe Munck's diary. Note dated June–July 1943. Diary pag. 104, Munck's archive. It appears from the diary that Rantzau formerly had been in Stockholm and had established contact with the Stockholmorganisation. Cf. the diary pag. 30.
31. Letter from Turnbull to Muus, undated (after content from July 1943). Duus Hansen's archive, folder 4.
32. Rf. this correspondence: 1) letter from Muus to Hollingworth 25/7–43. 2) Undated letter from Turnbull to Muus pag. 1. 3) Letters from Turnbull to Duus Hansen 15/7 –43 and 24/8–43 pag. 1 and 1. 4) Reports from Rantzau, forwarded through Duus Hansen. Duus Hansen's archive, folder 3, 4, 11 and 19. Cf. Muus: "Ingen tænder et lys" pag. 106–07.
33. Letter from Rantzau to Turnbull 28/7–43 pag. 2. Duus Hansen's archive, folder 19.
34. As mentioned the special "propagandadroppings", which Rantzau together with Seehusen was to have directed, came to nothing.
35. Cited letter pag. 6–7. Duus Hansen's archive, folder 3.
36. Op. cit., pag. 106–07.
37. Hecht Johansen's account pag. 3. Schoch's account pag. 7. Later on Schoch took over from Rantzau.

38. Letter from Turnbull to Duus Hansen 24/8–43 pag. 1 Duus Hansen's archive, folder 11.
39. Cf. above pag. 194 and pag. 203.
40. Cited account pag. 8 Cf. "Parl. Komm. Betænkn." VII, volume 1, pag. 264–65.
41. Arboe-Rasmussen: "Den første".
42. See account.
43. Op. cit. pag. 18.
44. Letter from Rantzau to Turnbull 28/7–43. Duus Hansen's archive, folder 19.
45. Letter from Muus to Hollingworth 28/7–43. Duus Hansen's archive, folder 3.
46. About the English material see "Danmark under besættelsen" III, pag. 137–40.
47. Letter from Muus to Hollingworth 30/4–43 pag. 4. Duus Hansen's archive, folder 3.
48. Letter from Hollingworth to Muus 17/5–43 pag. 4–6. Duus Hansen's archive, folder 2.

20. Sabotage Groups

1. "Besættelsestidens Fakta" II, pag. 1206.
2. Letter from Hollingworth to Muus 17/5–43. Duus Hansen's archive, folder 2.
3. "Besættelsestidens Fakta" II, pag. 1206.
4. See above pag. 94.
5. Børge Brandt & Kaj Christiansen: "Sabotage".
6. Ibid., pag. 34.
7. Op. cit. II, pag. 1203.
8. A great field of activity for local research is open. It is my opinion that local research should be carried into effect – which partly has been done – as long as the possibility still exists to obtain verbal information of a reliable character. It will hardly be possible to find essential documentary material any longer and in any case only sporadic examples of such material. Verbal information even today may help.
9. See above, chapter 8.
10. See above pag. 220 ff.
11. Op. cit., pag. 15–22.
12. Brøchner's account, pag. 1, Sonne's account, pag. 1.
13. See above pag. 139.
14. Knud E. Petersen's and Hans F. Hansen's accounts, pag. 7 and 14.
15. Lok Linblad's account, pag. 4.
16. Muus: "Ingen tænder et lys", pag. 90. Cf. letter from Muus to Hollingworth 30/4–43 pag. 3. Duus Hansen's archive, folder 3.
17. Accounts from: Balling, pag. 3–5. Møller Christensen, pag. 2–5. Diemer, pag. 5–6, Bach Frederiksen, pag. 3, I. F. Jacobsen, pag. 1. Paul Jensen, pag. 2–4, Verner Jensen, pag. 3, Verner Johansen, pag. 5–6 and Juncker, pag. 9–11. In Ebbe Munck & Børge Outze: "Danmarks Frihedskamp", which is planned to give a description of the resistance-movement county for county detailed information about the development of local groups can be found, albeit very often inaccurate information.
18. Juncker's account, pag. 9–11.
19. Diemer's account, pag. 5–6.
20. H. Schlanbusch's account, pag. 2.
21. "Chr. Ulrik Hansen" (ed. Elith Olsen & Inge Theut), pag. 19–20. Juncker's account, pag. 11–12.
22. Toldstrup: "Uden kamp ingen sejr" pag. 49.
23. Op. cit. pag. 54.
24. Bach Frederiksen states, that the names of people, with whom Geisler came into contact were given him from Copenhagen. Undoubted-

ly this has been the case in several circumstances, but some of the persons mentioned in Bach-Frederiksen's account can be traced back to Juncker's contacts.

25. Balling's account, pag. 4. Verner Johansen's account, pag. 5.
26. Stærmose's account, pag. 7.
27. Lok Linblad's account, pag. 4. Verner Johansen's account, pag. 7. Møller Christensen's account, pag. 2. Peter Carlsen's account, pag. 4. Georg Quistgaard: "Fængselsdagbog og Breve".
28. Cited account, pag. 4. Muus: "Ingen tænder et lys", pag. 110. About Quistgaard see the introduction to his "Fængselsdagbog og Breve" (ed. Elias Bredsdorff).
29. Paul Jensen's account, pag. 2–4.
30. Accounts from Møller Christensen, Balling, Juncker, Godske Pedersen, Søndergaard Pedersen and Schlanbusch.
31. Aage Møller Christensen's account, pag. 4. Schlanbusch's account, pag. 3. The reception took place medio October.
32. Peter Carlsen's account, pag. 4–5. Erik Frandsen's account, pag. 1. "Rapport om dannelsen af den første faldskærmsgruppe i Odense". Archive for the Funen-region.
33. Peter Carlsen's account, pag. 9. "Rapport om dannelsen af den første faldskærmsgruppe i Odense", pag. 3. Archive for the Funen-region.
34. Lok Linblad's account, pag. 4. Muus: "Ingen tænder et lys", pag. 90.
35. Fog's account, pag. 11–12. Cf. Muus: "Ingen tænder et lys", pag. 92–93.
36. The sabotage organisation "Holger Danske". See about this organisation the following.

37. The account omits a word.
38. Houmann's account, pag. 5.
39. E.g. account from Peter Carlsen, pag. 4–5.
40. Op. cit., pag. 92–93.
41. Letter from Muus to Hollingworth 25/7–43 pag. 10. Duus Hansen's archive, folder 3.
42. Muus: "Ingen tænder et lys", pag. 92–93.
43. See above pag. 236.
44. Peter Carlsen's account, pag. 5–6.
45. "Danmark under besættelsen" III, pag. 144.
46. Letter from Muus to Hollingworth 30/4–43 pag. 2. Duus Hansen's archive, folder 3.
47. Cf. that Lok Linblad in his account pag. 4 mentions that one of the first groups, "which was activated", was a communist group.
48. "Frit Danmarks hvidbog" II, pag. 334. Josef Petersen and Bob Jarset: "Holger Danske vågner" pag. 26–27. About Josef Søndergaard see last-named book, pag. 36–38. Cf. "Besættelsens Hvem, Hvad, Hvor", biography.
49. See above pag. 94.
50. About the materiel difficulties for the early "Holger Danske"-group see Josef Petersen and Bob Jarset: "Holger Danske vågner", pag. 27–31.
51. Op. cit. pag. 77–78, 84 ff. and 90. Incidentally the book is quite wrong as to information about SOE. Thus first droppings in Denmark are dated to July 1943. See pag. 82. On the "Holger Danske"-organisation and its connections with SOE see also Lillelund's account, pag. 2.

21. Sabotage

1. Brøchner's account, pag. 3.

2. Bach Frederiksen's account, pag. 4.

3. See above pag. 58 f.

4. Letters from Hollingworth to Muus 9/5–43, pag. 1 and 17/5–43, pag. 2. Duus Hansen's archive, folder 2.

5. See above pag. 58 f. Hollingworth's letter to Muus 17/5–43, note above.

6. The list appears in Muus's letter to Hollingworth 21/5–43. Duus Hansen's archive, folder 2.

7. Letter from Muus to Hollingworth 21/5–43, Duus Hansen's archive, folder 3.

8. There are examples in several of the archives. For instance in letters from Muus in Toldstrup's and Duus Hansen's archives.

9. Reports in Duus Hansen's archive.

10. Cf. accounts given by Paul Jensen, Haakon Lauritzen, Viggo Aasted, Einar Balling, Jens Godske Pedersen and Peter Carlsen and Erik Frandsen.

11. As for the Statements from the Naval Research Institute it holds true, that the sabotage concerned after negotiation with director Gerhard Hansen, who at the time elaborated the statements, is listed as "English explosives found" irrespective of the fact that it can be seen only indirectly in the statements.

12. "Besættelsestidens Fakta" II, pag. 1206 records the sabotage figures for the months January-August 1943 as the following: 14-29-60-70 -62-44-84-198. The list given, as mentioned by the authors of the book, is not complete. Several of the sabotage cases, mentioned in the statements from the technical departments, are not included in the list.

13. See above, chapter 18.

14. Toldstrup: "Uden kamp ingen sejr" pag. 46.

15. Cf. above chapter 18. Muus: "Ingen tænder et lys" pag. 110–11. "Den hvide brigade" pag. 105 and 110. About the attitude towards a first meeting with the parachutists see Josef Petersen & Bob Jarset: "Holger Danske vågner" pag. 77–78.

16. Interrogation in court of Werner Best. Frisch: "Danmark besat og befriet" I pag. 400.

17. Letter from Ebbe Munck to Christmas Møller 18/7–43, attached report, pag. 2. Munck's archive I, folder mrk. "Rapporter London I".

18. Foss: "Fra passiv til aktiv modstand" pag. 154, 164, 174 and 181.

19. Letter from Muus to Hollingworth 25/7–43, pag. 10. Duus Hansen's archive, folder 3.

20. Foss: "Fra passiv til aktiv modstand", pag. 181.

21. Resistance people at least aimed at a discontinuation of the government's policy of concessions, which under the given circumstances meant a break with Germany. They were willing to take the consequences of such a break and were relieved when the rupture came.

22. Cited account, pag. 6. Cf. information by Paul Jensen in Arboe-Rasmussen: "Den første", pag. 35.

23. Cited account, pag. 14.

24. Duus Hansen's account, pag. 12.

25. Muus: "Ingen tænder et lys", pag. 116–17. The essence of telegram and answer has been confirmed by Hollingworth and Colin Gubbins and by other competent English authorities.

26. In his account pag. 12 Duus Hansen mentions such a telegram.

27. As to the development here and as to the political development as a whole on to August 29th see P.

Munch: "Danmark under verdenskrig og besættelse" pag. 171–189. Frisch: "Danmark besat og befriet" I, pag. 319–336. Scavenius: Forhandlingspolitikken under besættelsen", pag. 176–195. The strikes are thoroughly investigated by H. Kirchhoff (unpublished manuscript) and by Aa. Trommer: "Besættelsestidens første folkestrejke" in "Historie", 1966, pag. 149–231.

28. Cited diary pag. 108, Munck's archive.

29. Letters from Hollingworth to Muus 9/5–43, appendix B, 17/5–43, pag. 2–3 and 26/7–43, appendix D. Duus Hansen's archive, folder 2.

30. Børge Brandt & Kaj Christiansen: "Sabotage", pag. 110 Cf. "Danmark under besættelsen" II, pag. 704–05. A more thorough description will follow in volume II and III.

31. E.g. Josef Petersen and Bob Jarset: "Holger Danske vågner" pag. 40–41 and 47.

32. Paul Jensen's account, pag. 6.

33. Aage Møller Christensen's account, pag. 4.

34. Peter Carlsen's account, pag. 8.

35. Lok Linblad's account, pag. 4.

36. Cited account, pag. 16–17.

37. Houmann's account, pag. 6.

38. Foss: "Fra passiv til aktiv modstand", pag. 256 ff. Cf. Schoch's account, pag. 3–4.

39. Letter from Hollingworth to Muus 17/5–43, pag. 7. Duus Hansen's archive, folder 2.

40. About "crack"-signals see above pag. 227.

41. Reference has been made above to entire descriptions of the political development. As to the situation for the army and the navy see "Danmark under besættelsen" I, pag. 387–402 and 409–442.

42. Letter from Frode Jakobsen to Christmas Møller 30/9–43 pag. 1. Munck's archive, I, folder mrk. "Rapporter London I". Political events during the crucial day, August 28th, are described in detail in Jørgen Hæstrup: "Til landets bedste" I, pag. 22–48.

22. Denmarks Freedom Council

1. Muus: "Ingen tænder et lys", pag. 93.

2. Cf. Dedichen's account, pag. 12.

3. See above pag. 190.

4. "Danmark under besættelsen" II, pag. 683–720.

5. Muus: "Ingen tænder et lys", pag. 125.

6. Dedichen's account, pag. 15.

7. Cf. Frisch: "Danmark besat og befriet" III, pag. 24–25.

8. Cited account, pag. 16.

9. Report, attached letter from Ebbe Munck to Christmas Møller 3/6–43. Munck's archive, I, folder mrk. "Rapporter London I".

10. "Frit Danmarks hvidbog" I, pag. 153–54.

11. Dedichen's account, pag. 19.

12. Muus was a member of the Freedom Council. See volume II, chapter 2.

13. Letter from Muus to Hollingworth 31/7–43 pag. 1. Duus Hansen's archive, folder 3.

14. See for instance "Bogen om Christmas Møller", pag. 196.

15. See above pag. 18 and pag. 77.

16. Spink's account, pag. 11.

17. Muus: "Ingen tænder et lys", pag. 125.

18. Dedichen's account, pag. 15.

19. Dedichen's account, pag. 16. Sf. Frisch: "Danmark besat og befriet" III, pag. 24 Cf. "Danmark under besættelsen" II, pag. 713, where Fog himself mentions the meetings.

Also Federspiel mentions, that he was kept informed of the meetings (his account, pag. 12).

20. Fog's account, pag. 12.
21. Muus left Denmark in the beginning of October 1943 and returned in December the same year, see volume II, chapter 3.
22. Houmann's account, pag. 6.
23. Muus: "Ingen tænder et lys", pag. 125–26.
24. Cited account, pag. 15–16.
25. "Frit Danmarks hvidbog" II, pag. 683–692. Frode Jakobsen's version
26. As to the creation of the Freedom Council see volume II, second chapter.
27. Early sources are: Foss: "Fra passiv til aktiv modstand", pag. 264–277. Houmann's exposition in "Frit Danmarks hvidbog" II, pag. 179–84 and Fog's exposition in "Danmark under besættelsen" II, pag. 683–692. Frode Jakobsen's version is given in his book: "I Danmarks Frihedsraad" I, pag. 48–55, a version mainly based upon his account from 1955.
28. The date for the meeting has been under discussion. Foss fixes the date to August (cited work, pag. 268), while Fog says June 5th ("Danmark under besættelsen" II, pag. 684). Frode Jakobsen insists upon an early date. The many questions behind the creation of the "Denmark's Freedom Council" – the question of name was only settled in September – has been the subject of an article by the author: "Tilblivelsen af Danmarks Frihedsråd" in the periodical, "Historie", 1973.
29. According to Foss's explanation it seems, as if he had no knowledge at the time of Fog's connections with SOE, but it seems, as if he

was aware of Schoch's connections.
30. Foss, op. cit., pag. 265–66. Cf. note 28.
31. Houmann's account, pag. 8.
32. Houmann's account, pag. 7.
33. Cited account, pag. 6–7.
34. Cited account, pag. 71–78.
35. According to Roland Olsen's account the meeting took place at "Davidsens Vinhus".
36. The resolution was published in the English "Frit Danmark" (paper, published by Danes in London, not to be confounded with the illegal paper of the same name) and in the same number an encouraging answer from "The Danish Council" was published. (The English "Frit Danmark" 30 July–43).
37. According to a generally accepted statement by Foss, it was Houmann, who proposed this name: "The word freedom was in the air and after a short discussion I suggested Denmark's Freedom Council, which Houmann altered to two words: Denmark's Freedomcouncil, and thus the matter was quickly settled and unanimously agreed upon" (Cited work, pag. 276).
38. Letter from Foss to Munck 25/9–43, Munck's archive, IV, folder mrk. "Korrespondancer med og vedr. Frihedsrådet".
39. Foss mentions in "Fra passiv til aktiv modstand" not Staffeldt, but professor Noe-Nygaard as the representative for the Danish Unity Party. Fog, however, relates in his exposition that Staffeldt took part in the meeting on September 16th (Cf. also Schoch's account, pag. 5) but that from the next meeting he was replaced by Noe-Nygaard. This is accordance with Noe-Nygaard's account. Cf. volume II, chapter 2.
40. "Frit Danmarks hvidbog" II, pag.

182.

41. Muus: "Ingen tænder et lys", pag. 122.

42. Letter from Muus to Turnbull 16/9–43, pag. 2. Duus Hansen's archive, folder 5.

43. Letter from Muus to Hollingworth 16/9–43, pag. 2. Duus Hansen's archive, folder 3.

44. Lok Linblad's account, pag. 5. Cf. Dedichen's account, pag. 20.

45. Muus: "Ingen tænder et lys", pag. 127–29.

Odense University Studies in History and Social Sciences